# PRIESTLY IDENTITY

# PRIESTLY IDENTITY

*A Study in the Theology of Priesthood*

Thomas J. McGovern

WIPF & STOCK · Eugene, Oregon

Wipf and Stock Publishers
199 W 8th Ave, Suite 3
Eugene, OR 97401

Priestly Identity
A Study in the Theology of Priesthood
By McGovern, Thomas J.
Copyright©2002 by McGovern, Thomas J.
ISBN 13: 978-1-60899-532-5
Publication date 3/26/2010
Previously published by Four Courts Press, 2002

# Contents

In memory of
Bishop Alvaro del Portillo (1914–1994)
Prelate of Opus Dei
who called me to share sacramentally
in the priesthood of Jesus Christ

# Introduction

It is generally accepted that since the end of Vatican II there has been a crisis in the Catholic priesthood. The symptoms were already well defined when the synod of bishops met in 1971 to discuss that very topic. The synod recognized that there was an identity crisis among priests because of the serious doubts raised subsequent to Vatican II about the essence of the priesthood and its purpose. In their response the bishops assessed the problem to be nothing less than a deep spiritual crisis arising from a defective theological understanding of the very nature of the priesthood. The way forward was clear: according to the synod:

> Priests ... find their identity to the extent that they fully live the mission of the Church and exercise it in different ways in communion with the entire People of God, as pastors and ministers of the Lord in the Spirit, in order to fulfil by their work the plan of salvation in history.[1]

A correct understanding of the nature of priestly ministry is therefore essential for conviction about, and commitment to, this vocation. Such understanding, the synod implied, could only be achieved through a sound ecclesiology and a deep awareness of how the ministerial priesthood is essentially at the service of the faithful.

The crisis is reflected in two areas in particular – defections from the priesthood and a serious decline in vocations.[2] Over the past thirty years more priests have abandoned their vocation than in any other similar period in the history of the Church.[3] This sad phenomenon has been referred to by the pres-

---

1 *De sacerdotio ministeriali,* pars II, AAS, 68 (1971) 909. 2 Despite the decline in vocations in Western Europe, North America and Oceania, there has been a significant growth in vocations over the past twenty years in Africa, South America, South East Asia, and Eastern Europe – cf. *Osservatore Romano,* 31 July 1996. See also Review of Church statistics for the period 1979-97 in *Seminarium,* XXXIX (1999), no. 4, *Dimensione quantitativa della Chiesa Cattolica alle soglie dell'Anno giubilare,* p. 652. 3 During the period 1964 to 1997, there were

ent Holy Father as a 'counter-sign', a 'counter-witness' and 'one of the set-backs to the great hopes for renewal aroused throughout the Church by the Second Vatican Council'.[4] It was largely a universal phenomenon, affecting both secular and religious priests, but one which was most marked in the developed countries of Western Europe and North America.

It is difficult to understand the onset of the crisis which affected so many priests since Vatican II. The identity of the priest is writ large on the pages of the Gospel, the record of the words and the works of Christ the Priest *par excellence*. We also have accounts of the lifestyle, preaching and teaching of the first generation of priests in the narratives of the New Testament. In addition, the Magisterium has always had a very clear conception of the role of the priest based on Scripture, the insights of the Fathers, and the exemplary lives of so many priests whose sanctity was publicly recognized by the Church. Particularly in this twentieth century, papal Magisterium has expressed its perception of the priesthood in many significant documents, covering every aspect of the vocation and the life of the priest. [5]

Why, we might ask, could such a clearly defined job specification as that of the priest become so blurred as to cause tens of thousands to lose sight of it and eventually abandon their commitment? While no one can answer for the very personal reasons involved in each case, theological and pastoral reflection on this phenomenon has identified some of the ideas which negatively influenced the perception of the priesthood during this period. In 1985 John Paul II, in an address to the council of European episcopal conferences, assessed the difficulties as follows:

> An analysis of the situation in Europe today shows, together with comforting signs of vitality and revival, a persistent *crisis of vocations* and

60,126 defections from the priesthood (diocesan and religious). See *Osservatore Romano*, 13/20 August 1997; *Seminarium*, op. cit., p. 646. 4 Address to priests at Maynooth, 1 October 1979. The addresses of the Holy Father to priests down through the years can be found in the pages of *Osservatore Romano* (English language weekly edition). A number of these, covering the first five years of his papacy (1978-83), are available in *A priest forever*, ed. Fr Seamus O'Byrne, Athlone, Ireland, 1984. To avoid overloading the footnotes with dates, when referring to a papal address, I simply give the date it was delivered, as the address can then be easily sourced in the relevant edition of the English weekly edition of *Osservatore Romano*. 5 Cf. *The Catholic priesthood: papal documents from St Pius X to Pius XII*, ed. Monsignor P. Veuillot, Dublin 1957. To mention but a few of the more important ones: St Pius X: Exhortation, *Haerent animo*, on priestly sanctity, 4 August 1908; Pius XI: Encyclical, *Ad Catholici sacerdotii*, on the Catholic priesthood, 20 December 1935; Pius XII: Apostolic exhortation, *Menti nostrae*, on the sanctification of priestly life, 23 December 1950; John XXIII: Encyclical, *Sacerdotii nostri primordia*, on priestly perfection, 1 August 1959; Paul VI: Encyclical, *Sacerdotalis caelibatus*, on priestly celibacy, 24 June 1967.

the painful phenomenon of *defections*. The causes of this painful phenomenon are multiple, and it will be necessary to face up to them with
vigour, especially those that can be traced back to a process of spiritual atrophy or to an attitude of corrosive dissent. Vocations are not born
in these environments. We should also keep in mind that it is not by
diminishing the formative and qualitative requirements of the apostle
that a more effective and incisive evangelizing action will be realized,
but quite the contrary. The 'memory' of the Church, regarding, for
example, the patron Saints of Europe, constitutes a significant lesson
in this regard.[6]

Anaemic spirituality, theological dissent, and deficient formation were thus
seen as catalysts in the process leading to the fall in vocations and the problem
of defections.

Organising the 1990 synod of bishops on the formation of seminarians and
priests was John Paul II's most significant response to the situation he outlined
in 1985. At the close of this same synod he suggested further reasons for the
crisis in the priesthood:

This crisis arose in the years immediately following the Council. It was
based on an erroneous understanding of – and sometimes even a conscious bias against – the doctrine of the Conciliar Magisterium.
Undoubtedly, herein lies one of the reasons for the great number of
defections experienced then by the Church, losses which did serious
harm to pastoral ministry and priestly vocations, especially missionary
vocations.[7]

## THEOLOGICAL INFLUENCES

Apart from the reasons adduced by the Pope for this crisis, other factors also
had an effect which have their roots in history. The sixteenth-century
Reformers eviscerated the traditional concept of priesthood in two respects.
Firstly, the essential distinction between the sacramentally ordained priesthood
and the universal priesthood of the laity was denied – and thus Holy Orders
was no longer considered a sacrament. Secondly, the cultic aspect of priesthood was replaced by a new emphasis on the ministry of the word. With the
rejection of the hierarchical structure of the priesthood and the jurisdiction

6 Address, 11 October 1985 (italics in original).   7 Discourse at the end of the 1990 synod
of bishops, 27 October 1990.

derived from it, ministers of the new religion were elected or deputed by the ecclesial community. In reply to arguments of the Reformers that there was no such thing as a special priestly office, Trent affirmed the hierarchical nature of Church office endowed with a specific spiritual jurisdiction. In response to the denial of the priestly character conferred on the priest through sacramental ordination, Trent emphasized the link between the visible sacrifice (the Mass) and priestly authority.[8] In doing so, it was simply maintaining the theology of the Middle Ages that the priesthood was to be understood primarily from the perspective of the priest's sacramental duties and powers. The celebration of the Mass was the key to the priest's role and identity, and the Church was understood primarily as a hierarchical structure with governing authority. The position of the laity in the Church was therefore a very secondary one, an attitude reflected clearly in 1917 code of canon law which described lay people as simply non clerics.[9] About the time of Vatican II, however, the theological pendulum began to swing back in the opposite direction towards the theology of the Reformers.

In his address at the opening of the 1990 synod of bishops, Cardinal Ratzinger affirmed that the post-Vatican II crisis in the priesthood was primarily due to the fact that

> the old arguments of the sixteenth-century Reformation, together with more recent findings of modern biblical exegesis – which moreover were nourished by the presuppositions of the Reformation – acquired a certain plausibility, and Catholic theology was unable to respond to them adequately.[10]

Theological ideas borrowed from Protestantism gave rise to a reinterpretation of the New Testament concept of priesthood, despoiling it of its unique sacral dimension. This change of perception of the essential nature of the priesthood questioned the idea of the priest as a man apart, as somehow 'different' from the rest of men. While the supporters of this new perspective admit the existence of various ecclesiastical functionaries in the New Testament such as bishops, deacons, and presbyters, they argue that the cultic dimension is totally lacking and, consequently, while they accept that they were administrators, they deny that they were priests. According to this thesis, only little by little, during the first centuries, was the element of cult added to the administrative and preaching function. In this way presbyters became priests. The priest was then seen as a

8 Cf. 'Decree concerning the sacrifice of the Mass' (22nd Session, 17 September 1562); 'Decree concerning the sacrament of Order' (23rd Session, 15 July 1563), in *The canons and decrees of the council of Trent,* trans. H. J. Schroeder, Rockfort, Il., 1978. 9 Cf. canon 107. 10 Address, 1 October 1990, in *Osservatore Romano,* 28 October 1990.

representative of the Church rather than as a representative of Christ. As a consequence, in recent decades the tendency has been to ground the identity of the priest ecclesiologically rather than christologically with an emphasis on functionalism.[11] The Lutheran model of priestly ministry was making ground at the expense of the identity of the Catholic priesthood as defined by Trent.

The Ratzinger critique was directed mainly at the model of priesthood proposed by the Schillebeeckx school of theology. The Dutch Dominican developed a theology of ministry based more on sociological criteria than on the living Tradition of the Church.[12] For Schillebeeckx, priesthood is the emergence of ministry from below driven by the social dynamics of the primitive Christian communities. He maintains that this original ministry gradually developed a cultic dimension which subsequently became the dominant characteristic. In particular circumstances he would say that the sacramental needs of the community could mandate the celebration of the Eucharist by a designated, non-ordained member of the faithful. He thus effectively denies the transmission of a sacred power through the apostolic succession as the foundation of the Catholic priesthood. From this we see that his concept of ministry is essentially Lutheran. In its 1983 Letter, *Sacerdotium ministeriale*,[13] the Congregation for the Doctrine of the Faith responded to a number of these errors, but Ratzinger's 1990 address to the synod of bishops was in part a follow-up to the document he signed in 1983.

## SECULARIZATION

The influences which caused the change in the perception of priesthood have not been theological only. Shifts in cultural and secular attitudes have also played their part. A characteristic of our time is the progressive secularization of society and the drifting of people away from the Church. Even in countries of long-standing Christian tradition people increasingly live without reference to the transcendent. Large numbers have abandoned following Christ as 'the way, the truth and the life' (Jn 14:6), and live by a relativistic and subjectivist ethic. Economic progress has become the primary goal of individuals and of society, an attitude which leads to practical atheism and drains the life from mystery.[14] Christian values are reflected less and less in society and political programmes are often implicitly hostile to Christian moral teaching. In a situ-

11 Anton Ziegenaus, 'Identidad del sacerdocio ministerial' in *La formación de los sacerdotes en las circunstancias actuales*, Pamplona, 1990, pp 81-86. 12 Cf. E. Schillebeeckx, *Ministry: a case for change*, London, 1981; idem, *The Church with a human face: a new and expanded theology of ministry*, London, 1985. See critique of Schillebeeckx's theory published by Albert Vanhoye and Henri Crouzel, 'The ministry in the Church: reflections on a recent publication', *Clergy Review*, 68, 1983, pp 155-74. 13 *Letter to the bishops of the Catholic Church on certain questions concerning the minister of the Eucharist*, 6 August 1983. 14 Cf. *Pastores*

ation where religion is relegated more and more to the sphere of private conscience, the traditional status and prestige of priests in society has considerably
diminished especially in urban areas. As a result, some priests have lost confidence in the effectiveness of the Christian message of salvation and in the
Church's ability to articulate a meaningful Gospel.

Because one of the current orthodoxies is that the expression of religious
values should be confined to the area of personal conscience, many people
today will affirm that Christian moral values should not be allowed to influence
public discourse or secular realities. Both the sacred and the profane have, of
course, their own authentic values and principles. But it was never part of
God's plan that man should live a sort of schizophrenic existence – that his
religious life on the one hand, and his professional, social and family commitments on the other, should be completely separate and compartmentalized
existences. Nevertheless, there is increasing social and legislative pressure to
copperfasten this compartmentalization.

Despite the efforts of Vatican II to recover the Gospel teaching of the universal call to holiness and of personal sanctification in and through secular
realities, a strong, materialistic influence has been active in many areas of society, erasing the notion of man made to the image and likeness of God with a
supernatural destiny. Many priests have been affected by this negative pressure, with the result that they tend to see their role as Christian social workers
rather than as priests endowed with the key to supernatural life whose principal task is to lead souls to eternal salvation. A side effect of this secularising
influence is that priests very rarely preach about the last things – death, judgement, heaven, hell. If redemption is seen to be closely related to the things of
this world, speaking about the last things loses its relevance.

CULTURAL INFLUENCES

Another side-effect of this loss of supernatural outlook is that priests are in
danger of taking their priorities from the political, academic and media elites.
Hence, some theologians have interpreted categories of sin, repentance and
grace in collective and social terms rather than in personal and spiritual ones.
In this way they have responded to the mission set for the Church by the world
rather than promote the mission of the Church which requires the world to
open out to the light of the Gospel. Since the fall of Communism the political
option has been stripped of its allure, and so the new enthusiasms are for
sundry versions of feminism, multiculturalism, and ecological correctness.[15]

*dabo vobis*, 7 (25 March 1992), subsequently abbreviated to PDV in the footnotes.   15 Cf. J.
Nuechterlein, 'Pastoral concerns', in *First Things*, no. 77, November 1997, p. 9.

The increased emphasis on the ideas of freedom and democracy in the general cultural environment has created a climate of opinion which critically questions religious authority and ultimately rejects it, especially in the area of moral norms. The fact that the dominant notion of freedom is detached from the concept of objective truth, and that the real nature of religious authority is poorly understood, aggravates the problem. Because the priest is part of a hierarchical structure which is not answerable to the human democratic process, and because he preaches a doctrine which draws its validity primarily from the authority of Revelation, he can feel increasingly uncomfortable in a society which is shaped less and less by the dynamics of Christian culture, and where relativism in doctrine and moral values are the defining theological characteristics.[16]

When Vatican II 'rediscovered' the notion of the common priesthood of the faithful, it changed the existing understanding of things which perceived priesthood in the Catholic Church only in terms of the clergy. However, because of a fundamental misunderstanding of the nature of the lay vocation (which is primarily to make the values of the Gospel present in secular society), the swing to the opposite pole has resulted in an increased clericalization of the laity in an effort to get them more involved in the work of the Church. The process of laity empowerment has been understood largely as a conferring of different ministries on them, tasks which previously were often carried out by the clergy. The result is a blurring of the identity of the priest both in the eyes of the clergy themselves as well as among lay people. That this creates problems in the Church at the present time is clear from the attention given to it in recent statements by Pope John Paul II and Vatican departments.[17] These practices 'give rise to a "functionalistic" conception of the ministry, which sees the ministry of "pastor" as a function and not as an ontological sacramental reality'.[18]

## JOHN PAUL II AND PRIESTHOOD

Since his election as Pope, John Paul II has made his own unique contribution to the theology of priesthood. He introduced the custom of writing a letter directly to all the priests of the Church for the feast of Holy Thursday, the day which he felicitously refers to as 'the birthday of priests'. This was an innova-

16 Cf. PDV, 8. See also Gisbert Greshake, *The meaning of Christian priesthood*, Dublin, 1988, pp 17-20. 17 Cf. Address, 21 Nov. 1998, no. 5; *Instruction on certain questions regarding the collaboration of the non-ordained faithful in the sacred ministry of priests*, 15 August 1997. 18 Cardinal Joseph Ratzinger, 'Reflections on the Instruction regarding the collaboration of the lay faithful in the ministry of priests - 6', *Osservatore Romano*, 29 April 1998.

tion in papal teaching, one which the Holy Father has used effectively over the past twenty three years to comment on many aspects of priestly ministry and as a means to make his own original contribution to the theology of priesthood.

Like all his other writings, these letters draw deeply from the Scriptures and are more often than not written in the form of a prayerful reflection rather than the traditional doctrinal dissertation. It is clear, too, that he brings the rich experience of his own priestly life to this annual communication with his brother priests. These letters, together with his 1992 document on the formation of priests, *Pastores dabo vobis*,[19] are, among other things, a response to some of the negative elements of contemporary culture which have, perhaps unconsciously, penetrated the formation and lifestyle of priests. Such elements include a certain rationalism which undermines conviction about the supernatural, and an aggressive individualism which makes binding and permanent commitments difficult. A social climate which is subversive of good human relationships leads inevitably to a type of loneliness which people try to satisfy by way of consumerism and a hedonistic approach to life. These corrosive influences of the cultural environment inevitably filtered into the attitudes of priests and their understanding of the priestly ministry. They also made the promotion of vocations more difficult. These, and other factors, were what suggested to John Paul II the need to renew and revitalize the priesthood in light of Vatican II's teaching on the universal call to holiness.[20]

Consequently, in October 1990 he called a synod of bishops to study the question of the formation of priests. This focussing on priestly formation was, perhaps, a tacit recognition of the fact that the problems giving rise to the crisis referred to above arose primarily from inadequate or defective formation in the seminary and subsequently. The Apostolic Exhortation, *Pastores dabo vobis*, is the most extensive document of the magisterium devoted to priestly formation and constitutes John Paul II's most comprehensive statement on the nature of priestly ministry. We can now rightly speak of a *magna carta* of the theology of the priesthood which will continue to be authoritative for the future of the Church.[21] It is a development of the Vatican II document *Optatam totius* on priestly formation.[22] It takes up the distilled wisdom of the 1990 synod to which the Holy Father adds many of his own penetrating insights on priestly formation. It points the way forward for a rediscovery and a reaffirmation of the priesthood of Christ as transmitted through the apostolic succession, and as enriched down through the centuries by the action of the

19 Post-synodal apostolic exhortation, *Pastores dabo vobis*, 25 March 1992. 20 Cf. George Weigel, *Witness to hope: the biography of John Paul II*, New York, 1999, p. 656. 21 In the text of *Pastores dabo vobis*, John Paul II specifically affirms the fact that he is issuing this document as 'Bishop of Rome and successor of Peter' (no. 4). 22 Decree on the training of priests, Vatican II, *Optatam totius*, 28 October 1965.

Holy Spirit in the Church. More recently, in the context of his weekly catechesis on the mystery of the Church, between March and September 1993, John Paul II devoted eighteen addresses to a discussion of different aspects of the priesthood which are a treasure of theology and a source of many practical recommendations.[23]

The following chapters on priesthood have in a special way been inspired by the teachings of the present Holy Father – that they draw heavily on his ideas will be clear from the multiple references to his writings. The conviction that a deeper awareness of this papal teaching will be of much benefit to priests is what has justified my putting this book together. At the same time I should point out that my purpose is not to present a comprehensive, systematic theology of the priesthood: there are many substantial volumes already available on this topic. Rather my objective is to draw attention to particular aspects of the priestly vocation which help to define the identity of the priest and which I feel need to be emphasized at the present time. The different chapters of this study are gathered together under three main headings – Theological, Spiritual, and Pastoral. These are not watertight compartments, reflecting the fact that in the priestly life itself the spiritual, theological, and pastoral overlap to a considerable degree and cannot be isolated from one another.

## THEOLOGICAL CONSIDERATIONS

A deep understanding of the theological nature of the priestly ministry is essential if we are to have a clear perception of how this ministry affects the life of the priest, and the way in which its exercise brings about his personal holiness. We therefore begin our enquiry into theology of ministry by looking in some detail at the priesthood of Christ. It is from this datum that all our subsequent considerations about priesthood derive.

In Chapter 1, 'The Priesthood of Christ and its development in the New Testament', we consider how Jesus' priesthood is the fulfilment of that prefigured in the Old Testament. We will discover how Christ has all the characteristics of priesthood, which began at the moment of the Incarnation and how, while he exercised his priestly office all during his life, it was on Calvary that it was consummated. The scriptural perception of Christ's priesthood cannot, however, be taken in isolation. It has to be completed by the insights of the liv-

23 Addresses of 31 March; 21 April; 5, 12, 19 and 26 May; 2, 9, 30 June; 7, 17, 21, 28 July; 4, 25 August; 1, 22, 29 September – all in 1993. These are available in the weekly English language edition of the *Osservatore Romano*, usually the week following delivery. A compendium of these addresses is also available under the title *Priests for the third millennium*, published by Midwest Theological Forum, Chicago, 1995.

ing Tradition of the Church. Through it the Holy Spirit, who is the living memory of the Church,[24] progressively leads her to a deeper level of self-understanding (cf. Jn 14:26; 16:13). From Scripture and Tradition we see how the profile of priestly ministry and hierarchical structure developed in the early Church, reflecting the priesthood and teaching of Christ. This is the content of Chapter 1.

One of the developments of the theology of priesthood in recent decades is a deeper awareness of the vital relationship between ministerial priesthood and the common or universal priesthood of the laity. This has come about as a result of the restatement of Catholic ecclesiology in *Lumen gentium*, the Vatican II dogmatic constitution on the Church. In summary this document says that the Church has received a unique mission from Jesus Christ, which is entrusted to all the members of the People of God. Through the sacraments of Baptism and Confirmation they have been made sharers in the priesthood of Christ to offer God a spiritual sacrifice, to bear witness to Christ before men, and to build up the Church, each according to his own vocation. The mission of the Church extends to all men and all times, and to fulfil it there is one priesthood – Christ's – in which all the members of the People of God share though in different ways. Together with the priesthood of all the baptized, God has willed that there also be a ministerial priesthood which shares in a unique way in the priesthood of Christ, and which differs essentially from the common priesthood of the faithful. This ministerial priesthood is at the service of the faithful since its primary purpose is to activate and empower the priesthood of all the baptized. Chapter 2, 'Ministerial priesthood', examines these complementary aspects of priesthood in some depth, and then goes on to look at basic theological concepts of priesthood such as consecration and mission, and the triple ministerial function of teacher, sanctifier and leader of the People of God. In recent years considerable attention has been given to the idea of *pastoral charity* as the dynamic and unifying principle in the ministry and spiritual life of the priest. We will be looking at different aspects of this important concept with special reference to John Paul II's articulation of it in *Pastores dabo vobis*.

PRIESTLY IDENTITY

With these reflections as context, the ground is now prepared to consider in some depth the theological dimensions of priestly identity. This, as we have seen, has been a much discussed question since Vatican II. It has also been

24 Cf. *Catechism of the Catholic Church*, 1099 (subsequently abbreviated to CCC).

referred to on many occasions by John Paul II. In his pastoral visits to different countries he has always made a point of speaking to priests and seminarians to confirm them in their vocation, and to show them how to find their true identity in Christ, the Eternal High Priest. He has repeatedly said that their lives will be authentic to the extent that they reflect Christ, in so far as they become *alter Christus*, other Christs.[25]

Priestly identity in the writings of John Paul II is the main theme of Chapter 3. It can be considered from many different angles. What I have done here is to examine it from the perspective of divine vocation and sacramental character, and the consequences these realities have for the life of the priest. Then follows a study of the Trinitarian identity of the priest with special reference to the christological dimension – this latter includes a consideration of the priest as icon of Christ. It will not be surprising that a fundamental theme running through this chapter is how the priest acts *in persona Christi* (in the person of Christ), a defining characteristic of priestly identity.

In this context the relational character of priesthood also needs to be considered, especially the priest's relationship with the Church, with his bishop, and with his brother priests. The theological concept of communion (*communio*), which has been developed more thoroughly since Vatican II, is the key used to penetrate more deeply into these relationships. In the final part of this chapter we examine some of the negative influences which tend to blur and obscure the clarity of priestly identity.

## CELIBACY

Many of those who left the priesthood in the post-Vatican II era claimed that the demands of celibacy were no longer tenable, theologically, psychologically, or at a practical level. The Vatican II decree on *The ministry and life of priests*[26] reaffirmed the Church's position on celibacy, and this teaching was cogently developed a few years later in Paul VI's encyclical (*Sacerdotalis caelibatus*) in 1967. The mind of the Church on priestly celibacy today was stated very clearly by the 1990 synod of bishops and was incorporated in John Paul II's synodal document on priestly formation, *Pastores dabo vobis*. In it he reiterates 'the Church's firm will to maintain the law that demands perpetual and freely chosen celibacy for present and future candidates for priestly ordination in the Latin rite'.[27]

There is justifiable sadness and, indeed, a certain scandal at reports of a priest's failure to keep his vow of celibacy. For many people his priesthood, in

25 Cf. Address, 23 October 1993. **26** *Presbyterorum ordinis*, 7 December 1965. **27** PDV, 29.

a very real sense, is worth what his celibacy is worth – this is a measure of the importance of this charism for the ordinary faithful. However, the intensity of media concentration on failures in this area is often a reflection of the anticlericalism which pervades much of the media ethos. Newspapers and TV are, by and large, committed to a permissive ethic in the area of sexual morality, and the only opposition which is offered to this agenda is the consistent moral teaching of the Catholic Church. One cannot help feeling at times that the active prosecution of failures in celibacy by the media is another way of attacking the Church's stand on sexual morality by trying to show it to be self-contradictory.

Since I have recently published a comprehensive study of celibacy,[28] it is not my intention to deal at length with this aspect of priesthood here. Much of what I say in that work is a development of important issues raised by John Paul II in an address to a group of Canadian bishops in 1993:

> Cultural considerations, and the scarcity of priests in certain regions, sometimes give rise to calls for a change in this discipline. *To give decisive weight to solutions based on criteria deriving more from certain currents of anthropology, sociology or psychology than from the Church's living tradition* is certainly not the path to follow. We cannot overlook the fact that the Church comes to know the divine will through the *interior guidance of the Spirit* (cf. Jn 16:13), and that the difficulties involved today in keeping celibacy are not sufficient reason to overturn the Church's conviction regarding its value and appropriateness, a conviction constantly reaffirmed by the Church's Magisterium, not least by the Second Vatican Council (cf. *Presbyterorum ordinis*, no.16). Like the Church in other countries, the Church in Canada is called to face this situation *with* faith and courage, trusting 'in the Spirit that the gift of celibacy ... will be generously bestowed by the Father, as long as those who share in Christ's priesthood through the sacrament of Orders, and in deed the whole church, humbly and earnestly pray for it' (ibid.).[29]

Our Chapter 4 – 'Body and soul to Christ: priestly celibacy' - will consider the main scriptural and theological arguments for this charism.

## SPIRITUAL DIMENSION

Having established a clearer idea of the theological identity of the priest, of his unique bonding with the Incarnate Word through sacramental consecration,

---

28 Thomas McGovern, *Priestly celibacy today*, Dublin and Chicago, 1998. 29 Address, 8 November 1993 (italics in original).

we can investigate more closely the nature of the personal relationship which the priest is called to have with Christ. *Pastores dabo vobis*, reviewing the doctrine of Vatican II, speaks about the priest's specific vocation to holiness, based on the sacrament of Holy Orders. And it makes the very valid point that, if all Christians are called to sanctity, then the priest has a particular responsibility to be holy if he is to act effectively *in persona Christi*, and be configured to Christ the Head and Shepherd.[30] While we priests certainly accept this in theory, in practice our attitude may often be one of just surviving spiritually rather than making a serious effort to follow the Master closely. One of the objectives the priest should have for his spiritual life is to try to interiorize the rich theological doctrine available about priesthood and priestly identity which we discuss in the first part of the book. By reflecting on this teaching in the presence of Christ, he will put down deep roots into the soil of his vocation and acquire a spiritual and emotional maturity which will be a solid defence against passing theological fads and temptations related to perseverance in vocation.

How should the priest respond to the extraordinary powers and the immense treasures of grace placed in his hands? Of its very nature the priestly vocation demands a deep friendship with Christ: 'I have called you friends'(Jn 15:15), he told his first priests at the Last Supper. Friendship with Christ, however, is not something that comes automatically as a consequence of ordination. It is a relationship that has to be cultivated in prayer in the seminary and allowed to mature progressively during the lifetime of the priest. The accumulated wisdom of the Church, and the witness of truly effective pastors down through the centuries, testifies to the fact that a committed prayer-life is the only sure means to acquire that intimacy with the Master which the priestly vocation demands.

*Pastores dabo vobis* gives central importance to the bonding between the priest's spiritual life and the exercise of the ministry.[31] Nevertheless, the integration of consecration and mission in the priest can only be achieved through unity of life. Here we are dealing with a fundamental element of priestly spirituality which was fully outlined in *Presbyterorum ordinis*[32] and subsequently developed in *Pastores dabo vobis*.[33] Given the fragmentation and dispersion which characterize the current social and ecclesial context, *Pastores dabo vobis* affirms that the demand for unity of life in the priest is even more urgent at the present time. Chapter 5, 'The spiritual life of the priest', discusses some practical ways in which priestly holiness can be related to ministry in the context of unity of life. It also draws out the implications priestly fraternity has not only for the spiritual life of the individual priest, but also for the diocesan presbyterate as a whole.

30 Cf. PDV, 20 and 21. 31 Cf. no. 24. 32 Cf. no. 14. 33 Cf. PDV, 23.

## EUCHARIST

In the course of an address delivered in 1993, John Paul II made the striking point that:

> In order to have an adequate understanding of the ordained priest-
> hood, and to deal correctly with every question concerning the identi-
> ty, life, service and ongoing formation of priests, it is necessary to be
> always aware of the sacrificial nature of the Eucharist, of which they
> are the ministers.[34]

The identity of the priest is inextricably linked with the Eucharistic sacrifice. To say that a priest is one who renews the sacrifice of Calvary is, in a very real sense, to have said everything significant about him. This affirmation grounds and supports every other theological statement that can be made in relation to him. It also defines the essence of his spirituality, and immediately leads to the assertion that the sum total of his ministry is to build up a Eucharistic com-munity. Chapter 6: 'Eucharistic identity, priest and victim', discusses, in the first place, the scriptural basis for these claims. It then proceeds to develop a eucharistic theology of priesthood, and its relevance for ministry and for the priest's own interior life. The chapter ends with a discussion of the implica-tions of Christ's role as Victim for the priest's spiritual life.

### PRIESTLY VIRTUES

St Augustine points out that unlike ordinary food, which after ingestion we change into ourselves, the food of the Eucharist assimilates us to Christ. By eating his Body each day we gradually acquire his attitudes and sentiments: we learn to see people and events through his eyes. Consequently, if priests have a deep Eucharistic life they will easily acquire the essential priestly virtues which we see reflected in Christ's life as we read the pages of the Gospel. At times some of these virtues – humility, spirit of service, compassion, etc. – will be underdeveloped and so they have to be worked at if priests are to acquire the attractive profile of the Master. Jesus had a perfect human nature, and St Mark adds that as a man he did everything well (cf. Mk 7:37). Despite his human lim-itations the priest has a duty to try to develop those natural virtues – cheerful-ness, generosity, empathy – which make his pastoral work more effective. Above all he needs to mature his talents for communication and social interac-tion so that his message comes across as credible and compelling despite all the

34 John Paul II, Address, 22 October 1993.

competing messages in the air waves. As *Pastores dabo vobis* points out, the priest's human personality should be a bridge for others to encounter Christ.[35] Chapter 7 looks as some of the more important human and Christian virtues which facilitate the priest reproducing in himself the image of the Good Shepherd.

### EVANGELIZER

A key role of the priest is to preach the word of God, to be an evangelizer. In the present cultural environment, where people are constantly bombarded with audio and visual images, it is difficult for the priest to make his voice heard above all the static in the air waves. His preaching is also challenged by the pervasive catechetical illiteracy. Since he is a bearer of the only message that will bring about personal happiness, following the example of St Paul he is asked to preach the good news of salvation in and out of season if he is to convince people that the attractions of this world do not in the long run provide redemption.

> As minister of the essential saving acts, he places at the service of all men not perishable goods, nor socio-political projects, but supernatural and eternal life, teaching how to read and interpret the events of history in a Gospel perspective. This is the primary task of the priest, even in the area of new evangelization, which requires priests who, as primarily responsible together with their Bishops for this renewed Gospel sowing, are 'deeply and fully immersed in the mystery of Christ'(*Pastores dabo vobis*, 18).[36]

In Chapter 8, 'The priest as evangelizer', some of the implications of this aspect of the pastoral role are developed. Since the thrust of evangelization and preaching is to help people discover their individual vocation in the Church, an integral part of the priest's role is to help those who are so called to discern vocation to the priesthood. Because of the radical decline in vocations this aspect of evangelization has now acquired a special urgency. John Paul II warns that priests can no longer adopt a passive role in relation to nurturing priestly vocations: he strongly encourages them to be proactive and to positively invite young men to follow Christ along this path. The chapter concludes by considering ways in which the priest can respond to the challenge of the vocations ministry.

35 Cf. PDV, 43. 36 John Paul II, Address, 23 October 1993.

CHASTITY, MARRIAGE

A sad feature of Western society over the past few decades has been the cor-
ruption of sexual moral values and the growth of a hedonistic culture even in
countries with a deep-rooted Christian tradition. This has had profound negative effects not only on individuals but also on families and society as a whole.
Therefore to preach about chastity in the present context is very much a
counter-cultural exercise. Yet even secular society is beginning to recognize the
bitter fruits being reaped from an amoral approach to human sexuality as
reflected in the rapid growth of unwed teenage pregnancies, abortion, sexual-
ly transmitted diseases, and the collapse of traditional family values. The
immense social cost of sexual irresponsibility is now forcing public authorities
to look again at traditional values in this area, even to the extent of organising
advertising campaigns which extol the value and advantages of virginity.

Since sexuality is such an integral constituent of the human personality,
and since it is a gift given by God for a very noble purpose, precisely because it
is a human capacity that can easily be misused and perverted we need to be regularly reminded of the moral dimension of sexual activity. Yet homilies about
God's plan for human sexuality, both inside and outside of marriage, are sel-
dom heard today. This may be due in part to the prevalent media hostility to
the Christian perception of chastity, and the Church's supposed over-concern
with sexual morality at the expense of other areas of moral action. Up to the
time of Vatican II there may have been a certain negative emphasis in preaching about chastity. However, it is a rare experience today to hear a homily on
this topic, and even rarer for married couples to listen to an explanation of
*Humanae vitae* from the ambo.

Chastity is not, of course, the first or the most important of the Christian
virtues. Yet because the proper ordering of sexuality has such profound consequences for the good of the family and society, it demands adequate attention
in any homiletic or catechetical programme. The extensive catechesis of John
Paul II at the beginning of his pontificate (1979-84) on 'the nuptial meaning of
the body' has left priests a wealth of material for preaching about chastity and
*Humanae vitae* in an encouraging and challenging way. He draws his doctrine
from scriptural sources and a rich Christian anthropology and, in so doing,
demonstrates how Catholic moral teaching on human sexuality is always pro-
love and pro-life. Chapter 9, 'Preaching about marriage, chastity and *Humanae
vitae*', is primarily a presentation of this teaching of John Paul II on the theology of the body, a teaching which provides the necessary context to make
Catholic doctrine on sexual morality credible and convincing. Because pastoral
work in relation to marriage and the family at the present time is so crucial for
the future of the Church, a point consistently made by the present Pope, I have

dealt not only with a number of key aspects of family apostolate, but have tried to give a clear statement of the underlying theological issues as well.

## HOLY SPIRIT, SIN, RECONCILIATION

The essence of the message of salvation is the invitation to respond to God's grace and to experience the adventure of being adopted children of God through baptism. Vatican II has reaffirmed the idea that Christ calls all his followers to holiness and to grow progressively in friendship with him. Yet this noble aspiration for sanctity in man is often thwarted by his sinful tendencies. Because his nature was damaged by original sin, he will continue to experience in his soul the barb of pride, selfishness and sensuality. Living in a materialistic and hedonistic environment, he will also have to do battle with many external enticements to sin.

To respond to this undoubted moral fragility, with the sacrament of Reconciliation Christ left us a formidable antidote to sin. On the very day of his resurrection, Jesus appeared to the apostles in the Cenacle and imparted to them the sacred power to forgive sins in his name. This extraordinary prerogative is linked by Christ to a special infusion of the Holy Spirit which he bestows on his apostles that first Easter evening (cf. Jn 20:21-23). To plumb the depths of sacramental power conferred on him by ordination the priest needs to be familiar with the action of the Holy Spirit both in his own soul and in the souls of those to whom he ministers. Chapter 10, 'Holy Spirit, sin, reconciliation', reviews this dimension of the priestly life with particular reference to the sacrament of Penance. It discusses some of the factors which have led to a loss of the sense of sin in contemporary Western culture, and the role of the Holy Spirit in 'convincing about sin'. It also suggests ways of addressing the dramatic fall-off in the use of the sacrament of confession.

## SPIRITUAL GUIDANCE

In *Pastores dabo vobis* John Paul II reminds priests that : 'It is necessary to rediscover the great tradition of personal spiritual guidance which has always brought great and precious fruits to the Church's life'.[37] The Vatican II decree on *The ministry and life of priests* also encouraged them to have a very high regard for this ascetical practice.[38] The aim of Chapter 11, 'Spiritual guidance for priest and laity', is to develop this point and to highlight some of the many

37 No. 46. 38 Cf. no.18.

practical advantages which the priest can derive from personal spiritual guidance. Not the least of these will be his increased effectiveness in giving spiritual direction to lay people.

Referring to role of the priest in giving personal attention to souls, the Holy Father reminds us that

> the community dimension of pastoral care cannot overlook the needs of the individual faithful ... The Council stresses the need to help each member of the faithful to discover his specific vocation as a proper, characteristic task of the pastor who wants to respect and promote each one's personality. One could say that by his own example Jesus himself, the Good Shepherd who 'calls his own sheep by name' (cf. Jn 10:3-4), has set the standard of individual pastoral care: knowledge and a relationship of friendship with individual persons. It is the presbyter's task to help each one to utilize well his own gift, and rightly to exercise the freedom that comes from Christ's salvation, as St Paul urges (cf. Gal 4:3; 5:1,13; see also Jn 8:36).[39]

Here we get a glimpse of the 'standard of individual pastoral care' expected of the priest, especially in the context of the universal call to holiness proclaimed by Vatican II.

The pastoral fruitfulness of spiritual guidance for the laity depends to a great extent on how well the priest understands the nature of the lay vocation in the Church. Recently the Pope felt obliged to clarify once again the theological character of this vocation as distinct from that of the priest. He reminds us that in the first place what Vatican II

> called for was lay involvement in the world of the family, commerce, politics, intellectual and cultural life – which are the proper field of specifically lay mission. The Council therefore stressed the essential secularity of the lay vocation (*Lumen gentium*, 31; cf also *Evangelii nuntiandi*, 70; *Christifideles laici*, 17). This does not mean that lay people have no special place or work to perform in the life of the Church *ad intra:* in many pastoral, liturgical and educational tasks, they clearly have. But the main focus of the lay vocation should be engagement in the world, while the priest has been ordained to be pastor, teacher and leader of prayer and sacramental life within the Church.[40]

In this chapter I have tried to summarize the main elements of lay spirituality

39 Address, 19 May 1993. 40 John Paul II, Address, 21 November 1998, no.5.

outlined in the documents of Vatican II as a context and a reference for priests so that the personal spiritual guidance they offer will be more effective.

## THE PRIEST AND THE LITURGY

The celebration of the liturgy is what defines the essence of the priest since his principal task is to renew on the altar Christ's sacrifice on Calvary. In recent decades, however, because the sacrificial aspect of the Mass has tended to be eclipsed by over-emphasis on other aspects of the Eucharist, an essential element of priestly identity – the sacrificial – has become somewhat shrouded and obscured. While Josef Pieper relates the crisis of priestly identity to a deficient faith in the sacrifice of the Mass,[41] Cardinal Ratzinger is of the opinion that the crisis in the Church as a whole is not unrelated to problems which have to do with the liturgy:

> A renewal of liturgical awareness, a liturgical reconciliation that again recognizes the unity of the history of the liturgy and that understands Vatican II, not as a breach, but as a stage of development: these things are urgently needed for the life of the Church. I am convinced that the crisis in the Church that we are experiencing today is to a large extent due to the disintegration of the liturgy, which at times has come to be conceived of *etsi Deus non daretur:* in that it is a matter of indifference whether or not God exists and whether or not he speaks to us and hears us.[42]

Loss of belief in the Real Presence is not just a consequence of deficient catechetics. The erosion of the numenous character of the liturgy over the past three decades also had its part to play. Unconsciously, perhaps, there was a dismantling of religious awe to encourage social participation in the liturgy. But as has been pointed out:

> The foundations of worship are fragile. Reverence is not hereditary ... It has to quicken anew in each generation. Consequently its modes of transmission have to be conserved and cherished. We need to be watchful not to dislodge a certain fear of the Lord – the trembling of the ancient psalmist – without which reverence cannot endure. It matters tremendously the things we choose as evocations of the divine

---

41 Josef Pieper, *In search of the sacred,* San Francisco, 1996, p. 30. 42 Joseph Cardinal Ratzinger, *Milestones: memoirs 1927-1977,* San Francisco, 1998, pp 148-9.

*mysterium.* So much depends on the settings we create for the life of prayer. *Lex orandi, lex credendi* (how we pray determines what we believe).[43]

In Chapter 12, 'The priest and the liturgy', I have tried to bring together the main theological principles underlying Catholic worship. I point out the continuity between the worship of the Old and the New Covenants, and some of the lessons to be learned from this. This chapter also deals with the nature of signs and symbols used in the liturgy, its sacramental dimension, participation of the laity in the liturgy, how silence and song are important elements of cult, and the influence of church art and architecture on the eschatological and doxological aspects of Catholic worship. A deeper sensitivity by the priest to these elements of the liturgy will enhance his role in the work of redemption.


ACKNOWLEDGMENTS

As I have already indicated, much of what I say in this book draws on the writings and teaching of John Paul II. It will be seen that his addresses to priests at many different times and places, the annual Holy Thursday Letters, and the apostolic exhortation *Pastores dabo vobis* are repeated sources of reference in the chapters which follow. On Trinity Sunday of 1982, with seventy-eight others, I had the privilege of being ordained to the priesthood by the present Holy Father in St Peter's in Rome. One way I feel I can show appreciation for this exceptional favour is by making more accessible some of the rich doctrine John Paul II has given us about the priesthood during his long and fruitful pontificate.

How one writes about priesthood is obviously influenced by personal perception and experience. All during my life I have had the good fortune to know priests who reflected in different ways the attractive image of Christ the Good Shepherd. Among these I would like to mention two in particular. The first is Blessed Josemaría Escrivá, founder of Opus Dei, whom I had the privilege to know personally. From him I learned many things, but especially what it means to be *alter Christus*, another Christ, as I saw it reflected in the generous example of his priestly life and in his rich theology of the priesthood. The second is Bishop Alvaro del Portillo, prelate of Opus Dei and successor to Blessed Josemaría. He called me to the priesthood, transmitted to me and my colleagues the benefit of his immense pastoral experience, and taught us how to love the priesthood as the greatest of God's gifts to mankind. From that pas-

43 Maureen Mullarkey, 'Worship gone awry', in *Crisis*, July/August 2000, p. 27.

toral and spiritual inheritance I have drawn deeply in writing this study, often times perhaps unaware that I am repeating their ideas and insights. It goes without saying that none of the limitations of this work can be held against them.

Since I am writing primarily for priests, occasionally I use 'we' rather than 'they' to avoid pedantic repetition and also where I feel such usage expresses more clearly what I am trying to say. Because the priesthood is the greatest gift I have received and the source of deepest personal fulfilment, I would find it difficult to discuss it in a totally detached, clinical way. I write, as it were, with my heart on my sleeve. However, I do not think that this approach will detract from its objectivity,

Among the bibliography referred to I wish to recognize the debt I owe to the material presented at the 1990 International Congress organized by the Theology Faculty of the University of Navarre, Pamplona (Spain). The topic of this congress was 'The nature of priestly formation as demanded by contemporary society'. In particular I would like to express my gratitude for the insights gained from the papers presented by Professors L. Mateo-Seco, J. L. Illanes, E. Borda, and A. Sarmiento.[44]

I would also like to thank the following who read through previous drafts of the text and who offered many helpful suggestions and ideas – Mgr Michael Manning, Fr James Gavigan, and Fr Tom O'Toole.

---

[44] These papers were subsequently published under the title: *La formación de los sacerdotes en las circunstancias actuales*, Pamplona, 1990.

# I

# The priesthood of Christ and its development in the New Testament

Since all priesthood stems from Jesus Christ, before we can develop a theology of priesthood we must first look to the life and teaching of the Master to learn from him what it means to be a priest. We can have access to the historical Jesus because the Christ who is with us in the Church is the same 'yesterday, today and forever' (Heb 13:8). Only if we take full account of his 'yesterday' can we grasp correctly the meaning of Christ's 'today', while at the same time being conscious that he is the eternal Christ. It is true that we find him in the Church, in the sacraments, in the liturgy, and in the life of Christians. But this experience has always to be interpreted and verified by reference to the source, especially the witness and testimony of those who knew Christ personally when he walked the earth. In this sense the Jesus of history must be an integral part of our faith.

Scripture scholars have investigated the historical Jesus in some depth, but with a tendency at times to lock him into the past, separating him from the Christ of faith we find in the Church. However, it was to the Church, the community of faith, that Christ said: 'he who hears you hears me; he who rejects you rejects me' (Lk 10:16). To open up the Scriptures we have to use a christological key under the light of the Holy Spirit. That christological key is constituted not only by what the Bible tells us about the Word made flesh. An essential part of its content is also the christological doctrine which the Magisterium, as authentic interpreter of sacred Scripture, has clarified down through the centuries and which is now an explicit part of the faith of the Church.[1] This is the perspective from which we now examine the New Testament in relation to what it tells us about the priesthood of Christ.

As we read the Gospels we gradually come to see how Jesus affirmed the basic elements of his priesthood. We notice how his actions, indeed his whole life, reflect the fact that as our Redeemer he was priest, prophet, and king. We draw especially on the witness of the Letter to the Hebrews to illustrate how

---

1 Cf. Vatican II constitution on Divine Revelation, *Dei verbum*, 7-10; Congregation for the Doctrine of the Faith, Declaration *Dominus Jesus*, 6 August 2000. See also Cardinal Joseph Ratzinger, *Sing a new song to the Lord*, New York, 1998, pp 3-15.

the implications of Christ's priesthood were clearly grasped by the first generation of Christian converts. By reviewing the Pauline corpus, and especially the Pastoral Letters, we see how the profile of the priest developed in the early Church. We will also reflect on how Christ continues his priestly activity through the Church which he established to channel and perpetuate the merits of his salvific work. Thus it is important for the priest to understand how he is grafted on to Christ through the mediation of this same Church in such a way that he represents both Christ and the Church.

One of the striking things about Jesus is that he does not call himself a priest, nor does he refer to priesthood when defining the role of his apostles. However, neither do we hear him explicitly call himself Messiah, Christ, Lord or Redeemer.[2] The reason Jesus avoids the title of priest is that his priesthood is very different from the hereditary Jewish priesthood. He was not part of the priestly tribe of Levi, but was a member of the tribe of Judah. It becomes clear, as his mission and teaching unfold, that his priesthood is of a different order to that of the Temple priesthood. Indeed, a characteristic of Jesus' public life is an ongoing confrontation with the outlook and mentality of the Jewish priests: it was obvious to everyone that he was not one of them. He lays down a significant marker about his priesthood with the declaration: 'I tell you, something greater than the Temple is here' (Mt 12:6). That Christ would consider himself superior to the Temple, the focus of Jewish worship and the centre of God's presence among the Hebrews, is a pointer to the radical difference of the New Covenant priesthood inaugurated by Christ and centred on him. This would also constitute the main charge brought by the Jews against Jesus at his trial. It confirms that his accusers understood clearly the import of Jesus' claim – that he was proposing to establish a new priesthood superior to that of the Temple (cf. Mt 26:61; Mk 14:28).[3]

## MEDIATOR

Christ comes as a priest-mediator offering the sacrifice of himself for sin, thus opening the way for us to participate in the divine life of the Trinity. He is the only mediator between God and man: 'No one', he tells us, 'comes to the Father, but by me' (Jn 14:6). Christ's power of mediation is grounded on the hypostatic union, but it is through his humanity that he mediates – his human nature is the bridge linking God and man

When we consider Christ's mediatorship, we immediately think of him as a mediator to reconcile God with men and men with God. But, as Scheeben

2 Cf. Jean Galot, *Theology of priesthood*, San Francisco, 1985, p. 32. 3 Cf. Galot, pp 34-5.

tellingly points out, this is only a single, subordinate factor in the God-man's mediatorship. As the only-begotten Son of the Father, he transmits to all who believe in him the power to become sons and daughters of God (cf. Jn 1:12). This is the fullest expression of the mediatory role of Christ. God draws so close to us that, with his grace, the immeasurable chasm which separates the creature from God is bridged and, in the grace of divine sonship, together with the extinction of guilt, an extraordinary supernatural union between God and man is established – we become, in the words of St Peter, *divinae consortes naturae,* sharers in the divine nature (cf. 2 Pet 1:4). By the price of the same blood by which Christ redeemed us from the slavery of sin, he also purchased our divine filiation, our admission into the sonship of God.[4]

To understand more clearly the notion of mediator we first need to look at this concept in the context of the Old Testament. Priests and prophets were mediators between Yahweh and the people of Israel in relation to the Old Covenant. The priests made it possible for man to enter into union with God by mediating divine blessings and presenting offerings for atonement and purification from sin. While the most important characteristic of the prophet was to impart revelation and to act as its authentic interpreter, his function also manifested itself as an office of interceding (cf. Jer 7:16; 14:11; Ezek 14:13-20), and as having access to God on behalf of individuals or for the people (cf. Amos 7:7; Dan 9:4-20). Moses was a mediator of the Old Covenant in so far as he interceded for the Chosen People (cf. Deut 9:18f) during the plagues of Egypt (Ex 8; 9; 10), and to appease the wrath of Yahweh (Num 14:13-20).[5]

The term mediator does not appear in the Gospels. It was created by the early Church in order adequately to express the place of Jesus in God's plan and in his work of salvation (cf. Gal 3:19f; Heb 7:6; 9:15; 12:24; 1 Tim 2:5). In Paul's first letter to Timothy (cf. 2:5) mediatorship is envisaged as operating in an upward direction. The redeemer represents men to God and must therefore be identified with them. Hence the strong emphasis on his humanity. United to his brothers and sisters in a common destiny, Jesus makes himself answerable for sin (cf. 2 Cor 5:21; Gal 3:13) and gives the 'ransom' which obtains pardon for them from God. As mediator he is also at the same time security – his blood is the purchase price (cf. 1 Cor 6:20; 7:23; Tit 2:14).

In the mediation of Jesus we can distinguish the triple office of Christ : pastoral or royal, prophetic or teaching, and priestly or sanctifying.[6] They are not separate functions but different aspects which support and enrich one another. In each and every action and word, Christ exercises his teaching

---

4 Cf. Matthias Joseph Sheeben, *The mysteries of Christianity,* St Louis, MO, 1946, p. 411.  5 Cf. J. B. Baur (ed.), *Encyclopedia of biblical theology,* vol. 2, London, 1970, pp 566-8.  6 Cf. Vatican II constitution on the Church, *Lumen gentium,* 13.

authority, his priesthood, and his kingship, but each of these three dimensions is expressed in a special way at particular moments in his life.[7]

## SHEPHERD, SERVANT, AND KING

Jesus claims to be the Good Shepherd of the new Christian community (cf. Jn 10:11). His mission, which he shares with his disciples, is to 'the lost sheep of the house of Israel' (Mt 10:6;15:24), and he is eager to recover those who have strayed (cf. Lk 15:3-7; Mt 18:12-14). In referring to himself as the good shepherd, Jesus is evoking an analogy with which the Jews were very familiar, that is, of Yahweh as the shepherd of his people (cf. Ezek 34).

Jesus speaks about his kingdom which has no end (cf. Lk 1:32-33). His kingship is proclaimed in the Old Testament (cf. Ps 2:6; Is 9:6) and equiparated to the status of shepherd of the people who are his flock (Is 4:9-11; Jer 3:15). Christ's kingship is not just a metaphor but a reality deriving from the hypostatic union, and by virtue of the fact that he is our Redeemer. As king he promulgates the New Law, institutes the Church and the sacraments, and is entrusted with the power of judgement (cf. Jn 5:22). He begins his preaching by proclaiming the arrival of the kingdom of God (cf. Mk 1:15). It is not of this world (cf. Jn 18:36), but is an essentially spiritual kingdom (cf. Lk 17:21). However, in so far as it is made up of men, it is a people – the Church.

Christ claims the title of king at his trial before the Roman authorities (cf. Jn 18:37). His is a kingship that imposes itself not through human power, but through sacrifice – the power of the good shepherd. Jesus never uses his divine power to his own personal advantage but, as his many miracles testify, always for the benefit of others. He has not come 'to call the righteous, but sinners to repentance' (Lk 5:32); he is 'a friend of tax collectors and sinners' (Mt 11:19). His power and authority are always expressed as pastoral charity: 'Greater love has no man than this, that a man lay down his life for his friends' (Jn 15:13). Hence his advice to his first priests: 'love one another as I have loved you' (Jn 15:12). His teaching in this regard is so radically different from the attitudes of the religious leaders of the Jews that Christ could justifiably say to his disciples that he was giving them 'a new commandment'(cf. Jn 13:34).

As the new Adam, Christ is head of regenerate mankind whom he vivifies with his own divine life. He has been anointed as king (Heb 1:8; Jn 18:37) and has full power over all that the messianic kingdom contains (Lk 22:29). Thus he is the head and origin of the new creation, founder and teacher of the New

7 Cf. F. Ocariz, L. Mateo Seco, J. A. Riestra, *The mystery of Christ*, Dublin, 1994, p. 141 (subsequently referred to as Ocariz et al.).

Covenant, head and ruler of the Church (Eph 4:15f). To be redeemed, man needs only to cleave to his person, 'to be in Christ' (1 Cor 1:30; Col 1:27).[8]

Christ's priesthood is, then, one of service, one of atonement. In trying to explain to his disciples that true greatness consisted in service to others, Jesus revealed one of the deepest sentiments of his heart: 'For the Son of Man also came not to be served but to serve, and to give his life as a ransom for many' (Mk 10:45; Mt 20:28). In this affirmation, which offers a striking model for the priestly service of those who would come after him, Jesus powerfully evokes the image of the suffering servant of Isaiah (Is 53). Priests exercise their ministry with the authority of Christ, but that authority is exercised very differently from the way the world perceives it: 'whoever would be great among you must be your servant, and whoever would be first among you must be slave of all' (Mk 10: 43-44).[9]

### PROPHET AND PRIEST

The public life of Jesus exemplifies the primacy of the teaching role. He had compassion on the multitude because, from the perspective of knowledge of eternal life, they were wandering aimlessly, untaught, with nobody to guide them. Christ's reaction was to invest a lot of time in their instruction (cf. Mk 6:34). At the beginning of his public life he describes his mission as the proclamation of the good news (cf. Lk 4:18-19). And summing up his life's work at his trial before Pilate, he declares that the whole purpose of his mission was 'to bear witness to the truth' (Jn 18:37).

But Jesus is more than a prophet. He is the master who teaches on his own authority (cf. Mt 5:22; 7:29; Jn 8.51). 'You', he tells the apostles, 'call me Teacher and Lord and you are right, for so I am' (Jn 13:10). He not only teaches the truth, but is Truth personified (cf. Jn 14:6). In fact all Christ's life was a continuous teaching which completes and perfects divine revelation.[10] He is the one who reveals the face of the Father: thus his reply to Philip, 'he who has seen me has seen the Father' (Jn 14:9; 12:45).

There are, as we have seen, several references in the Gospel where Jesus defines his role in relation to his followers as that of the good shepherd. But, as Christ himself points out, sacrifice is a characteristic act of the shepherd's mission: 'The good shepherd lays down his life for the sheep' (Jn 10:11). As a consequence of the Incarnation, the Word as man can offer his life to his Father God to win that more abundant life for the sheep (cf. Jn 10:11): his sacrifice of atonement brings about the redemption of fallen man. This, however,

8 Cf. Baur, p. 570.   9 Cf. Galot, p. 45.   10 Cf. Vatican II constitution on Divine Revelation, *Dei Verbum*, 4.

is a sacrifice which he freely offers: 'I lay [my life] down of my own accord' (Jn 10:18). Jesus claims the power to offer the sacrifice of his own life in the context of his mission as good shepherd. This is an expression of love which goes beyond human comprehension, the love with which Christ loved his disciples to the end (cf. Jn 13:1).

In Capernaum, towards the beginning of his public life, he intimated the ritual dimension of his vocation as good shepherd: 'Truly, truly, I say to you, unless you eat the flesh of the Son of Man and drink his blood, you have no life in you' (Jn 6:43): the good shepherd gives his life to nourish the flock. In his priestly prayer at the Last Supper he would be able to say: 'I have finished the work you have given me to do' (Jn 17:4). Hence, his life was an act of self-giving, an oblation which culminated on Calvary: 'not my will, but thine be done' (Lk 22:43).

### PRIESTHOOD OF JESUS CHRIST IN THE LETTER TO THE HEBREWS

One of the central concerns of the author of the epistle to the Hebrews is to demonstrate to Christian converts from Judaism the superiority of Christ's priesthood and sacrifice over the Temple ritual and worship. The basic affirmation of Hebrews is that, because of his own sacrifice, Jesus has been proclaimed for all time high priest of the order of Melchizedek (cf. Heb 5:6-10; 6:20; 7:17), a position which echoes the claim of Jesus himself during his trial (cf. Mt 24:64). Christ's priesthood is therefore a heavenly and eternal priesthood, immensely superior to the Levitical priesthood of the Old Law.

The author of Hebrews interprets the Christian exodus in terms of the sanctuary of Heaven, and he draws on the ritual of the Jewish liturgy, particularly as it was carried out in the desert, to set up an analogy for expressing the Christian mystery. In terms of this ritual the Letter presents an image of Christ the King entering the heavenly sanctuary as a priest. Risen from the dead he enters definitively into the eternal sanctuary, the place where God dwells (cf. Heb 9:12). The blood that gains him entry is not that of goats or calves but his own blood which has won us eternal redemption.[11] For Hebrews the drama of the redemption is a great liturgical action celebrated by Christ whose mission is thus seen as an essentially priestly one. He comes into the world so that he may return to the heavenly sanctuary as a priest, bringing with him the wounds of the sacrifice he con-

---

11 Because of its comparison with the Jewish liturgy of expiation, Hebrews lays more stress on Christ's bearing his blood into the presence of God than on the actual shedding on Calvary. This is because the slaughter outside the tent was secondary in the Jewish ritual; what constituted the sacrifice was the sprinkling of the blood in the Holy of Holies (cf. Heb 12:12). Cf. Colman O'Neill, *Meeting Christ in the sacraments*, Cork, 1964, p. 27.

summated on earth as a permanent expression of his eternal priestly mediation before the Father (cf. Heb 10:5-7).[12]

Hebrews gathers together the tradition of the Old Testament on priesthood and sacrifice. As early as Ps 110 the Messiah is described as a king-priest after the order of Melchizedek, a psalm which is frequently quoted in the New Testament as a messianic prophecy. There is a clear affirmation in the Old Testament, as seen especially in the poems of the Servant of Yahweh, that the Messiah would save his people through suffering. In other words, his death would be a redemptive one, a sacrifice in the strict meaning of the term. The author of Hebrews not only makes Christ's priesthood the central theme of the Letter, but portrays the entire messianic work of Jesus as priestly mediation, describing him as the great priest of the New Alliance, as the mediator of 'a new covenant' (Heb 9:15; cf. 8:6). Here it echoes Jesus' own words at the Last Supper where he invites his disciples to drink his blood, which is the blood of the New Covenant (cf. Mk 14:24; Mt 26:28).

Hebrews affirms a concept of priesthood in two passages in connection with sacrifice (Heb 5:1-2 and 8:3). It emphasises that in Christ are to be found all the essential characteristics of priesthood: real man, divine calling, consecration, connection with sacrifice (Heb 2:11-18; 9:26; 10:5-10). The Letter refers to Christ as priest under the following titles: a priest of the order of Melchizedek (5:6; 6:20; 7:11, 17); a high priest (5:10); a merciful and faithful high priest (2:17); a high priest of our confession (3:1); a great high priest (4:14); a high priest, holy, blameless, and unstained (7:16); a high priest of the good things to come (9:11).[13] The several references to Melchizedek demonstrate that the priesthood does not come to Christ through physical descent – it is an eternal priesthood which lasts forever (5:6; 6:20; 7:17). He is presented both as priest and victim on Calvary (cf. Heb 9:22-26).

The prophetic aspect of Christ's priesthood is underlined by the manner in which it is presented at the beginning of the letter: 'In many and various ways God spoke of old to our fathers by the prophets; but in these last days he has spoken to us by a Son, whom he appointed the heir of all things, through whom also he created the world' (Heb 1:1-2). Jesus is the very Word of God and not just the fulfilment of the prophecies of the past: he is in fact the complete and final revelation of the Father, 'the mediator and the sum total of Revelation'.[14]

In heaven he continues his mediation on our behalf 'as high priest of the good things to come' (Heb 9:11; cf. 7:25; 9:24) through the permanent consecration of the hypostatic union. Thus the work of Christ – the salvation of men – is carried out in three principal stages: the Incarnation (cf. Heb 2:10-

12 Cf. O'Neill, p. 26.   13 Cf. Ocariz et al., p. 167.   14 *Dei Verbum*, 2.

18), his death on the cross (cf. Heb 9:26-28), and his eternal glorification (cf. Heb 10:11-15). In the light of this unity it can be clearly seen that the totality of the mystery of Christ is priestly, that he is essentially a priest by his very constitution – the hypostatic union - and that all his work is nothing other than priestly mediation.[15]

## THE PRIESTHOOD OF JESUS IN THE WRITINGS OF ST PAUL

While St Paul does not refer to Christ as a priest, he does however speak of him from this perspective: 'Christ our passover has been sacrificed' (1 Cor 5:7). All the effects of the redemption are ascribed to the blood of Christ (cf. Eph 1:7; Col 1:20; Rom 5:9, etc.), who underwent the punishment which we merited on account of our sins (cf. Rom 4:25; 8:32). We have been ransomed by the shedding of his blood (cf. 1 Cor 6:20; 7:23), an offering pleasing to God (cf. Gal 2:20), which assuaged his justifiable anger (cf. Rom 3:25). By taking on human nature Christ became the representative and 'head' of all mankind – the 'New Adam' (1 Cor 15:20-22). His death is a perfect atonement for sin – Christ 'gave himself up for us, a fragrant offering and sacrifice to God' (Eph 5:2). His redemptive sacrifice is a divine initiative (Rom 5:19; 8:32), a free act of obedience prompted by love (Eph 5:2), which is accepted by the Father.

We have seen that one of the strongest arguments for affirming Christ's priesthood is the sacrificial nature of his death. It is superior to all the old sacrifices, not only because of the priest who offered it but also because of the victim offered. As a consequence of the identity between priest and victim there is thus a perfect unity between the *interior* sacrifice and the *exterior* sacrifice, which is always the purpose of the highest form of worship.[16] Because it was not only his body which was offered in sacrifice but also his soul, the correspondence between the external and internal sacrifice could not have been more perfect. So it was that the sacrifice on Calvary was a perfect holocaust.

Through the Incarnation the human nature of Jesus was raised to the highest possible degree of holiness because of its union with the person of the Word. Christ has been given grace not only because of his dignity as Son, but

15 Cf. Lucas F. Mateo-Seco, 'El ministerio, fuente de la espiritualidad del sacerdote', in *La formación de los sacerdotes* ..., Pamplona, 1990, p. 404. For a more detailed exegetical analysis of Hebrews, see Albert Vanhoye, *Old Testament priests and the new priest*, Petersham, Mass., 1986, pp 67-235. 16 'The unity in the sacrificial act between what is offered and the offerer brings to its fullness what is, in a sense, the universal law of all sacrifice. *External* sacrifice has meaning and value to the extent that it is the expression of the *interior* sacrifice by which the victim is offered to God for sin or as a sacrifice of praise ... External sacrifice is meritorious to the extent that it is the expression of interior sacrifice' (cf. Ocariz et al., p. 170).

also with a view to his mission as the new Adam and Head of the Church. As we read in *Mystici corporis*:

> Christ is the author and efficient cause of holiness; for there can be no salutary act which does not proceed from him as from its supernatural source ... From him flows into the Body of the Church all the light which divinely illuminates those who believe, and all the grace which makes them holy as he himself is holy.[17]

All during his hidden life on earth Jesus exercised his triple role of mediator (as shepherd, teacher and priest). This is because every human action of Christ, because it is a human action of God, has a transcendent value for our redemption and salvation.[18] Indeed, any single action of Jesus would have been sufficient of its own to redeem all mankind.[19] Christ's whole earthly life – his words and deeds, his silences and sufferings, his very manner of being and speaking, is revelation of the Father. His whole life is a mystery of redemption and recapitulation – all he said and suffered had for its aim restoring fallen man to his original vocation.[20] The hidden years of Jesus' life allow us to participate in the mystery of Christ through the most ordinary events of daily life.

### PASCHAL MYSTERY

The Paschal mystery of Christ's passion, death and Resurrection constitutes the core of the good news of salvation which the apostles and their successors were to proclaim to the world. Some incidents in his public life, such as his baptism in the Jordan and transfiguration on Mount Olivet, illustrate how his whole life was orientated to the Paschal mystery.

By his redemptive death Christ fulfilled Isaiah's prophecy of the suffering Servant (cf. Is 53:7-8; Acts 8:32-35). Indeed he explained the meaning of his life and death from this perspective after his Resurrection as he walked with the two disciples along the road to Emmaus (cf. Lk 24:25-27; 44-45). St Paul affirms that Jesus died 'in accordance with the scriptures' (1 Cor 15:40) – he sees the events of the Paschal mystery as a fulfilment of the prophecies and figures of the Old Testament.

> Christ's death is both the *Paschal sacrifice* that accomplished the definitive redemption of men, ... and the *sacrifice of the New Covenant*, which restores man to communion with God through the 'blood of the

17 Pius XII, Encyclical *Mystici corporis*, 49.  18 Cf. St Thomas Aquinas, S. Th., III, qq 31-48.  19 Cf. ibid., q 46, a. 6 in c.  20 Cf. CCC, 517-18.

covenant, which was poured out for many for the forgiveness of sins' (Mt 26:28).[21]

One of the very beautiful metaphors designating the relationship between Christ and his Church is that of Bridegroom and Bride. The spousal relationship of Yahweh with his people, as described by the prophets in the Old Testament, was a prefiguring of Christ's relationship with his Church. Jesus took up this idea specifically when he referred to himself as the 'bridegroom' (Mk 2:39). Paul in turn speaks of the whole Church, and of each of the faithful, members of his Body, as a bride 'betrothed' to Christ the Lord so as to become one spirit with him (cf. 1 Cor 6:15-17; 2 Cor 11:2).[22] This spousal relationship between Christ and his Church, with all that that implies in terms of self-giving and faithful, redemptive love, is to be the model for the relationship between husband and wife in marriage (cf. Eph 5:21-32), but more particularly, from our perspective, for the priest's love for the Church.[23]

## THE NEW TESTAMENT BASIS FOR PRIESTHOOD

Jesus gathered a group of twelve around him after an explicit invitation to share his company and to participate in his evangelizing mission. He formed them to be the foundation stones of his Church. After he had revealed to them the mysteries of the kingdom of heaven (Mk 4:11; Mt 13:11; Lk 8:10), he gave them a mission to preach and the power to cast out devils after the model of his own mission: Jesus sends out the Twelve as he was sent by the Father (Mk 9:37; Jn 20:21; Lk 10:16). The mission he gave the apostles was a continuation of his own mission: 'He who receives you receives me'(Mt 10:40; cf. Jn 20:21).[24]

At the same time he invests them with extraordinary authority: 'Truly, I say to you, in the new world, when the Son of man shall sit on his glorious

---

21 CCC, 613. 22 For a detailed analysis of St Paul's spousal theology, see John Paul II, Apostolic letter, *Mulieris dignitatem*, 23-27 (15 August 1988). 23 'The Church ... is held, as a matter of faith, to be unfailingly holy. This is because Christ, the Son of God, who with the Father and Spirit is hailed as "alone holy", loved the Church as his Bride, giving himself up for her so as to sanctify her (cf. Eph 5:25-26); he joined her to himself as his body and endowed her with the gift of the Holy Spirit for the glory of God. Therefore all in the Church, whether they belong to the hierarchy or are cared for by it, are called to holiness, according to the Apostle's saying: "For this is the will of God, your sanctification' (1 Thess 4:3; cf. Eph 1:4)' (*Lumen gentium*, 39). 24 'For the sake of his universal priesthood of the New Covenant Jesus gathered disciples during his earthly mission (cf. Lk 10:1-12) and with a specific and authoritative mandate he called and appointed Twelve "to be with him, and to be sent out to preach and have authority to cast out demons" (Mk 3:14-15)'(PDV, 14).

throne, you who have followed me will also sit on twelve thrones, judging the twelve tribes of Israel' (Mt 19:28). They have been given the mission and the power to rule over the Church, the new Israel. But as Luke points out, there is a connection between the power conferred and a life of commitment to sacrifice:

> You are those who have continued with me in my trials; as my Father appointed a kingdom for me, so do I appoint for you that you may eat and drink at my table in my kingdom, and sit on thrones judging the twelve tribes of Israel (Lk 22:28-30).

This leadership is combined with the mission to evangelize the whole world (Mt 28:18-20; Mk 16:16-18), the power to celebrate the Eucharist (Lk 22:19-21), and the power to remit all sins (Jn 20:20-22; Lk 24:47). In summary we can say that Christ transmitted his own priesthood to the Twelve, constituted by the triple office of shepherding, preaching and sanctifying.[25]

Jesus not only confers on the Twelve his own priesthood, but establishes the basic hierarchical structure that pertains to priesthood based on the idea of a gradation of sacred powers.[26] Peter was given the primacy of jurisdiction (Mt 16:16-19) and all that that involved in terms of being the rock on which the Church is grounded, ready to strengthen the faith of his brothers (Lk 22:31-32).[27] He is to be the universal shepherd of the flock (Jn 21:15-19), ready to lay down his life for it (Jn 10:11) just as Christ was ready to sacrifice his.

Apart from the Twelve there were seventy disciples endowed with Christ's authority to teach (Lk 10:16). There is a similarity in the powers conferred on the two groups – both can cast out devils (Mk 3:15). Christ thus shared with the wider group of his disciples the mission to preach the good news of the kingdom, and his power over the forces of evil. While the Twelve have a higher authority, the essential characteristics and powers attached to both missions are the same. Since the mission entrusted to the Twelve to evangelize the whole world (Mt 28:18-20) is so immense, something which will last to the end of time, the appointment of successors to the apostles and the seventy disciples is implicit in the task assigned by Christ. Under the guidance of the Holy Spirit, who will lead the apostles into all truth and recall for them all that Christ taught them (cf. Jn 14: 26; 16:13), the priestly power instituted by Christ would be transmitted to succeeding generations of bishops and priests.[28]

25 Cf. Aidan Nichols, *Holy Order*, Dublin, 1990, pp 5-34. 26 Cf. Galot, p. 77. 27 Congregation for the Doctrine of the Faith, 'The primacy of the successor of Peter in the mystery of the Church', *Osservatore Romano*, 18 November 1998. 28 Cf. Galot, pp 85-7.

## ST PAUL'S PRIESTHOOD

St Paul is deeply aware of the novelty of his own mission coming directly from Christ. He has been appointed a priest of Jesus Christ and is sent especially to evangelize the Gentile nations (Rom 15:15-16). He has been ordained 'minister of a new covenant' (2 Cor 3:6) which implies two specific responsibilities. Firstly he has to reveal the mystery and the glory of Christ (2 Cor 4:6), God's plan to bring salvation to man. This theme runs right through Paul's letters, reaching its fullest development in Ephesians. The other characteristic of his ministry emphasized by Paul is that of 'reconciliation' (2 Cor 5:18). Our Lord entrusted the apostles with the 'message of reconciliation' (2 Cor 5:19) to pass it on to all men. Hence Paul's pressing appeal, 'We beseech you on behalf of Christ, be reconciled to God' (2 Cor 5:20).

Paul underlines the nature of his priestly vocation by his teaching on the renewal of the Eucharistic sacrifice (1 Cor 11:17-32). Taken in conjunction with a previous text in the same letter to the Corinthians (10:14-22), the Apostle spells out some basic truths about the Eucharist – that it was instituted by Christ himself; that it is a sacrifice; that Christ is really present in the Eucharist under the appearances of bread and wine. He also affirms the institution of the priesthood by Christ with the words 'Do this in remembrance of me' (v.24), by which our Lord charged that the sacrament of his sacrifice on Calvary be enacted until the end of time (cf. Lk 22:19).[29] He emphasises that everything he passed on to the Corinthians he has received from the Lord himself through the apostolic Tradition (v.23). All of this shows that the apostolic and priestly ministry is clearly distinguished from the gifts and charisms common to ordinary faithful.[30]

29 The Council of Trent teaches that 'Our Lord Jesus Christ, that his priesthood might not come to an end with his death (cf. Heb 7:24), at the Last Supper ... offered up to God the Father his own body and blood in the form of bread and wine, and under the forms of those same things gave to the Apostles, whom he then made priests of the New Testament, that they might partake, commanding them and their successors in the priesthood to do likewise: *Do this in remembrance of me* (Lk 22:19; 1 Cor 11:24f), as the Catholic Church has always understood and taught' (22nd Session, *Doctrine concerning the sacrifice of the Mass*, Ch. 1). In this context it is worth noting that the word 'remembrance' is charged with the meaning of the Hebrew word used to convey the essence of the feast of the Passover – the commemoration of the exodus from Egypt. For the Israelites the Passover rite reminded them of a bygone event: they were conscious of making that event present, reviving it, in order to participate in it, in some way, generation after generation (cf. Ex 12:26-27; Deut 6:20-25). So when our Lord commands his Apostles to 'do this in remembrance of me', it is not a matter of merely recalling his supper but of renewing his own Passover sacrifice of Calvary, which already, at the Last Supper, was present in an anticipated way (see *The Navarre Bible: Corinthians*, Dublin, 1991, p. 118). 30 Cf. Cardinal Joseph Ratzinger, 'The nature of priesthood', in *Osservatore Romano*, 29 October 1990.

### STEWARDS OF THE MYSTERIES OF GOD

Paul reacts strongly to any interpretation of his ministry as acting in his own name. He proclaims himself as 'a servant of Christ and a steward of the mysteries of God' (1 Cor 4:1). 'Stewards of Christ' are those to whom he has entrusted his property – his teaching and his sacraments – for them to protect faithfully and to transmit intact. As Paul stresses, a basic qualification of being a servant or steward is trustworthiness (1 Cor 4:2).[31] He is also God's co-worker, a builder of the Church's foundations (cf. 1 Cor 3:10) in the different communities he evangelized. The authority of Paul in relation to the Christian community comes across very clearly in his First Letter to the Corinthians (1 Cor 4:21), even to the extent of threatening excommunication (1 Cor 5:5)

Paul doesn't offer a systematic doctrine of the priesthood, but his writings indicate that he has a priestly conception of the nature of his own apostolic activity and vocation which is grounded on the priesthood of Christ. When describing his ministry he includes in it all the essential features of the ministerial priesthood – the ministry of salvation and remission of sins, the proclamation of the word, steward of God's mysteries, authority to rule and build up the Christian community, Eucharistic worship. His whole ministry is imbued with a deep pastoral charity derived from his imitation of Christ.[32] In Paul's testimony to the apostolic ministry we find the same sacramental structure as that made known by Christ in the Gospels.

31 The Magisterium of the Church has often applied these words (cf. 1 Cor 4:1-2) to the Catholic priesthood: 'The Apostle of the Gentiles thus perfectly sums up what may be said of the greatness, the dignity and the duty of the Christian priesthood: "This is how one should regard us, as servants of Christ and stewards of the mysteries of God" (1 Cor 4:1). The priest is the minister of Christ, an instrument, that is to say, in the hands of the divine Redeemer. He continues the work of the redemption in all its universality and divine efficacy, that work that wrought so marvellous a transformation in the world. Thus the priest, as is said with good reason, is indeed "another Christ", for , in some way, he is himself a continuation of Christ: "As the Father has sent me, even so I send you" (Jn 20:21), is spoken to the priest, and hence the priest, like Christ, continues to give "glory to God in the highest, and on earth peace among men with whom he is well pleased" (Lk 2:14). A priest is appointed "steward of the mysteries of God" (cf. 1 Cor 4:1) for the benefit of the members of the mystical body of Christ, since he is the ordinary minister of nearly all the sacraments – those channels through which the grace of the Saviour flows for the good of humanity. The Christian, at almost every important stage of his mortal career, finds at his side the priest with power received from God, for the purpose of communicating or increasing that grace which is the supernatural life of his soul' (Pius XI, encyclical, *Ad catholici sacerdotii,* 20 December 1935). 32 Cf. Galot, p. 102.

## THE DEVELOPMENT OF THE PRIESTLY
## MINISTRY IN THE EARLY CHURCH

Presbyters were established in the newly evangelized communities. We are told that Paul and Barnabas 'appointed elders for them in every church' (Acts 14:13) after passing through Iconium, Lystra, Derbe, and Antioch in Pisidia. Titus also appointed elders in every town as directed by Paul (Tit 1:5). In the first epistle to Timothy, access to the ministry is explicitly linked to the laying on of hands (1 Tim 4:14; cf. also 2 Tim 1:6).[33]

The Pastoral Letters of St Paul tell us much about the functions of Church ministers in the early Christian communities. Paul gives Timothy and Titus a very definite and fixed role in the churches of Ephesus and Crete. Presbyters exercise authority in the local churches as shepherds (Acts 11:30; 20:28-33). Paul encourages the presbyters of Ephesus to be on guard for the flock and to feed the church of God (Acts 20:28). Peter's exhortations to the elders (cf.1 Pet 5:3) recall those of our Lord when he spoke about the good shepherd (Jn 10:1ff), and when he told Peter after the Resurrection, 'Feed my lambs ... Feed my sheep' (Jn 21:15-17). The Vatican II constitution on the Church draws inspiration from these same texts of Scripture when reminding pastors of their duties:

> As to the faithful, they (priests) should bestow their paternal attention and solicitude on them, whom they have begotten spiritually through Baptism and instruction (1 Cor 4:15; 1 Pet 1:23). Gladly constituting themselves models of the flock (cf. 1 Pet 5:3), they should preside over and serve their local community in such a way that it may deserve to be called by the name which is given to the unique People of God in its entirety, that is to say, the Church of God (cf. 2 Cor 1:1 and *passim*).[34]

Paul's pastoral letters emphasize the teaching function of the presbyter (1 Tim 5:17). An essential part of their mission is the preaching of the word of God and the instruction of the people. In relation to this ministry, Paul tells Timothy that he must strive 'to convince, rebuke and exhort' (2 Tim 4:2), devote himself to teaching, and work hard at evangelization (cf. 2 Tim 4:5). In liturgical assemblies he should attend to the reading of the sacred books and to preaching (cf. 1 Tim 4:13). Candidates for the episcopacy-priesthood must be competent teachers (1 Tim 3:2; 2 Tim 2:24); they must be faithful men if they are to pass on intact the doctrine they themselves have received (2 Tim 2:2).

---

33 Cf. Galot, p. 155. 34 *Lumen gentium*, 28; see also idem, no. 41.

The expressions 'sound doctrine' and 'sound teaching' are features of the Pastoral Letters and occur frequently (1 Tim 6:3; 2 Tim 1:13; 4:3; Tit 1:9; 1:13; 2:1-2).

In 1 Tim 1:14 Paul refers to the laying on of hands which Timothy received from the elders, that is, the rite of priestly ordination (cf. also 1 Tim 5:22; 2 Tim 1:6). He is to take charge of liturgical matters (cf. 1 Tim 2:1-12; 4:13). In his letter, James tells us that the presbyters are called to anoint the sick and to pray over them (Jas 5:14).


### APOSTOLIC SUCCESSION

By the end of the apostolic era the offices of 'presbyter' (the name coming from the Jewish tradition) and of 'bishop' and 'deacon' (titles taken from the secular world) had emerged as a clearly defined structure. This can be seen in two particular texts. In his address to the presbyters of Asia Minor Paul admonishes them,

> Keep watch over yourselves and all the flock of which the Holy Spirit has made you overseers. Be shepherds of the Church of God which he bought with his own blood (Acts 20:28).

As Ratzinger points out,

> two notions which up until this point were unconnected, that is, 'presbyter' and 'bishop', are here equated; the traditions of Christians stemming from those of a Jewish background and those of Christians who entered from paganism coalesce and are explained as a single ministry of apostolic succession.[35]

Entry into the ministry is by way of a call, a gift of the Holy Spirit, that is, a sacramental consecration, a ministry by which the duty of the apostles to feed the flock is continued. The ministry of priests and bishops as regards its spiritual essence is thus shown to be the same as the ministry of the apostles.

The same principles enunciated by St Paul are affirmed in the First Letter of St Peter (5:1-4):

> So I exhort the elders (presbyters) among you, as a fellow elder and a witness of the sufferings of Christ as well as a partaker in the glory that

35 Cf. Ratzinger, 'The nature of priesthood'.

is to be revealed: Tend the flock of God that is your charge, not by constraint but willingly, not for shameful gain but eagerly, not as domineering over those in your charge but being examples to the flock. And when the Chief Shepherd is manifested, you will obtain the unfading crown of glory.

In the very first words we find Peter affirming an identity between the apostolic and presbyteral ministry, thereby establishing 'a theological link between the ministry of the apostles and that of the presbyters'.[36] By referring to himself as a fellow elder or co-presbyter with the presbyters, Peter acknowledges that they are constituted in the same ministry, and thus firmly establishes the principle of apostolic succession. Thus *Pastores dabo vobis* summarizes:

> In their turn, the Apostles appointed by the Lord, progressively carried out their mission by calling, in various but complementary ways, other men as Bishops, as priests and as deacons, in order to fulfil the command of the Risen Jesus who sent them forth to all people in every age. The writings of the New Testament are unanimous in stressing that it is the same Holy Spirit of Christ who introduces these men chosen from among their brethern into the ministry. Through the laying on of hands (cf. Acts 6:6; 1 Tim 4:14; 5:22; 2 Tim 1:6) which transmits the gift of the Spirit, they are called and empowered to continue the same ministry of reconciliation, of shepherding the flock of God and of teaching (cf. Acts 20:28; 1 Pet 5:2).[37]

### CONCLUSION

Reflecting on divine revelation in the New Testament we see that the priesthood of Christ is clearly etched there, both in what he did and what he taught. He is mediator between God and men, and this is reflected in his exercise of the role of Good Shepherd, Priest and Teacher. His life is one of total self-giving to the will of the Father and, at the same time, one of unlimited service to the flock to lead them to salvation. This service finds its consummation in the sacrifice of his life on Calvary.

In Hebrews we see how the priestly institution of the of the Old Covenant finds its fulfilment in the mystery of Christ, a priest of a radically different kind from that of the Temple priests. For the author of Hebrews the new liturgy does not consist in ceremonies but in a real event, the death of Christ, which completely changes the religious situation of mankind, because it transforms

36 Ibid. 37 PDV, 15.

man and introduces him into the intimate life of God. The sacrifice of Christ is the one true sacrifice which, unlike the old, leads to true communion with God. Christ is also the one true priest in that he brought priestly mediation to its conclusion. By his total and perfect self-offering he establishes the New Covenant with God in the centre of human hearts.[38]

We have noted how Christ transmitted to his disciples a share in his authority and power as prophet, priest and king. He consecrated them as priests and entrusted them with the same mission which he had received from the Father (cf. Jn 20:21). They were to go to the ends of the earth to evangelize and baptize, building up the new People of God. As good shepherds they were to be ready to lay down their lives for the flocks entrusted to their care. In the early Christian communities we have seen how the episcopal and presbyteral offices took shape, containing in embryo all the essential elements of the Catholic priesthood of today.

---

38 Cf. Vanhoye, pp 232-3.

# 2

# Ministerial priesthood

To outline a theology of priestly identity it will first of all be necessary to review briefly the ecclesiology of Vatican II as developed in the constitution on the Church, *Lumen gentium*. The Council affirmed a new and enriched vision of the Church both from the point of view of its structure and mission. Before the Church is hierarchical we are reminded that it is first of all the People of God. This point is well made by the very sequence of the different chapters in *Lumen gentium*. The first chapter considers the mystery of the Church, and the second deals with the Church as the People of God. It is only when we come to chapter three that we are introduced to the Church as hierarchical, not as an end in itself, but in service to the faithful to bring them to salvation. This conciliar document spells out the equal dignity of all the faithful, including priests, stemming from Baptism.[1] The proclamation of the universal call to holiness in the same document redresses the lack of balance in previous Church teaching on the vocation of the laity.[2]

The theology of the priesthood of the lay faithful was a clear doctrine of the early Church, but it was lost sight of in later centuries when priority was given to monastic and religious spiritualities as a paradigm for the holiness of the laity. In the Book of Revelation we are told that Jesus 'made us a kingdom, priests to his God and Father' (Rev 1:6). St Peter develops this concept of the common priesthood of the faithful. They are to be 'a holy priesthood', offering 'spiritual sacrifices' (1 Pet 2:5), 'a chosen race, a royal priesthood, a holy nation, God's own people' (1 Pet 2:9). Here the titles applied to Israel in the Old Testament find their full meaning. This same theme is taken up by Vatican II:

> Christ the Lord, high priest taken from among men (cf. Heb 5:1-5), made the new people 'a kingdom of priests to his God and Father' (Rev 1:6; cf. 5:9-10). The baptized, by regeneration and the anointing of the Holy Spirit, are consecrated to be a spiritual house and a holy

---

1 Cf. *Lumen gentium*, 10. 2 Cf. ibid., 30-41.

priesthood, that through all the works of Christian men and women they may offer spiritual sacrifices and proclaim the perfection of him who has called them out of darkness into his marvellous light (cf. 1 Pet 2:4-10).[3]

This theology of a priestly people is based on the divine promise in Exodus to the people of Israel as a whole: 'You shall be to me a kingdom of priests and a holy nation' (Ex 19:6).

In this people there is only one priest, Jesus Christ, and one sacrifice, that which he offered on the cross and which is renewed in the Mass. But all Christians, through the sacraments of Baptism and Confirmation, obtain a share in the priesthood of Christ, and are thereby equipped to mediate in a priestly way between God and man and to take an active part in divine worship. Because of this baptismal anointing, they are priests of their own lives and can turn all their secular activities – family, social, professional, etc. – into a pleasing offering to God and thus make of them a way to holiness.[4] Theirs is a true priesthood although it is essentially different from the ministerial priesthood of those who receive the sacrament of Order.[5]

St Paul reinforces this idea of Simon Peter's. He encourages the first Christians to worship God 'by offering your living bodies as a holy sacrifice, truly pleasing to God' (Rom 12:1). We find the same concept in Hebrews (cf. Heb 13:15-16), an exhortation to offer a continual sacrifice of praise, doing good and sharing resources.[6] In Christ's own teaching we discover echoes of the notion of a universal priesthood offering spiritual worship, as, for example, in his conversation with the Samaritan woman about worshipping the Father in spirit and in truth (cf. Jn 4:23). John Paul II sums up this teaching as follows:

> With the one definitive sacrifice of the Cross, Jesus communicated to all his disciples the dignity and mission of priests of the new and eternal Covenant. And thus the promise which God had made to Israel was fulfilled: 'You shall be to me a kingdom of priests and a holy nation' (Ex 19:6). According to St Peter, the whole people of the New Covenant is established as a 'spiritual house', 'a holy priesthood, to offer spiritual sacrifices acceptable to God through Jesus Christ' (1 Pet 2:5). The baptized are 'living stones' who build the spiritual edifice by keeping close to Christ, 'that living stone ... in God's sight chosen and precious' (1 Pet 2:4). The new priestly people which is the Church not only has its authentic image in Christ, but also receives from him a real

3 Cf. ibid., 10. 4 Cf. ibid., 34; *Christifideles laici*, 14; Blessed Josemaría Escrivá, *Christ is passing by*, Dublin, 1982, no. 96. 5 Cf. *Lumen gentium*, 10; *Presbyterorum ordinis*, 2. 6 Cf. Galot, p. 113.

ontological share in the one eternal priesthood, to which she must conform every aspect of her life.[7]

The scope of the apostolate of the laity was articulated by Vatican II in light of this new vision of their baptismal vocation. While the *Decree on the lay apostolate* outlined how the laity could cooperate directly in ecclesial activities,[8] the central thrust of this document is that their primary apostolic role is to transform the world from within by bringing Gospel values to bear on family life, education, media, culture, the world of work, politics, etc.[9] And the primary role of the priest is to unfold this baptismal grace.[10] It would seem, however, that much of this doctrine has been side-tracked, and thus the apostolate of the laity tends to be promoted primarily as a participation in ecclesial activities and ministries, many of which were previously carried out by the priest. This clericalization of the laity creates its own difficulties, not least for priests trying to identify clearly their role in the Church.[11]

## VATICAN II TEACHING ON PRIESTHOOD

The documents of Vatican II developed and enriched the concept of ministerial priesthood articulated by Trent. This counter-Reformation council defines the essence of the priesthood of the New Testament as the power of consecrating and offering the body and blood of Christ, and the power of forgiving sins.[12] In response to the Lutheran view that the priesthood consisted essentially in preaching, Trent insisted that it could not be reduced to this ministry alone. While the preaching and pastoral roles are implicit in the decrees of Trent, Vatican II made them explicit, thereby recovering for the Church a more scripturally grounded concept of priesthood.

*Lumen gentium* expressed its vision of ministerial priesthood within the context of the mission of the whole People of God which is carried out through a sharing in the office and mission of Christ.[13] The role of the priest has a triple dimension – a participation in the mission of Christ as Priest,

7 PDV, 13. 8 Cf. *Apostolicam actuositatem*, 10. 9 Cf. ibid., 11-17. 10 Cf. CCC, 1547. 11 The point has been well made that 'to the extent that this participation is presented as a "promotion" of the laity, we risk losing sight of the proper mission of the laity played out at the heart of the world, in the spheres of work, family, economy, communication, and politics. The laity have no need to become clericalized in order to be appreciated. To see their promotion in pastoral roles is a final residue of clericalism': Marc Ouellet, 'Priestly ministry at the service of ecclesial communion', in *Communio* 23 (Winter 1996), p. 680. The apostolate of the laity is discussed in greater detail in Chapters 8 and 9 below. 12 Cf. Council of Trent, 23rd Session on the Sacrament of Order, Chapter I (DS 1764). 13 Cf. *Lumen gentium*, 10.

Prophet, and King. It is not a question of three different functions, but of different aspects of the one mission of Christ which are closely linked, and which clarify and condition one another. As a consequence of Baptism all the faithful share in the mission of Christ. However, some members of the People of God, firstly as baptized Christians, and subsequently as priests through the sacrament of Order, witness to Christ in a special way in the Church and before the world.[14]

The priestly ministry, the mission of the Church, and the priesthood of Christ are realities which are so closely related that the consideration of any one of them requires that the others be keep clearly in focus at the same time. The mission of the Church consists in prolonging in space and time the mission of Christ, and the priestly ministry contributes in a very particular way to the realisation of that mission.[15] Thus, when considering the nature of the priestly ministry, the first point of reference is the mission of Christ and of the Church. The other indispensable co-ordinate for understanding the priesthood is the ontological component of consecration, since mission and consecration are inseparable in Christ, and Christ is always the central point of reference for priesthood in the Church.

> The priest shares in Christ's consecration and mission in a specific and authoritative way, through the Sacrament of Holy Orders, by virtue of which he is configured in his being to Jesus Christ, Head and Shepherd, and shares in the mission of 'preaching the good news to the poor' in the name and person of Christ himself.[16]

Through baptism every Christian is so configured to Christ that they can be called other Christs. But Christ is essentially a priest from whom all priesthood derives. Hence the baptismal consecration is a priestly consecration. As a consequence, all Christians are endowed and sent to carry out the mission in the Church which corresponds to them, according to that participation in the priesthood of Christ which they have received.[17] The participation correspon-

---

14 Cf. *Lumen gentium*, 28; *Holy Thursday Letter* (henceforth HTL), 1979, no. 3.  15 Cf. *Lumen gentium*, 1- 8.  16 PDV, 18. Cf. Augusto Saramiento, 'Elementos configuradores del la espiritualidad del sacerdote secular', in *La formación de los sacerdotes ...* Pamplona, 1990, p. 563.  17 From the Pauline doctrine of incorporation in Christ through baptism (cf. Rom 8:29; 13:14; Phil 3:10; 3:21; Gal 3:27; Col 3:10) and, as a consequence, becoming like him (cf. Rom 6:1-11; Col 1:19; 3:1-4; Eph 2:5-6: 4:13), the early tradition developed a conception of baptismal anointing which saw all Christians sharing in the gift and mission of Christ. Thus St John Damascene: 'Oil is used in Baptism to indicate our anointing, which makes us anointed ones, or christs' (*De fide orthodoxa*, 4, IX: PG 94, 1125 B), and St Augustine: 'All who have been anointed by his chrism we can rightly call christs and yet there is but one Christ: the whole body with its Head' (*De civitate Dei*, 17, IV: PL 41, 532).

ding to the sacrament of Order presupposes and requires that first insertion in Christ's priesthood acquired through baptism. But the consecration received through Holy Orders is qualitatively different from that of baptism, to the point that Vatican II says that it differs essentially, and not only in degree, from the common priesthood of the faithful.[18]

Thus in the ministerial priesthood there is a double participation in the priesthood of Christ. Exploring this particular configuration with Christ through the sacrament of Order allows us also to discover the nature of the priestly ministry:

> The ministerial priesthood in the People of God is something more than a holy public office exercised on behalf of the community: it is primarily a configuration, a sacramental and mysterious transformation of the person of the man-priest into the person of Christ himself, the only mediator (1 Tim 2:5). In effect, the priests of the New Alliance 'through that sacrament, by the anointing of the Holy Spirit, are signed with a special character and so are configured to Christ the priest' (*Presbyterorum ordinis*, 2). The mission and life of the priest are so configured to Christ's mission and life, that the sacrament of Order wonderfully equips a man (who has all the inherent weakness of the human condition) to act in the name of Christ himself, the head of the Church (cf. Council of Trent, 22nd Session, ch. 2; Pius XII, encyclical letter, *Mediator Dei*, 20 November 1947: AAS 39 (1947) 553; *Lumen gentium*, 10 and 28; *Presbyterorum ordinis*, 2), and to share in the authority 'by which Christ himself builds up and hallows and rules his Body'(*Presbyterorum ordinis*, 2).[19]

However, from St Thomas onwards the theology of priesthood acquired a new emphasis based on the concept of sacramental character, causing the traditional theology of anointing and the triple *munera* (teaching, sanctifying, shepherding) to recede considerably. The notions of character and grace now became the dominant elements in the theology of priesthood, and the idea of ministerial priesthood came to be exclusively related to divine worship with a parallel undervaluing of the baptismal priesthood. This theological imbalance was accentuated by the dynamics of the Reformation controversy when the reality of the ordained priesthood had to be energetically defended against the Lutheran denial of the essential difference between the ministerial priesthood and the common priesthood of the faithful. It was not until the beginnings of the twentieth century that there was a recovery of the concept of the common priesthood as a true and proper priesthood, which reached its full flowering in the theology of baptismal anointing as a true priestly anointing in Vatican II (see Antonio Aranda, 'The Christian, *alter Christus, ipse Christus*, in the thought of Blessed Josemaría Escrivá', in Belda et al. (ed.), *Holiness and the world*, Dublin, 1997, pp 132-48). 18 Cf. *Lumen gentium*, 10. 19 Alvaro del Portillo, *On priesthood*, Chicago, 1974, p. 45.

Participation in the priesthood of Christ proper to the sacrament of Order consists, then, in a configuration with Christ the Head of the Church which, at the same time, gives shape and form to the ministerial function and activity – that is, to act in the name of Christ, with the authority of Christ, in the person of Christ. The configuration and participation of priests in the unique and eternal priesthood of Christ is described by the Council not in itself but in relation to the mission they have received as a consequence of their consecration, that is, in so far as they are sent to build up the Church.[20] This perspective allows us to penetrate the deepest meaning of the priestly ministry: the ministerial activity is the activity of Christ and of the Church; the authority of the priest, which is that of Christ, has to be exercised in and for the Church.[21]

Consideration of the ontological components of the ministerial priesthood leads us to the conclusion that it is foreign to its very structure to try to establish a dichotomy between consecration and mission, cult and evangelization, adoration of God and service to men. Consequently, in referring to the priestly ministry, it is more correct to speak of the triple dimension of the service and mission of Christ rather than of three distinct functions. In a homily to a group of young men he was about to ordain to the priesthood John Paul II reminded them:

> The consecration which you are going to receive will qualify you for *the service, for the ministry of salvation*, in order to be, like Christ, 'consecrated of the Father' and 'sent into the world' (cf. Jn 10:30). Your service to men is not a distinct part of your priesthood; it is the consequence of your consecration ... Don't fear that in this way you will become separated from your faithful, from those to whom your mission is destined. Rather, it is forgetfulness or carelessness about the consecration which distinguishes your priesthood that would separate you from them.[22]

### CONSECRATION

The discussion of priesthood in *Presbyterorum ordinis* is carried out in the light of the rich ecclesiology developed in *Lumen gentium* which we have outlined above. The first chapter of the decree describes the meaning of priesthood in the mission of the Church, and the way the priest is most effectively present in the world in the ordinary lives of the faithful. The decree emphasizes the fact

20 Cf. *Presbyterorum ordinis*, 2, 4-6. 21 Cf. Saramiento, op. cit., pp 565-7. 22 John Paul II, Homily at a priestly ordination ceremony, Valencia, Spain, 8 November 1982 (italics in original).

that the priest, as a consequence of sacramental ordination, is a *consecrated* person who shares in the ministerial priesthood of Christ. In the Old Testament Aaron and his successors were initiated into the priestly office by a special form of consecration (cf. Ex 29:1-37; Lev 8) in which there were two stages – anointing and offering of sacrifice. The rite of anointing with oil showed that the man was being dedicated exclusively to the service of the Lord (cf. Ex 29:1-9). The whole ceremony of consecration of priests was expressive of the high degree of sanctity inherent in their office (cf. Lev 8–9). By his sacrificial death Christ consecrated both himself and those whom he commanded to renew his sacrifice: 'For their sake I consecrate myself, that they also may be consecrated in truth' (Jn 17:19).

Vatican II texts emphasise that consecration is an essential element of priestly ordination: 'they are consecrated priests of the New Testament', *Lumen gentium* tells us.[23] *Presbyterorum ordinis* develops this idea:

> The purpose for which priests are consecrated by God through the ministry of the bishop is that they should be made sharers in a special way in Christ's priesthood and, by carrying out sacred functions, act as his ministers who through his Spirit continually exercises his priestly function for our benefit in the liturgy.[24]

Later the same document adds:

> They are consecrated to God in a new way in their ordination and are made the living instruments of Christ the eternal priest, and so are enabled to accomplish throughout all time that wonderful work of his which with supernatural efficacy restored the whole human race.[25]

But this is no new terminology. *Sacerdotes consecrantur*, St Thomas tells us, priests are consecrated.[26]

The consecration of the priest is accomplished by 'God through the ministry of the bishop'.[27] It is this consecration through the sacrament of Order which constitutes the candidate as a priest by bringing about an ontological participation of the man-priest in the priesthood of the God-man. The priest is thus transformed into a *persona sacra*, a sacred person.[28] But this is still not the essence of the priesthood. What constitutes a man a priest of Jesus Christ is that he becomes endowed with the *sacra potestas*, a sacred

---

23 *Lumen gentium*, 28: *Presbyteri consecrantur ut veri sacerdotes Novi Testamenti.* 24 *Presbyterorum ordinis*, 5. 25 Ibid., 12. 26 *S. Th.* III, 67, 2; *Summa contra gentes*, 4, 77. See Josef Pieper, op. cit., p. 56. 27 *Presbyterorum ordinis*, 5. 28 Cf. Pieper,, p. 62.

power.[29] And the core of this unique endowment is the power to consecrate the Eucharist acting *in persona Christi* for the universal Church.[30] As a result of his consecration he shares in the eternal mediation of the Man who was God.[31]

> The priest, a consecrated man, has a special quality, the quality of something holy, for his sacramental consecration endows him with a sacred character. He can no longer behave as if this special quality did not exist. He is a man of God, belonging no longer to himself but to God alone. His life is not his own, for he surrendered it when he responded to the divine call, so he cannot act as if it still belonged to him. He has no right to attempt to gain his life for, if he does, he will unquestionably lose it. On the other hand, if he gives it up completely, keeping nothing back for himself, then indeed he will gain it for ever, both here and hereafter. If he really lives for the fulfilment of God's will in himself and in others, if he makes his priesthood his whole life, if his dedication to the mission entrusted to him genuinely occupies every fibre of his being, then he will truly experience how the divine promise of a hundred-fold return becomes an authentic reality.[32]

The office of priesthood is transmitted by the bishop's imposition of hands on the head of the ordinand, and by the consecratory prayer imploring the outpouring of the Holy Spirit and his gifts proper to the priestly ministry. In this way the priest is incorporated into the apostolic succession. The effects of the sacrament are well summarized by the *Catechism of the Catholic Church*:

> Through the sacrament of Holy Orders priests share in the universal dimensions of the mission of Christ entrusted to the apostles. The spiritual gift they have received in ordination prepares them, not for a limited and restricted mission, 'but for the fullest, in fact the universal mission of salvation "to the ends of the earth"' (*Presbyterorum ordinis*, 10), 'prepared in spirit to preach the gospel everywhere' (*Optatam totius*, 20).[33]

Although a priest is incardinated in a particular diocese, the grace of ordination gives him a perspective on his mission which extends beyond the boundaries of a particular diocese or country.

Priesthood is then a gift from Christ which is to be put at the service of the

---

29 Cf. *Lumen gentium*, 10. 30 Cf. *S. Th.*, III, 82, 1. 31 Cf. *S. Th.*, III, 22, 1. 32 Federico Suarez, *About being a priest*, Dublin, 1979, pp 12-13. 33 No. 1565.

community of believers. Thus 'the ministry of the priest is entirely on behalf of the Church; it aims at promoting the exercise of the common priesthood of the entire people of God'.[34] The *Catechism of the Catholic Church* explains it this way:

> Intrinsically linked to the sacramental nature of ecclesial ministry is *its character as service*. Entirely dependent on Christ who gives mission and authority, ministers are truly 'slaves of Christ'(cf. Rom 1:1), in the image of him who freely took 'the form of a slave' for us (Phil 2:7). Because the word and grace of which they are ministers are not their own, but are given to them by Christ for the sake of others, they must freely become the slaves of all (cf. 1 Cor 9:19).[35]

### TEACHERS OF THE WORD

In *Presbyterorum ordinis* the mission of the priest is described under the three main headings of teacher of God's Word, minister of the sacraments, and ruler of God's People.[36] To put the ministry of the word into perspective it will be useful to consider the nature of divine Revelation to which it is so closely linked.

Out of his goodness God revealed himself to men in order to adopt us as his children. His will is that we should have access to the Father through Jesus Christ, the Word made flesh, and become sharers of the divine nature.[37] The purpose of this revelation, shown through God's words and works, is to make us capable of knowing and loving him far beyond our natural capacity[38] and thus enter a relationship of deep friendship with the persons of the Blessed Trinity. Divine revelation culminated in the person and mission of Jesus Christ who proclaimed the mystery of God's plan that all should be 'saved and come to the knowledge of the truth' (1 Tim 2:4). So that this living Gospel would always be preserved in the Church, Christ ensured that the apostolic preaching would be preserved in a continuous line of succession until the end of time. In this way the Church 'transmits to every generation all that she herself is, all that she believes'.[39] Serving this continuity defines the purpose, content and context of the ministry of the word.

---

34 PDV, 16. A consequence of this is that 'the ordained priesthood ought not to be thought of as existing prior to the Church, because it is totally at the service of the Church. Nor should it be considered as posterior to the ecclesial community, as if the Church could be imagined as already established without the priesthood' (PDV, 16). 35 CCC, 876 (italics in original). 36 Cf. nos. 4-6. 37 Cf. *Dei Verbum*, 2. 38 Cf. CCC, 52. 39 Cf. *Dei Verbum*, 8; CCC, 98.

Christ, during his public life, preached the good news of salvation – God's plan of redemption for sinful man. He walked the length and breadth of Palestine, proclaiming a Gospel message for people to live by and inviting all to repentance. He spoke to small groups and large crowds, but he paid particular attention to individual souls. To all he revealed the mystery of God's love for man. We see from the reaction to Christ's preaching, and from the history of evangelization, that 'the Gospel preached by the Church is not just a message but a divine and life-giving experience for those who believe, hear, receive and obey the message'.[40] Preaching is therefore an instrument of the Church by means of which Christ acts in us with his Spirit.

For the priest, proclaiming the Gospel is a ministry derived from the sacrament of Orders and is exercised with the authority of Christ. To do it effectively he first needs to reflect on the Word of God in his personal prayer and assimilate it into his own life. In this way he will speak with conviction about the power of the love of God. When people see the image and sentiments of Christ etched clearly in the life of the priest, when they experience him as a father in their personal dealings with him, then they will take notice when he invites them to conversion and holiness. Personal familiarity with Christ through prayer and regular meditation on the New Testament will make his preaching persuasive, coherent and convincing. Attentive daily reading of the Breviary is also important in this context because it will help him 'to interiorize and become familiar with biblical, patristic, theological and magisterial teaching' which he can subsequently use to illustrate and embellish his preaching.[41]

One of the principal objectives of evangelization is to help people bring to maturity their baptismal vocation, to communicate to them the reality of a personal call to holiness from God. To promote this sense of individual vocation, so strongly affirmed by Vatican II,[42] it is essential to educate the faithful in an awareness of the most fundamental truth about their lives – that, as adopted children of God in Baptism, they are truly daughters and sons of a loving Father[43]. This is the context in which they have to be encouraged to strive for holiness, struggle against evil, do battle with their sinful tendencies, and accept the contradictions of life. Together with inculcating a deep conviction that there is a divine, paternal providence ruling every aspect of their lives, this will facilitate a positive and optimistic mode of preaching, drawing men and women to an appreciation of the goodness, truth and beauty in God and in the Christian message.[44]

40 Congregation for the Clergy, Letter to bishops: *The priest and the third Christian millennium*, II, (19 March 1999). 41 Cf. ibid. 42 Cf. *Lumen gentium*, 40; *Apostolicam actuositatem*, 2. 43 Cf. Gal 4:4–6; Rom 8:14–17; see also Blessed Josemaría Escrivá, *Friends of God*, Dublin 1981, no. 26. 44 These aspects of preaching are covered in more detail in Chapter 8 below.

For preaching to be effective it requires preparation and planning. Apart from the scriptural text, the *Catechism of the Catholic Church* is an essential preaching resource. Not only will it provide the priest with deep insights on the message of the Gospel, but its very structure will enable him cover all the basic elements of the Church's teaching in a progressive way – the content of the faith, the sacraments as sources of Christian vitality, the commandments as principles of moral life, and prayer as the expression of friendship with, and dependence on, God. These four constitutive elements have always been the pillars of Christian catechesis and will continue to be so. However, to respond to the specific needs of the faithful, at different times in the history of the Church it has been necessary to emphasise specific aspects of Christian teaching for which priests should be well prepared.[45]

### MINISTERS OF THE SACRAMENTS

To put the sacramental role of the priest in context, let us first review briefly the theology of the sacramental economy. The Church was instituted by Christ to provide historical continuity for the work of redemption. With the sending of the Holy Spirit the 'age of the Church' began.[46] The Church was born primarily from Christ's total self-giving for our salvation, and promulgated to the world at Pentecost. The Lord's work of salvation is communicated to mankind through the liturgy of the Church, which revolves around the Eucharistic sacrifice and the sacraments. In this new age of the Church, Christ acts through the sacramental economy by means of which the Paschal mystery is communicated to men. Thus the Vatican II decree on the liturgy tells us that,

> Christ is always present in his Church, especially in her liturgical celebrations. He is present in the Sacrifice of the Mass not only in the person of its minister ... but especially in the Eucharistic species. By his power he is present in the sacraments so that when anybody baptizes it is really Christ himself who baptizes.[47]

In each celebration of the Paschal mystery there is an outpouring of the Holy Spirit which sanctifies the People of God, brings us into communion with Christ and thus builds up his Body. The sacraments, 'the masterworks of God',

---

45 'If priests are to give adequate answers to the problems discussed by people at the present time, they should be well versed in the statements of the Church's magisterium and especially those of the Councils and the Popes' (*Presbyterorum ordinis*, 19).  46 Cf. CCC, 1076.  47 *Sacrosanctum Concilium*, 7.

are, therefore, actions of the Holy Spirit at work in the Body of Christ, the Church, which is ever-living and life-giving.[48]

In the liturgy it is the whole community, the Body of Christ united to its head, which celebrates. Here the common priesthood of the faithful, a participation in the priesthood of Christ, is activated in a special way. In its role of being at the service of this baptismal priesthood, the ordained priesthood guarantees that it really is Christ who acts in the sacraments through the Holy Spirit.

The administration of the sacraments is the life-blood of the priestly ministry.[49] In the liturgy the priest acts in a unique way *in persona Christi* because he is a living instrument of Christ the Priest, feeding the flock and leading it to holiness. The sacraments are privileged moments for communicating the divine life to man, but are also particularly important opportunities for evangelization. Often, preparation for, and administration of the sacraments is the only effective opportunity to transmit the contents of the faith to those who are irregular in their practice. Many who have lost contact with the Church occasionally participate in the liturgy for family reasons – Baptisms, First Communions, Confirmation, marriages, ordinations, funerals, etc. Consequently the priest needs to prepare the ceremony well – the explanation of the rite, the homily, the liturgical celebration – so that the administration of the sacraments is an effective catechesis and an invitation to respond to the grace of faith. It goes without saying that the personal faith of the priest, reflected in what he says and in the way he administers the sacraments, is a powerful influence in drawing people to a deeper participation in the work of salvation.[50] The sacramental ministry of the priest is most frequently exercised in the celebration of the Eucharist and the sacrament of Reconciliation.[51]


## LOVING PASTORS OF THE FLOCK


In *Pastores dabo vobis* the theology of priesthood and priestly formation is presented from the outset within the scriptural profile of the good shepherd. John Paul II takes God's promise made through the prophet Jeremiah – 'I will give you shepherds after my own heart' (Jer 3:15) – as the context in which to develop what is arguably the most comprehensive magisterial statement on the priestly

48 Cf. CCC, 1116. 49 As Nichols points out, it is in terms of the mystery of Christian worship that the *Catechism of the Catholic Church* primarily presents the life of the priest. The complementary offices of teaching and pasturing are thus properly understood when seen in relation to the sacred liturgy which is the priest's principal defining task (cf. Aidan Nichols, *The service of glory*, Edinburgh, 1997, p. 85). 50 Cf. *Presbyterorum ordinis*, 12. 51 The sacramental ministry is more fully developed in Chapters 5, 6 and 10 below.

ministry.[52] While the Pope uses several analogies to develop a theology of priesthood (e.g. the priest as servant and spouse, as icon of Christ, etc), without doubt the dominant image running through the whole of *Pastores dabo vobis* is the priest's configuration to Christ as Head and Shepherd. This is the basic reference for the description of the nature and mission of the priest (Chapter II),[53] and the background against which the theological foundations of the priest's spiritual life are discussed (Chapter III).[54] As we shall see, the significance of this analogy is underlined by the importance which the concept of *pastoral charity* has for the whole document. John Paul II uses it not only as an essential element for the theological and ascetical definition of priesthood, but also as an interpretative key in relation to the on-going formation of priests.[55]

The image of the Good Shepherd recalls a favourite theme of the Old Testament prophetic literature: the chosen people are the flock and Yahweh is their Shepherd (cf. Ps 23). Kings and priests are also described as shepherds or pastors. Jeremiah has harsh words for those pastors who let their sheep go astray and, in God's name, promises new shepherds who will graze their flocks properly so that they will not be harassed or anxious (cf. Jer 23:1-6; also 2:8; 3:15; 10:21). Isaiah speaks of the shepherd who would carry the lambs in his arms, and bind up the broken limbs (cf. Is 40:1-11). Ezeckiel reproaches pastors for their misdeeds and sloth, their greed and neglect of responsibility – Yahweh will take the flock away from them and he himself will look after the sheep. Indeed, a unique shepherd will appear, descended from David, who will graze them and protect them (cf. Ezek 34). Jesus presents himself as this shepherd who looks after his sheep, seeks out the strays, cures the crippled and carries the weak on his shoulders (cf. Mt 18:12-14; Lk 15:4-7), thereby fulfilling the ancient prophecies. *Pastores dabo vobis* elaborates as follows:

> The figure of Jesus Christ as *Shepherd of the Church, his flock*, takes up and re-presents in new and more evocative terms the same content as that of Jesus Christ as Head and Servant. Fulfilling the prophetic proclamation of the Messiah and Saviour joyfully announced by the psalmist and the Prophet Ezechiel (cf. Ps 22-23; Ezek 34:11ff), Jesus presents himself as the 'good shepherd' (Jn 10:11, 14) not only of Israel but of all humanity (Jn 10:16). His whole life is a continual manifestation of his 'pastoral charity', or rather, a daily enactment of it. He feels compassion for the crowds because they are harassed and helpless, like sheep without a shepherd ( (cf. Mt 9:35-36). He goes in search of the straying and scattered sheep (cf. Mt 18:12-14) and joyfully celebrates their return. He gathers and protects them. He knows them

52 Cf. PDV, 1 and *passim.* 53 Cf. PDV, 11-18. 54 Cf. ibid., 19-33. 55 Cf. ibid., 70, 82.

and calls each one by name (cf. Jn 10:3). He leads them to green pastures and still waters (cf. Ps 22-23) and spreads a table for them, nourishing them with his own life. The Good Shepherd offers this life through his own Death and Resurrection, as the Church sings out in the Roman Liturgy.[56]

The good shepherd is the image of pastoral care proposed by St Peter in his First Letter (cf. 1 Pet 5:1-4), as well as by St Paul in his advice to the presbyters of the church of Ephesus (cf. Acts 20:28-29).

This same biblical image, with a strong christological emphasis, is used in *Lumen gentium* to describe the dignity and duties of priests:

> in virtue of the sacrament of Orders, after the image of Christ, the supreme and eternal priest, they are consecrated in order to preach the Gospel and shepherd the faithful ... they sanctify and govern that portion of the Lord's flock assigned to them ... as good shepherds [they] seek after those too (Cf. Lk 15:4-7) who, whilst having been baptized in the Catholic Church, have given up the practice of the sacraments, or even fallen away from the faith.[57]

John Paul II underlines a specific element of this role:

> Thanks to the priestly character, you share in a *pastoral charism*, which is a sign of a special relationship of *likeness to Christ, the Good Shepherd*. You are precisely marked with this quality in a very special way. Although care for the salvation of others is and must be a task of every member of the great community of the People of God, ... nevertheless you priests are expected to have a care and commitment which are far greater and different from those of any lay person.[58]

Because the priest is mediator of the mercy of God (according to the Curé of Ars, the priesthood is 'the love of the heart of Jesus'),[59] he will endeavour, as Christ did, to get to know his flock individually and treat them with care and compassion. At the core of his leadership role is his responsibility to lead the

---

56 PDV, 22. 57 *Lumen gentium*, 28. See also, Lawrence B. Porter, 'Sheep and shepherd: an ancient image of the Church and a contemporary challenge', in *Gregorianum* 82, 1 (2001), pp 51-85. 58 HTL, 1979, no. 5 (italics in original). The *Holy Thursday Letters* are all available in the English language edition of *Osservatore Romano*. A very useful compendium is *Letters to my brother priests: 1979-1999*, published by the Midwest Theological Forum, Chicago, 1999. 59 HTL, 1986, no. 4.

flock to rich pastures, that is, to provide them with the spiritual nourishment and moral guidance which will enable them mature to the fullness of their baptismal vocation. In addition he has to protect them from the wolves of false doctrine and bad example. This he will do by alerting them to the negative influences which can undermine personal and family life. Because they know that he is not a hireling but one who feels personal responsibility for their spiritual well-being, they will listen to his voice and follow his advice because they recognize that he has only their good at heart (cf. Jn 10:11-13).

> *Jesus Christ* is in our midst and he says to us: 'I am the Good Shepherd'(Jn 10:11,14). It is precisely he who has *'made' shepherds* of us too. And it is he who goes about all the cities and villages (cf. Mt 9:35), *wherever we are sent* to in order to perform our priestly and pastoral service ... It is precisely he, Jesus Christ, who continually feels compassion for the crowds and for every tired and exhausted person, 'like a sheep without a shepherd'(cf. Mt 9:36). Dear Brothers! *Let us ask Christ* for just one thing: that each of us may learn to *serve* better, more clearly and more effectively, *his presence as Shepherd* in the midst of the people of today's world. This is also most important for ourselves, so that we may not be ensnared by the temptation of 'uselessness', that is to say, the temptation to feel that we are not needed. Because it is not true. *We are more necessary than ever, because Christ is more necessary than ever!* The Good Shepherd is more than ever necessary![60]

The priest has always enjoyed a certain prestige in communities which appreciate his role as icon of Christ and who experience in their lives his service as Good Shepherd. It is a source of support and consolation for the priest to know that he is appreciated by the people because he reflects Christ to them.

### PASTORAL CHARITY

Discussion of the role of the priest as shepherd of souls leads on logically to a consideration of the concept of pastoral charity. This idea is referred to in a general way in *Lumen gentium*[61] and in a more developed sense in *Presbyterorum ordinis*.[62] In the case of the priest, charity is qualified as 'pastoral' charity, an interior dynamic which impels him to follow Christ as the Good Shepherd.

---

**60** HTL, 1984, no. 5 (italics in original). **61** Cf. no. 41. **62** It is referred to six times in *Presbyterorum ordinis* but particularly in no. 14.

The adjective 'pastoral' gives an intrinsic determination to the charity of the priest which unfolds by means of a growing pastoral love – the charity of the priest is the love proper to a pastor of souls.

In giving this concept such a central role in its exposition of the spiritual life of the priest, the Council proclaimed, on the one hand, that his interior life has to flow from the same root by which all Christian existence is nourished – the love of God which is communicated in and through the gift of the Holy Spirit, and which is called on to inform the whole range of the priest's activities. On the other hand, the charity infused by God is personalized in each subject according to his or her participation in the mission of the Church. Thus in the case of the priest, it is a 'pastoral' charity, a charity which imbues the exercise of the ministry and which receives from this ministry its characteristic tone.[63]

The priest, like every Christian, is called to love and, more specifically, to love in a way which makes present the love Christ has for his Church. This means that his style of life should be geared to building up the community and each of the faithful in Christ. Participation in the love of Christ for his Church also presupposes in the priest a love for Christ himself, and, in Christ, for the Father. But these two loves do not function in parallel: they are fused together. Incorporated into that intimate relationship between Christ and his Church, the priest finds himself referred to both. His constant going and coming from Christ to the Church and from the Church to Christ reinforces his links with both.[64]

## PASTORAL CHARITY AND THE HEADSHIP OF CHRIST

*Pastores dabo vobis* devotes three paragraphs to the topic of pastoral charity and begins by summarising the theological presuppositions of priesthood:

> By sacramental consecration the priest is configured to Jesus Christ as Head and Shepherd of the Church, and he is endowed with a 'spiritual power' which is a share in the authority with which Jesus Christ guides the Church through his Spirit.[65]

Having affirmed these dogmatic foundations, the post-synodal document then goes on to apply them to the spiritual life of the priest:

63 For a detailed analysis of the conciliar texts where the concept of pastoral charity appears, see G. Colombo, 'Fare la verità del ministerio nella carità pastorale', in *La vita spirituale del presbitero diocesano oggi: Problemi e prospettive*, Bergamo, 1989, pp 57 ff. 64 Cf. J. L. Illanes, 'Vocación sacerdotal y seguimiento de Cristo', in *La formación de los sacerdotes ...*, op. cit., p. 620. 65 PDV, 21.

By virtue of this consecration brought about by the outpouring of the Spirit in the Sacrament of Holy Orders, the spiritual life of the priest is marked, moulded and characterized by the way of thinking and acting proper to Jesus Christ, Head and Shepherd of the Church, and which are summed up in his pastoral charity.[66]

*Pastores dabo vobis* makes extensive use of the concept of pastoral charity to describe the identity, activity, and spirituality of the priesthood.[67] As one commentator has pointed out,

the Pope's novel, repeated and insistent use of the term makes it one of the most important contributions of *Pastores dabo vobis* to the Church's understanding of the ordained priesthood.[68]

Pastoral charity, then, as a virtue has its source in the sacrament of Orders[69] and, as a consequence, is a participation in Christ's own love for the Church because he is configured in a special way to Christ the Head and Shepherd of the Church. As has been pointed out,[70] the idea of the Headship of Christ is an important key for understanding the specific nature of pastoral charity. In the documents of Vatican II there is already significant emphasis on the connection between the ministerial priesthood and the Headship of Christ.[71] In *Pastores dabo vobis* John Paul II develops this idea, making the configuration of priests to Christ the Head one of the central themes of the whole document. Through sacramental ordination priests become instruments of Christ's Headship to create communion and to fulfil Christ's mission, gathering all the faithful of the Body in union with the Head. The expression *in persona Christi Capitis* (in the person of Christ the Head) emphasises the very close relationship between the priest and Jesus Christ, a relationship which consists in making the Lord present in a way analogous to that by which an instrument makes the principal cause present.[72]

Although all the baptized participate in Christ's relationship with the Father through grace, only the priest shares in Christ's relationship with the Church as a sacramental sign of Christ the Head.[73] But to truly represent the

66 Ibid. 67 The term 'pastoral charity' occurs approximately thirty times in the document and appears in every chapter of *Pastores dabo vobis*. 68 Cardinal Francis George, 'Pastoral charity rooted in priestly fraternity' in *Priests for a new millennium*, USCC, Washington DC, 2000, p. 68. 69 Cf. PDV, 23. 70 Cf. George, ibid., p. 70. 71 Cf. *Lumen gentium*, 28; *Presbyterorum ordinis*, 2, 6, 12. 72 Cf. *Presbyterorum ordinis*, 12; John Paul II, Address, 26 May 1993, no. 5. 73 'Through the ordained ministry, especially that of bishops and priests, the presence of Christ as head of the Church is made visible in the midst of the community of believers' (CCC 1549). The description of the priest as acting *in persona Christi Capitis* (in the person of Christ the Head) is also used by John Paul II in his apostolic exhortation,

Head he should strive to make his life one of total service to the Body, mod-
elled on the *kenosis* of Christ (cf. Phil 2:7-8).[74] For John Paul II, pastoral charity is what ensures fidelity in the priest's representing Christ, her Head, to the
Church, 'the force which animates and guides the spiritual life of the priest in
as much as he is configured to Christ the Head and Shepherd'.[75]

PASTORAL CHARITY AND LOVE FOR THE CHURCH

Pastoral charity can also be viewed as an expression of the priest's spousal love
for the Church. The doctrine about Christ as spouse of the Church was developed by St Paul in his letter to the Ephesians. This is another theological prism
through which to examine the pastoral charity of Christ which John Paul II
takes up in *Pastores dabo vobis*, starting from the idea that Christ's gift of himself to the Church is analogous to that unique gift of self made by the
Bridegroom to the Bride.[76] The Holy Father, referring back to some of his previous statements on pastoral charity, draws out the rich implications of this
aspect of the priest's love for the Church under the rubric of 'gift of self':[77]

> The essential content of this pastoral charity is the *gift of self*, the total
> gift of *self to the Church*, following the example of Christ. 'Pastoral
> charity is the virtue by which we imitate Christ in his self-giving and
> service. It is not just what we do, but our gift of self, which manifests
> Christ's love for his flock. Pastoral charity determines our way of
> thinking and acting, our way of relating to people. It makes special
> demands on us...' (Homily, Seoul, 7 October 1989). The gift of self,
> which is the source and synthesis of pastoral charity, is directed
> towards the Church. This was true of Christ who 'loved the Church

*Christifideles laici*, 22 (30 December 1988). We find it too in previous documents of the magisterium – in Pius XII's encyclical, *Mediator Dei*, AAS, 39 (1947) 556; and in the declaration of the Congregation for the Doctrine of the Faith, *Inter insigniores*, 5 (15 October 1974).
Since all the faithful share in the priestly, prophetic and kingly office of Christ, they can be
said to act in some way *in persona Christi*. Consequently to describe the role of the priest as
acting *in persona Christi Capitis* is to point to the essential difference between the ministerial priesthood and the priesthood of all the baptised. Cf. John P. McIntyre, '*In persona Christi
Capitis*: a commentary on canon 1008', *Studia canonica*, 30 (1996) pp 372-3. 74 Cf. PDV,
21. 75 PDV, 23. See George, ibid., pp 71-3. 76 Cf. PDV, 22. The spousal love of the priest
as related to celibacy is discussed in Chapter 4 below. 77 The concept of 'the person as gift'
is a core idea of the anthropology of John Paul II; cf. Karol Wojtyla, *Love and responsibility*,
London, 1981, *passim*. See also Thomas J McGovern, 'The Christian anthropology of John
Paul II: an overview', in *Josephinum Journal of Theology*, 8, no. 1, Winter/Spring, 2001, pp
132-47.

and gave himself up for her' (Eph 5:25) and the same must be true for the priest. With pastoral charity, which distinguishes the exercise of the priestly ministry as an *amoris officium*, 'the priest, who welcomes the call to ministry, is in a position to make this a loving choice, as a result of which the Church and souls become his first interest, and with this concrete spirituality he becomes capable of loving the universal Church and that part of it entrusted to him with the deep love of a husband for his wife'(Address, 4 November 1980). The gift of self has no limits, marked as it is by the same apostolic and missionary zeal of Christ, the Good Shepherd.[78]

The priest, then, loves and gives himself to the Church as the Body and Bride of Christ. However, he will only be able to do this in so far as the person of Jesus Christ is the central reference and love of his life. It is from this primary relationship that he will be able to draw the necessary spiritual energy and apostolic zeal to exercise those virtues which are implicit in the spousal love for the Church which his vocation demands.

### ROLE OF THE PRIEST IN THE WORLD

For centuries the concept of *secular* clergy was primarily a canonical one, distinguishing those priests who belonged to the hierarchical structure of the Church from monastic or religious clergy. Yet this canonical distinction was compatible with a marked theological and, especially, ascetical indistinction. The ascetical paradigm for secular priests was in general the religious model and indeed, until recent times, the idea of secularity was not considered as a point of reference for priestly spirituality.[79]

In chapter IV of the Vatican II constitution on the Church, which deals with the role of the laity, the point is made 'Their secular character is proper and peculiar to the laity'.[80] This quasi identification between secularity and the lay condition in the Church lead to some theological currents adopting the figure of the laity as the point of reference for defining the secularity of the priest. This perception of priestly secularity inevitably gave rise to some adverse arguments about celibacy and to questionable suggestions about the priest working in a civil task from the point of view of personal fulfilment.[81]

*Lumen gentium* tells us that 'by reason of their special vocation it belongs to the laity to seek the kingdom of God by engaging in temporal affairs and

---

78 PDV, 23. **79** Cf. J.M. Pero-Sanz, 'Existe una secularidad sacerdotal?' in *La formación de los sacerdotes ...*, p. 99. **80** *Lumen gentium*, 31. **81** Cf Pero-Sanz, pp 102-3.

directing them according to God's will'.[82] But as John Paul II clarified, 'all the members of the Church are sharers in this secular dimension but in different ways'.[83] Because lay people are called by vocation to sanctify themselves in the world and impregnate all temporal realities with the values of the Gospel,

> for the lay faithful, to be present and active in the world is not only an anthropological and sociological reality, but in a specific way, a theological and ecclesiological reality as well.[84]

Thus when lay people order temporal realities to the glory of God they are, at the same time, building up the Church.[85] As the laity fulfil their principal task *in the Church* when they work in the world, directing temporal affairs according to God's plan, in an inverse way the secular priest builds up the world precisely through the exercise of his sacred ministry. This is his authentically secular presence in society.[86]

While it is true that priests by ordination are set apart (cf. Heb 5:1), this is not to separate them from people but so that they be completely consecrated to the task for which God chooses them. At the same time, the diocesan priest has to live in the world, in the midst of ordinary life. For this is the environment he has to purify and to sanctify – removing the stain of sin from people's lives is a substantial part of his ministry. In doing this he is simply following the example of the Master who, after working as a carpenter in Nazareth, travelled the cities and towns of Palestine to preach the Gospel, living in the real world. At the Last Supper Christ prayed for his disciples who were 'in the world ... They are not of the world, even as I am not of the world ... As thou didst send me into the world, so I have sent them into the world' (Jn 17:11, 16, 18).

The priest, therefore, has to be in the world, but not as somebody belonging to it. Indeed, he has to learn 'to be more and more *in the* world but less and less *of the* world'.[87] He lives, as it were, on the frontiers of two worlds, teaching people how to bring to God all the human realities among which they live and work. Christ laid down a marker for priests about involvement in worldly affairs when he refused to become a judge in a dispute about property which had arisen between two brothers (cf. Lk 12:13-14). The priest does, of course, have a clear role in teaching the moral principles of justice and in helping people to judge things from a Christian perspective. He should never see the affairs of the world as intrinsically opposed to the kingdom of God because creation is God's gift to man and, in the light of the theology of the redemption, he

---

82 *Lumen gentium*, 31. 83 Apostolic Exhortation, *Christifideles laici*, 15 (30 December 1988). 84 Ibid. 85 Cf. Pero-Sanz, op. cit., p. 108. 86 Cf. ibid., p. 109. 87 John Paul II, Message to priests, 19 June 2000, no. 5 (italics in original).

knows that it is the role of the laity to impregnate the world of the family, work, culture, the media, politics, etc. with the values of the Gospel, recovering them for Christ.[88] While standing apart from these interests himself, he has to provide the pastoral leadership, and the resources of grace and formation, to enable the laity sanctify their work in the world, that is, to sanctify the world from within.

Nevertheless, it is inevitable that the priest will always be, to some extent, a sign of contradiction as Christ was. He is a living witness to 'another world' which sin causes man to want to forget about. For those who would build a paradise on this earth, the presence of the priest is an uncomfortable reminder that man was made for something greater than the ephemeral pleasures of this world. He is often an embarrassment to those who no longer live by Christian moral values. This is because, following the example of Christ, he dares preach about 'poverty of spirit' (cf. Mt 5:3) in a world drugged by an aggressive materialism, and about 'purity of heart' (cf. Mt 5:8) in a culture where sexual permissiveness is accepted as the norm. A priest who is faithful to his responsibilities to preach Christ cannot expect to be universally popular at the present time. Because he is an instrument of redemption he has to challenge people with the full truth about their lives. This calls for courage as well as being prepared for some negative reaction. In his instruction to his first priests Christ forewarned us about this: 'If the world hates you, know that it hated me before it hated you. If you were of the world, the world would love its own; but because you are not of the world, but I chose you out of the world, therefore the world hates you' (Jn 15:18-19). While most priests are blessed with congregations who respect the priesthood, they cannot expect to avoid some disfavour if they are faithful witnesses of Christ.

Such reaction, however, is never a reason to be defensive or inhibited in proclaiming the Gospel, and this for two reasons. Firstly, the priest has the conviction that, in a world of bankrupt ideologies, the teaching of Christ is the only truth with will satisfy the deepest desires of the human heart. Secondly, Christ has told us, 'Be of good cheer, I have overcome the world' (Jn 16:33). He confirmed this reason for optimism when he said: 'I will see you again and your hearts will rejoice, and no one will take your joy from you' (Jn 16:22). The priest will always win out in his battles for God if he is faithful to Christ and the demands of his priesthood. Nevertheless, he needs to be strong in his convictions and fortified by a solid prayer-life to avoid being deceived by the wisdom of the world. 'Don't be conformed to the world' (Rom 12:2), St Paul warns. The priest does not transform the world by allowing himself become secularized through a dilution of his priestly identity. He should not be sur-

---

88 Cf. *Lumen gentium*, 31, 33; *Apostolicam actuositatem*, 7; *Christifideles laici, passim*; John Paul II, Homily in Limerick, 1 October 1979.

prised that at times he may feel on the periphery of things: that is of the very
nature of his vocation. But it is the power of Christ working through him, not
his own talents or secular involvements, which maintains and reinforces the
Christian commitment of his community.


SALVATION OF SOULS


In the post-Vatican II era a new vocabulary has developed in the context of
priestly ministry which has undoubtedly helped to define more precisely and
more relevantly the nature of the Catholic priesthood and the service which it
offers. But this has perhaps at times been at the expense of terms and phrases
which, through continued usage, have been invested with immense theological
and pastoral richness, and which are bywords for priestly identity. It may be
passé to describe the essential role of the priest as 'the saving of souls'. While
it does not fully express the positive contribution and richness of the priestly
ministry, nevertheless it would be difficult to find an equivalent phrase which
penetrates more accurately to the very core of his vocation. On the one hand,
it is an immediate and salutary reminder of the irrelevance of over-concern
about the things of this world, and, on the other, confirmation of the fact that
priesthood is essentially in function of a wondrous eschatological design –
man's supernatural salvation and his eternal happiness which are permanently
at risk. The responsibility and the dignity of the priesthood are best seen in the
light of this awesome panorama. It follows logically that the main thrust of
priestly pastoral activity should be directed to helping the faithful live their
lives in charity with God, in 'the state of grace', that is, to providing the doctrine and the sacramental support which will enable people discover the true
meaning of their Christian vocation.

John Paul II does, however, speak this language when he reminds us that
'our vocation is a singular *solicitude for the salvation of our neighbour*', that 'this
solicitude is a special *raison d'être* of our priestly lives', what 'gives it meaning',
and that only through it can 'we find the full significance of our own life'.[89]
Seeing so many souls living away from God, he comments:

> Unfortunately we witness the moral pollution which is devastating
> humanity, disregarding especially those very little ones about whom
> Jesus speaks. What must we do? We must imitate the Good Shepherd
> and give ourselves without rest for the salvation of souls. Without for-
> getting material charity and social justice, we must be convinced that

89  HTL, 1979, no. 5 (italics in original).

the most sublime charity is spiritual charity, that is, the commitment for the salvation of souls. And souls are saved with prayer and sacrifice. This is the mission of the Church![90]

But the priest's mission cannot be defined or limited to the idea of saving souls – he is also called to sanctify them. This is the whole thrust of the universal call to holiness of Vatican II, and of the pastoral programme for the new millennium outlined by John Paul II.[91]

**90** Address, 14 August 1979. **91** Cf. Apostolic Letter, *Novo millennio ineunte*, 30–31 (6 January 2001). See also Chapters 8 and 11 below.

# 3

# Priestly identity – other Christs

In his very first address after his election, Pope John Paul II said that one of the principal objectives of his papacy would be to put the doctrine of Vatican II into effect in the Church.[1] During the past two decades he has been indefatigable in doing just that, in his writings and pastoral initiatives, and in his journeys to all parts of the world. Yet it is hardly an exaggeration to say that, of all the areas of Church life he has had to deal with, the spiritual well-being of priests has been a preferential and continuous concern. His documents and addresses on this topic are too numerous to mention. Whether in Maynooth or Manila, Philadelphia or Fulda, he has explained again and again different aspects of Vatican II teaching on the priesthood. In doing so he has shared with priests his own truly original insights on this topic, and spoken to them in language which conveys his profound veneration for the priestly vocation. In a recent message to priests he said:

> Dear friends, in fulfilment of the Petrine *munus* (office), I intend to strengthen your faith in the identity of Christ and in your own identity as *other Christs*. Take a holy pride in being *called*, and be especially humble before so great a dignity, in the awareness of your human weakness.[2]

Perhaps the most significant expression of this esteem for the priesthood is, as we have already noted, the custom he initiated, a few months after his election, of writing each year a special letter to all the priests of the Church for Holy Thursday to celebrate 'the birthday of priests'. In these letters he has reaffirmed once and again the substance and the identity of the priesthood. He has explored different aspects of the priestly mission and, in doing so, gives us the benefit of his own immense priestly experience, sharing with us also the insights of a man of uncommon intellectual calibre who has followed very closely in the footsteps of Christ. However, his most complete statement of the

1 Cf. Address, 22 October 1978. 2 John Paul II, Message to priests, 19 June 2000, no. 5.

christological identity of the priest is given in *Pastores dabo vobis*. What he says in this and other documents deserves close consideration to enable priests grow in their vocation and, where necessary, recover conviction about the dignity and greatness of their calling.

## PRIESTLY IDENTITY

*Pastores dabo vobis* analyses in some depth the nature of the priesthood from the perspective of priestly identity to provide answers to questions which have been raised about the crisis of identity in the priesthood in recent decades.[3] What precisely does the word 'identity' mean, and what significance does it have in the present context? 'Identity' denotes equality with what one is or ought to be. Consequently it evokes a content very similar to what is implied by the words 'nature' or 'essence'. But 'identity' also has an existential resonance which 'nature' and 'essence' lack, one which is closer to that which it has acquired in the field of psychology. From this perspective, when speaking about identity one is referring to the image a person has of themselves – in particular if one feels satisfied or identified with what one is, or with one's place in society and what others expect of him. A crisis of identity arises when one ceases to feel at ease with what one is or does, or when there is a rupture or discontinuity between reality and the image a person has of themselves.

In the genesis of a crisis of identity exterior factors generally play a part – a change in life or environment, having to cope with greater difficulties than normal, problems of adaptation, etc. But the decisive factor is always an interior one – a debility or weakness which prevents the subject facing up to a situation in order to recover his own proper identity. Overcoming the difficulty implies a perception of the factors which provoked it so that the subject can squarely confront reality by means of a deeper self-knowledge. Awareness of identity and, where necessary, overcoming a crisis of identity has, then, its roots at the level of affectivity or, more precisely, at the very core of the person. Consequently, intuition of identity transcends the merely intellectual perception of things, although it is closely linked to it.[4]

It is fairly clear that where the priestly life is concerned there is a close interaction between theology and psychology. Hence it is not surprising that *Pastores dabo vobis* begins its analysis of the nature and mission of the ministerial priesthood with an exposition of the demands which the contemporary culture and social context impose on the priest. Indeed it refers to the question of the priestly identity crisis in this context, and goes on to underline the

3 Cf. PDV, 11-18. 4 Cf. J. L. Illanes, 'Naturaleza y figura del ministerio sacerdotal' in J. L. Illanes and M. Belda Plans, *Teología espiritual y sacerdocio*, Mexico City, 1995, pp 62-5.

importance which a deep grasp of the truth about the priesthood has to play in the formation of priests and in priestly life in general. As the post-synodal document assures us:

> A correct and in-depth awareness of the nature and mission of the ministerial priesthood is the path which must be taken in order to emerge from the crisis of *priestly identity*.[5]

Hence, a deep understanding of the reality of the priesthood, both at the intellectual and existential levels, is the only solid foundation for an authentic priestly life. Priests cannot carry out their exacting ministerial service without a clear and deep-rooted conviction of their identity: the priesthood has to be the primary and unifying element of their existence.[6] It would, the Holy Father suggests, be a pointless exercise to have recourse to the social sciences, or to try to find the authentic image of the priest reflected in the results of social surveys. We should rather 'humbly question the Divine Master and ask him who we are, what he wishes us to be, what is, in his eyes, our true identity'.[7]

### CALLED BY CHRIST

Looking to Christ to find the answer to priestly identity, we see that the history of our priesthood begins, as in the case of the apostles, with a divine call. The vocation of the twelve in St Mark's narrative has a special nuance: 'And he called to him those whom he desired, and they came to him' (Mk 3: 13f). 'These words', it has been pointed out, 'fix the origin of New Testament ministry, where and how it takes shape'.[8] Christ himself took the initiative. To be called by Christ means to be loved by Christ. It is a sign of special predilection, a call to participate in Christ's friendship at the deepest level (cf. Jn 15:15).[9]

> The vocation of each one is fused, to a certain degree, with his own being: it can be said that the vocation and the person are made the same thing. This signifies that, in the creative initiative of God, there is present a particular act of love for those called, not only to salvation, but to the ministry of salvation.[10]

Our response to this call, John Paul II affirms, marks 'the highest moment in the use of freedom' and 'has brought about the great and irrevocable option of

5 PDV, 11 (italics in original). 6 Cf. John Paul II, Address, 2 March 1979. 7 Address, 2 July 1980. 8 Joseph Ratzinger, *Priestly ministry: a search for its meaning*, New York, 1971, p. 8. 9 Cf. John Paul II, Address, 2 July 1980. 10 Ibid.

our life and, therefore, the finest page in the history of our personal experience'.[11] Christ called the first twelve in a specific way: 'Follow me and I will make you become fishers of men' (Mk 1:18). Following Christ meant living with Christ, learning from him, and living his style of life. This was both attractive and demanding.

At the Last Supper, after three eventful years in his company, he would remind his disciples again of the fundamental reason for their remaining with him: 'You did not choose me, but I chose you' (Jn 15:16), underlining the point that priesthood was not something they had a right to aspire to on their own initiative but was rather a free gift of the Lord. While all the baptized share in the common priesthood of the faithful, and all are called to holiness,[12] the priestly vocation is a specific call:

> Every vocation to the priesthood has an individual history of its own, related to quite specific moments in the life of each one of us. When he called his Apostles, he said to each one of them: 'Follow me!' (Mt 4:19; 9:9; Mk 1:17; 2:14; Lk 5:27; Jn 1:43; 21:19). For 2,000 years he has continued to address the same invitation to many men, especially young men. Sometimes he calls them in a surprising way, even though his call is never completely unexpected. Christ's call to follow him usually comes after a long preparation. Already present in the mind of the young person, even if later overshadowed by indecision or by the attraction of other possible paths, when the call makes itself felt once more it does not come as a surprise. No wonder then that this calling prevails over all others, and the young person is able to set out on the path shown him by Christ: he takes leave of his family and begins his specific preparation for the priesthood.[13]

There is a typology of priestly vocation which has a clear expression in the New Testament. With the words, 'Follow me!', Christ called men of very different backgrounds – fishermen like Peter and the sons of Zebedee; Levi the tax collector; Saul the persecutor of the early Christians (Acts 9:1-19). The image of vocation handed down by the Gospels is particularly related to the figure of the fisherman. Indeed, Jesus defined the apostolic mission by using terminology identified with the task of fishing, such as boats, nets, catches, putting out into the deep, etc. After the miraculous catch, when Peter could only say in wonder to the Master, 'Depart from me for I am a sinful man,' Christ reaffirmed Simon's vocation with the words: 'Henceforth you will be catching men' (Lk 5:10). The significance of this event would never be lost on Peter and his companions. The first call is, then,

11 Ibid. 12 Cf. *Lumen gentium*, 10, 31. 13 HTL, 1996, no. 3.

the beginning of a journey which continues until death, a journey
which is 'vocational' at every step ... Over and above the tasks which
are the expression of priestly ministry, there always remains the underlying reality of 'being a priest'. The situations and circumstances of
life constantly call upon the priest to confirm his original choice, to
respond ever anew to God's call. Our priestly life, like every other form
of Christian existence, is a succession of responses to God who calls.[14]

Hence a vocation is not something static: it has an inherent dynamic. We constantly fulfil and confirm our vocation to the extent that we live faithfully the
mystery of God's covenant with man, especially in the Eucharist. We reinforce
our vocation every time we try to increase our love for the priesthood.

The priesthood is a special call to give glory to God, to render him an *officium laudis*, a work or office of praise.[15] When celebrating the Eucharist or the
other sacraments the priest is always giving praise to God. This *officium laudis*
includes not only the daily recital of the breviary,

but is above all the unceasing discovery of what is true, good and beautiful, which the world receives as a gift from the Creator ... God's
glory is written in the order of creation and redemption; the priest is
called to live this mystery in its fullness in order to participate in the
great *officium laudis* which is unceasingly taking place in the universe.
Only by living in depth the truth of the redemption of the world and
of humanity can he come close to the sufferings and problems of individuals and families and fearlessly face as well the reality of evil and
sin, with the spiritual strength necessary to overcome them.[16]

## SACRED CHARACTER

With the rite of sacramental ordination priests are initiated and consecrated to
a new kind of life which in a particular way separates them from everything (cf.
Heb. 5:1) and unites them to Christ 'with an original, ineffable and irreversible
bond'.[17] There is no question here of a mere juridical title. The priest's mission is not one delegated by the ecclesial community which can be revoked at
will by the same community. His service is not a part-time one, a priesthood *ad
tempus*. On the contrary, because of the real, ontological change wrought in the
soul by the sacrament of Order, he is marked by a permanent *seal* or *character*
configuring him to the Lord, which enables him to act *in persona Christi* ('This

14 Ibid., no. 5. 15 Cf. ibid., nos. 6, 7. 16 Ibid., no. 6. 17 John Paul II, Address, 2 July 1980.

is my Body'; 'I absolve you from your sins'), the ultimate source of the dignity of priests.[18]

In his 1970 homily at the canonization of St John of Avila, a model of
priestly holiness, Paul VI referred explicitly to the identity crisis which had
invaded the ranks of the clergy after Vatican II, and drew a parallel with what
had happened in the sixteenth century.[19] To confront the crisis of priestly
identity which arose as a consequence of the Reformers' doctrine, Trent
solemnly affirmed that Christ had instituted an external and visible priesthood
in the Church, and that the priestly character was an indelible sign imprinted
on the soul by sacramental ordination[20] by reason of which it could not be
repeated.[21] So the priestly character is not something added on to that received
in Baptism and Confirmation.[22] What it does is to deepen 'the mark already
there by imprinting on the self the project of a priestly life that is to come to
fruition with the help of graces conferred during the exercise of the ministry'.[23] But it is something more than a capacity to engage in priestly activities.
It is primarily a relationship to God by which Christ takes possession of the
being of the priest to imprint his own reflection on him.[24]

The sacred character affects the priest so deeply that his whole being is
directed to a priestly purpose: he is always God's minister, even when dealing
with things of a temporal nature. Consequently, 'in him everything, even what
is secular, must become priestly as in Jesus, who was always a priest, and always
acted as a priest, in all the expressions of his life'.[25] To such an extent does
Christ identify the priest with himself in the exercise of the powers he has conferred on him, that it can be said 'the sacrament of Order in effect equips the
priest to lend our Lord his voice, his hands, his whole being. It is Jesus Christ
who, in the Holy Mass, through the words of consecration, changes the substance of the bread and wine into his Body, Blood, Soul and Divinity'.[26] The
character received through priestly ordination impresses on the priest the likeness of Christ such that all his actions can resemble those of the Good

18 Cf. *Presbyterorum ordinis*, 2. 19 Homily, 31 May 1970. 20 Cf. Council of Trent, 7th
Session, 3 March 1547; 23rd Session, 15 July 1963. 21 Cf. Council of Trent, Session 7 on
Sacraments in General, Canon 9 (DS 1609). 22 'The three characters conferred by baptism,
confirmation and orders reveal both an anthropology and an ecclesial structure. By way of
anthropology, we can say that each character provides the ground (*fundamentum*) for a
specifically personal relationship to each of the three Persons in the Trinity. First of all, by
baptism we are made children of a common Father... Secondly, the sacrament of confirmation seals us in the Spirit of Christ. ... Thirdly, the character of orders puts the priest in
direct relationship with Christ the High Priest' (McIntyre, op. cit., p. 377). 23 Galot, op.
cit., p. 204. 24 As the Holy Father wrote to priests on Holy Thursday, 1979: 'You are always
and everywhere bearers of your specific vocation' (no. 6). 25 John Paul II, Address, 2 July
1980. 26 Blessed Josemaría Escrivá, *A priest forever*, London 1975, p. 6, quoted by John Paul
II in Address of 2 July 1980.

Shepherd. It engages all his human activities so that he may raise them too up to the supernatural level. This configuration to Christ defines the role of the priest in the heart of the People of God, enabling him to act *in persona Christi Capitis* (in the person of Christ the Head) teaching, ruling and sanctifying.[27]

The relationship between priestly service and the character imprinted on the priest's soul at ordination is explained as follows by Cardinal Ratzinger:

> The word 'character' describes the ontological nature of the service to Christ that lies in the priesthood, while illustrating what is meant by sacramentality. Only from this perspective can we understand why St Augustine describes the character — both functionally and ontologically — as 'the right of giving' (*ius dandi*), the necessary pre-condition for valid administration of the sacraments To belong to our Lord, who has become a servant, is to belong to those who are his. This means that now the servant can, under the sacred sign, give what he could never give on his own. In fact, he can give the Holy Spirit, absolve from sins, make present the sacrifice of Christ, and Christ himself in his sacred Body and Blood, which are all rights reserved to God, which no man can acquire by himself or by delegation from any community. So if 'character' is an expression of community service, it shows, on the one hand, that it is ultimately always our Lord who is acting, and on the other hand, that he nevertheless acts in the visible Church by means of men. Character thus guarantees the 'validity' of a sacrament, even in the case of an unworthy servant, but at the same time stands in judgement on the servant, and obliges him to live the sacrament.[28]

The priest then, 'always, and in an unchangeable way, finds the source of his identity in Christ the priest. It is not the world which determines his status, as though it depended on changing needs or ideas about social roles. The priest is marked with the seal of the Priesthood of Christ in order to share in his function as the one Mediator and Redeemer'.[29] Because of this bond an immense field of service to souls opens up to the priest, for their salvation in Christ and in the Church.

Since the pastoral mission is grounded on an indelibly sacramental character, it can therefore be exercised with greater continuity and efficacy. This obviously enhances the structural stability of the Church since the pastoral ministry demands the engagement of the whole being of the priest. The char-

27 Cf. Congregation for the Clergy, *Directory on the ministry and life of priests*, 7, 31 January 1994. See also *Presbyterorum ordinis*, 12; PDV, 15. 28 Cardinal Joseph Ratzinger, 'The ministry and life of priests', in *Homiletic and Pastoral Review*, August-September 1997, p. 12. 29 HTL, 1986, no. 10.

acter empowers the priest to exercise the ministry after the manner of Christ the shepherd. So despite the variety of circumstances which the passage of time throws up, the priest can always respond to events in keeping with the image of Christ which he has impressed on the core of his being.

## TRINITARIAN IDENTITY

To ensure that the priest's conviction about his own identity is not undermined by the pervasive secularism in which he has to live out his vocation, it is essential that he have a profound appreciation of its theological basis. Since we tend to look at things primarily in their horizontal dimension, the priest must never lose sight of the vertical axis of his vocation which is what gives it its essential meaning. Hence a firm grasp of the theology of priestly identity is a fundamental requirement for perseverance and fidelity.

Sacramental identification with the Eternal High Priest inserts the priest in a very specific way into the Trinitarian mystery. It is this special communion with the Father, the Son, and the Holy Spirit which defines the identity of the priest.[30] If every Christian through baptism acquires a relationship with the three divine Persons, sacramental ordination reinforces this Trinitarian communion in the soul of the priest in a new way. This relationship, John Paul II tells us, is the foundation of 'our identity, our true dignity'.[31]

> Indeed, the priest, by virtue of the consecration which he receives in the Sacrament of Orders, is sent forth by the Father through the mediatorship of Jesus Christ, to whom he is configured in a special way as Head and Shepherd of his people, in order to live and work by the power of the Holy Spirit in service of the Church and for the salvation of souls.[32]

This point is developed later in the same document:

> We derive our identity ultimately from the love of the Father, we turn our gaze to the Son, sent by the Father as High Priest and Good

---

30 When John Paul II explained in his apostolic letter, *Ordinatio sacerdotalis* (22 May 1994), that the reservation of the ministerial priesthood to males is irreformable doctrine, he spoke of the way God had planned it through Trinitarian relationships: 'Christ chose those whom he willed (cf. Mk 3:13-14; Jn 6:70), and he did so in union with the Father, "through the Holy Spirit" (Acts 1:2), after having spent the night in prayer (cf. Lk 6:12)'. See also George W. Rutler, *A crisis of saints*, San Francisco, 1995, p. 74. 31 PDV, 18. See *Directory on the ministry and life of priests*, nos. 4-15 (subsequently abbreviated to DMLP). 32 PDV, 12.

Shepherd. Through the power of the Holy Spirit, we are united sacramentally to him in the ministerial priesthood. Our priestly life and
activity continue the life and activity of Christ himself. Here lies our
identity, our true dignity, the source of our joy, the very basis of our
life.[33]

Therefore the theology of priestly identity needs to investigate these
Trinitarian relationships and see how they link with the Church and its saving
mission.

The priest has an essential relationship to the salvific love of the Father
expressed in the ministry of the word and sacraments. He receives from the
Holy Spirit the power to generate a multitude of new children of God. As a
consequence of his celibacy the priest acquires a 'true and real spiritual paternity which has universal dimensions'.[34] Thanks to this total self-giving which
the priest freely embraces, and the foregoing of a paternity according to the
flesh, he receives in return a notable enrichment through the gift of spiritual
paternity. This renunciation is rooted in his love for Christ and for his Church,
a love which the priest develops in his care and concern for people:

> The nuptial meaning of the Redemption impels each of us to guard
> our fidelity to this vocation, by means of which we are made sharers in
> the saving mission of Christ, priest, prophet and king ... We freely
> renounce marriage and establishing our own family in order to be bet-
> ter able to serve God and neighbour. It can be said that we renounce
> fatherhood 'according to the flesh' in order that there may grow and
> develop in us a fatherhood 'according to the Spirit' (cf. Jn 1:13).[35]

Fecundity, generation and fruitfulness are a feature of the Scriptures from the
'increase and multiply' of Genesis (1:22) to the Tree of Life of the book of
Revelation that bears fruit twelve fold (cf. Rev 22:2). In the same spirit St Paul
could write to the Corinthians: 'For I became your father in Christ Jesus,
through the gospel' (1 Cor 4:15). The priest foregoes the possibility of father-
ing children of the flesh so that he can devote himself fully to a higher form of
generation – the begetting of children in Christ through his preaching and
administration of the sacraments. Scheeben describes this fruitfulness of the
priest with a marian analogy:

> In accordance with its office the priesthood must bring Christ to birth
> anew in the bosom of the Church, both in the Eucharist and in the
> hearts of the faithful, by the power of Christ's Spirit reigning in the

33 PDV, 18.  34 DLMP, 59.  35 HTL, 1988, no. 5.

Church. Priests must build up the organism of Christ's mystical body, as Mary, by the power of the same Holy Spirit, brought forth the Word in his own humanity, and gave him his physical body. The miraculous conception of Christ and his birth from the womb of the Virgin is the model and also the basis of the further spiritual conception and birth of Christ in the Church through the priesthood. And this priesthood stands in a relationship to the God-man similar to that of Mary to the Son of God who descended into her and was born of her. The two mysteries are complementary; they illuminate and set off each other.[36]

Christ is born anew through the priesthood by a continuation, as it were, of his miraculous birth from Mary. The activity of the priesthood in the Church, in St Paul's terms, amounts to this: to fashion Christ in his members, to unite them to Christ, to conform them to him, to build them up to the fullness of the stature of Christ (cf. Eph 3:14-19; 4:11-16). If he is faithful to his priestly vocation, he will become the father of a multitude of children of the spirit.[37]

John Paul II had already thought a lot about fatherhood when he wrote his encyclical *Dives in misericordia* on God the Father.[38] He had profound and grateful memories of life with his own father, and his experience of the spiritual paternity of Cardinal Sapeiha, Archbishop of Krakow, who ordained him a priest, was a constant reference point in his priestly life.[39] How deeply the importance of this idea was rooted in his mind is intimated in his play, *Reflections of fatherhood*, where he says,

> everything else will turn out to be unimportant and inessential except for this: father, child, love. And then, looking at the simplest things, all of us will say: could we have not learned this long ago? Has this not always been embedded at the bottom of everything that is?[40]

For John Paul II, Christ's parable of the Prodigal Son is a powerful statement of the mercy of God, of the fact that we are children of a loving Father who restores our lost dignity. The Prodigal Son represents every human being burdened by the 'awareness of a squandered sonship',[41] but recovered by the grace of a merciful Father who never forgets his children, and who loves them no matter how far they may have wandered from him. The spiritual fatherhood of the priest has in a special way to draw its inspiration from this parable:

36 Scheeben, op. cit., p. 546. 37 Cf. Fulton Sheen, *The priest is not his own*, London 1964, pp 45-7. 38 Encyclical letter, *Dives in misericordia*, on the Mercy of God, 30 November 1980. 39 Cf. Weigel, ibid., p. 387. 40 K. Wojtyla, 'Reflections on fatherhood' , in *The collected plays and writings on theater*, Berkeley, University of California Press, 1987, p. 368. 41 *Dives in misericordia*, 5.

The priest is the witness and instrument of divine mercy! How important in his life is the ministry of the confessional! It is in the confessional that his *spiritual fatherhood* is realized in the fullest way. It is in
the confessional that every priest becomes aware of the great miracles
which divine mercy works in souls which receive the grace of conversion.[42]

It is not surprising then that a priest would experience a certain emptiness in
his life if he does not have the opportunity regularly to bring about this regeneration of souls through the sacrament of Reconciliation. Any priest who
assiduously promotes and carries out the apostolate of confession and spiritual guidance will feel a deep sense of fulfillment in his vocation as the Holy
Father points out.[43]

## CHRISTOLOGICAL DIMENSION:
### 'IN PERSONA CHRISTI' (IN THE PERSON OF CHRIST)

Continuing our enquiry into the insertion of the priest in the Trinitarian mystery, we can say that the christological dimension of the priest's identity
springs directly from the sacrament of Order which configures him ontologically with Christ the Priest, Teacher, Sanctifier, and Pastor of his people.[44]
This is a participation in the public dimension of mediation and authority
related to the threefold office of Christ in sanctifying, teaching and guiding the
faithful. In this unique identity with Christ, the priest must be conscious that
his life is a mystery totally grafted on to the mystery of Christ and the Church.
However, the primary reference is always to Christ:

> The priest finds the full truth of his identity in being a derivation, a
> specific participation in and continuation of Christ himself, the one
> High Priest of the new and eternal Covenant. The priest is a living and
> transparent image of Christ the Priest. The priesthood of Christ, the
> expression of his absolute 'newness' in salvation history, constitutes
> the one source and essential model of the priesthood shared by all
> Christians and the priest in particular. Reference to Christ is thus the
> absolutely necessary key for understanding the reality of priesthood.[45]

Jesus Christ associates the priest with his own mission: 'As the Father has
sent me, I also send you' (Jn 20:21). The priest should be an authentic repre-

---

42 John Paul II, *Gift and mystery: on the fiftieth anniversary of my priestly ordination*, London,
1996, p. 86 (italics in original). 43 For a detailed discussion of this topic, see Chapters 5, 10
and 11 below. 44 Cf. *Lumen gentium*, 18, 28; *Presbyterorum ordinis*, 2. 45 PDV, 12.

sentative and messenger such that Christ is able to say of him, 'He who hears you hears me' (Lk 10:16). This has profound implications not only for the quality of his preaching, but for the impact his whole life-style and personality have on the people entrusted to his care.[46] Acting *in persona Christi* he is the mediator of the message of salvation and the means to achieve holiness.[47]

> Priests as ministers of the sacred mysteries, especially in the sacrifice of the Mass, act in a special way in the person of Christ who gave himself as a victim to sanctify men.[48]

During the post-conciliar period of deepest crisis in the priesthood, the expression *in persona Christi* to define the identity of the priest, frequently used by Vatican II,[49] was ignored or rejected.[50] Here it is worth noting that the expression *in persona Christi* was not invented to exalt the priestly ministry, but was an ineluctable requirement of the nature of Christ's mediation. Precisely because the mediation, priesthood and sacrifice of Christ are unique, the actions of the priest are not added to or juxtaposed to the actions by which Christ gathers and sanctifies his Church. Rather they are instrumental actions by means of which Christ himself continues to exercise his priesthood.[51] As Vanhoye points out,

> the priest is the sacrament of the presence of Christ the mediator in the ecclesial community; he is a sign and instrument of the mediation of Christ. He acts, in fact, *in persona Christi*. The sacraments are actions of Christ himself, and not of the priest as man.[52]

This relationship achieves a deep mysterious union in the Sacrifice of the Mass when Christ the Priest is offered through the hands of the man-priest who serves as a free and willing instrument. What is clear is that the primary objective of the sacramental character with which the priest is sealed is to make possible this *impersonation* or *personification* of Christ:

> The priest offers the Holy Sacrifice *in persona Christi*; this means more than offering 'in the name of' or 'in the place of' of Christ. *In persona*

---

46 Cf. PDV, 18. 47 The phrase *in persona Christi* originated in the Vulgate translation of 2 Cor 2:10 where Paul says he pardons the community 'in the person of Christ'. See also St Thomas, *S. Th.* III, 82, 1. 48 *Presbyterorum ordinis*, 13. 49 Cf., for example, *Lumen gentium*, 10, 21, 25, 27, 28; *Sacrosanctum Concilium*, 33; *Presbyterorum ordinis*, 2, 12, 13. 50 Cf. Mateo-Seco, op. cit., p. 389. 51 Cf. Mateo-Seco, p. 389; M. Evans, '*In persona Christi*: the key to priestly identity', in *Clergy review*, 71 (1986), 117-25. 52 A. Vanhoye, 'Sacramentalidad del ministerio y su repercusión en la persona ordenada', in *Espiritualidad del presbítero diocesano secular*, Madrid, 1987, p. 77.

means in specific sacramental identification with the eternal High
Priest who is the Author and principal Subject of this sacrifice of his,
a Sacrifice in which, in truth, nobody can take his place. Only he – only
Christ – was able and is always able to be the true and effective 'expiation for our sins and ... for the sins of the whole world'(1 Jn 2:2; cf.
4:10).[53]

This configuration of the minister with Christ the Priest, and the resulting
capacity to act *in persona Christi*, is a consequence of, and, at the same time,
manifests the unicity of the priesthood of Christ. For this very reason it is
Christ, present in the liturgical action, who renders cult to the Father and
offers his body to men through priests. This is the context in which the fundamental role of the ministerial priesthood in the economy of salvation has to
be seen.[54] By means of it Christ can continue his work of Redemption, and
through it he, the Head, remains inseparably united to his Church, his
Mystical Body, and continues to channel to her that divine sap which vitalizes
his members. Hence the identity of the priest comes from a specific participation in the priesthood of Christ:

> In the Church and on behalf of the Church, priests are a sacramental
> representation of Jesus Christ, the Head and Shepherd, authoritative-
> ly proclaiming his Word, repeating his acts of forgiveness and his offer
> of salvation, particularly in Baptism, Penance and the Eucharist,
> showing his loving concern to the point of a total gift of self for the
> flock, which they gather into unity and lead to the Father through
> Christ and in the Spirit. In a word, priests exist and act in order to pro-
> claim the Gospel to the world and to build up the Church in the name
> and person of Christ the Head and Shepherd.[55]

---

53 John Paul II, HTL, 1980, no. 8. See also *The Navarre Bible: St Matthew's Gospel*, Dublin,
1988, pp 210-12. 54 'The deepest reason for the distinctive role of the priest in the
Eucharist lies in the fact that only God can offer worthy sacrifice to God: the Christian God
is so transcendent to the world, so holy, that no act of human religion is adequate in his presence. Only the incarnate Son of God can make the suitable offering and exchange. The
priest must speak and act *in persona Christi*, because only Christ can act in the appropriate
way in the presence of the Father; in what other name could the Church speak and act? The
offering of the Son of God is not just mentioned or remembered in the Eucharist but
expressed and actuated in the Son's own words. The community, in adoration and thanks,
joins in this offering, but the offering is first there through the action of Christ, who uses
the words and actions of the priest to re-enact his perfect offering sacramentally' (Robert
Sokolowski, *Eucharistic presence: a study in the theology of disclosure*, Washington DC, 1994,
p. 18). 55 PDV, 15. The priest, acting *in persona Christi* in the Eucharist, is considered in

In his apostolic exhortation on *Reconciliation and penance*, John Paul II under-lines the fact that the priest acts in the sacrament of confession in the person of Christ in whose name he absolves the penitent.[56] This sacramental configu-ration which causes Christ to be present among men, not only in the liturgical action but also in pastoral work, leaves its mark on the spirituality of the priest. To act fully *in persona Christi* requires a coherent personal, ascetical, and psy-chological union with Him whom he is making present to others.[57]

### THE PRIEST AS ICON OF CHRIST

As Saward points out, in *Pastores dabo vobis* the language of representation is used interchangeably with that of imaging.[58] The priest represents Christ in a manner similar to that by which an icon represents its subject. As explained in the *Catechism*: 'the ordained minister is, as it were, an "icon" of Christ the Priest ...(through him) the presence of Christ as head of the Church is made visible in the midst of the community of believers'.[59] Before developing this point it may be useful to recall some general aspects of iconic theology which has a particular importance in Eastern Catholicism and in Orthodoxy.[60]

The icon is art, but it is above all liturgical art. It is a theology of images in that it completes the liturgy and explains it. As Cardinal Schönborn has pointed out, 'the Eastern Church sees the icon as a *condensed* version of the Creed'.[61] St Basil the Great tells us that what the icon shows by artistic repre-sentation corresponds to what the word in Scripture communicates by sound.[62] Thus the icon portrays the divine beauty and glory in ways which are visible to the eyes. It incorporates specific forms of artistic expression which are charac-teristic of the icon alone and distinguish it from all other images. In Eastern theology the icon is venerable and holy because it is a sacramental of a person-al presence. It participates in the holiness of its prototype and, through the icon, we in turn participate in this holiness through our prayers. It is the grace of the Holy Spirit which sustains the holiness both of the represented person and of its icon, and it is in this grace that the relationship between the faithful and the saint is brought about through the intermediary of the icon.[63] The

---

more detail in Chapter 6 below. **56** Cf. *Reconciliatio et paenitentia*, 29. See also, Address to Apostolic Penitentiary, 31 March 2001, no. 4. **57** Cf. Mateo-Seco, op. cit., pp 391-2. **58** Cf. John Saward, *Christ is the answer: the Christ-centred teaching of Pope John Paul II*, Edinburgh, 1995, pp 118-125. **59** CCC, 1142, 1549. **60** Cf. Leonid Ouspensky, *Theology of the icon*, Crestwood, NY, 1978; Michel Quenot, *The icon: window on the kingdom*, London, 1991. **61** Christoph Schönborn, *God's human face*, San Francisco, 1994, p. 137 (italics in original). **62** Cf. Hom. 19, on the Forty Martyrs, PG 31: 509A. **63** Cf. Ouspensky, p. 191.

Incarnation is, of course, the basis for the icon because Christ is the icon of the invisible Father. The icon *par excellence* is then the icon of Christ himself.[64]

> The Church, after having for centuries examined and proclaimed the divine glory of Christ, his consubstantiality with the Father, could do only one more thing: profess that *this human countenance*, the face of Jesus of Nazareth, holds in itself the complete mystery of God.[65]

While the New Testament tells us that Christ is the icon of the Father (cf. Jn 12:45; 14:9), at the very beginning of the Old Covenant we discover the fundamental anthropological principle which undergirds the whole of iconic theology: 'Let us make man to our own image and likeness' (Gen 1:27). Man sullied this image through original sin, but the divine image was reconstituted in man by Christ who reincorporated us into the divine life. In Christ this likeness is realized in a perfect, total degree through the Incarnation.[66]

The priest as icon and representative of Christ has a long history in the Tradition of the Church, beginning with the New Testament. Jesus himself affirms the intimate solidarity, even a kind of identity between himself and his disciples: 'he who receives anyone whom I send, receives me; and he who receives me receives him who sent me' (Jn 13:20). St Paul reminds his beloved Galatians how they had received him as if he were Christ Jesus himself (cf. Gal 4:14). He asks the Corinthians to 'be imitators of me as I am of Christ' (1 Cor 11:1). The Apostle imitated Christ not by copying his gestures and words, but by integrating himself completely into the life of Christ - by letting Christ live in him (cf. Gal 4:20; 2 Cor 13:5; Rom 8:10). The same idea runs through the Fathers with St John Chrysostom referring to the priest as a 'symbol' of Christ.[67] But it was as a result of the iconoclastic controversy in the eight century that the notion of the priest as icon of Christ was more clearly defined, with particular reference to the concept of character or seal imprinted on the soul of the priest.

For St Thomas, the priest 'bears the image of Christ, in whose person and by whose power he pronounces the words of consecration'.[68] And it is precisely because the priest has to be the sign and image of Christ that only men can be ordained to the priesthood.[69] By virtue of sacramental ordination the priest acquires an ontological identification with Christ which objectively imprints Christ's image on his soul irrespective of his personal moral qualities. However, to be a true icon of Christ the priest has a duty to become spiritual-

64 Cf. Quenot, p. 35. 65 Schönborn, p. 133 (italics in original). 66 Cf. Ouspensky, p. 187. 67 Cf. Schönborn, p. 169. 68 *Summa theologiae*, III, 83, 1, ad 3. 69 Cf. John Paul II, Apostolic letter, *Ordinatio sacerdotalis*, 22 May 1994; Congregation for the Doctrine of the Faith, Instruction, *Inter insigniores*, 15 October 1976.

ly assimilated to Christ so that subjectively he increasingly reflects his objective identity. In the papal magisterium of the twentieth century, the description of the priest as 'another Christ' (*sacerdos alter Christus*) became quite commonplace.[70] We also find it in the writings of John Paul II.[71] He describes this expression 'created by the intuition of the Christian people', not just as a metaphor, but as 'a marvellous reality'.[72]

The Vatican II document on the training of priests uses iconic theology when it outlines the foundations for the spiritual formation of seminarians: 'Those who are to take on the likeness of Christ the priest by sacred ordination should form the habit of drawing close to him as friends in every detail of their lives'.[73] *Pastores dabo vobis* expands on this teaching, pointing out that the commitment to acquire the image of Christ should focus on those sources where the Master can be found in a direct and fruitful way – the Eucharist, *lectio divina*, personal prayer, and regular confession.[74]

### INTIMACY WITH CHRIST

After Vatican II, when the vision of priestly identity became clouded over in some sectors of the Church, dissenting voices suggested that, among other things, priests should be free to engage in a secular occupation or to dedicate themselves to politics. Other aspects of the priestly life-style which were also questioned included the commitment to celibacy, the wearing of priestly attire, and the reading of the breviary.

Because priests share in Christ's priestly consecration it is only logical that they should look to the lifestyle of Christ as a model of how to live their consecration. The primary role of the priest, like that of Christ, is to be an instrument of holiness in the world, and so his mode of life should facilitate that goal. Since the priest belongs entirely to Christ, he is asked for the unconditional commitment which the Lord requested of his first disciples – that readiness to leave home, family, wife and children for his sake (cf. Mt 10:29; Lk 18:19; 14:26). Down through history, guided by the light of the Holy Spirit, the Church has determined in each generation how this wholehearted following of

70 Cf. St Pius X, Encyclical, *E supremi apostolatus*, ASS 36 (1903–4), p. 135; Apostolic exhortation, *Haerent animo*, ASS 41 (1908), p. 569; Benedict XV in an address to the Roman Clergy, AAS 11 (1919), p. 113; in a letter to the bishops of Czechoslovakia, AAS 13 (1921), p. 555; Pius XI, Encyclical, *Ad catholici sacderdotii*, AAS 28 (1936), p. 10; in a letter to the bishops of the Philippines, 18 January 1939; Pius XII, in Apostolic letter, *Haud mediocrem*, to Bolivian bishops, AAS 34 (1942), p. 234; Apostolic exhortation, *Menti nostrae*, AAS 42 (1950), p. 659; Paul VI, Address to Roman clergy, 26 March 1968. See Aranda, op. cit., pp 150–1. 71 Cf. HTL, 1991. 72 Cf. Address, 2 July 1980. 73 *Optatum totius*, 8. 74 Cf. PDV, 46–8.

our Lord expresses itself in particular detail. The underlying structure is, however, unchanging because the fundamental means to personal holiness do not
vary: prayer, sacraments, the Cross, zeal for souls.

The Catholic priesthood of its very nature demands a particular intimacy
with Christ, as the Master himself reminded his first priests in the Cenacle.
During the Last Supper he had washed their feet one by one in a ceremony
which left itself indelibly imprinted on the mind of the Beloved Disciple (cf.
Jn 13:2-17). Now they could understand clearly the full significance of what he
meant when he told them, 'No longer do I call you servants, ... but I have
called you friends, for all that I have heard from my Father I have made known
to you' (Jn 15:15). Without this special friendship it would be difficult to envis-
age Christ entrusting men with the sacrament of his Body and Blood. Absent
this intimate relationship, we cannot imagine the Risen Lord, on Easter
Evening, saying to the Apostles, 'Receive the Holy Spirit. If you forgive the
sins of any, they are forgiven' (Jn 20:22-23). Such friendship involves a commitment and, the Holy Father reminds us, should instil in us a holy fear of not
remaining faithful to it.[75] It should also evoke a deep sense of gratitude to be
sharers in this enduring affection, for 'having loved his own who were in the
world, he loved them to the end' (Jn 13:1). As Aquinas felicitously puts it:
*Christus est maxime sapiens et amicus* (Christ is our wisest and best friend).[76]

If ordination creates a special bonding between the priest and Christ, it
needs to be worked on to develop its full potential:

> (This bond) demands to be assimilated and lived out in a personal, free
> and conscious way through an ever richer communion of life and love
> and an ever broader and radical sharing in the feelings and attitudes of
> Jesus Christ. In this bond between the Lord Jesus and the priest, an
> ontological and psychological bond, a sacramental and moral bond, is
> the foundation and likewise the power for that 'life according to the
> Spirit' and that 'radicalism of the Gospel' to which every priest is
> called today and which is fostered by ongoing formation in its spiritu-
> al aspect.[77]

Priests are, in a very real sense, an extension of Christ's sacred humanity
because they continue to perform in souls the same miracles which he himself
worked while on earth: restoring spiritual sight to the blind; giving back supernatural life to those who have died through mortal sin; nourishing hungry souls
with the Eucharistic bread.[78]

75 Cf. HTL, 1988, no. 3.   76 *S. Th.*, I-II, 108, 4, *sed contra*.   77 PDV, 72.   78 The priest's
relationship with the Holy Spirit is considered in Chapter 10 below.

## RELATIONAL CHARACTER OF THE PRIESTHOOD: CONSEQUENCE OF *COMMUNIO*

We now come to the concept of the Church as a communion (*communio*)[79] which provides another context for looking at priestly identity. This is a theological prism which sheds new light on the mystery of the priesthood. Sacramental ordination establishes a relationship of communion with the Blessed Trinity, 'with the Father, the ultimate origin of all his power; with the Son, in whose redemptive mission he participates; with the Holy Spirit, who gives him the power for living and fulfilling that pastoral charity which qualifies him in a priestly way'.[80] By virtue of his participation in the Trinitarian communion, the fundamentally relational dimension of priestly identity by which he enters into communion with the Church, the bishop, his brother priests and the Christian community, can be better understood:

> The nature and mission of the ministerial priesthood cannot be defined except through this multiple and rich interconnection of relationships which arise from the Blessed Trinity and are prolonged in the communion of the Church, as a sign and instrument of Christ, of communion with God and of the unity of all humanity (cf. *Lumen gentium*, 1). In this context the ecclesiology of communion becomes decisive for understanding the identity of the priest, his essential dignity, and his vocation and mission among the people of God and in the world.[81]

Hence we can understand the insistence of theology on the *communio* in its different manifestations, not just for reasons of efficiency or public order, but because it is demanded by the very nature of the ministry which has as its objective the building up of communion in the Church. Ecclesial communion cannot be reduced to any other form of community such as the family, a culture, a nation, or simply the human community.[82] A consequence of this communion and upbuilding of the Church is that, as instructors of the people in the faith, it is the priest's responsibility to see to it

79 Articulated by Vatican II (cf. *Lumen gentium*, 4, 8, 13-15, 18, 21, 24-25; *Dei Verbum*, 10), the concept of *communio* was developed more fully in the document *Communionis notio: Letter to bishops on some aspects of the Church understood as communion*, Congregation for the Doctrine of the Faith, 28 May 1992. 80 DMLP, 20. 81 PDV, 12. 82 In Scripture the expression *communio sanctorum* (communion of the saints) has a triple meaning. In the first place it is mystical: communion with God; secondly it is sacramental and eucharistic: it is communion with Christ; and thirdly it is ecclesiological: it is the communion of the particular Churches (cf. Cardinal Godfried Danneels, 'Una eclesiología de comunión' in *Iglesia universal, Iglesias particulares*, Pamplona, 1990, p. 726).

that each member of the faithful shall be led in the Holy Spirit to the full development of his own vocation in accordance with the Gospel teaching, and to sincere and active charity, and the liberty with which Christ has set us free.[83]

It is a question of ensuring that each individual reaches Christian maturity according to his or her personal circumstances.[84] This commitment will in turn help the priest to mature spiritually, since the effort to care for all the Christian community at a personal level will enlarge his heart after the manner of the Good Shepherd, deepening his sentiments of mercy and universal love, with a preferential option for the needs of the poor, children, and the sick.[85]

RECIPROCAL RELATIONSHIP WITH CHRIST AND THE CHURCH

As already discussed, the priest's fundamental relationship is to Jesus Christ, Head and Shepherd,[86] and consequently the identity of the priest can only be understood from this perspective. The priest, however, relates to Christ in another way – as one who is an instrument of Christ the Head to communicate this divine life to Christ's Body the Church:

> Reference to the Church is … necessary, even if it is not primary, in defining the identity of the priest. As a *mystery, the Church is essentially related to Jesus Christ.* She is his fullness, his body, his spouse. She is the 'sign' and living 'memorial' of his permanent presence and activity in our midst and on our behalf.[87]

Since the Church is the Spouse of Christ, the priest's spousal relationship with the Church is an integral part of his identity. Both relationships, to Christ and to the Church, are inseparable. Indeed one could say that they are two aspects of the one relationship. They are, in fact, 'interiorly united in a kind of mutual immanence.'[88] *Pastores dabo vobis* describes the relationship as follows:

> Inasmuch as he represents Christ the Head, Shepherd and Spouse of the Church, the priest is placed not only *in the Church* but also *in the forefront of the Church.* The priesthood, along with the word of God and the sacramental signs which it serves, belongs to the constitutive elements of the Church. The ministry of the priest is entirely on

83 *Presbyterorum ordinis*, 6. 84 In Chapter 11 below the role of the priest in developing the individual Christian vocation is examined. 85 Cf. Mateo-Seco, op. cit., pp 419-21. 86 Cf. PDV, 16. 87 PDV, 12 (italics in original). 88 PDV, 16.

behalf of the Church; it aims at promoting the exercise of the common priesthood of the entire people of God; it is ordered not only to the particular Church but also to the universal Church (cf. *Presbyterorum ordinis*, 10), in communion with the Bishop, with Peter and under Peter.[89]

In the theology of priesthood traditionally the expression *in persona Christi* is often accompanied by another when referring to the priestly ministry: *in persona* or *in nomine Ecclesiae* (in the name or person of the Church).[90] The reach of the priestly action *in persona Christi* is not the same as *in persona Ecclesiae.* The signification of the latter phrase defines the reference of the priestly ministry to the *communio*, that is, to his bonding with his bishop, his brother priests and the Christian community.

> The priest is a *servant of the Church as mystery* because he actuates the Church's sacramental signs of the presence of the Risen Christ. He is a *servant of the Church as communion* because – in union with the Bishop and closely related to the presbyterate – he builds up the unity of the Church community in the harmony of diverse vocations, charisms and services. Finally, the priest is a servant of the Church as *mission* because he makes the community a herald and witness of the Gospel.[91]

However, many times when acting *in persona Christi*, he is also acting *in nomine totius Ecclesiae* (in the name of the whole Church). In the priestly ministry, then, the ecclesiological dimension is inseparable from the christological one.[92]

As we have already seen, the priest's relationship with the Church is described by the three pastoral offices, the triple *munera Christi* – teacher, priest, and shepherd.[93] *Pastores dabo vobis* does not use this exact typification of the pastoral offices, but refers to 'the threefold ministry of word, sacrament and pastoral charity'.[94] Elsewhere the same document refers to 'the ministry of reconciliation, of shepherding the flock of God and of teaching (cf. Acts 20:28; 1 Pet 5:2)',[95] which is expanded on as follows:

---

89 Ibid. (italics in original). 90 St Thomas defines the relationship between the two ideas as follows: 'In reciting the prayers of the Mass, the priest speaks *in persona Ecclesiae*, to which he remains united. In consecrating the sacrament, however, he speaks *in persona Christi*, whose place he takes in this by virtue of the power of Holy Orders. If, therefore, a priest cut off from the unity of the Church celebrates Mass, since he does not lose the power of Holy Orders, he consecrates the true Body and Blood of Christ. But, because he is separated from the unity of the Church, his prayers are not effective' (*S. Th.*, III, 82, 7, ad 3). 91 PDV, 16 (italics in original). 92 Cf. Mateo-Seco, p. 393. 93 Cf. *Presbyterorum ordinis*, 4-6, and CCC, 888-96. 94 PDV, 26. 95 PDV, 15.

In the Church and on behalf of the Church, priests are a sacramental representation of Jesus Christ, the Head and Shepherd, authoritatively proclaiming the word, repeating his acts of forgiveness and his offer of salvation, particularly in Baptism, Penance and the Eucharist, showing his living concern to the point of a total gift of self for the flock, which they gather into unity and lead to the Father through Christ and in the Spirit. In a word, priests exist and act in order to proclaim the Gospel to the world and to build the Church in the name and person of Christ the Head and Shepherd.[96]

Thus the priest not only acts in the name of Christ before the faithful, but also in the name of the whole Church, especially when presenting the Eucharistic sacrifice to God.[97]

While the priest's relationships with Christ and the Church define the role and identity of the priest, there is a third important relationship to be considered. It is not so much a new dimension as making explicit what is already implicit in the relationships already discussed – the bonding between the priest and the college of bishops and with his own presbyterate. *Pastores dabo vobis* tells us that,

By its very nature, the ordained ministry can be carried out only to the extent that the priest is united to Christ through sacramental participation in the priestly order, and thus to the extent that he is in hierarchical communion with his own Bishop ... The ministry of priests is above all communion and a responsible and necessary co-operation with the Bishop's ministry, in concern for the universal Church and for the individual particular Churches, for whose service they form with the Bishop a single presbyterate.[98]

Each priest is united to the other members of this presbyterate on the basis of the sacrament of Holy Orders and by particular bonds of apostolic charity, ministry and fraternity.[99]


## BLURRING OF PRIESTLY IDENTITY

As a recent Vatican document points out, there has been a propensity over the past decades to eliminate differences in roles between priest and laity.[100] This

96 Ibid. 97 Cf. CCC, 1552-3. 98 PDV, 17. See also PDV, 28. 99 For a detailed discussion of priestly fraternity, see Chapter 5 below. 100 Cf. *Instruction on certain questions regarding the collaboration of the non-ordained faithful in the sacred ministry of priests*, 15 August 1997.

leads to a levelling off of functions, a tendency which is not uninfluenced by appeal to a more 'democratic' model of the Church.[101] As a consequence, the distinction between the ministerial priesthood and the common priesthood of the faithful is often blurred. John Paul II refers to 'a tendency to obscure the theological basis of this difference' which 'can lead to a faulty clericalizing of the laity and a laicizing of the clergy'. What is now clear, he tells us, is that 'where the essential difference between the priestly and lay vocations is ignored, vocations to the priesthood all but disappear, and this is certainly not Christ's will nor the work of the Holy Spirit'.[102] Neither was this the mind of Vatican II when it encouraged greater lay involvement in the life of the Church:

> What the Council called for was lay involvement in the world of the family, commerce, politics, intellectual and cultural life – which are the proper field of specifically lay mission. The Council therefore stressed *the essential secularity of the lay vocation* (*Lumen gentium*, 31; cf. also *Evangelii nuntiandi*, 70; *Christifideles laici*, 14) ... The main focus of the lay vocation should be engagement in the world, while the priest has been ordained to be pastor, teacher and leader of prayer and sacramental life within the Church. His grace and responsibility is above all to act in the sacraments in *persona Christi*.[103]

Reaffirmation of the respective roles of priest and laity in line with Vatican II teaching is essential for several reasons, not least to guarantee an authentic perception of priestly identity and to facilitate the promotion of vocations with a clear conviction about the role of the priest in the Church.

*Christifideles laici* articulated an exciting vision of a laity fully living its mission of bringing Gospel values into the family, society, culture and the world of work. In this way they exercise their common priesthood as an expression of the universal call to holiness. This call is 'intimately connected to mission and to the responsibility entrusted to the lay faithful in the Church and in the

---

101 'The priest is first and foremost the leader of the people entrusted to him. The Church's structure transcends both the "democratic" and "autocratic" models, because it is founded on the Father's "sending" of his Son and on the conferral of a "mission" through the gift of the Holy Spirit to the Twelve and to their successors (cf. Jn 20:21) ... This is an authority which does not originate from below and therefore its extension and exercise cannot be defined by any assembly from below ... The ordained minister carries out this mission with an authority and grace which do not come from knowledge and skill, however necessary, but from ordination' (John Paul II, Address, 15 October 1998, no. 4). 102 Cf. Address, 21 November 1998, no. 5. 103 Ibid. (italics in original). See also *Report of interdicasterial meeting with representatives of the Australian bishops*, no. 23, released on 14 December 1998.

world'.[104] Their task is to continue Christ's saving mission in the world 'which is the place and means for lay faithful to fulfil their Christian vocation'. The sanctification of the world – society, culture, work – is the distinctively 'secular' vocation of the laity.[105]

The temptation to clericalize the laity by adjusting their vocation into involvement in priestly activities should be resisted for the sake of the integrity and dignity of the lay vocation. The assumption that they can adequately fulfil their vocation by assuming clerical responsibilities undermines the grace of baptism, from which the laity derive their mission to the world, and falsifies the reality of the Church as communion.[106] What is at stake here is the fundamental ecclesiological principle articulated by Vatican II – on the one hand, that of the unity of the Church's mission in which all the baptized participate, and on the other, the essential difference between the priestly ministry, rooted in the sacrament of Orders, and the role of the laity in the Church deriving from the sacraments of Baptism and Confirmation. The primary apostolic context for the laity is not the sacristy but the family, work, politics, the media, fashion, sport – fields of human endeavour which in their own right they try to bring to God. The consciousness of their baptismal mission in the world will lead them to imbue all these areas with Christian principles, thus raising them to the supernatural order. The dignity and primacy of the human person, social solidarity, the sanctity of marriage, responsible freedom, respect for justice at all levels – all this is the business of the laity.[107] They sanctify the world through their secular tasks, sharing in the one mission of Christ by means of the different vocations they have received. And so,

> precisely in order to exercise fully this prophetic, priestly and royal function of Christ, the baptized need the help of the ministerial priesthood that confers the gift of divine life received from Christ, Head of the Body, in a privileged and tangible way. The more Christian and conscious people are of their dignity and of their vital role in the Church, the more urgently they feel the need for priests who are truly priests.[108]

The new evangelization encouraged by John Paul II demands a Church which has transcended clericalism.[109] The primary reason for the Church's hierarchical structure is to serve the needs of the mission of the laity to the world. Weigel describes John Paul II's teaching on the vocation of the laity, like

---

104 *Christifideles laici*, 17 (30 December 1988). 105 Cf. ibid., no. 15. 106 Cf. ibid., nos. 23-24. 107 Cf. *Lumen gentium*, 36; *Christifideles laici*, 17. 108 John Paul II, Address, 6 October 1986. 109 Cf. Weigel, ibid., p. 554.

his catechesis on the theology of the body, as well in advance of current Catholic thinking:

> When the life of the Church catches up with *Christifideles laici*, that fact will alter the face of world Catholicism, by reviving dimensions of New Testament Christianity among evangelically assertive Catholics who are far more passionate about service than about ecclesiastical power.[110]

On 9 June 1987, during a pastoral visit to his native country, John Paul II ordained fifty priests in the university city of Lublin where he himself had taught as a professor of philosophy. In his homily, among other things, he asked the new priests to avoid the dangers of clericalism:

> Your task, my dear new priests, will be to collaborate with lay people aware of their responsibility for the Church, and for a Christian form of life in society.

Their specific priestly role was:

> To serve God – to serve man: *to liberate* in man the consciousness of royal priesthood, of that dignity proper to man as a son or daughter of God himself and proper to the Christian of whom it is said that he is 'another Christ'.[111]

Intelligent solutions have been found for the collaboration of the lay faithful in the pastoral ministry of priests which respect sacramental limits and the differences of charisms and pastoral roles. However, at the same time a functionalist conception of Holy Orders has developed in the Church which, John Paul II warns, is causing serious damage to the theological identity of both laity and the clergy, and consequently to the whole work of evangelization.[112]

In this context he has also pointed out that the use of the word 'ministries' for those offices exercised by the lay faithful in the Church can lead to doubt and confusion, obscuring the essential difference between the ministerial priesthood and that of all the baptized. Hence there is an urgent pastoral need to clarify terminology, not for the purpose of defending clerical privileges, but out of the need for obedience to Christ's will and respect for the essential constitutional structure impressed by him on the Church.[113] Where there is a

---

110 Cf. ibid., p. 555. 111 Cf. ibid., p. 545. 112 Address, 24 April 1994, no. 2. 113 Cf. ibid., no. 4. The importance of using precise terminology in this context was emphasized by the Cardinal Prefect of the Congregation for the Sacraments and Divine Worship. Writing

shortage of vocations, the solution, John Paul II reminds us, is not to look for alternatives partially supplied by lay ministries, but rather to focus efforts on making the call of Christ heard again in families, parishes, and schools.[114]


PRIESTLY DRESS

One expression of this blurring of differences is the tendency to avoid wearing the distinctive clerical garb which immediately identifies the priest publicly for what he is. While the Church reaffirms the equal dignity of all the baptized, she cannot deny the hierarchical structure entrusted to her by Christ himself. Hence it is only natural that she would give importance to the symbols of that structure which distinguish the ministerial priesthood from the common priesthood of the faithful, and which for priests is expressed through the wearing of clerical dress.

For a priest to dress in lay attire is to disguise the fact that his very *raison d'être* is to draw souls to Christ. He has a representative role which is, as a consequence of ordination, part of his very being. To dress as a priest is to give witness to the total commitment of one's life and to manifest the presence of Christ among men. If the priest has been formed in the social virtues; if he has a spirit of service linked to a deep conviction about the value of his vocation, he will rarely find that the external expression of his ministry will be a barrier to his social assimilation. On the contrary, he will discover that his very visible priesthood is a positive means to attract people, and to engage their interest and response at the level of their deepest concerns. Priestly garb is never an obstacle to the kind of friendship which the priest can and needs to have with those souls entrusted to his care.

People can easily detect how a priest responds to the gift of his own vocation and to what extent he appreciates it. They expect that his awareness of his apostolic mission will be reflected in his conversation and in his attitude to

about the ICEL's proposed retranslation of *De ordinatione episcopi, presbyterorum et diaconorum*, he says, 'Prominent among the problems is the decision of the translators to break with common Catholic usage and translate the Latin "presbyteri" into English not with "priests" but with "presbyters". This cannot meet with the Holy See's consent since it risks being misunderstood by the people and represents an unacceptable theological tendency. In particular it constitutes a retreat from a term that carries with it the history of the development of the faith, in favour of a term which does not' (Cardinal Jorge Medina Estévez, letter to Bishop Anthony Pilla, 20 September 1997, in *Inside the Vatican* 6:1 [January 1998]: 22). See Kevin M. Quirk, 'With apologies to Shakespeare: What's in the name "priest"?' in *Josephinum Journal of Theology*, 8, no. 1, Winter/Spring 2001, pp 148–55. 114 Cf. Address, 24 April 1994, nos. 4, 6. See also Leo Scheffczyk, 'Laypersons, deacons and priests: a difference of ministries' in *Communio*, 23, Winter 1996, pp 639–55.

them. They may have little Christian commitment; they may even be agnostic or have anticlerical tendencies, but, in spite of all of this, the priest dressed as a priest will generally have for them a certain prestige if he lives his vocation with elegance, affability and a spirit of service; if it is seen that he is open-minded and has a welcoming spirit. The objective reality of his vocation is that he has been chosen, personally, to participate in the eternal priesthood of Christ for the benefit of all. The awareness of this distinction should be reflected in a natural way in his external life-style as an expression of this new configuration of his personality to that of Christ. His own reverence for his priesthood will induce him to demand the appropriate respect for it from others. He will have the courage and the conviction to explain the reasons why, where necessary. However, by his behaviour and his attitudes, he will always communicate to others something of the dignity of his vocation, and invariably there will be little need to for him to speak in his own defence.

The actor, Alec Guinness, recalling the different influences which guided him to the Catholic Church, describes a revealing incident on his spiritual journey to Rome. He was on location in Burgundy filming *Fr Brown*. One evening, dressed in a soutane, he walked from the set to his hotel, a few miles outside the village. It was getting dark.

> I hadn't gone far when I heard scampering footsteps and a piping voice calling, 'Mon père!' My hand was seized by a boy of seven or eight, who clutched it tightly, swung it and kept up a non-stop prattle. He was full of excitement, hops, skips and jumps, but never let go of me. I didn't dare speak in case my excruciating French should scare him. Although I was a total stranger he obviously took me for a priest and so to be trusted. Suddenly with a 'Bonsoir, mon père', and a hurried sideways sort of bow, he disappeared through a hole in the hedge. He had had a happy, reassuring walk home, and I was left with an odd calm and sense of elation. Continuing my walk I reflected that a Church which could inspire such confidence in a child, making its priests, even when unknown, so easily approachable could not be as scheming and creepy as so often made out. I began to shake off my long-taught, long-absorbed prejudices.[115]

Often today our service as priests takes place in a secularized society where there is a gradual decline in the sense of the sacred and a progressive elimination of religious values. Such a society has all the more need of the sign value of the priesthood, of this witnessing to the unseen world of the supernatural.

115 Alec Guinness, *Blessings in disguise*, London, 1985, p. 36.

In a culture where most ideas are transmitted at the visual level its relevance is
even more obvious. A priest in lay garb is, in a certain sense, a sign of a dying
Church. On the other hand, the priest who does not hide his identity is confirmation for his people of the vitality of the faith. 'The priestly personality',
Pope John Paul II wrote to priests in 1979, 'must be *for others* a clear and plain
*sign and indication*'.[116] That indelible character, imprinted on the soul by the
sacrament of Order, cannot be privatized because it was given by the Church
for the service of others. The faithful not only have a need of the sign value of
a priest dressed as a priest, but have a right not to be deceived in this respect:

> In a secularized and materialistic society, where the external signs of
> sacred and supernatural realities tend to disappear, it is particularly
> important that the community be able to recognize the priest, man of
> God and dispenser of his mysteries, by his attire as well, which is an
> unequivocal sign of his dedication and his identity as a public minis-
> ter. The priest should be identifiable primarily through his conduct,
> but also by his manner of dressing, which makes visible to all the faith-
> ful, indeed and to all men, his identity and his belonging to God and
> the Church ... Outside of entirely exceptional cases, a cleric's failure
> to use this proper ecclesiastical attire could manifest a weak sense of
> his identity as one consecrated to God.[117]

As we have already seen, a concomitant danger of the trend to clericalize
the laity is the risk of secularizing the service of the priest. The Holy Father
tells us that attempts to make the priest more like the laity are damaging to the
Church, and offers us the example of St John Mary Vianney as a model of how
to be close to the laity. 'It is essential to the Church', he affirms, 'that the identity of the priest be safeguarded, with its vertical dimension. The life and personality of the Curé of Ars are a particularly enlightening and vigorous illustration of this'.[118]

In his 1982 Holy Thursday letter, John Paul II prays: 'May no place be
found in our souls for those currents of ideas which diminish the importance
of the ministerial priesthood, those opinions and tendencies which strike at the
very nature of the holy vocation and service to which you, O Christ, call us
within your Church ... Save us', he concludes, 'from *grieving your Spirit*'(cf.
Eph. 4:30): – by secularism and by wishing at all costs to conform to the mentality of this world; by whatever shows itself as a desire to hide one's priesthood before men and to avoid all external signs of it.' [119]

---

116 HTL, 1979, no. 7 (italics in original).  117 DMLP, 66.  118 HTL, 1986, no. 10.  119
HTL, 1982, no. 4.

The idea that the priest, by dressing no differently from others, will more effectively convince lay people of his closeness to them, reflects a fundamental error of human psychology if not a profound inferiority complex as well. Our pastoral activity requires 'that we should be close to people and all their problems, whether these problems be personal, family or social ones, but it also demands that we should be close to all these problems "in a priestly way".'[120] If we are to be of real assistance to others, an essential precondition is that we remain ourselves, that we retain our identity, because the best and the only effective contribution we can make to the solution of these human problems is from 'the perspective of eternal life'.[121]

Our brothers in the faith, and unbelievers too, expect us always to be able 'to show them this perspective, to become real witnesses to it, to be dispensers of grace, to be servants of the word of God'.[122] Experience shows that priests who try to be more useful by doing what they think will make them more popular, end up by being neither supernaturally useful nor humanly popular. They have been given the capacity to be salt and light through their priestly service but, by an inversion of values, will fail to deliver the one thing which is uniquely theirs to give. 'The personal experience of each of us', John Paul II affirms, 'is that our joy and fruitfulness in the priestly life come from a full acceptance of our priestly identity'. We must not only love our priesthood but also be seen to do so:

> Let your people see that you are men of prayer. Let them see that you treat the sacred mysteries with love and respect ... Let everyone see that you love the Church, and that you are of one mind and heart with her. What is at stake is the credibility of our witness![123]

These are counsels which as priests we need to reflect on, to pray about frequently so that we never forget that we are always *other Christs*, and can never afford to be less than this to people. Our service to the Church is related essentially to man's eternal salvation.[124] If we were ever to lose sight of that fundamental objective, there is a grave danger that our lives would become suffused with mere activism, with solving human and social problems, at the expense of that unique *diakonia* which, as Christ's priests, we alone can offer in the cause of man's definitive, supernatural happiness.

120 HTL, 1979, no. 7.  121 Ibid.  122 Ibid.  123 Address, 31 May 1982.  124 HTL, 1979, no. 2.

CONCLUSION

In his 1991 Holy Thursday letter, the Holy Father returns to the question of priestly identity. He is strongly of the opinion that the current dearth of vocations in many places should help to overcome the existing crisis in the priesthood. At the same time he reminds us that 'the experience of recent decades shows even more clearly how much the priest is needed both in the Church and in the world, not in some "laicized" form, but in the form which is drawn from the Gospel and the rich Tradition of the Church'.[125] In summary we can say with John Paul II:

> Priestly identity is important for the presbyter; it is important for his *witness among people*, who, in him, seek only the priest: *a true 'homo' Dei*, who loves the Church as his Bride; who is a *witness to God as the Absolute* and to invisible realities for the faithful; who is a *man of prayer* and, because of this, *a true teacher, guide and friend*. Before a priest like this, it is easier for believers to kneel and confess their sins; it is easier for them when they participate in the Mass, to be aware of the anointing of the Holy Spirit, granted to the priest's hands and heart through the sacrament of Holy Orders. Priestly identity implies *fidelity* to Christ and to the People of God to whom we are sent. It is not only something intimate which concerns the priest's self-awareness. It is *a reality that is constantly examined and verified by men*, because the priest is 'taken from among men and made their representative before God to offer gifts and sacrifices for sins' (Heb 5:1).[126]

This will always be the source of the true identity of the priest. The more we look at Christ, the more we meditate on his presence in the Gospel and in the Tabernacle, the more clearly will the sentiments and features of the Master be reflected in our words and works, in our dealings with all those entrusted to our care.

125 HTL, 1991, no. 2. 126 Address, 27 October 1995, no. 6 (italics in original).

# 4

## Body and soul to Christ – priestly celibacy

Priestly celibacy has been a topic of active discussion for a number of years. In the past it rarely drew attention to itself because it was accepted as a normal part of the lifestyle of the priest. However, for different reasons it has become a subject of keen media interest, not least because of some high profile failures in commitment to this discipline in recent years. Several questions are being asked about celibacy at the present time. It is suggested that it creates a barrier between priest and people, especially married people with whose difficulties, we are told, he can have little empathy. Some contend that celibacy leads to emotional and psychological isolation. Others see it as a repression of natural feelings and inclinations, with a stunting of the normal growth of personality.

It is frequently affirmed that celibacy is a burden for most priests, a cause of loneliness and lack of fulfilment. Indeed one newspaper editorial quoted with approval 'research' which suggested that 'a mere two percent who pledge celibacy achieve it'.[1] In any case, it is asserted, since celibacy is not a precept of divine law but rather a matter of ecclesiastical discipline, it can be changed at any time. Many consider it the main cause of the significant drop in candidates for the priesthood, and hence a barrier to attracting the right kind of young men into seminaries. For all these reasons it is affirmed that the Church should make celibacy an optional requirement for ordination, because otherwise it will have to face serious manpower difficulties in the future. As a backdrop to this scenario, the shadow of John Paul II is seen to be cast over the present impasse because of his perceived traditionalist brand of Catholicism, and his refusal to accommodate law to 'reality'.

From another perspective it is affirmed that, with the development of the theology of marriage since Vatican II, it is no longer tenable to consider priesthood as a 'higher' calling, and that there is, therefore, a need to 'demythologize' the traditional concept of ministry to bring it into line with the requirements of modern society. For some, the Catholic priesthood, as at present constituted, is seen as a privileged position characterized by the exercise of 'power' without responsibility. It is also claimed that, precisely through the insistence

1 Cf. *Irish Times*, 21 September 1996.

of the Church on a celibate priesthood, this 'power' is perpetuated for the domination of the rest of the Christian faithful.

Some of these objections at first sight may seem to have a certain validity, but there are others which betray a patent ideological bias. It is clear too that, underlying many of the arguments against what is sometimes referred to as 'compulsory' celibacy, there is an understanding of priesthood which differs radically from the traditional concept of ministry which developed in the first millennium and a half of the Church's life, and as articulated by the Council of Trent and Vatican II.[2]

## CHURCH TEACHING ON CELIBACY

Let us first of all briefly define what the Church teaches about celibacy. Vatican II affirmed the tradition of celibacy in the Western Church as follows:

> By persevering in virginity or celibacy for the sake of the kingdom of heaven (cf. Mt 19:12) priests are consecrated in a new and excellent way to Christ (cf. 1 Cor 7:32-34). They more readily cling to him with undivided heart and dedicate themselves more freely in him and through him to the service of God and of men. They are less encumbered in their service of his kingdom and of the task of heavenly regeneration. In this way they become better fitted for a broader acceptance of fatherhood in Christ. By means of celibacy, then, priests profess before men their willingness to be dedicated with undivided loyalty to the task entrusted to them, namely that of espousing the faithful to one husband and presenting them as a chaste virgin to Christ (cf. 2 Cor 11:2). Moreover they are made a living sign of that world to come, already present through faith and charity, a world in which the children of the resurrection shall neither be married nor take wives (cf. Lk 20:35-6).[3]

Based on this teaching Paul VI developed a rich theology of celibacy in his 1967 encyclical, *Sacerdotalis caelibatus*.[4] Although this document didn't receive an enthusiastic reception in some quarters, four years later his teaching was reaffirmed by the 1971 synod of bishops:

2 The material for this chapter is taken from my *Priestly celibacy today*, Four Courts Press, Dublin, 1998, pp 248. This volume gives a detailed account of celibacy from the historical, scriptural, theological, and anthropological perspectives. It also has chapters on 'Formation for celibacy', 'Celibacy a way to holiness', 'Witnesses and testimonies to celibacy', and a chapter answering objections to this charism. 3 *Presbyterorum ordinis*, 16. 4 Published on

Because of the intimate and multiple coherence between the pastoral
function and a celibate life, the existing law is upheld: one who freely
wills total availability, the distinctive character of this function, also
freely undertakes a celibate life. The candidate should feel this form of
living not as having been imposed from outside, but rather as a manifestation of his free self-giving, which is accepted and ratified by the
Church through the bishop. In this way the law becomes a protection
and a safeguard of the freedom wherewith the priest gives himself to
Christ and it becomes 'an easy yoke'.[5]

The same position was adopted in the 1983 revised Code of Canon Law:

Clerics are obliged to observe perfect and perpetual continence for the
sake of the Kingdom of heaven, and are therefore bound to celibacy.
Celibacy is a special gift of God by which sacred ministers can more
easily remain close to Christ with an undivided heart, and can dedicate
themselves more freely to the service of God and their neighbour. [6]

In the build-up to the 1990 synod of bishops there was a lot of pressure to
introduce optional celibacy. However, the mind of the Church on priestly
celibacy was stated very clearly in the post-synodal document on priestly formation, *Pastores dabo vobis*, published on 25 March 1992. As if anticipating the
current speculation and unrest, John Paul II affirmed that

The Synod does not wish to leave any doubts in the mind of anyone
regarding the Church's firm will to maintain the law that demands
perpetual and freely chosen celibacy for present and future candidates
for priestly ordination in the Latin rite.[7]

This, in outline, is the status of celibacy in Church teaching at present. What
are the theological arguments for this demanding discipline? Why has the
Church continued to affirm the appropriateness of this charism for the exercise of the priestly ministry? To find out let us first of all review the scriptural foundations and witness to celibacy.

### SCRIPTURAL FOUNDATIONS FOR CELIBACY

While there are a number of biblical texts which describe the spiritual and theological value of virginity or celibacy *in genere*, at first sight there does not
appear to be any specific text which directly links celibacy with the ministers

24 June 1967. 5 Synodal document, *The ministerial priesthood*, Part Two, Section I, no.4 c).
6 Canon § 271:1. 7 PDV, 29.

of the Church.[8] At the same time the scriptural validation of priestly celibacy derives more from the convergence of meaning of a number of different texts, and the cumulative thrust of their signification, rather than from the probative value of individual texts. The different insights drawn from various scriptural passages, as understood by Tradition and proposed by the Magisterium, constitute the biblical case for priestly celibacy.[9] The Church has never claimed that this case is a definitive one, but it consistently refers to particular texts as an affirmation of the intimate affinity between the charism of celibacy and the exercise of the priestly ministry *in persona Christi*. We will now examine the more important of these texts.[10] Nevertheless, above and beyond the textual support for priestly celibacy, there is the Gospel witness to the celibacy of Jesus himself, God become a priest in the humanity of Christ. This is the most powerful of all scriptural statements in favour of priestly celibacy.

## CHRIST PREACHES ON CELIBACY

When Christ called his first apostles to make them 'fishers of men' (Mt 4:19; Mk 1:17), they 'left everything and followed him' (Lk 5:11; cf. Mt 4:20,22; Mk 1:18, 20). It was Peter who recalled this aspect of the apostolic vocation when one day, with characteristic frankness, he said to Jesus, 'we have left everything and followed you' (Mt 19:27) and asked what the rewards would be. The Master in his reply opened up unexpected horizons of self-giving. His call envisaged that his disciples would leave behind home, property, and loved ones – family, wife, children – 'for my name's sake' (Mt 19:29; cf Lk 18:29-30). Indeed, on another occasion he makes the same point in even more demanding language: 'Whoever loves father or mother more than me is not worthy of me' (Mt 10:37), all pointing to the fact that practical renunciation is an essential element of the apostolic vocation. This clear scriptural doctrine, John Paul II has pointed out, provides the context for Christ's teaching on celibacy.[11]

8 Cf. Ignace de la Potterie, 'The biblical foundation of priestly celibacy' in *For love alone: reflections on priestly celibacy*, Maynooth, 1993, p. 14. 9 Cf. *Dei Verbum*, no.9 for the relationship between Scripture, the living Tradition of the Church, and the Magisterium. See also *Instruction on the ecclesial vocation of the theologian*, nos. 13-24, published by the Congregation for the Doctrine of the Faith, 24 May 1990. 10 A review of the significant documents of the Magisterium on priestly celibacy since the beginning of the twentieth century shows that the following texts are consistently referred to: Lev 8:33-35; Mt 19:10-12; Mt 22:30; 1 Cor 7:7; 1 Cor 7:25-33; 2 Cor 11:2; Eph 5:25-32. Thus, for example, we find in Vatican II (*Lumen gentium*, 42; *Presbyterorum ordinis*, 16) the following references: Lk 20:35-36; Mt 19:11-12; 1 Cor 7:7; 1 Cor 7:32-34; 2 Cor 11:2; in *Sacerdotalis caelibatus*: Mt 19:11; Mt 22:30; 1 Cor 7:29-31; 1 Cor 7:32-33; Eph 5: 25-27; in *Pastored dabo vobis*: Mt 19:11; 1 Cor 7:7; 1 Cor 7:32-34; in the *Catechism of the Catholic Church*: Mt 19:12; 1 Cor 7:32. 11 Cf. Address, 17 July 1993.

From St Matthew we see that Christ recommends celibacy in the same setting in which he affirms the indissolubility of marriage (cf. 19:10-12). The disciples had reacted strongly to Christ's forbidding a man to put away his wife: 'If such is the case of a man with his wife', then, they concluded, 'it is not expedient to marry'(19:10). Christ's reply was challenging:

> Not all men can receive this precept, but only those to whom it is given. For there are eunuchs who have been so from birth, and there are eunuchs who have been made eunuchs by men, and there are eunuchs who have made themselves eunuchs for the sake of the kingdom of heaven. He who is able to receive this, let him receive it (Mt 19:11-12).

As Galot points out, this text has a marked Semitic structure similar to other *logia* of Jesus in the Sermon on the Mount. Yet, in the context of the contemporary Jewish mentality, the idea is a complete innovation.[12] The eunuch, born thus or made so, was an outcast, denied by Jewish law the right to bring offerings to the Temple (cf. Lev 21:17-20) and excluded from the assembly of Yahweh (cf. Deut 23:2), because it seemed improper that a person deprived of the power of transmitting life would associate with the God of life.[13] There are, however, words of praise for the eunuch who does no evil and who is faithful to the covenant (cf. Wis 3:14; Is 56:3).

But Christ goes further than merely show benevolence. He dares to portray eunuchry as a freely chosen state, something unthinkable for Jews who look on marriage and the procreation of children as a religious obligation, and who considered lack of descendants as one of the greatest misfortunes. In trying to explain why Jesus would use the pejorative word 'eunuch', some exegetes suggest that this was probably because Jesus' enemies had used it about him and his disciples to chide them on their renunciation of marriage. Jewish tradition regarded a celibate as somebody less than a man.[14]

12 'This saying is traceable to words spoken by Jesus himself. Its form exhibits a marked Semitic colouring, and its structure discloses an ascending rhythm in three steps found elsewhere, as in markedly Semitic *logia* embodied in the Sermon on the Mount (cf. Mt 5:22; 5:39-41). There is also an opening admonition and a matching warning at the end. In vocabulary and style, we note expressions similar to those current among the Jews. Yet, compared to the Jewish mentality of the day, the idea is new, and the way of expressing it is paradoxical, which is an index of authenticity. In a genuinely Semitic idiom, a revolutionary thought is being expressed' (Galot, *Theology of the priesthood*, p. 232). 13 Some Israelites were castrated so that they could work with the harem of Israelite or foreign kings (cf. 2 Kings 9:32; Esther 2:3; 4:4-5). 14 Cf. Galot, ibid., p. 235.

CELIBACY A TURNING POINT IN SALVATION HISTORY

Consequently, from the perspective of the Old Testament, Christ's affirmation of celibacy for a supernatural motive marks a turning point in salvation history. As John Paul II reminds us, it directs attention to 'the eschatological "virginity" of the risen man, in whom will be revealed the absolute and eternal nuptial meaning of the glorified body in union with God himself'.[15] Hence, earthly continence for the sake of the Kingdom is a testimony to the truth that the end of the body is not the grave, but glorification, and in this sense it anticipates a future resurrection (cf. Rom 8:22-23). Ultimately celibacy derives from the will of Christ as manifested in the Gospel. The link between celibacy and priesthood was first established in him, which shows that, in its most perfect realisation, the priesthood involves the renunciation of marriage.

Christ's celibacy was appropriate to his universal love and his spiritual engendering of a new humanity. It did not distance him from people – on the contrary it enabled him to draw close to every human being. Through his humanity he was able to reveal the infinite love of the Father for all mankind, expressed in so many different ways in the Gospel narrative – his compassion on the crowds who followed him, his sharing of the successes and disappointments of his disciples, his grief at the death of his friend Lazarus, his affection for children, his experience of all human limitations except sin. By freeing himself from the claims of family Christ was totally available to do his Father's will (cf. Lk 2:49, Jn 4:34), to constitute the new and universal family of the children of God. Accordingly 'his celibacy was not a defensive reaction against anything, but an enhancement conferred upon his life, a greater closeness to his people, a yearning to give himself unreservedly to the world'.[16]

This new vision implicit in Christ's celibacy had already been set in train by Mary's virginal motherhood and by Joseph's sharing in the same virginal mystery.[17] While the mystery of the conception and birth of Christ was hidden from his contemporaries, it was a totally new departure in relation to the Old Testament tradition which, because of its exclusive favouring of marriage, rendered continence incomprehensible. Mary and Joseph were therefore the first and intimate witnesses to a 'fruitfulness different from that of the flesh, that is, of a fruitfulness of the spirit', realized in the gift of the incarnation of the Eternal Word.[18] This mystery was only gradually revealed to the eyes of the Church on the basis of the witness of the infancy narratives in the gospels of Matthew and Luke. The divine maternity of the Virgin Mary helps us to understand more fully, on the one hand, the sanctity of marriage and, on the other, the mystery of continence for the sake of the Kingdom of Heaven.[19]

15 Address, 24 March 1982, no. 1. 16 Galot, ibid., p. 232. 17 Cf. John Paul II, Address, 24 March 1982, no. 2. 18 Cf. ibid. 19 Cf. ibid., no. 4.

Here again we see two correlative aspects of the one baptismal vocation to holiness.

### CHRIST CALLS TO CELIBACY

When Christ first opened the horizon of celibacy to his disciples, the example of his own life would have given them a clear reference point for this supernatural life-style which they would associate directly with the kingdom which Christ was preaching. From Christ's words it is obvious that a special grace is necessary to understand the meaning of celibacy and to respond to it. 'He who is able to receive it', he tells his disciples, 'let him receive it' (Mt 19:12). Celibacy is therefore a response to the experience of God's kingdom as made present in the example and teaching of the Master. It is not, and can never be, a human initiative alone, nor is there ever a question of obligation to it. It must be appropriated as an expression of personal freedom in response to a particular grace. It is not merely a question of understanding the vocation to celibacy; there is also associated with it a motivation in the will to follow this way drawn by the example and the mystery of Christ.

Response to a celibate vocation is a decision based on faith. Nevertheless, the calling does not eliminate the sacrifice involved in giving up the attraction to conjugal love in this life, a renunciation which is implied in Christ's teaching in Matthew 19:10-12. Yet, acceptance of it is based on the conviction that by following this life-style one can make a particular contribution to the realisation of the Kingdom of God in its earthly dimension, with the prospect of a higher and definitive level of self-fulfilment in the next life.

Implicit in the response to God's call is the readiness to share in the sacrifice involved in Christ's redeeming work. It is therefore a decision based on love but, as John Paul II reminds us, 'it is natural for the human heart to accept demands, even difficult ones, in the name of love for an ideal, and above all in the name of love for a person'.[20] A commitment to celibacy is in no way a rejection of the value of human sexuality; rather it respects the 'duality' inherent in man's being made to the image and likeness of God.[21] Indeed, the Holy Father makes the challenging point that it is precisely the person who understands the full potential for self-giving that marriage offers who can best make a mature offering of himself in celibacy.[22] By choosing continence for the sake of the Kingdom of Heaven, a man fulfils himself differently and, in a certain sense,

20 Address, 28 April 1982, no. 1. 21 Cf. Address, 7 April 1982, no. 2. 22 Cf. Address, 5 May 1982, nos. 2. As John Paul II points out (cf. ibid., no.3), this renunciation is, paradoxically, at the same time an affirmation of the value from which the person abstains. Thus he reminds us that the vocation to celibacy is, in a certain sense, indispensable so that the nup-

more fully than through marriage.[23] This is the implication of Christ's response to Peter's very honest question about the rewards to be expected by those who had left everything to follow the Master (cf. Mk 10:29-30).


## PAULINE TEACHING

In reply to questions about virginity and celibacy from the early Christian communities, St Paul, in his first Letter to the Corinthians, gives a magisterial and, at the same time, a pastoral interpretation of the doctrine of Christ. The uniqueness of Paul's teaching is that, while transmitting the truth proclaimed by the Master, he gives it his own personal stamp based on the experience of his missionary activity. In the Apostle's doctrine we encounter the question of the mutual relationship between marriage and celibacy or virginity, a topic which created difficulties among the first generation of converts from paganism at Corinth.

He emphasises with great clarity that virginity, or voluntary continence, derives exclusively from a counsel and not from a command: 'With regard to virgins, I have no command from the Lord, but I give my opinion' (1 Cor 7:25). But it is an opinion of 'one who by the Lord's mercy is trustworthy' (ibid.). At the same time he gives his advice to those already married, to those who have still to make a decision in this regard, and to those who have been widowed (cf. 1 Cor 7, *passim*). In his explanations Paul tries to give reasons why those who marry do 'well', and why those who decide on a life of continence or virginity do 'better' (cf. 1 Cor 7:38).[24]

From the perspective of apostolic zeal, celibacy allows a man to be concerned about 'the affairs of the Lord' and thus be able 'to please the Lord with all his heart' (cf. 1 Cor 7:32). By contrast St Paul points out that the married man doesn't have the same availability to devote himself to the things of God (cf. 1 Cor 7:33). He was celibate himself (cf. 1 Cor 7:7) and recommends celibacy as a way of having the freedom to love God totally and unconditionally. The perishability of human existence ['I tell you this, brothers: the time is already short ...'(1 Cor 7:29)], and the transience of the temporal world ['the form of this world is passing away' (1 Cor 7:31)] should, he tells the Corinthians, cause 'those who have wives to live as though they had none' (1 Cor 7:29). In this way Paul prepares the ground for his teaching on continence.[25]

Christ's doctrine on celibacy 'for the sake of the kingdom of Heaven' (cf.

tial meaning of the body may be more easily recognized in conjugal and family life. And this is because the key to understanding the sacramentality of marriage is the spousal love of Christ for his Church, so eloquently described by St Paul in his letter to the Ephesians (cf. Eph 5:22-33). **23** Cf. Address, 7 April 1982, no. 2. **24** Cf. Address, 23 June 1982. **25** Cf. Address, 30 June 1982, nos. 1-5.

Mt 19:12) finds a direct echo in the Apostle's teaching that 'the unmarried man is anxious about the affairs of the Lord, how to please the Lord' (1 Cor 7:32). This concern of Paul's to serve God finds similar expression in his 'anxiety for all the Churches' (2 Cor 11:28) and his desire to serve all the members of the Body of Christ (cf. Phil 2:20-21; 1 Cor 12:25). The unmarried person is concerned about all this, and this is why Paul can be, in the full sense of the term, an 'apostle of Jesus Christ' (1 Cor 1:1) and minister of the Gospel (cf. Col 1:23), and would wish that others would be like him (cf. 1 Cor 7:7). At the same time, apostolic zeal and pastoral activity ('anxiety for the affairs of the Lord') does not exhaust the content of the Pauline motivation for continence. The root and source of this commitment is to be found in the concern 'how to please the Lord' (1 Cor 7:32). This is a desire to live a life of deep friendship with Christ, expressing at the same time the spousal dimension of the vocation to celibacy.[26]

St Paul observes that the man who is bound by marriage 'is divided' (1 Cor 7:34) by reason of his family obligations, implying that the commitment 'to please the Lord' presupposes abstention from marriage. This state of being unmarried allows virgins to be 'anxious about the affairs of the Lord, to be holy in body and spirit' (1 Cor 7:34). In biblical terms, especially in the Old Testament setting, holiness implies separation from what is 'profane', of this world, in order to belong exclusively to God.[27]

In his affirmation of the value of virginity or celibacy, some of the phrases used by St Paul in reference to marriage, if taken out of context, could suggest that he sees marriage primarily as a remedy for concupiscence.[28] Nevertheless, we have to understand Paul's observations on marriage in light of what he says: 'I wish that all were as I myself am. But each has his own special gift from God, one of one kind, one of another' (1 Cor 7:7). Consequently the vocation to marriage is a gift of God, a grace proper to this way of living. In light of the situation in pagan Corinth, Paul, as regards marriage, adverts to the reality of the concupiscence of the flesh, but at the same time he stresses its sacramental character.[29] He will develop this teaching more completely in Ephesians 5, where he removes any doubts about understanding marriage as a residual vocation.[30]

---

26 Cf. ibid., nos. 6-10. 27 Cf. Address, 7 July 1982, nos. 1-5. 28 'To the unmarried and the widows I say that it is well for them to remain single as I do. But if they cannot exercise self-control, they should marry. For it is better to marry than to be aflame with passion' (1 Cor 7:8-9); 'Because of the temptation to immorality, each man should have his own wife and each woman her own husband' (1 Cor 7:2). 29 Cf. Address, 7 July 1982. 30 Cf. Address, 14 July 1982, nos. 2 -6.

## PRIESTHOOD, CELIBACY AND SERVICE

There are further texts of St Paul which, taken in conjunction with other passages of the New Testament, fill out our appreciation of the relationship between priesthood, celibacy, and service. Priesthood has to be considered in light of the fact that God himself became a priest in the sacred humanity of Christ and instituted a new priesthood in the temple of his body (cf. Jn 2:21). He offered himself to God (cf. Heb 9:11), 'and wished to perpetuate his sacrifice to the end of time (cf. Lk 22:19; 1 Cor 11:24) through the action of other men whom he made and makes sharers in his supreme and eternal priesthood (cf. Heb 5:1-10; 9:11-28)'.[31]

So rich is the bonding with Christ which comes as a result of sacramental ordination that the priest can make his own the words of St Paul, 'For to me to live is Christ' (Phil 1:21), and, again, 'it is no longer I who live but Christ who lives in me' (Gal 2:20).[32] Hence, as the priest grows in his understanding of the content and meaning of his vocation, he sees how appropriate his celibacy is in the light of the Gospel. He finds the deepest meaning of his life not only in the example of Christ but also in the Master's reply to Peter: 'Truly, I say to you, there is no man who has left house or wife or brothers or parents or children for the sake of the kingdom of God, who will not receive manifold more in this time, and in the age to come eternal life' (Lk 18:29-30). Matthew (cf.19:29) and Mark (cf.10:28-30) report a similar response from Christ in different contexts. Clearly the question of celibacy was so counter-cultural that it came up several times in our Lord's discussions with his disciples.

We have already seen that the Catholic priesthood is intimately bound up with the ministry, life and growth of the Church, the Virginal Spouse of Christ (cf. Rev 19:7; 21:2; 22:17; 2 Cor 11:2). Because of the nature of his service to the Church,

> the priest is father, brother and servant of all; his person and his life belong to others, they are the property of the Church who loves him with nuptial love; and her relationship with, and rights against, the priest are such as no one else may share in ... For this very reason one can understand the suitability of celibacy (which better guards the unity of the human heart: cf. 1 Cor 7:33) for protecting, filling and enriching the bonds of nuptial love which unite the Christian priesthood with the spouse of Christ.[33]

This is the complementary aspect of celibacy: just as Christ, and his priests,

---

31 Alvaro del Portillo, *On priesthood*, Chicago, 1974, p. 44. 32 Cf. *Presbyterorum ordinis*, 16. 33 del Portillo, p. 48.

have a spousal relationship with the Church, so the Church as virginal spouse of Christ has in a very real sense exclusive nuptial rights over the priest as icon of Christ.

As he exercises his ministry the priest discovers the greatness of his vocation: 'his capacity for affection and love is filled by the pastoral and paternal task of engendering the people of God in faith, training them and bringing them "as a chaste virgin" to the fullness of life in Christ'.[34] Looking at the priesthood from this perspective we understand more deeply the affection that fills Paul's heart for his beloved Corinthians, and why he asks them to overlook his seeming foolishness in his expression of affection for them. 'I feel a divine jealousy for you', he tells them, 'for I betrothed you to Christ to present you as a pure bride to her one husband' (2 Cor 11:2). His celibacy allows Paul, as it does the priest, to receive and exercise in a special way his paternity in Christ. It elevates and extends, the better to fulfil his ministry of regeneration, 'the need the priest, like every man, has of exercising his capacity for generation and leading to maturity those children who are the fruit of his love'.[35]

## MAN OF ONE WIFE: *UNIUS UXORIS VIR*

To understand the history of celibacy from today's perspective it is necessary to realize that in the West, during the first millennium of the Church, a large number of bishops and priests were married men, something which today is quite exceptional. However, a precondition for married men to receive Orders as deacons, priests, or bishops was that after ordination they were required to live perpetual continence or the *lex continentiae* (law of continence). They had, with the prior agreement of their spouses, to be prepared to forego conjugal life in the future.

St Paul laid down a norm stipulating that bishops (1 Tim 3:2), priests (Tit 1:6) and deacons (1 Tim 3:12) be *unius uxoris vir* (the husband of one wife), as a special requirement for exercising the ministerial priesthood.[36] At first sight this condition for ordination would seem to be puzzling. Yet the interpretation of these texts in the tradition of the Church is that a man who remarried after the death of his first wife could not be a candidate for Orders because such remarriage would be considered a contra-indication to his capacity to practise the perfect continence that would be required after ordination. This was the authoritative interpretation of these Pauline texts given by Pope Siricius in his *Cum in unum* decretal issued after the synod of Rome in 386.[37] The same inter-

---

34 Ibid. 35 Ibid. 36 'Now a bishop must be above reproach, the husband of one wife (1 Tim 3:2); 'A priest must be blameless, the husband of one wife' (Tit 1:6);' Let deacons be the husband of one wife' (1 Tim 3:12). 37 PL 13, 1160a–61a, as quoted in Christian Cochini, *Apostolic origins of priestly celibacy*, San Francisco, 1990, p. 11.

pretation is found in a number of patristic writers.[38] For example, St Epiphanius of Salamis affirms that:

> Since the Incarnation of Christ, the holy Word of God doesn't admit to the priesthood monogamists who, after the death of their wives, have remarried; this is so because of the exceptional honour of the priesthood. This is observed with great exactitude, without failing, by the holy Church of God. But the man who goes on living with his wife and begetting children is not admitted by the Church as deacon, priest or bishop, and subdeacon, even if he married only once, but only the one who, being monogamous, observes continence or is a widower; above all in those places where the ecclesiastical canons are very precise.[39]

In other words, a man who had married a second time after his first wife died could not be considered as a prospect for ordination, as the fact of his remarriage would be regarded as a clear indication that he would not be able to observe the perfect continence which was required afterwards. It is important to remember that Paul uses this formula *unius uxoris vir* only in relation to ministers of the Church, and never to lay Christians, a fact which has been too little noted.[40]

This authoritative interpretation made by Pope Siricius, and afterwards by Pope Innocent I,[41] was a reference datum during the subsequent centuries. The *Glossa Ordinaria* to the *Decretum* of Gratian explains that remarriage by a man whose first wife died would be regarded as a sign of incontinence, and therefore he would not qualify as a candidate for ordination.[42] As recently as 1935, Pius XI, in his encyclical *Ad catholici sacerdotii* on the priesthood, interprets *unius uxoris vir* as an argument in favour of priestly celibacy.[43]

The Pauline prohibition on the admission to Orders of a man who had

---

38 Thus St Ambrose: 'The apostle is a master of virtue; he teaches how to convince the contradictors patiently; he orders that the bishop be the husband of only one wife, not in order to exclude in such a way one who would not have been married (this is indeed above the law), but so that, through conjugal chastity, he keeps the grace of his baptism; on the other hand the apostolic authority is not an invitation to beget children during his priesthood; the apostle spoke about a man who already had children, but not about one who is begetting them or who contracts a new marriage' (*Ep.*, 63:62; PL 16, 1205, as quoted in Cochini, ibid., note 18 on p. 12). 39 *Panarion (Adversus haereses) Haer.* 79,4. CGS 31, 367 as quoted in Cochini, p. 12. 40 Cf. de la Potterie, op. cit., p. 21. 41 Cf. Alfons M. Stickler, *The case for clerical celibacy: its historical development and theological foundations*, San Francisco, 1995, pp 32-3. 42 Cf. ibid., pp 91-2. 43 Published 20 December 1935. He quotes the passage from St Epiphanius given above, and in footnote no. 89 adds a reference to the relevant texts in St Paul's letters - 1 Tim 3:2; Tit 1:6; 1 Tim 3:12.

remarried after the death of his first wife was strictly preserved throughout the centuries, and was still to be found among the irregularities for Orders in the 1917 Code of Canon Law (can. 984,4).[44]

## THEOLOGY OF CELIBACY

More than three decades have elapsed since the publication of Pope Paul VI's encyclical *Sacerdotalis caelibatus* on priestly celibacy. At the time the document was published, just two years after the Council, theological confusion and defections among the clergy had begun to accelerate. The Pope's clear articulation of the meaning and value of clerical celibacy, at a time of doubt and hesitation, was a great light and support to priests. Its teaching and pastoral encouragement continue to be as relevant as ever.

The encyclical takes up the doctrine on celibacy of the Vatican II decree on the ministry and life of priests[45] and develops it. John Paul II has returned to this theme several times during his pontificate, particularly in his first Holy Thursday letter to priests in 1979, and more recently in his apostolic exhortation *Pastores dabo vobis* on the formation of priests. It shouldn't come as a surprise that Popes have felt it necessary frequently to reaffirm the value of the charism of celibacy. On the one hand the wisdom of the world has always been hostile to the Christian virtue of chastity, and to priestly celibacy in particular, and so the priest needs to be reminded of the purpose of this gift and its essentially supernatural meaning. On the other hand, precisely because celibacy is a commitment which goes to the very root of the priest's being, he needs to reflect regularly on the fact that celibacy 'for the sake of the Kingdom' is a wellspring of spiritual energy that enables him, with the help of God's grace, to have a truly fruitful priesthood and to overcome all the difficulties that can arise in being faithful to this commitment.

The moral environment in which priests have to live out their celibacy has, doubtless, become more difficult over the past twenty-five years. While the increasing thrust in modern society towards hedonism and sexual permissiveness aggravates the situation, a more humanistic approach to priesthood has tended to undermine theological convictions about celibacy and to see it as an unnecessary burden. In a culture which promotes a short theological memory and an over-concern with the existential present, it is important that the accumulated wisdom of Christian tradition about celibacy be restated and reaffirmed to enable priests give an intelligible explanation for the hope they cherish. Celibacy cannot be assessed at the human level alone. It involves not only the sexual nature of man but is, above all, a work of grace, a response to a

44 Cf. Stickler, op. cit., p. 92. 45 *Presbyterorum ordinis*, 16

divine initiative. In a secularized society people easily lose sight of the transcendent and thus of the ontological connection between the sacrament of Orders and priesthood. Hence it is necessary to recall the theological reasons which underpin the practice of celibacy.

## CHRISTOLOGICAL SIGNIFICANCE

The priesthood, Paul VI tells us in his encyclical *Sacerdotalis caelibatus*,[46] can be understood only in the light of the newness of Christ who instituted the Catholic priesthood as a real ontological participation in his own priestly being. Christ is therefore the model and prototype of the Catholic priesthood. By means of the paschal mystery he gave birth to a new creation (cf. 2 Cor 5:17; Gal 6:15); man was reborn to the life of grace which transformed the earthly condition of human nature (cf. Gal 3:28).

Christ, as mediator between heaven and earth, remained celibate throughout his life signifying his total dedication to God and man. This deep connection between celibacy and the priesthood of Christ is reflected in the life of the man-priest – the freer he is from the bonds of flesh and blood, the more perfect is his participation in the dignity and mission of Christ.[47] By remaining celibate Jesus went against the socio-cultural and religious climate of his time since, as we have seen, in the Jewish environment no condition was so much deprecated as that of a man who had no descendants. Yet Christ freely willed to combine the virginal state with his mission as eternal priest and mediator between heaven and earth.

We have already considered the fact that by sacramental ordination every priest is configured to Jesus and shares in his priesthood in such an intimate way that he acts *in persona Christi*. From this identification with the Master it follows that the man who wishes to imitate Christ in his priesthood assents to becoming his witness and to adhering strictly to the ontological connotations of that priesthood. It is on the strength of this 'essential, ontological and existential assimilation to Christ' that the relevance and appropriateness of priestly celibacy can and should be judged. The priest, in as much as he is an *alter Christus*, finds his true identity in this intimate, personal relationship with Christ.[48] As we have already seen, the ontological bond which unites the priesthood to Christ is the source of priestly identity.[49]

Because Christ is 'the same yesterday, today and forever' (Heb 13:58), at a fundamental level sociological interpretations or changing fashions have little to tell us about the relevance of celibacy to the lifestyle of the priest. It is by reflection on the mystery of Christ, his life and his work, and the experience of

46 Cf. no. 19. 47 Cf. *Presbyterorum ordinis*, 16. 48 Crescenzio Sepe, 'The relevance of priestly celibacy today', in *For love alone*, op. cit., pp 69-70. 49 Cf. PDV, 12.

celibacy as lived in the Church through the centuries under the guidance of the Holy Spirit, that we can come to valid conclusions in this regard. The call to priesthood, and the charism of celibacy offered with it, is a gift of God, a supernatural reality to which no individual has a right. To follow it calls for a committed, but not impossible, effort on the part of the priest. As John Paul II reminds us in *Pastores dabo vobis*, this charism brings with it the graces that are necessary for the recipient to be faithful to it throughout his life.[50]

The reason for celibacy, as previously discussed, is dedication to Christ in order to build up the kingdom of Heaven on earth in response to a divine vocation. By living it authentically the priest manifests that Christ is sufficiently rich and great to fill the heart of man. In his own way the priest gives witness that Christ is the one to whom ultimately all love refers. By his celibacy he lets it be known that henceforth he expects everything from God, the Creator of all love, in whose hands he places his human completion and his human fruitfulness. Consequently celibacy makes a constant appeal to the priest to live in intimacy with Christ.

The Holy Father developed this point in an address to an international symposium on *Pastores dabo vobis*. Perpetual and freely chosen celibacy can only be fully understood in a Christological context. And 'therefore the ultimate reasons for the discipline of celibacy are not to be sought in psychological, sociological, historical or legal areas, but in those which are essentially theological and pastoral, that is within the ministerial charism itself'.[51]

ECCLESIAL CONSIDERATIONS

The consecrated celibacy of the priest is a sign and manifestation of the virginal love of Christ for his Spouse the Church. It is therefore a visible reminder of the virginal and supernatural fruitfulness of this marriage by which the children of God are engendered.[52] If the Incarnate Word left himself free of all human attachments, no matter how noble they might have been, so as to facilitate his total availability for his ministry, we can easily understand how appropriate it is that the man-priest would do the same, renouncing freely, through celibacy, something which is good and holy in itself so that he might more easily unite himself to Christ (cf. Mt 19:12; 1 Cor 7:32-34), and, through Him, dedicate himself with complete freedom to the service of God and of souls.

The priesthood, with its associated charism of celibacy, is a gift bestowed by the Holy Spirit, not for the use of the person who receives it, but for the

50 Cf. PDV, 50. 51 Address, 28 May 1993. 52 Cf. *Lumen gentium*, 42; *Presbyterorum ordinis*, 16.

benefit of the whole Church. John Paul II explains the ecclesiological implications of the intimate relationship between celibacy and priesthood as follows:

> It is especially important that the priest understand the theological motivation of the Church's law on celibacy. In as much as it is a law, it expresses *the Church's will*, even before the will of the subject expressed by his readiness. The will of the Church finds its ultimate motivation in the *link between celibacy and sacred Ordination*, which configures the priest to Jesus Christ the Head and Spouse of the Church.[53]

While vocation to the priesthood is a personal grace, it belongs to the Church to choose those whom she judges to be qualified. The Church will never try to impose a charism on anyone, but she does have the right to lay hands exclusively on those who have received the free gift of chastity in the celibate life from the Holy Spirit. The priestly vocation, therefore, is not simply a subjective self-giving on the part of the individual, but also requires clear signs of a calling which only the bishop is deputed to ascertain and confirm.

### SPOUSAL DIMENSION OF CELIBACY

Christ's spousal relationship with his Bride the Church is very beautifully developed by St Paul in chapter five of his Letter to the Ephesians. Now the sacrament of Order gives the priest a share not only in the mystery of Christ as Priest, Teacher and Shepherd, but in some way also in his role as Servant and Spouse of the Church.[54] The spousal love of Christ is manifested by his willingness to die for his Bride, by the fact that he nourishes and cares for her, and continually beautifies her (cf. Eph 5:25-27). The priest as icon of Christ has to love the Church with the same spousal love, which is supernatural and gratuitous, giving himself generously to the needs of the Church. This spousal love has to be exercised not in an overbearing way but with all the refinement, generosity and patience of an *amoris officium*,[55] remembering always that Christ came 'not to be served but to serve' (Mk 10:45).

Probably nobody has done more than John Paul II himself to penetrate the nuptial dimension of Christology.[56] He highlights how central to our understanding of the faith is the spousal aspect of the Redemption, and consequently the spousal dimension of the priest as icon of Christ. The notion of spousal love is one which the Holy Father has explored in several of his writings, espe-

---

53 PDV, 29 (italics in original). 54 Cf. PDV, 3. 55 St Augustine, *In Johannis Evangelium tractatus.* 123, 5: *CCL*, 36, 678, as quoted in PDV, 23 and 24, and in DMLP, 16 (*amoris officium* rk or office of love). 56 Cf. John Saward, *Christ is the answer: the Christ-centred*

cially at the beginning of his pontificate in his detailed commentary on chapters 2-4 of Genesis related to 'the nuptial meaning of the body'.[57] He returned to the same theme in *Mulieris dignitatem* in 1988.[58] This is a letter which has special significance for our understanding the nuptial meaning of the Redemption wrought by Christ as the Bridegroom of the Church, and therefore also for our understanding of priestly celibacy.

The priest is the living image of Jesus Christ, the Spouse of the Church. But Christ is Spouse in a special way in the sacrifice of Calvary, because the Church as Bride 'proceeds like a new Eve from the open side of the Redeemer on the Cross'.[59] Christ's supreme priestly act is then a spousal one, as St Paul explains when he encourages husbands and wives to love each other 'as Christ loved the Church and gave himself up for her' (Eph 5:25). This is why 'Christ stands "before" the Church, and "nourishes and cherishes her" (Eph 5:29), giving his life for her'.[60]

In *Mulieris dignitatem*, John Paul II affirms the spousal mystery of the Mass, 'the Sacrament of the Bridegroom and of the Bride', which 'makes present and realizes anew in a sacramental manner the redemptive act of ... Christ the Bridegroom towards the Church the Bride'.[61] As Saward, following Pope John Paul, points out, this spousal theology of the priesthood has a direct bearing on two much discussed aspects of priesthood at the present time: the fact that only men can be priests, and the theological reasons for celibacy.[62]

The priest is an image of the nuptial love of Christ for his Church because 'in virtue of his configuration to Christ, the Head and Shepherd, the priest stands in a spousal relationship with regard to the community'.[63] Hence,

> in his spiritual life he is called to live out Christ's spousal love towards the Church, his Bride. Therefore the priest's life ought to radiate this spousal character which demands that he be a witness to Christ's

*teaching of Pope John Paul II*, Edinburgh, 1995, pp 65-7; 125-8. **57** Cf. John Paul II, *Original unity of man and woman: catechesis on the book of Genesis*, Boston, 1981. This is a series of twenty-three addresses given at the Wednesday audiences, between 5 September 1979 and 2 April 1980. **58** Apostolic letter on the dignity of women, 15 August 1988. **59** PDV, 22. **60** Ibid. **61** *Mulieris dignitatem*, 26. **62** 'Since Christ is Priest as Bridegroom and Bridegroom as Priest, his maleness is an essential part of his redemptive mission. It follows that those who are his sacramental representatives and icons must also be male, if there is to be that 'natural resemblance' proper to sacramental signification. This is of the very essence of the sacrament of Holy Order as willed and instituted by Jesus Christ. For this reason, the Church insists that she does not have the power to admit women to the priesthood. Women's ordination is not simply undesirable or inexpedient; as the *Catechism* firmly states, it is impossible (cf. *CCC*, 1577). "A woman cannot receive the Sacrament of Orders and, therefore, cannot fulfil the proper function of the ministerial priesthood" (*Christifideles laici*, 51)' (Saward, op. cit., p. 126). **63** PDV, 22.

spousal love, and thus be capable of loving people with a heart which is new, generous, and pure, with genuine self-detachment, with full, constant and faithful dedication and at the same time with a kind of 'divine jealousy' (cf. 2 Cor 11:2), and even with a kind of maternal tenderness, capable of bearing 'the pangs of birth' until 'Christ be formed' in the faithful (cf Gal 4:19).[64]

Therefore the priest's total self-giving to the Church finds its validation in the fact that she is the Body and the Bride of Christ.[65] In this spousal commitment we discover the fundamental theological reason for celibacy. Following Christ, the Church as Bride is the only woman the priest can be wedded to, the only Body over which he can have nuptial rights. He has to love her with an exclusive, sacrificial love which results in all the fruitfulness of spiritual paternity. For the priest, Christ is the source, the measure, and the impetus of his love for the Spouse and service of the Body.[66]

Therefore John Paul II can affirm: 'the Church, as the spouse of Jesus Christ, wishes to be loved by the priest in the total and exclusive manner in which Jesus Christ her Head and Spouse loved her. Priestly celibacy, then, is the gift of self *in* and *with* Christ *to* his Church and expresses the priest's service to the Church in and with the Lord'.[67] The demands of such a love clearly suggest the incompatibility of any other nuptial commitment on the part of the priest, giving rise to the most compelling reason for the celibacy of the priesthood.[68] In the same way that the sacrificial love of Christ for his Spouse is consummated on Calvary, so in the Eucharist, the sacrifice of the Mass, the priest *in persona Christi* represents and makes present once more his love for the Church, and from it derive the grace and obligation of the priest to give to his whole life a 'sacrificial' dimension.[69]

Because bishops are ordained with the fullness of the priesthood, they image Christ the Bridegroom in a paramount way. This is why they wear a

---

64 Ibid. 65 Cf. ibid., no. 23. 66 Cf. ibid. 67 PDV, 29 (italics in original). 68 'As a child of the God of abundant life, every human person desires to procreate new life. For the priest, celibacy is neither a rejection nor a repression of his sexuality, but a positive choice to be spiritually life-giving for the larger family of faith. A celibate priest is 'unmarried' only in that he is not married to a particular, individual woman in the wonderful union created in the Sacrament of Matrimony. But he is – through the indelible mark conferred through the Sacrament of Orders, which leaves him forever configured to the celibate Christ – married to His Bride, the Church. As such, he becomes a sign to those in the married state of the radical love God asks of them. It is in recognition of his vocation as a husband to the believing community he serves that we traditionally call priests "father". In this way, we who are born into the Church through Baptism express our love for those who are wedded to our Mother the Church' (Archbishop Charles J. Chaput, Pastoral letter, 8 September 1999). 69 Cf. PDV, 23.

wedding ring and are always celibate in both East and West. In Church history there is no precedent for a bishop obtaining a dispensation to marry on being laicized, as Talleyrand discovered to his chagrin when in 1801 he tried to get the Vatican to ratify his civil marriage.[70]

Since one can only go a certain distance in deriving a theology of celibacy by means of a logic of propositions, there is frequent recourse to symbolism in *Pastores dabo vobis* to describe the relationship between the priest and Christ. Hence he is considered under the more suggestive titles of 'representative', 'image', and 'icon of the Lord Jesus'. Because the gift of celibacy is such an integral part of the mystery of Christ, its understanding requires not only intellectual reflection but, above all, contemplation in prayer and adoration to achieve that deeper disclosure of its fuller meaning which only comes through the light of the Holy Spirit, the ultimate source of this charism.

## SPIRITUAL PATERNITY

Celibacy, then, is not just an external constraint imposed on the priestly ministry, nor can it be considered as a merely human institution established by law. Rather 'this bond, freely assumed, has theological and moral characteristics which are prior to the juridical characteristics, and is a sign of that spousal reality present in sacramental Ordination'.[71] Through it the priest acquires a 'true and real spiritual paternity which has universal dimensions'.[72]

Celibacy has a deep inner affinity with the calling to be a priest and, consequently, it is misleading to speak of the 'burden of celibacy' as if priesthood and celibacy were in some sense irreconcilable. The priest who lives for Christ and from Christ usually has no insurmountable difficulties in living out this charism. He is not immune to the normal temptations of the flesh but, as a result of his ascetical training, the daily cultivation of his spiritual life, and the distancing of himself from anything which could constitute a danger to his chastity, he will encounter joy in his vocation and experience a deep spiritual paternity in bringing supernatural life to souls. As Fr Stanley Jaki comments:

> A priest has compensations for celibacy which a married man (or woman), who in St Paul's divinely inspired observation is always divided between earthly and heavenly concerns, can but vaguely suspect. That compensation is the spiritual fatherhood which a priest may experience on not a few occasions. He may do so above all when he celebrates Mass with the extraordinary faith that thereby he enters into

70 This judgement is given by Cardinal Ercole Consalvi, Secretary of State to Pius VII, in his reply to Talleyrand, dated 30 June 1802. It is quoted in Stanley L. Jaki, *Theology of celibacy*, Front Royal, VA, 1997, pp 196–7. 71 DMLP, 58. 72 Ibid.

*cary sinh*

the closest imaginable symbiosis with the crucified Christ. If his faith makes him see in that symbiosis the highest life-giving role available to man, he will have the only truly positive perspective in which priestly celibacy can be seen. It will become for him the implantation of St Paul's experience of being 'crucified with Christ'. It takes no degree in New Testament Greek to perceive that experience as the deepest living truth available to priests.[73]

Jaki illustrates this with a graphic example:

> Margaret Bosco, a desperately poor, largely uneducated, and incredibly hard-working peasant woman, saw far deeper than most recent authors on Mass and priesthood when she walked the long miles home with her son, the future saint, after his first Mass. Suddenly she said to him: 'So now you are a priest, John, my son, and will say Mass every day. You must remember this: beginning to say Mass means beginning to suffer. At first you won't notice it, but in time, one day, you will see your mother is right... Henceforth think of nothing but the saving of souls and don't worry about me.' Such was the inner logic of spiritual fatherhood, a logic accurately perceived by a simple Christian widow.[74]

Thanks to this total self-giving which the priest freely embraces, and the renunciation of a paternity according to the flesh, he receives in return a notable enrichment of a paternity according to the spirit. This renunciation is rooted in a spousal love for Christ and his Church, a love which develops in its care and concern for people, and which makes possible a better pastoral service.[75] In virtue of this renunciation for the kingdom of heaven, the priest realizes existentially that which he already is ontologically through the grace of the sacrament: he becomes 'a man for others'.[76]

This is a reality which he makes visible and operative in the total dedica-

73 Stanley L. Jaki, 'Man of one wife or celibacy', in *Homiletic and Pastoral Review*, January 1986, p. 20.  74 Ibid., p. 21.  75 'The Church is virgin because she guards whole and pure the faith given to the Spouse. Christ, according to the teaching contained in the Letter to the Ephesians (cf Eph 5:32), is the Spouse of the Church. The nuptial meaning of the Redemption impels each of us to guard our fidelity to this vocation, by means of which we are made sharers in the saving mission of Christ, priest, prophet and king. The analogy between the Church and the Virgin Mother has a special eloquence for us, who link our priestly vocation to celibacy, that is, to "making ourselves eunuchs for the sake of the kingdom of heaven". We freely renounce marriage and establishing our own family in order to be better able to serve God and neighbour. It can be said that we renounce fatherhood 'according to the flesh' in order that there may grow and develop in us a fatherhood "according to the Spirit" (cf. Jn 1:13) which, as has already been said, possesses at the same time maternal characteristics' (HTL, 1988, no.5).  76 'Our celibacy manifests on its part that we

tion of his person to the good of the community of the faithful entrusted to him:

> The celibacy of the priest does not have only an eschatological signif-
> icance, as a witness to the future Kingdom. It also expresses the pro-
> found connection which unites him to the faithful, in so far as the
> community of faith is born from his charism and is intended to sum
> up all the capacity for love which the priest bears within himself.[77]

That priestly charity, which flowers in the heart thanks to celibacy, knows no barriers of time or place nor does it make any exception of persons. It ought to be a universal charity, a reflection of the pastoral charity of Christ the priest for all men and for each one.

Observing celibacy for the sake of the kingdom of heaven does not mean being any less a man. As a consequence the heart is free to love Christ and to love others in an inclusive way.

> By *freely choosing priestly celibacy* the priest renounces earthly father-
> hood and gains a share in the Fatherhood of God. Instead of becom-
> ing father to one or more children on earth, he is now able to love
> everybody in Christ. Yes, Jesus calls his priest to carry his Father's ten-
> der love for each and every person. For this reason, people call him
> 'Father'.[78]

### ESCHATOLOGICAL AND SALVIFIC MEANING

While celibacy is a sign of the kingdom of God on earth, it is above all a sign of future glory where, as Christ said, 'in the Resurrection they neither marry nor are given in marriage but are all like angels in heaven' (Mt 22:30). In this sense celibacy proclaims on earth the final stages of salvation (cf. 1 Cor 7:29-31), and as such acts as a reminder for all that we don't have here a lasting city but are mere pilgrims on the way to our definitive homeland. This witness is essential at a time when there is so much pressure to give absolute value to concerns of the present life at the expense of interest for eternal salvation.

*Pastores dabo vobis* emphasised that priestly celibacy was a prophetic sign for today's world, a sign of the kingdom which is to come where marriage will

are entirely consecrated to the work to which the Lord has called us. The priest, seized by Christ, becomes "the man for others", completely available for the kingdom, his heart undivided, capable of accepting fatherhood in Christ' (Address, 30 May 1980, no. 8). 77 Homily, 4 November 1980. 78 Mother Teresa of Calcutta, 'Priestly celibacy: sign of the charity of Christ' in *For love alone*, ibid., p. 212.

no longer be a feature.[79] The celibate priest is thus not only able to speak about the world to come, but bears witness to it by his lifestyle, giving hope to believer and non-believer alike in the resurrection to a future life of glory. Priestly celibacy is then a witness to the conviction that man does not find the deepest meaning of his life within the apparent self-sufficiency of the present world. The priest's ministry should be a constant reminder to people that this life has real value only in so far as it an opportunity to realize one's baptismal vocation and establish one's Christian identity. The celibate priest points to the value of the one thing necessary (cf. Lk 10:42) – personal holiness which is achieved through the power of God's grace and our response to it.[80]

The world, as the Holy Father has frequently affirmed, is in great need of re-evangelization especially the countries of the affluent West. If this new evangelization is to be effective, it requires the radical Gospel commitment which was always the basis of winning souls for Christ in the past. Historically one of the most important elements in this work of evangelization was the dynamic of priestly celibacy. It will continue to be so in the future.

### CELIBACY AND MARRIAGE

We can see then that, in its deepest Christian sense, celibacy cannot be reduced to the mere fact of not getting married – it is a response to a particular vocation from God to devote oneself fully, body and soul, to his service. Although marriage is a 'great sacrament' (Eph 5:32) and is blessed by the Church as a way to holiness, the same Church clearly affirms that celibacy for the sake of the kingdom of heaven is *of itself* superior to marriage.[81] This doesn't imply in any way a disdain for human sexuality, or that those who are married are called to a lesser or second-rate holiness. To reason in this way would reveal a truncated understanding of the Incarnation and its implications. Certainly Vatican II has a very different perception of the case in that it recommends priestly celibacy in the context of affirming marriage as a vocation and a way to holiness.[82] And so John Paul II can testify, 'Virginity and apostolic celibacy not only do not contradict the dignity of marriage but presuppose it and confirm it'. They are in fact 'two ways of expressing the one mystery of the covenant of God with his people'. More specifically, 'virginity keeps alive in the Church the awareness of the mystery of marriage and defends it against all attempts to impoverish it or reduce its importance'.[83] Priests have a duty of fidelity to Christ, to the Church, and especially to those who are married. In his first Holy Thursday Letter to Priests, John Paul II counselled:

79 Cf. PDV, 29.  80 Cf. *Novo millennio ineunte*, 30, 31.  81 Cf. Council of Trent, *De sacramento matrimonii*, can.10, DS 1810. See also HTL, 1979, no. 9.  82 Cf. *Lumen gentium*, 11 and 41; *Gaudium et spes*, 48 and 52.  83 *Familiaris consortio*, 16.

Our brothers and sisters joined by the marriage bond have the right to expect from us, Priests and Pastors, good example and the witness of fidelity to one's vocation until death, a fidelity to the vocation that we choose through the sacrament of Orders just as they choose it through the sacrament of Matrimony. Also in this sphere and in this sense we should understand our ministerial priesthood as 'subordination' to the common priesthood of all the faithful, of the laity, especially of those who live in marriage and form a family.[84]

The Pope emphasized this point again in his very first encyclical, *Redemptor hominis*, in the context of reminding us that fidelity to vocation in general was an expression of the 'kingly service' arising from our baptism:

Married people must be distinguished for fidelity to their vocation, as is demanded by the indissoluble nature of the sacramental institution of marriage. Priests must be distinguished for a similar fidelity to their vocation, in view of the indelible character that the sacrament of Orders stamps on their souls. In receiving this sacrament, we in the Latin Church knowingly and freely commit ourselves to live celibacy, and each one of us must therefore do all he can, with God's grace, to be thankful for this gift and faithful to the bond that he has accepted forever. He must do so as married people must, for they must endeavour with all their strength to persevere in their matrimonial union, building up the family community through this witness of love and educating new generations of men and women, capable in their turn of dedicating the whole of their lives to their vocation, that is to say to the 'kingly service' of which Jesus Christ has offered us an example and the most beautiful model.[85]

Celibacy is then a commitment which is similar to the fidelity which spouses reciprocally offer each other in marriage.[86] It is, in fact, a 'duty which demands of priests a fidelity to death'.[87]

This self-giving to God does not emasculate or neutralize the celibate.[88] There is a radical difference between sexual repression and a conscious, free self-giving to Christ which, informed by grace, enables the priest to forego the demands of the flesh and give himself, body and soul, to the Lord. In responding to his vocation to celibacy the future priest is not unaware of the difficulties which this commitment involves. He also becomes conscious, as he grows in his priesthood, of the danger that, surreptitiously, other sources of human

---

84 HTL, 1979, no. 9. 85 Encyclical *Redemptor hominis*, 4 March 1979, no. 21. 86 Cf. ibid. 87 Cf. HTL, 1979, no. 9. 88 Cf. Dietrich von Hildebrand, *Celibacy and the crisis of faith*, Chicago, 1971, p. 38.

fulfilment (over-involvement in sport, social activities, etc.) could begin to substitute themselves for the renunciation of marriage, commitments which contradict and could even undermine the real reason for his celibacy.

When we hear talk of the so-called 'burden of celibacy' it should also be
remembered that Christ promised a more abundant recompense, even in this
life, to those who would leave home, family, wife and children for the sake of
the kingdom of God (cf. Lk. 18:29-30). In words which showed that human
perception alone was insufficient to grasp the mystery involved, he recommended a more perfect consecration to the work of spreading the kingdom of
heaven by means of celibacy, as a special gift (cf. Mt 19:11). It is perhaps the
most radical sign of the new creation brought about by Christ.

## CELIBACY, FREEDOM AND FAITH

Because apostolic celibacy gives the priest a total freedom to love the Lord with
body and soul, it is important that he understand the nature of freedom from
a human and supernatural point of view to really make sense of this charism.
It cannot be enforced by law; it is a gift freely offered by God and freely accepted by the seminarian as a precondition to his ordination.

The Holy Father says that the widespread view that priestly celibacy in the
Catholic Church is imposed by law is the result of misunderstanding, if not of
downright bad faith. Commitment to celibacy is, in the first place, a consequence
of a free decision after a number of years of preparation; it is a lifelong commitment accepted with full personal responsibility. It is, as John Paul II emphasises,
'a matter of keeping one's word to Christ and the Church'. This is a duty which
is an expression of inner maturity, a maturity which is shown particularly when
this free decision 'encounters difficulties, is put to the test, or is exposed to temptation', which like any other Christian the priest is not spared.[89]

Cardinal Joachim Meisner, archbishop of Cologne, made a number of very
relevant points in this context:

> Celibacy, he says, is plausible only if one believes in Jesus Christ. For
> a person who does not experience the existence of Jesus Christ, for a
> person who does not believe in him, the celibate is, in fact, a madman
> or somebody who is sick. Consequently they do not even conceive or

---

89 Cf. HTL, 1979, no. 9. John Paul II developed this point the following year in an address
to priests at Fulda in Germany. He reminded them that they had perceived the call of God
from the depths of their own weakness, and that the constant awareness of this weakness
should never be a reason for being unfaithful to that call. He continued: 'Christ has taught
us that man has above all a right to his greatness, a right to that which really towers above
him. For it is precisely here that his special dignity emerges: here is revealed the wonderful

tolerate that others can live it. It is not a problem related to canon law or to dogma, but to faith in God; a man can come so close to God that he prefers union with God to any other type of union. Celibacy cannot be explained by sociological, psychological or pedagogical reasons, but only by spiritual and theological ones. Without prayer, without dialogue with God, celibacy makes no sense. I repeat: if a person does not take God seriously, he will not be able to understand the essence of celibacy. At times I have the impression that criticism of celibacy is only an alibi for those who want to dispense themselves from that radical change of lifestyle which the following of Christ demands.[90]

Indeed the priesthood is so charged with potential for self-realisation that, through the grace of God, it can give to the man who has chosen this life a fullness which is often lacking in the lives of others. In the judgement of a psychiatrist who has worked closely with priests for many years:

Spiritual fatherhood, the power to bind and loose, the joy of bearing, with his own hands, the supreme gift of God himself to others: these place the priestly dignity on so high a plane in the hierarchy of human

power of grace: our true greatness is a gift deriving from the Holy Spirit. In Christ man has a right to such greatness. And the Church, through the same Christ, has a right to the gift of man: to a gift by which man offers himself totally to God, in which he also opts for celibacy "for the Kingdom of Heaven" (Mt 19:12) in order to be the servant of all' (Address, 17 November 1980). 90 Cf. *Osservatore Romano*, 25 October 1992. The Cardinal went on to say: 'Celibacy is too sacred and too important an issue to be subjected to the judgement of public opinion which is fundamentally non-Christian.' He recalled the gospel scene of Jesus in Bethany when Mary anointed his feet with a very expensive perfume which provoked the criticism of Judas. But Jesus defended Mary's generosity, and Meisner comments : 'I ask those narrow-minded people – doesn't the Lord merit that men would give their lives totally to him? Isn't it also possible that if they didn't do this they could squander their lives? On the contrary, isn't it normal that the mean-spirited, the Judases ... distance themselves from him? People do not understand celibacy, but what really escapes them is not why so many answer yes, but rather why in fact God calls them. Love responds only to love'. Meisner affirms that celibacy will continue to exist: 'God is always magnanimous and we cannot deceive him with our limited human conceptions of things. Celibacy is a gift of that loving God, a precious gift for his Church. This gift has enriched the Church down through the centuries, and to reject it would mean an impoverishment. The Church will continue to be faithful to its spouse Jesus Christ, and one particular form of that fidelity is to give oneself completely to Christ in celibacy, to say *yes* without reserve to that God who makes us capable of it and who offers it to us as a gift. There are other ways of giving oneself to God, in Christian marriage, for example, or by entering a monastery or responding to some other type of vocation. We know that God is not giving us a loan of something, but rather a present which is not just for today or tomorrow, but forever. For those who know this, celibacy presents no problem'.

possibilities that it cannot be compared with anything else whatsoever and leaves no room for frustration.[91]

God has given priests the power to be dispensers of divine mysteries which surpass the privileges of his angels. The consequent responsibility to be pure of mind and body is graphically described by St John Chrysostom:

> For the office of the priesthood is executed upon earth, yet it ranks amongst things that are heavenly, and with good reason. For it was neither an angel or an archangel nor any created power, but the Paraclete Himself that established that ministry, and commanded that men yet abiding in the flesh should imitate the functions of angels. Wherefore it behoves the priest to be as pure as if he stood in heaven itself amidst those Powers ... For when you behold the Lord immolated and lying on the altar, and the priest standing over the sacrifice and praying, and all the people purpled by the precious blood, do you imagine that you are still on earth amongst men?
>
> For if you consider what it is for a man yet clothed in flesh and blood to approach that pure and blessed nature, you will easily understand to what a dignity the grace of the Holy Spirit has raised priests. For by them these things are accomplished, and others not inferior to these pertaining to our redemption and salvation ... It is to priests that spiritual birth and regeneration by baptism is entrusted. By them we put on Christ, and are united to the Son of God, and become members of that blessed Head. Hence we should regard them as more august than princes and kings, and more venerable than parents. For the latter begot us of blood and the will of the flesh, but priests are the cause of our generation from God, of our spiritual regeneration, of our true freedom and sonship according to grace.[92]

Chrysostom's was probably the first theological treatise written on the priesthood. He doesn't write in abstract theological concepts but in language that is fruit of personal meditation and wide pastoral experience. At the same time he roots all his understanding of priesthood in Scripture, just as John Paul II does in *Pastores dabo vobis*. In his treatise Chrysostom never discusses the issue of celibacy. It is clear, however, that he takes for granted that celibacy/continence is an integral part of that vocation.

---

91 Wanda Poltawaska, 'Priestly celibacy in the light of medicine and psychology' in *For love alone*, p. 89.   92 Cf. St John Chrysostom, *On the priesthood: a treatise*, Westminster MD, 1943, PP 43-4.

# 5

## The spiritual life of the priest

Over the past twenty years Pope John Paul II has preached consistently about the priesthood. In every country he has travelled to in that time he has never missed an opportunity to speak to priests and seminarians, to share with them his joy in the priesthood, and to open up new apostolic and pastoral horizons for them. His style is always to encourage priests in the face of difficulties, transmitting to them a share in his enduring optimism and faith.

His love for priests is patent. In the very first year of his pontificate he would write: 'I think of you all the time. I pray for you, with you I seek the ways of spiritual union and collaboration, because by virtue of the sacrament of Orders ... you are my brothers'.[1] As we have noted, a particular expression of this affection is his annual Holy Thursday letters to priests which provide an abundance of material for prayer and meditation. He writes these letters because of 'our shared love for Christ and his Church, a love that springs from the grace of the priestly vocation, the love that is the greatest gift of the Holy Spirit'.[2]

The Holy Father's faith and his support for priests have confirmed many in their vocation at a time when they have been subjected to negative influences both of a doctrinal and a practical nature. Yet it is obvious that the primary source of his conviction about the priesthood is the dynamic of his own interior life, his deep love for the person of Christ, and his personal commitment to holiness. This facet of the Holy Father's priesthood comes through again and again. It is therefore worthwhile reflecting on aspects of priestly holiness which he has emphasized all through his pontificate.

### PRIESTLY HOLINESS

In *Pastores dabo vobis*, John Paul II, taking up the teaching of Vatican II, reminds us that the priest has a specific vocation to holiness.[3] He affirms that the conciliar decree on *The ministry and life of priests* offers a particularly rich

1 HTL, 1979, no. 1.  2 HTL, 1979, no. 2.  3 Cf. PDV, 20.

synthesis of our 'duty to become saints'.[4] If lay people are called and obliged to holiness, then this applies to priests even more so in view of their special consecration to God through ordination.[5] It is in this context of the duty of the priest to aspire to sanctity that his spiritual life takes on its full character and significance.

From the perspective of the universal call to holiness, Baptism is ultimately the basis of the Christian vocation for everyone[6], and this is specified subsequently in different ways depending on the particular forms of participation in the mission of the Church.[7] For secular priests what this means is that the baptismal vocation is given a particular orientation through the sacrament of Orders. Although there is this double configuration grounding priestly sanctity, the priest has still only one vocation to holiness, that which derives from Baptism and which is complete in itself.[8]

Expanding on the teaching of the conciliar document, the Holy Father says we must seek the holiness characteristic of priests through the exercise of the many tasks that belong to our vocation and pastoral ministry.[9] If the purpose of his ministry is the sanctification of others, it goes without saying that the priest must himself have a commitment to personal holiness:

> He cannot stand aside, John Paul II affirms, he cannot dispense himself from this commitment, without condemning himself thereby to a life that is not authentic, or, to use the words of the Gospel, without changing from a 'good shepherd' into a 'hireling'.[10]

These are strong words, but they are inspired by Christ's own uncompromising teaching about the responsibility of the good shepherd (cf. Jn 10:12-13).

At the Last Supper Jesus prayed to his Father that his disciples would be holy, so that they in turn would bring about faith in future believers (cf. Jn 17:17, 19-20). The holiness of the people is then a measure of, a reflection of the holiness of the priest. This is a reality confirmed time and again in the history of the Church.[11] The new evangelization, John Paul II affirms, needs

4 Ibid. 5 Cf. ibid. 6 Cf. *Lumen gentium*, 40. As PDV points out, 'the ministerial priesthood does not of itself signify a greater degree of holiness with regard to the common priesthood of the faithful' (no. 17). 7 Cf. *Lumen gentium*, 32, 41, etc. 8 Cf. ibid., no. 40. 9 Address, 2 March 1979. 10 Ibid. 11 Bishop Fulton Sheen has some thought-provoking comments about the relationship between priestly holiness and the level of sanctity in the world: 'Politics does not ultimately determine war and peace. What is decisive is the spiritual state of the Church living in and leavening the world. To read the Old Testament is to recognize that history is in the hand of the Lord who blesses and punishes nations according to their deserts. What we do to sanctify ourselves sanctifies the world. When the shepherd is lazy, the sheep are hungry; when he sleeps, they are lost; when he is corrupt they grow sick; when he is unfaithful, they lose their judgement. If the shepherd is not willing to be a victim for

priests who are seriously striving for holiness so that in turn they can [
isters of holiness' to the people entrusted to their care.[12]

## HOLINESS AND FOLLOWING CHRIST

In virtue of the sacrament of Orders the priest makes Christ present before the community and before the world. Through his ministry, and by the example of his personal life, he mediates Christ to men and, through Christ, shows them the way to the Father. If this is the role of the priest, how should it be reflected in his spiritual life?

Since priestly spirituality presupposes the universal call to holiness, it is not possible to form priests without forming at the same time, or indeed in the first place, the Christian on whom the priesthood had been conferred. How, then, is the spiritual life to be developed in the specific case of the priest? Down through the centuries, several styles of priestly spirituality have emerged in different periods related to particular pastoral, ecclesiastical or spiritual contexts. All affirm, however, that Christ and his priesthood is the central reference point for priestly spirituality.[13] For the lay person who is called to sanctify himself in ordinary life by manifesting the dynamic of the Gospel in his work, family and social commitments, the hidden years of Christ's life in Nazareth have a special resonance since they bear testimony to the sanctifying value of everyday life. On the other hand, the public life of Christ and the events of his glorification have a particular significance and are a fundamental point of reference for the spiritual life of the priest.[14]

Priests will achieve holiness 'by following in the fulfilment of their ministry the example of Christ the Lord, whose meat was to do the will of him who sent him that he might perfect his work'.[15] These words of the decree *Presbyterorum ordinis*, central to the message which Vatican II wished to give about the spiritual life of priests, underline, among other things, the connection between priestly vocation and the following of Christ. While the conciliar document is only reaffirming traditional doctrine, it gives its own emphasis to this teaching by highlighting two points, firstly, that this adherence to Christ has to be a radical commitment and, secondly, that the priest's following of

his sheep, the wolves come and devour them. Each morning we priests hold in our hands the Christ who shed blood from his veins, tears from his eyes, sweat from his body to sanctify us. How we should be on fire with love, that we may enkindle it in others!'(Fulton Sheen, *The priest is not his own*, London, 1964, p. 69). 12 Cf. PDV, 82; HTL, 1995, no. 8. 13 Cf. J. Esquerda Bifet, *Historia de la espiritualidad sacerdotal*, Burgos, 1985. 14 Cf. J. L. Illanes, 'Rasgos distintivos de la espiritualidad sacerdotal', in *Teología espiritual del sacerdocio*, pp 79-86. 15 *Presbyterorum ordinis*, 14.

Christ is influenced in very specific ways by his ministry and the manner in which he carries it out. The concept of following Christ brings us back to the community formed by the disciples who accompanied Jesus along the roads of Judea and Galilee, listening to his teaching and sharing his life. From the pages of the New Testament we see that to follow Christ is to share his sentiments (cf. Phil 2:5), to have the same availability to do the will of the Father (cf. Jn 4:34), and to be ready to give one's life for the love of the brethren (cf. Jn 15:12-13).[16] As *Pastores dabo vobis* points out, the spiritual life of the priest should be 'marked, moulded and characterized by the way of thinking and acting proper to Jesus Christ, Head and shepherd of he Church'.[17]

If the priest's spiritual life is to develop in the exercise of his ministry, he needs to grow in his 'awareness of being a minister of Jesus Christ'.[18] As Cardinal Ratzinger has trenchantly affirmed:

> If bearing witness to Jesus Christ before men is the task of the priest-hood, then it is the presupposition of this task that the priest first know him, that the priest live and find the real centre of his existence in a way of being that is in fact a being-with-him. For the man who, as priest, attempts to speak to his fellow men of Christ, there is nothing of greater importance than this: to learn what being-with-him, existing in his presence, and following him mean, to hear and see him, to grasp his style of being and thinking. The actual living out of priestly existence and the attempt to prepare others for such an existence demand growth in the ability to hear him above all the static, and to see him through all the forms of this world. To do this is to live in his presence.[19]

It is not without significance that the Church addresses the following invitation and admonition to the priest on the day of his ordination: 'Live the mystery that has been placed in your hands'. This mystery, of which the priest is steward, is, of course, Jesus Christ himself. The Church has always taught that the salvific effects of priestly ministry derive from the action of Christ who becomes present in the sacraments. However, the level of holiness of the priest has a real influence on the effectiveness of his ministry. Vatican II reiterates, in relation to the priest, that

> God normally prefers to show his wonders through those men who are more submissive to the impulse and guidance of the Holy Spirit and

16 Cf. J.L. Illanes, 'Vocación sacerdotal y seguimiento de Cristo', in *La formación de los sacerdotes en las circunstancias actuales*, p. 609. 17 Cf. PDV, 21. 18 PDV, 25. 19 Joseph Ratzinger, *Priestly ministry: a search for its meaning*, New York 1971, p. 9.

who, because of their intimate union with Christ and their holiness of life are able to say with St Paul, 'It is no longer I who live, but Christ who lives in me' (Gal 2:20).[20]

The lives of countless holy priests down through the centuries confirm this truth. It is sufficient to recall the memory of men like St John Fisher, the Curé of Ars, St John of Avila, St Charles Borromeo, Blesssed Josemaría Escrivá, and the extent of their pastoral achievements.

### MINISTRY AND THE SPIRITUAL LIFE

As we have noted, the Vatican II decree on priestly life outlines the mission of the priest under the three headings of ministry of the word, ministry of the sacraments, and the care of souls. It emphasises that it is precisely in the generous and sincere carrying out of these functions that priests will acquire holiness in their own distinctive way.[21] As one experienced pastor has put it:

> In effect, the conscientious practice of the three great ministerial functions requires and promotes the personal holiness of the priest; in this truth he finds the basis of the unity and harmony of all aspects of his life. Evangelization and preaching are inseparable from calm meditation of the divine Word. Devout, sincere celebration of Mass brings the priest to a vivid understanding of what his life is about: it is sacrifice and communion, a life fully consecrated to the Father and fully sent, given and communicated to men and to the world. The guidance of the Christian community, which the bishop has entrusted to him, draws from the priest the virtues proper to a good pastor – charity without limits, to the extent of complete unselfishness; faith, which illuminates and stimulates hope and perseverance; complete obedience, which is at the same time intelligent, active, and responsible; humility and meekness which combine firmness with understanding; perfect continence, which leaves his heart completely free to adore God and serve others; patience which enables him to suffer in silence and to pardon; poverty which is a lesson in happiness and hope for all men. In effect he needs an evangelical and profoundly priestly spirituality.[22]

In summary, an intimate bond exists between the priest's spiritual life and the exercise of his ministry.[23]

20 *Presbyterorum ordinis*, 12. 21 Cf. Ibid., no. 13. 22 del Portillo, ibid., p. 36. 23 Cf. PDV, 24.

Consequently the priest develops his spiritual life, not as something added on to, or different from, his ecclesiastical functions. Neither is priestly spirituality a matter of importing or adapting the three evangelical counsels which are characteristic of the religious state with its specific ascetical requirements. On the contrary, his spirituality should support the different aspects of his priestly consecration, and his exercise of the ministry has to become his way of approaching holiness to which he, like all Christians, is called.[24]

> For it is through the sacred actions they perform every day, as through the whole ministry they exercise in union with the bishop and their fellow-priests, that they are set on the right course to perfection of life.[25]

The relationship between a priest's spiritual life and the exercise of his ministry can also be explained on the basis of the pastoral charity stemming from sacramental ordination, a charity which is both the source and the spirit of his service and self-giving. Because his ministry is an *amoris officium*,[26] of its very nature it demands that the reality of this service be supported by a life of love, a life of deep intimacy with Christ the Good Shepherd whose minister he is. Indeed,

> every ministerial action, while it leads to loving and serving the Church, provides an incentive to grow in ever greater love and service of Jesus Christ the Head, Shepherd and Spouse of the Church, a love which is always a response to the free and unsolicited love of God in Christ.[27]

### UNITY OF LIFE

One of the most important sections of *Presbyterorum ordinis* is paragraph fourteen which deals with the priest's unity of life. It is an issue of great practical relevance for the spirituality of priests and, at the same time, a topic of deep theological significance. Vatican II approached this much discussed question indirectly when in *Lumen gentium* it underlined the radical equality of all the People of God and the call to holiness of all the faithful, and when, in the case of the laity, it pointed out that they should achieve sanctity in and through the secular activities with which their lives are so closely connected.[28]

24 Cf. del Portillo, ibid., pp 68-9. 25 *Presbyterorum ordinis*, 12. 26 Cf. PDV, 23, 24. 27 PDV, 25. 28 Cf. *Lumen gentium*, 31. The concept of unity of life for the lay faithful is developed in some detail by John Paul II in his apostolic exhortation *Christifideles laici* – cf. Chapter 11 below for a discussion of this theme.

In *Presbyterorum ordinis* the same ecclesiological and anthropological doctrine is present as a subtext: the ordinary ministerial occupations of the priest, the conciliar document affirms, are the locus, the scene of his encounter with God and, consequently, their multiplicity ought not to be an obstacle for the development of his interior life. What *Presbyterorum ordinis* shows is that through pastoral charity priests can achieve unity of life by their identification with the consecration and mission received:

> By adopting the role of good shepherd, they will find in the practice of *pastoral charity* itself the bond of priestly perfection which will reduce to unity their life and activity. Now this *pastoral charity* flows especially from the Eucharistic sacrifice … To enable them to make their unity of life a concrete reality, they should consider all their projects to find what is God's will – that is to say, how far their projects are in conformity with the standard of the Church's Gospel mission. Faithfulness to Christ cannot be separated from faithfulness to his Church. Hence *pastoral charity* demands that priests, if they are not to run in vain, should always work within the bond of union with the bishops and their fellow priests. If they act in this manner, priests will find unity of life in the unity of the Church's own mission. In this way they will be united with their Lord, and through him with the Father in the Holy Spirit, and can be filled with consolation and exceedingly abound with joy.[29]

Hence, by virtue of pastoral charity the essential and permanent demand for unity between the priest's interior life and the obligations of his ministry can be properly fulfilled, a demand which, John Paul II affirms, is 'particularly urgent in a socio-cultural and ecclesial context strongly marked by complexity, fragmentation and dispersion'. Only when he is motivated by the ambition to 'give his life for the flock' can the priest guarantee this unity which is indispensable for his interior harmony and spiritual balance.[30]

It has been well said about the Curé of Ars that his intense priestly min-

29 *Presbyterorum ordinis*, 14 (emphasis added). The same idea is repeated in the *Directory on the ministry and life of priests*: 'There exists, in fact, an intimate rapport between the centrality of the Eucharist, pastoral charity, and the unity of life of the priest, who finds in this rapport the decisive indications for the way to holiness to which he has been specifically called. If the priest lends to Christ, Most Eternal High Priest, his intelligence, will, voice, and hands so as to offer, through his very ministry, the sacramental sacrifice of redemption to the Father, he should make his own the dispositions of the Master and, like him, live those *gifts* for his brothers in the faith. He must therefore learn to unite himself intimately to the offering, placing his entire life upon the altar of sacrifice as a revealing sign of the gratuitousness and anticipatory love of God' (no. 48). 30 Cf. PDV, 23. See also ibid., 72.

istry never constituted a danger to his growth in holiness. He achieved unity of his spiritual life in and through the unity of his ministry. As a consequence, his example opens up for us a way to sanctity which passes through the heart of the pastoral life.[31]

## SHEPHERDS OF THE PEOPLE OF GOD

While it is clear how the ministry of the word and the ministry of the sacraments would contribute to the sanctification of the priest[32], it is not immediately obvious that his wider pastoral activity does the same. For many spiritual writers over the centuries, the care of souls as a way and a means to holiness for priests suffered the same misunderstanding as secular activities in relation to the holiness of the laity. The priest's involvement with the world was perceived as an obstacle to living a contemplative life and not as a source of holiness. Only with Vatican II was the call to holiness of the laity, expressed through the sanctification of family, social, and work related activities, recognized and reaffirmed by the Church. Similarly, in the theology of priestly holiness articulated by the Council, the counter-posing of action and contemplation was seen to be a false antinomy. A new direction was given to developing a spirituality of secular priests, showing how they could, and indeed must, sanctify themselves in caring for their flocks if their spirituality was to be an authentic one, grounded on pastoral charity. Vatican II is unambiguous in its defence of secularity as a characteristic of the fullness of Christian life, both for laity as well as for priests.[33] As regards priests, *Presbyterorum ordinis* refers specifically to this dimension:

> The priests of the New Testament are, it is true, by their vocation to ordination, set apart in some way in the midst of the People of God, but this is not in order that they should be separated from that people or from any man, but that they should be completely consecrated to the task for which God chooses them. They could not be the servants of Christ unless they were witnesses and dispensers of a life other than that of this earth. On the other hand, they would be powerless to serve men if they remained aloof from their life and circumstances. Their very ministry makes a claim on them not to conform themselves to this

31 Cf. Mateo-Seco, ibid., pp 424-5. 32 How the priest sanctifies himself through the ministry of the word is developed in Chapter 8 below. In Chapters 6 and 10, we consider the holiness of the priest from the perspective of the exercise of the sacramental ministry. 33 Cf. especially *Lumen gentium*, Chapter V (*The call to holiness*), and *Presbyterorum ordinis*, 3, 6 and 13.

world (cf. Rom 12:2); still it requires at the same time that they sh
live among men in this world, and that as good shepherds they shou
know their sheep and should also seek to lead back those who do not
belong to this fold.[34]

The secular condition pertains to the very structure of the pastoral ministry, in a manner analogous to that by which secularity pertains to the Church
in so far as it is sent into the world. It is in the context of this secularity that
the priest encounters Christ, specifically in his role as Good Shepherd. As spiritual leaders, priests are encouraged to imitate the pastoral charity of Christ the
Good Shepherd, being ready to spend their lives, day by day, for the flock
entrusted to their care:

> As rulers of the community they cultivate the form of asceticism suit-
> ed to a pastor of souls, renouncing their own convenience, seeking not
> what is to their own advantage but what will benefit the many for sal-
> vation (cf. 1 Cor 10:33), always making further progress towards a
> more perfect fulfilment of their pastoral work and, where the need
> arises, prepared to break new ground in pastoral methods under the
> guidance of the Spirit of love who breathes where he will (cf. Jn 3:8).[35]

After outlining the principal characteristics of Jesus's life as servant of the
Church out of love and manifested in pastoral charity, *Pastores dabo vobis* concludes:

> The spiritual life of the ministers of the New Testament should there-
> fore be marked by this fundamental attitude of service to the People of
> God (cf. Mt 20:24ff; Mk 10:43-44), freed from all presumption or
> desire of 'lording over' those in their charge (cf. 1 Pet 5:2-3). The
> priest is to perform this service freely and willingly as God desires. In
> this way the priests, as the ministers, the 'elders' of the community,
> will be in their person the 'model' of the flock, which, for its part, is
> called to display this same priestly attitude of service towards the
> world, in order to bring to humanity the fullness of life and complete
> liberation.[36]

The daily effort to fulfil these pastoral objectives is, the Holy Father
reminds us, the raw material, the *proprium* of priestly holiness.[37] Priestly ministry and spiritual life energize and support one another. Attention at the cele-

---

34 *Presbyterorum ordinis*, 3. 35 Ibid. 36 PDV, 21. 37 Cf. Address, 2 March 1979.

acraments carefully prepared and administered, sound
rd of God, regular visiting of the sick and the aged – all
rior life of the priest and bring about that unity of life
to integrate action and contemplation.[38]

## ECCLESIAL CONTEXT OF THE SPIRITUAL LIFE

*Pastores dabo vobis* describes how the bond between the spiritual life of the priest and the exercise of his threefold ministry of word, sacrament and governance is mutual and manifest.[39] Priestly spirituality should then be rooted in the grace which flows from the sacrament of Orders, and which has as its basic frame of reference the specific service that the priest provides to the particular church in which he is incardinated. The deepening of the spiritual life of the priest is, then, directly related to his effort to develop and enrich those bonds of communion which he acquires through sacramental ordination – with the Vicar of Christ, with his bishop and brother priests, and with the ecclesial community entrusted to his care.[40]

Thus we can say that priestly spirituality is a spirituality of dedication to the particular church in which the priest exercises his ministry:

> The priest needs to be aware that his 'being in a particular church' constitutes by its very nature a significant element in his living a Christian spirituality. In this sense, the priest finds precisely in his belonging to and dedication to the particular church a wealth of meaning, criteria for discernment and action which shape both his pastoral mission and his spiritual life.[41]

However, dedication to a particular church does not limit the ministry of the priest to that church because the priest shares in the universality of the mission entrusted by Christ to the Apostles. Hence the spiritual life of the priest should be deeply marked by a missionary zeal and dynamism.[42]

The spirituality of the priest is, then, closely related to the Church, to its structure and mission. This ecclesial context of the priest's spiritual life, and its essential reference to the implications of *communio*, are a guarantee against subjectivism in priestly spirituality and link it directly to the building up of the Church. The Church, however, cannot be the ultimate reference for speaking about priestly spirituality. The final reference is, of course, Christ himself,

38 Cf. del Portillo, p. 73. 39 Cf. PDV, 26. 40 Cf. PDV, 17. See also E. de la Lama and L.F. Mateo-Seco, 'Sobre la espiritualidad del sacerdote secular', in *Scripta Theologica*, 31 (1999), I, p. 162. 41 PDV, 31. 42 Cf. PDV, 32.

since it is only in relation to him that both the Church and the priesthood acquire their fullest meaning. In the light of what we have already considered, we see that key aspects of priestly spirituality include the following: secularity as an integral part of the vocation of the diocesan priest; the exercise of the ministry as source of priestly holiness; pastoral charity as the unifying principle of the life of the priest; and *communio* as an inherent demand of the priestly character and ministry. Let us now examine some other fundamental aspects of the spiritual life of the priest to which John Paul II gives particular significance.

### LIFE OF FAITH

By virtue of his mission the priest has the demanding task of winning others over to Christ. Men and women of today are immersed in a technological and materialistic culture which tends to anaesthetize the life of the spirit and thus make faith inert and ineffective. It causes people to be blind to mystery and to the wonders of the supernatural life, and drives them to slake their spiritual thirst in pools of self-indulgence, sensuality and self-esteem. The priest, if he is going to have an influence on people who live in such circumstances, must himself be a man of faith. Thus John Paul II tells us that the priest 'will be able to give light to people in darkness only to the extent that he himself has accepted the light of the Teacher, Jesus Christ'. Speaking at an ordination ceremony in Nagasaki he reminds us:

> As priests your basic service is to proclaim to everyone Christ the Truth and the truths of faith, to foster faith constantly, to strengthen it where it is weak and to defend it against every threat ... Needless to say you will be better instructors in the faith to the extent that you yourselves have a deep-rooted, mature, courageous and contagious faith.[43]

After describing how Christ fostered the faith of the Twelve by his miracles and conversations (cf. Jn 2:11; 11:15; etc.), the Holy Father encourages priests to 'be disciples with a tried and mature faith, firmly anchored in the words of the Teacher and ready for combat'.[44]

For Holy Thursday of 1982, the Pope's letter took the form of a prayer. It is a moving example of what a priest's prayer can, and perhaps ought to be, including the different elements of thanksgiving, petition, and contrition.

43 Address, 25 February 1981. 44 Ibid.

'Save us from "grieving your Spirit" (cf. Eph 4:30)', the Holy Father prays, 'by our lack of faith and lack of readiness to witness to your Gospel "in deed and in truth" (1 Jn 3:18)'.[45] We can identify with these sentiments. And yet we know that it is faith informed by charity (cf. Gal 5:6) which makes us capable of winning the struggle to extend the kingdom of God: 'this is the victory which overcomes the world; your faith' (1 Jn 5:4). Faith makes formidable obstacles fall: those in ourselves in the first place, and then those barriers which make the work of evangelization difficult – impenitence, materialism, infidelity and instability in marriages, the stultifying and debilitating effects of an indiscriminate diet of TV, the lust and hedonism of a drug culture which corrupts souls and bodies even from a very young age.

The priest may well feel inadequate when faced with such circumstances: it is perhaps then that the full import of Christ's words – 'without me you can do nothing' (Jn 15:5) – penetrate to the very depths of his soul. It has been well said that

> there is a temptation which perennially besets every spiritual journey and pastoral work, that of thinking that the results depend on our ability to act and to plan. God of course asks us really to co-operate with his grace and therefore invites us to invest all our resources of intelligence and energy in serving the cause of the Kingdom. But it is fatal to forget that without Christ we can do nothing (cf. Jn 15:5).[46]

This should not, however, cause the priest to lose heart. It will, on the contrary, prepare him to rely more on God's grace in the future, and then he will be encouraged by those other words of the Master, 'everything is possible for him who believes' (Mk 9:23). The only real guarantee of pastoral success is intimacy with the Lord through faith. Pastoral strategies, structures and the rest will be just so much activism if they are not backed up by a deep personal piety. Only if the branch is united to the vine will it bear fruit, fruit that will endure (cf. Jn 15:5).

In his 1980 address to the clergy of Paris in Notre Dame cathedral, John Paul encouraged them to counter the many difficulties they faced by really living their faith:

> Do we not believe that Christ has sanctified and sent us? Do we not believe that he dwells with us, even if we bear this treasure in fragile vessels, and ourselves need his mercy whose ministers we are? Do we not believe that he acts through us, at least if we do his work, and that

45 HTL, 1982, no.4.  46 John Paul II, Apostolic letter, *Novo millennio ineunte*, 6 January 2001, no. 38.

> he will cause to grow what we have laboriously sown according to his
> Spirit?[47]

The answers to these questions will certainly be 'yes' at the intellectual level.
But is supernatural faith really operative in our lives? Does it make us see that
God's grace is all-powerful and prevent us being inhibited by human respect
or timidity in preaching the full demands of Christ's gospel? Have we the
courage to challenge people to live the great adventure of a committed
Christian life?[48]

Faith generates realistic optimism. Conversions, renewal of religious practice, return to the sacrament of Reconciliation, marriages which are generously open to new life – these will become a reality if the priest prays and has faith.
History confirms that such are the enduring fruits of the ministry of holy
priests. This was particularly the case in the life of the Curé of Ars. Here was
a priest who had little of the human and intellectual qualities required for such
a difficult assignment, but his faith and love of God transformed not only Ars,
but countless thousands of souls from all over France and from many other
countries as well. From a consideration of the ministry of this unique pastor of
souls the Holy Father suggests what our approach should be:

> Sometimes it is a simple presence, over the years, with the silent wit-
> ness of faith in the midst of non-Christian surroundings; or being near
> to people, to families and their concerns; there is a preliminary evan-
> gelization that seeks to awaken to the faith unbelievers and the luke-
> warm; there is the witness of charity and justice shared with Christian
> lay people, which makes the faith more credible and puts it into prac-
> tice. These give rise to a whole series of undertakings and apostolic
> works which prepare or continue Christian formation. The Curé of
> Ars himself taxed his ingenuity to devise initiatives adapted to his time
> and his parishioners. However, all these priestly activities were centred
> on the Eucharist, catechesis and the Sacrament of Reconciliation.[49]

In saying this, John Paul II is reflecting not only the life of Jean Marie Vianney,
but is also giving us the benefit of his own immense priestly experience.[50]

People learn from the faith of the priest, and, in a very real sense, live off
it. Cardinal Ratzinger explains why this is so:

> The priest must be a believer, one who converses with God. If this is
> not the case, then all his activities are futile. The most lofty and impor-

47 Address 30 May 1980. 48 Cf. *Novo millennio ineunte*, 31. 49 HTL, 1986, no.6. 50 Cf.
Weigel, ibid., Chapters 3 to 6.

tant thing a priest can do for people is first of all being what he is: a believer. Through faith he lets God, the Other, come into the world. And if the Other is not at work, our work will never be enough. When people sense that one is there who believes, who lives with God and from God, hope becomes a reality for them as well. Through the faith of the priest, doors open up all around for the people: it is really possible to believe, even today. All human believing is a believing-with, and for this the one who believes before us is so important. In many ways this person is more exposed in his faith than the others, since their faith depends on his and since, at any given time, he has to withstand the hardships of faith for them … The priest has to believe before others, but he also must be humble enough again and again to imitate and to co-operate with their faith. He strengthens their faith, but he also constantly receives faith from them.[51]

There is then a profound connection between the prayer-life of the priest and his faith, a consideration which leads logically to our next topic.

### PRAYER LIFE

If we are Christ's in a special way, we need to express this friendship by giving him some of our time completely for himself, in 'coming apart' (cf. Mk 6:31). In Getsemane Christ's heart was filled with anguish and grief (cf. Mt 26:37). 'Could you not watch one hour with me?'(cf. Mt 26:55) was the question he put to Peter, James and John, gently rebuking them for their somnolence at a time when he most needed their support. It goes without saying that this watching with Christ can only be achieved with the help of daily prayer which is the core of every effort to be converted again: 'Watch and pray that you may not enter into temptation' (Mk 14:38). John Paul II has emphasized the point that in recent years there has been too much discussion about the priest's identity, the value of his presence in the world, etc., and too little actual praying:

> It is prayer that shows the essential style of the priest; without prayer this style becomes deformed. Prayer helps us always to find the light that has led us since the beginning of our priestly vocation, and which never ceases to lead us, even though it seems at times to disappear in the darkness. Prayer enables us to be converted continually, to remain in a state of continuous reaching out to God, which is essential if we wish to lead others to him.[52]

51 Ratzinger, *A new song for the Lord*, pp 46-7.  52 HTL, 1979, no. 10. In an address to

We grow to spiritual maturity by modelling ourselves on Christ so that we begin to reflect him in our way of thinking and working. But how do we achieve this? By regularly meditating on the life and teachings of the Master, and by familiarising ourselves with the sentiments of his heart as reflected in the inspired words of Scripture – in a word, by contemplating the face of Christ.[53] This is not a merely speculative exercise but, under the promptings of grace, it leads to acts of love and contrition, and to practical resolutions which can channel our apostolic and pastoral ambitions. In our meditation we gather up all the different strands of our day and, by reflecting on them in the presence of God, develop those instincts which facilitate an adequate response to the demands of each moment.

At times we can allow ourselves to be harassed by worries, doubts and discouragement. Yet when we consider these burdens in prayer before the Tabernacle they acquire less intimidating proportions. We then begin to appreciate more deeply that there is an active providence of God at work (cf. Lk 12:7). This conviction about the intimate concern the Lord has for each of us personally will renew our generosity, and raise us above the level of our own defects and the irritations stemming from daily clashes with the selfishness and small-mindedness inherent in every human situation. So it is that

> prayer unifies the priest's life which so often risks being fragmented by the multiplicity of the tasks he must undertake; prayer makes what you do authentic, because it draws from the Heart of Christ the sentiments that motivate your work. *Do not be afraid to dedicate time and energy to it*; indeed, strive to be men of diligent prayer, enjoying the silence of contemplation and the devout daily celebration of the Eucharist and the Liturgy of the Hours which the Church has entrusted to you for the good of Christ's entire Body. The priest's prayer is also a requirement of his pastoral ministry, since Christian communities are enriched by the witness of the prayerful priest who proclaims the mystery of God with his words and with his life.[54]

priests at Maynooth, John Paul II developed the same idea and warned that 'a constant danger with priests, even zealous priests, is that they become so immersed in the work of the Lord that they neglect the Lord of the work. We must find time, we must make time, to be with the Lord in prayer ... It is only if we spend time with the Lord that our sending out to others will also be a bringing of him to others' (Address, 1 October, 1979). 53 Cf. *Novo millennio ineunte*, 16–28. 54 John Paul II, *Message to Third International Meeting of Priests*, held at the Basilica of our Lady of Guadalupe, Mexico, dated 29 June 1998, no. 3 (italics in original).

The wisdom of the saints makes it clear that there is no holiness without regular dialogue between the soul and its Creator. Between two people in love, a smile, a gesture can speak volumes. The same applies to the relationship between the priest and his Christ who has called him to a more intimate friendship (cf. Jn 15:15). But, like all true friendships, it needs to be cultivated; it cannot be taken for granted. We develop it by trying to avoid coming to our period of meditation with distracted minds and empty hearts. We learn to gather up the incidents of each day and bring them to Christ to share our joys and sorrows with him, asking him to filter out the dross of self-interest and pride which seem to cling to everything we do. In prayer before the Tabernacle Christ draws us out; he questions our excessive interest in news and sport; he enquires how much we really know about the things of God and the message of salvation. He asks us about the souls entrusted to our care and how effective we are at forming them to be committed Christians; he sounds us out on our own commitment to holiness.[55]

In addition, since true friendship of its very nature demands sincerity, we need to learn how to be frank both with God and with ourselves. This means a willingness to recognize our failures, to go to the root of our infidelities, and to uncover them before our forgiving Lord. As one spiritual writer has pointed out:

> We should not be surprised to find in our body and soul, the needle of pride, sensuality, envy, laziness, and the desire to dominate others. This is a fact of life, proven by our personal experience. It is the point of departure and the normal context for winning in this intimate sport, this race towards our Father's house.[56]

The benefits of daily meditation are inevitable if we persevere despite aridity, tiredness or distractions. As Boylan says, mental prayer has one, unique effect:

> A man may blind his conscience to the serious danger of mortal sin – he may even go farther – and still carry out all his other religious exercises and duties. *But he cannot persist in any such infidelity and still persevere in the daily practice of mental prayer. One thing or the other must give way.*[57]

Without daily meditation we are in danger of becoming prisoners of our own time and surroundings. Only by such prayer will we avoid the danger of assim-

55 Cf. Fulton Sheen, *Those mysterious priests*, New York, 1974, p. 181. 56 Blessed Josemaría Escrivá, *Christ is passing by*, Dublin, 1982, no. 75. 57 E. Boylan, *The spiritual life of the priest*, Westminster MD, 1959, p. 34 (italics in original).

ilating the values of a materialistic and sensate culture which is the context of our lives.[58]

John Paul II devotes his 1987 Holy Thursday Letter to the subject of the priest's prayer-life, with particular reference to Christ's prayer in the Garden of Getsemane before his Passion. He relates this prayer to the institution of the Eucharistic sacrifice to help us understand how our priesthood must be deeply rooted in prayer.[59] Because the sacramental and ministerial priesthood is a special sharing in the priesthood of Christ, it will not develop or bear fruit unless it is grounded in him. And it is through prayer that we become engrafted into Christ and his Paschal mystery, through prayer and vigilance which will be our best defence when we are faced with the 'scandal of the Cross'. In the same way that Christ's prayer in the Garden precedes the supreme fulfilment of his priesthood, we will more effectively discover our identity as priests when we reflect in prayer on the demands and responsibilities of our vocation.

> It is prayer which ... constantly reminds us of the primacy of Christ and, in union with him, the primacy of the interior life and of holiness. When this principle is not respected, is it any wonder that pastoral plans come to nothing and leave us with a disheartening sense of frustration. We then share the experience of the disciples in the Gospel story of the miraculous catch of fish: 'We have toiled all night and caught nothing' (Lk 5:5). This is the moment of faith, of prayer, of conversation with God, in order to open our hearts to the tide of grace and allow the word of Christ to pass through us in all its power: *Duc in altum*! On that occasion it was Peter who spoke the words of faith: 'At your word I will let down the nets' (ibid.). As this millennium begins, allow the Successor of Peter to invite the whole Church to make this act of faith, which expresses itself in a renewed commitment to prayer.[60]

Prayer has then to be the cornerstone of our priestly existence. As a consequence 'it will enable us to harmonize our lives with our priestly service, preserving intact *the identity and authenticity* of this vocation which has become our special inheritance in the Church as the community of the People of God'.[61]

---

58 'The ascetical tradition has already pointed out – and in certain sense prescribed – to priests certain means of sanctification, particularly the appropriate celebration of Mass, the punctual recitation of the Divine Office, visits to the Blessed Sacrament, daily recitation of the Rosary, daily meditation and periodic reception of sacramental Penance. These practices are still valid and indispensable' (John Paul II, Address, 26 May 1993, no. 4). 59 Cf. HTL, 1987, no.7. 60 John Paul II, Apostolic letter, *Novo millennio ineunte*, 38. 61 HTL, 1987,

MINISTRY OF PRAYER AND THE SACRAMENTS

The *Liturgy of the Hours*, the official prayer of the Church, precisely because it is united in a priestly way to the prayer of Christ the High Priest, enjoys a special objective efficacy. We are reminded by *Presbyterorum ordinis* that when priests recite the Divine Office:

> they lend their voice to the Church which perseveres in prayer in the name of the whole human race, in union with Christ who 'always lives to make intercession for them' (Heb 7:25).[62]

It is worth emphasising that priestly prayer, especially the Liturgy of the Hours, is authentic priestly ministry. This conviction will help priests avoid the tendency to reduce it to a mere private devotion as if time devoted to prayer, even private prayer, were somehow time robbed from the ministry. It is no accident that *Presbyterorum ordinis* quoted Heb 7:25 in this context. In doing so it wanted to remind us that Jesus Christ continues the exercise of his priesthood in heaven by means of an eternal prayer. In his personal prayer the priest identifies himself with the heavenly prayer of Christ and, at the same time, he embraces the whole world in this prayer.[63] Here also we see the confluence of the double representative role of the priest. In his prayer the priest not only identifies himself with the prayer of Christ, but 'he offers his voice to the Church, which perseveres in prayer'.[64] This prayer, united always ontologically to Christ the priest, infallibly renders to God the honour which he is due, and opens up to us ready access to the divine mercy.[65]

The Psalms, which constitute the major portion of the Liturgy of the Hours, are the prayers of the psalmist to God which we make our own.[66] As a devout Israelite, Jesus would have made time every day to pray the Psalms, Canticles and readings from the Old Testament prescribed for observant Jews, both in the Temple and in the synagogues of his country. St Augustine reminds

no.10 (italics in original). **62** *Presbyterorum ordinis*, no. 12. **63** 'Whoever prays the psalms in the Liturgy of the Hours does not say them in his own name so much as in the name of the whole body of Christ, in fact in the person of Christ himself' (*General instruction on the Liturgy of the Hours*, 108). **64** Cf. Pius XII, Encyclical, *Mediator Dei*, 40. **65** Cf. Mateo-Seco, ibid., pp 414-15. See also C. Dillenschneider, *Teología y espiritualidad del sacerdote*, Salamanca, 1964, pp 263-4. **66** St Ambrose explains the meaning of the psalms as follows: 'In the psalms there is an opportunity for the people to bless and praise God; the psalms express the admiration that people feel and what the people want to say; in them the Church speaks, the faith is professed in a melodious way and authority finds a ready acceptance; there too is heard the joyful call of freedom, the cry of pleasure and the sound of happiness. The psalm soothes anger, frees from care and drives away sadness. It is a weapon by night and a teacher by day: it is a shield in times of fear, an occasion of rejoicing for the holy, a us that, in the Psalter, Jesus continues to pray every day in us.[67] As we have seen, the Divine Office is not a private or individual prayer:

> It is the very prayer which Christ himself together with his Body addresses to the Father ... Hence all who take part in the Divine Office are not only performing a duty for the Church, they are also sharing in what is the greatest honour for Christ's Bride; for by offering these praises to God they are standing before God's throne in the name of the Church, their mother.[68]

In the *General instruction on the Liturgy of the Hours*, the purpose of the Breviary is spelled out as follows:

> The Liturgy of the Hours is entrusted to sacred ministers in a special way ... in order that at least through them the duty of the whole community may be constantly and continuously fulfilled and the prayer of Christ may persevere unceasingly in the Church.[69]

Because of the obligation of priests to seek holiness, the Church expects them to recite the Divine Office each day.[70] Apart from the regular spiritual nourishment provided by these prayers, the daily recital of the Breviary also strengthens the bonds of communion with priests throughout the world. Whenever the opportunity arises, praying some of the Hours with fellow-priests can enhance considerably the effectiveness of this means of priestly holiness.

---

mirror of tranquillity: it is a pledge of peace and harmony, for with the aid of the harp the psalm makes one melody from a number of different notes. The beginning of the day hears the sound of the psalm and the end of the day hears its echoes. In the psalm teaching is combined with charm; for it is sung for pleasure but learnt for instruction. Is there anything that does not come to mind as you read the psalms? It is there I read: 'A Song for the Beloved', and at once I am on fire with a desire for divine love. There too I see the secret of revelations, the evidence of the resurrection, the gifts that have been promised. In the psalms I learn to avoid sin and I forget the shame of sins now repented ... The psalms teach us to shape our lives and our actions by the study of higher things, so that material pleasures may not arouse our bodily passions, by which the soul is weighed down instead of being redeemed' (*Discourse on the Psalms* – see the Office of Readings, for Saturday of Week 10).
67 Cf. Archbishop E. Curtiss, 'Liturgy of the Hours in our lives of prayer', in *Osservatore Romano*, 5 August 1998 (Letter to priests of the archdiocese of Omaha, for Holy Thursday 1995). 68 Constitution on the Liturgy (*Sacrosanctum Concilium*), 84-5. 69 No. 28. 70 Cf. Code of Canon Law, no. 276:2:3. See also, Congregation for Divine Worship and Discipline of the Sacraments, *Responses on the obligation attaching to the recitation of the Liturgy of the Hours*, 15 November 2000.

PRIESTLY FRATERNITY

Priestly fraternity is another topic which John Paul II has frequently addressed in the context of the spiritual life of the priest. The root of priestly fraternity is to be found in the spirit of unity, or communion, which is a defining characteristic of the priestly vocation: unity of the priest with Christ, with the Church, with his own bishop, with his brothers in the priesthood and with the faithful.[71] This unity is rooted in the very core of the priest and, ultimately, derives from the priest's unity of life. The theological basis of priestly fraternity is summarized clearly in a text from *Lumen gentium*:

> In virtue of their sacred ordination and of their common mission, all priests are united together by bonds of intimate brotherhood, which manifests itself in a spontaneously and gladly given mutual help, whether spiritual or temporal, whether pastoral or personal, through the medium of reunions and community life, work and fraternal charity.[72]

This statement highlights two fundamental points: firstly, the sacramental root of the fraternal unity of priests, and, secondly, that unity of mission is a demand and a manifestation of this fraternal communion.

*Presbyterorum ordinis* affirms that even though priests may be assigned different duties, 'they fulfil the one priestly service for people', and all 'are sent to co-operate in the same work'.[73] This unity of the ministry from an ecclesiological point of view is a direct consequence of the fundamental unity of the mission of the Church.[74]

> The ministry of priests is above all communion and a responsible and necessary cooperation with the Bishop's ministry, in concern for the universal Church and for the individual particular churches, for whose service they form with the Bishop a single presbyterate. Each priest ... is united to the other members of this presbyterate on the basis of the sacrament of Holy Orders and by particular bonds of apostolic charity, ministry, and fraternity.[75]

Despite the variety of activities and circumstances, because of the common mission there is a real communion with all priests. In other words, the unity of the mission of the Church postulates the unity of its priesthood because of a

71 Cf. PDV, 17. 72 *Lumen gentium*, 28. 73 *Presbyterorum ordinis*, 8. 74 'The mission of the Church ... is one and the same everywhere and in all situations, although, because of circumstances, it may not always be exercised in the same way' (*Ad gentes*, 6). 75 PDV, 17.

theological demand inherent in the very concept of mission.[76] The priest's mission by its very nature is a universal one, since it participates in the priesthood of Christ, the unique and universal cause of the salvation of the human race.[77]

From the unity and universality of the priestly mission derives the practical consequence of cultivating in seminarians 'that truly Catholic spirit which habitually looks beyond the boundaries of diocese, country or rite, to meet the needs of the whole Church, being prepared in spirit to preach the Gospel everywhere'.[78] In effect, although the priest carries out a specific pastoral task, the whole of the mission of the Church finds support in it, and through it the priest communicates with the broader mission of the Church. Priestly fraternity has, then, a clear theological reference in the fact that all priests, as co-operators of the episcopal body, share the one mission of building up the Mystical Body of Christ and leading it to completion. Mutual co-operation between priests, and their union with the bishop, is not only an indispensable condition for the human and supernatural effectiveness of their work, but is also a specific presupposition of pastoral charity. As the decree on the ministry and life of priests points out:

> Hence pastoral charity demands that priests, if they are not to run in vain (cf. Gal 2:2), should always work within the bond of union with the bishops and their fellow priests.[79]

### SACRAMENTAL ORIGIN OF PRIESTLY FRATERNITY

However, for a fuller explanation of the theological nature of the deep bond of communion which unites priests, we need to consider the sacramental dimension of this unity. *Presbyterorum ordinis* points the way when it affirms the sacramental foundation of priestly fraternity:

> All priests, who are constituted in the order of priesthood by the sacrament of Order, are bound together by an intimate sacramental broth-

---

76 Cf. 'La Fraternidad Sacerdotal de los Presbíteros: Fundamentos y Formación de los candidatos' by Enrique Borda, in *La formación de los sacerdotes* ..., 1990, pp 623-37. 77 'The spiritual gift which priests have received in ordination does not prepare them merely for a limited and circumscribed mission, but for the fullest, in fact the universal mission of salvation "to the end of the earth' (Act 1:8). The reason is that every priestly ministry shares in the fullness of the mission entrusted by Christ to the Apostles' (*Presbyterorum ordinis*, 10). 78 *Optatam totius*, 20. 79 *Presbyterorum ordinis*, 14.

erhood; but in a special way they form one priestly body in the diocese to which they are attached under their own bishop.[80]

Priestly fraternity can then be defined as a *sacramental* fraternity because it has a sacramental origin. In this way an ontological bonding is established which touches the core of the priestly personality, transforming and structuring its existence. As a consequence of the relationship between the sacrament and the fraternal bond, the priest finds in the specific grace of Holy Orders the principal source for developing his fraternal relationship with other priests. In addition, priestly fraternity, even though it is grounded on the sacrament of Order, is a relationship which has to be built up day by day. As John Paul II encouraged a group of priests:

> I wish to remind you that you cannot live or work in an isolated manner. With the aid of all, diocesan and religious priests, you must build up the presbyterate as a family and as a sacramental brotherhood, as a place where the priest finds all the specific means of sanctification and evangelization. Your presbyterate will be the efficacious sign of sanctification and evangelization when one can see in it the characteristics of the Cenacle, that is to say, prayer and apostolic brotherhood with Mary the Mother of Jesus (cf. Acts 1:14).[81]

One of the fundamental ideas developed by the Holy Father in his theology of the body is the relational aspect of the human person, a concept which has its source in Trinitarian theology.[82] In *Pastores dabo vobis* he applies this same idea to the sacramental relationship of the priest with the bishop and the other priests, as a basis for continuing Christ's mission to the Church. Priestly fraternity is then a constitutive dimension of the sacrament of Orders intrinsic to the mission the priest receives at ordination. Hence,

> if the sacrament of Orders configures a priest to Christ the Head, inserts him into an apostolic community of faith and mission (the presbyterate), and bestows on him the grace of pastoral charity as both a gift given and a call to be lived, then it must be in the visible priestly fraternity that a priest will best be able to respond to the call to live out the pastoral charity of Christ for the sake of the Church's mission. This belief has practical implications for the 'living out' of priesthood. Like pastoral charity, priestly fraternity is both a gift in ordination and a task to be lived throughout the life of the priest.[83]

80 Ibid., 8.  81 Address, 29 January 1985.  82 Cf. John Paul II, *The theology of the body: human love in the divine plan*, Boston, 1997.  83 George, ibid., p. 75.

Fraternity, then, forms part of the very priestly vocation itself and it is also the appropriate climate in which vocation matures, develops and reaches its fullness. Consequently, preparing young men for the priesthood implies not only communicating to them an awareness of this reality, but also helping them acquire the attitudes and experiences which will equip them to live this fraternity in their priestly ministry.

While the quest for personal holiness is the specific responsibility of each, in virtue of sacramental fraternity every priest has the right to be helped by his brothers in this task and has the duty to offer his assistance to others. Fraternal correction, spiritual guidance, and the sacrament of Reconciliation have a singular importance in this context and greatly contribute to reinforcing the bonds of fraternity.[84]

There is one other important dimension of the theology of priestly fraternity. Priests, together with the bishop, constitute the diocesan presbyterate which is a sign of the unity of the priestly ministry of Christ.[85] But the Council expresses the relations between the priests and the bishop in terms of filiation-paternity:

> By reason of this sharing in the priesthood and mission of the bishop, the priests should see in him a true father and obey him with all respect. The bishop, on his side, should treat the priests, his helpers, as his sons and friends (cf. Jn 15:15).[86] The diocesan clergy have a primary role in the care of souls because, being incardinated in or appointed to a particular church, they are wholly dedicated in its service to the care of a particular section of the Lord's flock, and accordingly form one priestly body and one family of which the bishop is the father.[87]

Without this reference to the spiritual paternity of the bishop, authentic priestly fraternity would not be possible. Hence, unity with the bishop, expressed in terms of filiation, is an inseparable element of fraternity and reinforces at the same time the bonds of fraternal union between priests. From ancient times this bonding is signified liturgically by the fact that priests present at an ordination are invited, after the ordaining bishop, to impose hands on the head of the new priest. Diocesan fraternity is also expressed in a special way when priests concelebrate with their bishop at the Chrism Mass on Holy Thursday.

On the other hand, one of the bishop's primary responsibilities is the spiritual and material welfare of his priests. Priest's should experience a real pater-

---

84 Cf. *Presbyterorum ordinis*, 8; PDV, 74; DMLP, 93.  85 Cf. *Lumen gentium*, 28; *Presbyterorum ordinis*, 8.  86 *Lumen gentium*, 28.  87 *Christus Dominus*, 28.

'est by the bishop in the human as well the spiritual aspects of their lives – ensuring that their living conditions are adequate, that they do not feel isolated, that they get appropriate support when difficulties arise in the parish, etc. In particular the bishop will have a concern for young and recently ordained priests to guarantee that they receive the necessary spiritual formation to grow in holiness and mature in their vocation.[88]

Since everyone needs human affection and affirmation, fraternity is an important dimension of the priest's life. Friends are an essential requirement for human flourishing, not just to exchange opinions with or to chat about current affairs. The imperative to communicate goes much deeper, especially in relation to events which bring particular joy, sorrow, or distress. As T.S. Eliot remarked: 'Human kind cannot bear very much reality'.[89] Every soul needs an outlet to alleviate sorrow or somebody to rejoice with. The sharing of confidences calls for friendship, understanding and mutual trust: we only open out to people who can empathize fully with our situation. Since friendship requires not only reciprocal confidence, but also a certain equality, it is clear that if a priest is to reveal the intimate aspects of his personality he will normally only be able to communicate his deepest self to another priest, because all his vital concerns will necessarily be related to his position as a priest or his pastoral role. Friendships with priests, mutual exchanges on problems arising from one's pastoral ministry, and personal guidance at the level of spiritual direction – these are all fundamental aspects of priestly fraternity.[90]

John Paul II, looking back on half a century experience of priesthood, has no doubt about the exceptional importance of this aspect of the priestly vocation:

> On the fiftieth anniversary of my priestly ordination, my thoughts go in a special way to the presbyterate of the *Church of Cracow*, of which I was a member as a priest and then as its head as Archbishop. So many outstanding parish priests and curates come to mind that it would take too long to mention them one by one. Then and now, bonds of deep friendship have united me to many of them. The example of their holiness and pastoral zeal has been immensely edifying to me. Certainly they have had a profound influence on my priesthood. From them I have learned what it means in practice to be a pastor. I am deeply convinced of the decisive role that the diocesan presbyterate plays in the personal life of every priest. The community of priests, rooted in true sacramental fraternity, is a setting second to none for spiritual and pastoral formation. The priest, as a rule, cannot do with-

88 Cf. ibid., 16, 28. 89 T.S. Eliot, *Four quartets (Burnt Norton)*, London, 1978. 90 Cf. Federico Suarez, *About being a priest*, Dublin, 1979, p. 198.

out this community. The presbyterate helps him in his growth towards holiness and is a sure support in times of difficulty. On the occasion of my Golden Jubilee, how can I fail to express my gratitude to all the priests of the Archdiocese of Cracow for everything that they have contributed to my priesthood?[91]

Such fraternity creates that necessary sense of belonging which all priests require. But the conviction of being part of a family needs to be nourished by the genuine care priests demonstrate for the good health and material needs of their brothers. It will, among other things, reflect itself in traditional priestly hospitality and in practical support for those who are sick or overworked.[92] If it is a question of a brother priest who is experiencing difficulties in his vocation, the obligations of priestly fraternity run deeper. A priest in spiritual need should not lack the extra prayer and penance of his brothers, and, where appropriate, 'the refined evangelical practice of fraternal correction'.[93] Are there not perhaps vocational failures which could have been avoided if priests had been more alert to the human and spiritual needs of their brothers?

> The fraternal character of church office needs to be more intensively put into practice, particularly today. In a society which is becoming ever more 'worldly', the priest needs a closer personal connection with, and a lifestyle marked by, fraternal and friendly relationships in which he can live as a Christian and a priest. Jesus did not call his disciples to leave their families in order to isolate them, but in order to introduce them into his 'new family'.[94]

The human, spiritual and pastoral support deriving from a well lived priestly fraternity can hardly be overstated. In this context it is worth noting that associations which promote priestly fraternity as well as holiness through the exercise of the ministry are especially encouraged by the Church.[95]

### DEVOTION TO MARY

For the priest the Marian example of faith is a light which illuminates every step of his spiritual journey.[96] Commenting on John Paul II's encyclical,

---

**91** John Paul II: *Gift and mystery: on the fiftieth anniversary of my priestly ordination*, London 1996, pp 67-68 (italics in original). **92** Cf. *Presbyterorum ordinis*, 8. **93** *Directory on the ministry and life of priests*, 93. **94** Gisbert Greshake, *The meaning of Christian priesthood*, Dublin, 1988, pp 162-3. **95** Cf. *Presbyterorum ordinis*, 8; PDV, 31, 81; DMLP, 29, 88. **96** Cf. Ratzinger, *A new song for the lord*, p. 48.

*Redemptoris Mater*, Ratzinger emphasizes two aspects of our Lady's 'obedience of faith'– its significance for the Incarnation, and again at the foot of the Cross:

> In Mary's 'yes' to the birth of the Son of God from her womb through the power of the Holy Spirit, she makes her body, her whole self available as the place for God's action. In this word, Mary's will and the will of the Son coincide. In the harmony of this 'yes', 'a body you have prepared for me', the incarnation, the birth of God, becomes possible. For God's entry into this world, for God's birth to come about, there must be this Marian yes, this coincidence of our wills with his will over and over again.[97]

On Calvary, 'the darkness in which Mary stands is the completion of the communion of wills with Christ. Faith is the community of the cross, and only on the cross does it become complete'.[98] We can say with conviction that one of the surest ways for the priest to deepen his faith is through devotion to the Mother of God.

> Mary was uniquely associated with Christ's priestly sacrifice, sharing his will to save the world by the cross. She was the first to share spiritually in his offering as *Sacerdos et Hostia*, and did so perfectly. As such, she can obtain and give grace to those who share in her Son's priesthood on the ministerial level, the grace moving them to respond ever more fully to the demands of spiritual oblation that the priesthood entails: in particular, the grace of faith, hope and perseverance in trials, recognized as a challenge to share more generously in the redemptive sacrifice.[99]

Some years ago John Paul II posed the following question in an address to priests, 'What should we ask of Mary as "Mother of priests"?' His unequivocal reply on their behalf was: 'Today, as and perhaps more than at any other time, the priest must ask Mary particularly for the grace of knowing how to accept God's gift with grateful love..; the grace of purity and fidelity in the obligation of celibacy, following her example as the "faithful Virgin"'.[100] His prayer for priests is as follows:

> With tender affection I entrust each of you to the Virgin, given to us in an extraordinary way as Mother of the Eternal Priest. For each of

97 Ibid., pp 48–9. 98 Ibid., p. 49. 99 John Paul II, Address, 30 June 1993. 100 Ibid.

you I place in her clasped hands a humble request for perseverance and for the commitment to leave as a legacy to your brethren at least one who will continue that unique priesthood that lives and springs from love within us.[101]

While the offering of the sacrifice of the Mass is for the priest an essentially christocentric activity, he can never forget the Mother who gave life to the Body which is sacrificed. This daily experience should create a unique bonding between the priest and Mary and give her a special presence in his life as Mother.[102] Priests are called to offer to the Eucharistic Body of Christ the service Mary rendered to the Body of her Child. In an ancient liturgical hymn in praise of the Real Presence of Christ, the Church affirms the direct connection between our Lady and the Eucharist: *Ave, verum corpus natum ex Mariae virgine,* Hail, the true Body born of the Virgin Mary.[103] Since Christ took his humanity totally from Mary, in the Eucharist we receive not only the *verum corpus natum ex Mariae virgine* but, in a very real sense, Mary's own flesh and blood for our nourishment.

The priest needs to have Mary as the woman at the centre of his life to fill his heart. If he has a genuine devotion to our Lady he will experience her maternal warmth and support every day. In his effort to live celibacy, the priest, as one spiritual writer has put it,

> must lift his eyes and his heart to the mother, companion and bride of his Lord, to that Queen of Virgins who is not only the archetype of humanity in the divine ordering of the world, but also embodies the purest and most perfect ideal of womanhood, virgin, mother, maid and queen. It is to her, the prudent, the mighty, the kindly and faithful Virgin that the priest should turn; it is with her, the pure, gentle Mother of Christ, the Mother of divine Grace, that he should place himself under instruction ... In a fashion wholly unique she unites in herself every noble trait of womanhood, and the priest who venerates her will transfer to all her sisters something of her graciousness and nobility. In every woman he encounters in his life he will seek to discover, or awaken some glimmer, of that womanly dignity which shines forth in Mary.[104]

The passions of the human heart need to be refined and purified if we are to be able to distinguish clearly between self-seeking and self-giving. Because

101 Message to priests, 19 June 2000, no. 5. 102 Cf. HTL, 1995, no. 3. See also PDV, 83.
103 Cf. James T. O'Connor, *The hidden manna: a theology of the Eucharist*, San Francisco, 1988, pp 341-53. 104 Josef Selmair, *The priest in the world*, London, 1954, p. 210.

of human weakness we can easily confuse these two contrary dispositions, and so, as Newman says, we need the 'cool breath of the Immaculate'[105] to help us be sincere with ourselves and recognize our self-seeking for what it really is.


## STUDY AND SPIRITUAL READING

Priestly life runs the risk of being emptied of its meaning through routine and a loss of pastoral charity.[106] Thus the effort to maintain a deep interior life is an essential antidote to this danger. Hence, to avoid a reductive approach to pastoral tasks, the priest should have a regular input of fresh ideas through study and spiritual reading. We all need to be challenged by the accumulated wisdom of Christian tradition seen through the prism of present-day needs. It is also necessary to reflect on the experience of Christian life lived heroically by men and women in the most diverse circumstances, so that we in turn can have a vision of how to inspire others to holiness. For this, regular spiritual reading is essential.[107]

The Vatican II decree on the priesthood reminds us that in order to touch the hearts of people we need to apply the eternal truth of the Gospel to the concrete circumstances of life. To preach in this way requires reading, reflection and study. In his 1979 Holy Thursday Letter, John Paul II strongly recommends on-going study:

> We must link prayer with continuous work upon ourselves: this is the *formatio permanens* ... This formation must be both interior, that is to say directed towards the deepening of the priest's spiritual life, and must also be pastoral and intellectual (philosophical and theological). Therefore, since our pastoral activity, the preaching of the word and the whole of the priestly ministry depend upon the intensity of our interior life, that activity must also find sustenance in assiduous study. It is not enough to stop at what we once learned in the seminary, even in cases where those studies were done at university level ...This process of intellectual formation must last all one's life, especially in modern times, which are marked – at least in many parts of the world – by the widespread development of education and culture. To the people who enjoy the benefits of this development we must be *witnesses* to Jesus Christ, and properly qualified ones. As teachers of truth and morality, we must tell them, convincingly and effectively, of the hope

---

105 John H. Newman, *Discourses to mixed congregations*, London, 1886, p. 376. 106 Cf. PDV, 57. 107 Cf. *Novo millennio ineunte*, 41.

that gives us life (cf. 1 Pet 3:15). And this also forms part of the process of daily conversion to love, through the truth.[108]

Every priest should have a good commentary on Sacred Scripture which combines the exegetical wisdom of the Fathers with the best in modern biblical studies. In this context it is worthy of note that, after several decades of over-emphasis on the historical-critical approach to biblical exegesis, there is a return to a greater appreciation of the merits of traditional exegesis as represented by the scriptural commentaries of the Fathers.[109]

As part of their on-going formation, priests are encouraged to acquire a deeper understanding of the biblical foundations of the priesthood and to become more familiar with the patristic commentaries on priestly life. In addition a lot is to be gained from reading biographies of zealous priests.[110] The documents of the Magisterium are always a useful source of doctrine for personal piety as well as for preaching. In addition, the priest should keep up-to-date with the principal writings of the Holy Father. His annual Holy Thursday Letters can be used regularly for spiritual reading and personal prayer. Encyclicals like *The splendour of truth*,[111] and *The gospel of life*[112] give an updated statement of Christian moral teaching. The Pope's post-synodal exhortations on *Reconciliation and penance*,[113] *The Vocation and mission of the lay faithful in the Church and the world*,[114] and *The Christian Family*[115], constitute a significant pastoral resource for preaching on confession, the vocation of the laity, and the sanctification of married life. The priest should also be familiar with John Paul II's letters on the *Dignity of women*,[116] on *Suffering*,[117] and on *Keeping the Lord's Day holy*.[118]

---

108 HTL, 1979, no. 10. *Pastores dabo vobis* notes the direct connection between pastoral charity and formation: 'The heart and form of the priest's ongoing formation is pastoral charity: the Holy Spirit, who infuses pastoral charity, introduces and accompanies the priest to an ever deeper knowledge of the mystery of Christ which is unfathomable in its richness (cf. Eph 3:14ff) and, in turn, to a knowledge of the mystery of Christian priesthood. Pastoral charity itself impels the priest to an ever deeper knowledge of the hopes, the needs, the problems, the sensibilities of the people to whom he ministers, taken in their specific situations, as individuals, in their families, in society, and in history' (PDV, 70). 109 Cf. Henri de Lubac, *The sources of revelation*, New York, 1968. 110 'Among his reading material, the primary place must be given to Sacred Scripture; and then the writings of the Fathers, classical and modern spiritual Masters, and the Documents of the Magisterium, which constitute the authoritative and updated source of permanent formation. Priests should study them and deepen their understanding of them (directly and personally) in order to adequately present them to the lay faithful' (*Directory on the ministry and life of priests*, 87). 111 *Veritatis splendor*, 6 August 1993. 112 *Evangelium vitae*, 25 March 1995. 113 *Reconciliatio et paenitentia*, 2 December 1984. 114 *Christifideles laici*, 30 December 1988. 115 *Familiaris consortio*, 22 November 1981. 116 Apostolic letter, *Mulieris dignitatem*, 15 August 1988. 117 Apostolic letter, *Salvifici doloris*, 11 February 1984. 118 Apostolic letter, *Dies Domini*, 31

CONCLUSION

When the Holy Father went to Ars to celebrate the bicentenary of the birth of Jean-Marie Vianney he gave a retreat to thousands of priests and seminarians on 6 October 1986. That he would do so highlighted more than anything else the importance he gives to the spiritual life of the priest. It was, in a very real sense, a personal invitation by the Holy Father to the priests of France and of the world to strive for holiness after the model of the saintly Curé of Ars. The three meditations he gave that day were in fact a summary of much of what he has been saying to priests in many different parts of the world over the past twenty years. The ideas he affirmed there are summarized by way of conclusion.[119]

He reminded priests that to act effectively as ministers of Christ we had to become assimilated to the Master in our thoughts, the attachments of our heart, and in our conduct. He once again emphasized the idea that, while all the baptized are called to holiness, our consecration and mission make it a particular duty to aspire to sanctity by means of the riches inherent in our priesthood and the requirements of our ministry within the People of God. He pointed to the fact that the Curé d'Ars was a priest who was not satisfied with the mere external performance of the acts of redemption, but that he shared in them 'in his very being, in his love of Christ, in his constant prayer, in the offerings of his trials or his voluntary mortifications', and that he still remains for all priests 'an unequalled model of the carrying out of the ministry and the holiness of the minister'.[120]

St Jean-Marie Vianney's stated reason for becoming a priest was 'to win souls for the good God'. He worked and mortified himself to the point of exhaustion to wrest from the Lord the graces of conversion for them. This was the context of the Holy Father's second meditation. Speaking to the bishops and priests assembled at Ars from sixty different countries, John Paul observed:

> Many of our contemporaries seem to have become indifferent to the salvation of their souls. Are you sufficiently concerned about this loss of faith? ... Our love for mankind cannot be resigned to seeing them deprive themselves of salvation ... We must invite our faithful to conversion and to holiness; we must speak the truth, warn, advise, and make them desire the sacraments that re-establish them in the grace of God.

May 1998. 119 The texts of these three meditations are published in *Osservatore Romano*, 10 November 1986. 120 First meditation, no. 2.

The Holy Father was appealing to, begging priests to devote more effort to the ministry of the confessional to recover souls for God.

The Curé of Ars, the Pope continued, was totally committed to this ministry, and he recalled the warning of this great priest: 'If a pastor remains dumb when he sees God outraged and souls wandering away, woe to him'. He referred to the saint's courage in proclaiming the demands of the Gospel, in denouncing sin, and inviting men to make good the evil they had committed. He reminded his listeners that the Curé spent ten to fifteen hours a day in the confessional harvesting souls for God, and that while we simply couldn't transpose this immense pastoral activity into the rhythm of our priestly lives, we needed to be vigorously challenged by his attitude and motivation.

Reflecting on the fact that there had been a considerable fall-off in attendance at the sacrament of Reconciliation, Pope John Paul strongly urged priests to do everything they could to promote this sacrament despite the difficulties. Jean-Marie Vianney, he said, overcame the same difficulties as a result of his priestly holiness. If priests 'burned with the mercy of Christ', they in turn would attract many more penitents to conversion and forgiveness.

The Holy Father's final address encouraged priests to work for spiritual renewal through fidelity to the daily practice of prayer despite the weaknesses and difficulties they encountered in themselves. This spiritual rejuvenation would give a deeper meaning to those virtues particularly appropriate to Christ's ministers – celibacy, real poverty, obedience, fortitude, voluntary mortification and the ascetical struggle of every day. By perseverance in this daily effort, which was also a characteristic of the life of Jean-Marie Vianney, the Church would again have priests of the spiritual and apostolic quality which are so necessary today.

# 6

## Eucharistic identity: priest and victim

John Paul II's Jubilee year visit to Israel in March 2000 left an indelible imprint not only on those who were present at the different ceremonies, but on all who followed the progress of his trip by means of the television broadcast. To see the Vicar of Christ journey in the footsteps of Jesus through different towns and cities of the Holy Land was an unforgettable experience. Bethlehem, Nazareth, Caesarea Philippi, the Mount of the Beatitudes, the Garden of Olives, Golgotha, the Holy Sepulchre – all of these names and locations on the Holy Father's itinerary are pregnant with meaning for Christians

The celebration of Mass in the Cenacle was a particularly emotional occasion for the Pope and had a special resonance for all priests. To this very room, where Christ instituted the Eucharist and ordained his first priests, we can trace the genealogy and origin of our priesthood. Here too, on 23 March 2000, John Paul II signed his Holy Thursday Letter addressed to priests for the Jubilee year. In this letter he allows us to share the thoughts and sentiments he experienced on that evocative and historic occasion. Thinking back through two thousand years to all that took place within those walls on that evening charged with mystery, the Holy Father recalls the scene of Jesus and the Apostles seated at table, the spirit of service of the Master washing the feet of the Twelve, and the new commandment of love which he gave them. The Apostles were no longer servants but truly friends of Christ, because he had revealed to them all that his Father had entrusted to him (cf. Jn 15:15). In this atmosphere of deep intimacy and self-giving, Jesus instituted the Blessed Eucharist and made his Apostles priests of the New Covenant, bonding them to himself in a new and unique way.

Hence, to really understand our vocation, to keep before us an authentic vision of the meaning of our priestly identity, and to be inspired to live out the full implications of our special intimacy with Christ, we too, like the Holy Father, need to return frequently in spirit to the Upper Room to reflect on the events of that historic evening which have engraved themselves indelibly on our priesthood. In this way our lives become progressively deep-rooted in the priesthood of Christ, and we grow in our appreciation of the intimate connection between the new commandment of love (pastoral charity), the Eucharist (sacrament and sacrifice), and our ministry (good shepherd) – elements which represent the key co-ordinates of our priestly existence. However, to put all this into perspective, we must first revert to Jesus' discourse on the 'bread of life' in Capernaum. We also need to note aspects of the divine pedagogy at work in this teaching, because it is paradigmatic for the response of the priest to his own vocation, especially at the level of faith.

In the preamble to his Eucharistic discourse, Jesus reveals himself as the bringer of messianic gifts by his reference to the manna which God provided every day to feed the Israelites in the desert (Jn 6:25-34). He then tries to lead his listeners to make an act of faith in him so that he can openly reveal to them the mystery of the Eucharist (vv. 35-47). Here we learn that faith is a coming to Christ drawn by the interior action of the Father; it is not something blind or untutored but a response to grace and the objective evidence of the infinite power of God. The previous day, with striking demonstrations of power, Jesus has prepared his audience for what he would shortly reveal to them. With five barley loaves and two fish he fed a hungry crowd of five thousand men (cf. Jn 6:5-14). And that very night, showing his command over nature, he came to the disciples walking on the sea to calm the storm which threatened their boat (cf. Jn 6:16-21). The scene was now set for him to make the astonishing revelation that the bread of life he is talking about was his own flesh and blood. By eating and drinking this food we receive the principle of supernatural life (6:35) and become intimately identified with Christ (6:56). His words have such realism about them that they cannot be interpreted in a figurative way. If he is not really present under the species of bread and wine, the discourse at Capernaum makes no sense.

Christ's hearers understand perfectly well that he means exactly what he says. If they had grasped it in a metaphorical way there would have been no need for them to be surprised. But in response to their protests Jesus only becomes more emphatic and, indeed, more shocking to Jewish feelings in light of the blood prohibitions of Leviticus.[1] When he says that eating his flesh is a pre-condition to share his divine life, the original Greek verb used has the stronger connotation of 'chewing' to show that Communion is a real meal.[2]

1 'If any man of the house of Israel or of the strangers that sojourn among them eats any blood, I will set my face against that person who eats blood and cut him off from among his people. For the life of the flesh is in the blood; and I have given it for you upon the altar to make atonement for your souls; for it is the blood that makes atonement, by reason of the life. Therefore I have said to the people of Israel, No person among you shall eat blood, neither shall any stranger who sojourns among you eat blood' (Lev 17:10-12). 2 *The Navarre Bible: St John's Gospel*, Dublin, 1987, p. 105. Sokolowski offers an insightful explanation of the sacramentality of the Eucharist: 'The choice of bread and wine as the embodiment of the memorial of our Redemption furnishes an image of the Incarnation: as the Son took on

There is no room here for speaking symbolically – this is why his 'flesh is food indeed' (6:56). Because many of his disciples refused to accept the reality of Jesus' words at their face value, his teaching for them became 'a hard saying' (6:60).[3] But Peter and the Eleven did accept them, not because they understood them any more clearly than those who had walked away. The difference was that they had learned to have faith in the words of Jesus, a faith magnificently expressed by Simon Peter: 'Lord, to whom shall we go? You have the words of eternal life; and we have believed, and have come to know, that you are the Holy One of God' (6: 68–69). This is not just an expression of human solidarity, but a statement of genuine supernatural faith. Jesus himself says we cannot accept the mystery of the Eucharist if we think in too human a way.

Like the disciples who listened in astonishment to our Lord's discourse at Capernaum, we also find this language difficult to understand (cf. Jn 6:61) and might sometimes be tempted to give it a reductive interpretation. But this would distance us from Christ, like the disciples who no longer walked in his company. It would also make us less sensitive to preaching about the appropriate moral dispositions necessary to receive the Body of Christ worthily.[4] Precisely because it is the *verum corpus, natum ex Mariae virgine*, the true Body of Christ born of the Virgin Mary, priests have a serious responsibility to avoid the danger of sacrilege being committed by people approaching this sacrament unworthily. This danger is not a remote one at a time like the present when faith in the Eucharist is weak, when catechetical illiteracy is pervasive, and when reception of Communion is routine for everybody.[5]

Only if we receive Christ's words as revelation will we have 'spirit and life' (6:63). Like Peter and the Eleven, the priest's faith in the Eucharist is at the core of his identity and mission. The more deeply he appreciates the grandeur of this mystery of faith, the more clearly will he understand the meaning of his priesthood as the definition of his existence and all that it implies in terms of love and service to the flock.

---

human flesh and assumed it into the life of God, so the common material elements of bread and wine become transformed into signs and vehicles of that same life. And the fact that bread and wine are food confirms the sacrament's involvement in the distribution of life. It is in being fed that our life is sustained. The Eucharist is the most material of all the sacraments; it establishes a sacramentality in eating. The bread and wine given to us to be consumed are palpable images of the life that is conveyed to us in and through the Church' (Robert Sokolowski, *Eucharistic presence: a study in the theology of disclosure*, Washington DC, 1993, p. 37). 3 For a history of this failure of faith in the Eucharist down through the centuries, see James T. O'Connor, *The hidden manna*, pp 94–177. 4 Cf. John Paul II, Homily, 22 June 2000, no. 4. 5 Cf. *The priest and the third millennium*, III, 2.

## INSTITUTION OF THE EUCHARIST

Jesus sent Peter and John to prepare the Passover meal (cf. Lk 22:8), and it was during this solemn and ceremonial occasion that he instituted the Blessed Eucharist and the sacrifice of the New Covenant. What was the annual memorial of the liberation from Egypt was given a new direction.[6] The Passover meal followed a very specific pattern. Before eating the lamb the religious meaning of the feast was explained. Then the food was eaten interspersed with hymns and psalms. At the end came a solemn prayer of thanksgiving. Throughout the meal, marking its main stages, the diners drank four glasses of wine mixed with water. St Luke mentions two of these, the second being that which our Lord consecrated (cf. Lk 22:17).[7] The Synoptics and St Paul[8] describe the events which took place in the Upper Room and which contain three essential truths of faith about the mystery of the Eucharist:

1) the institution of this sacrament and Christ's Real Presence in it. The whole tradition of the Church, in the words of St Ignatius of Antioch, professes that 'the Eucharist is the flesh of our Saviour Jesus Christ, the flesh which suffered for our sins and which the Father, of his kindness, brought to life'.[9]

2) the institution of the Christian priesthood. After celebrating the first Eucharist, Jesus instructed the Apostles to perpetuate what he had done. The Church has always understood Christ's words: 'Do this in remembrance of me' (Lk 22:19; cf. 1 Cor 11:24-25) to mean that he thereby made the Apostles and their successors priests of the New Covenant, endowing then with the power to renew the Sacrifice of Calvary in an unbloody manner in the celebration of Mass.[10] The Eucharistic sacrifice, celebrated by the priest, makes present in every Christian generation, in every corner of the earth, the work accomplished by Christ. The enduring guarantee of the Eucharistic presence is the Holy Spirit who transforms the bread and wine into the Body and Blood of Christ, the same Spirit who was 'breathed' on the Apostles in the Upper Room that first Easter evening, and who after Pentecost impelled them to go to the ends of the earth to proclaim the Word and build up the Church.[11]

6 Cf. *The Eucharist and freedom*, Pontifical Committee for International Eucharistic Congresses, Rome, in *Osservatore Romano*, 13 November 1996, no. 13. 7 Cf. *The Navarre Bible: St Luke's Gospel*, Dublin, 1987, p. 226. 8 Cf. Mt 26:26-29; Mk 14:22-25; Lk 22:19-20. See also 1 Cor 11:23-26. 9 Cf. Paul VI, Encyclical letter, *Mysterium fidei*, 5 (3 September 1965). 10 'In the biblical concept of remembering, events are not simply the object of mental recall. Rather are they by divine action called up, evoked, into the present in all their saving significance and power. In the formula of eucharistic consecration, for instance, the words "Do this in memory of me" could as well be translated "Do this to bring me into your present"' (Aidan Nichols, *The service of glory*, pp 15-16). 11 Cf. HTL, 2000, nos. 12 and 13.

3) the Eucharist as the Sacrifice of the New Testament. At the Last Supper, Christ – miraculously and in an unbloody manner – brought forward his Passion and Death. Every Mass from then on renews the Sacrifice of our Lord on the Cross, Jesus Christ once again offering his life to the Father on our behalf as he did on Calvary.[12] In Matthew's account – 'For this is the blood of the Covenant, which is poured out for many for the forgiveness of sins' (26:28) – we see the fulfilment of the Isaian prophecies (chapter 53) which spoke of the atoning death of Christ for all men. Only Christ's sacrifice is capable of atoning to the Father, and the Mass has all this power because it is that very sacrifice.[13]

The words of consecration of the chalice (cf. Mk 14:23-25) clearly show that the Eucharist is a sacrifice: the Blood of Christ is poured out, sealing the new and definitive covenant of God with men. This covenant remains sealed forever by the sacrifice of Christ on the Cross, in which Christ is both priest and victim. The words pronounced by Christ over the chalice must have been very revealing for the Apostles, because they show that the sacrifices of the Old Covenant were in fact a preparation for and anticipation of Christ's sacrifice.[14] In the Last Supper Christ already offered himself voluntarily to his Father as a victim to be sacrificed. Thus the Supper and the Mass constitute with Calvary one and the same unique and perfect sacrifice, for in all three cases the victim offered is the same – Christ; and the Priest is the same, Christ.[15] He brings the Passover to fulfilment with his redeeming death and his resurrection, according to the world of St Paul: 'Christ our paschal lamb has been sacrificed'(1 Cor 5:7).

12 'The Last Supper, which anticipated the death of Jesus; the eucharistic sacrifice, which re-enacts it; the biblical narratives which describe it; and even the prophecies and events of the Old Testament, which prefigured it, as well as the terrible vision itself on Calvary, are the various disclosures or appearances, the views within which the saving action performed by Christ toward the Father is made manifest and glorified. All these appearances are important; all are essential. It is not for us to argue which of these God might have dispensed with. They are all part of the manifestation of the sacrifice of the cross, and all must be theologically recognized' (Sokolowski, op. cit., p. 62). 13 Cf. James T. O'Connor, *The Father's Son*, Boston, 1984, pp 200-4. 14 We can find no better explanation of the sacrificial character of the Eucharist than in chapters eight and nine of the letter to the Hebrews. 15 The only difference is that the Supper, which takes place prior to the Cross, anticipates the Lord's death in an unbloody way, and offers a victim soon to be immolated; whereas the Holy Mass offers also in an unbloody manner the victim already immolated on the Cross, the Risen Christ who now exists forever in heaven. On Golgotha, Christ made his own life an offering of eternal value, a redemptive offering which has forever opened the path of communion with God which had been blocked by sin. This means that at the centre of Christ's entire activity stands the bloody sacrifice he offered on Calvary – the sacrifice of the New Covenant, prefigured in the sacrifices of the Old Law by Abraham (cf. Gen 15:10; 22:13), and by Melchizedek (cf. Gen 14;18-19; Heb 7:1-28). See *The Navarre Bible: St Mark's Gospel*,

## THE NEW COMMANDMENT

With his teaching on the new commandment (Jn 13:34) at the Last Supper, Jesus helps the Twelve to understand the fuller implications of sharing in the divine life of grace through the Eucharist. By comparison with the old commandment of loving one's neighbour (cf. Lev 19:17), Christ's commandment is 'new' because of the entirely novel standard against which its demands have to be measured – 'as I have loved you' (Jn 13:34; 15:12) – Christ's unlimited love for his disciples. Three times during the Last Supper our Lord entrusts to the Apostles the new commandment of love (cf. Jn 13:34; cf. 15:12; 17). If this is to be the distinguishing mark of all Christ's followers, it has to characterize Christ's priests in a special way. This is the style of pastoral charity that has to impregnate their mission, which in the first place is the guarantee of real priestly fraternity. The image of Christ surrounded by his own at the Last Supper should fill us with a vibrant sense of brotherhood and communion.[16]

As the disciples listened to Jesus in the Cenacle that evening, the memory of similar teachings would have been recalled to their minds, not least his doctrine about the good shepherd (cf. Jn 10:1-21). With this parable they were instructed about an essential part of their future ministry to souls – they would have to seek out the strays, cure the crippled, and carry the weak on their shoulders (cf. Mt 18:12-14; Lk 15:4-7). But it is not only a question of physical care. Beyond the resonance of Old Testament references, Christ introduced new traits in the role of the shepherd – that of intimate mutual knowledge and affection between the shepherd and the sheep, and the ideal of pastoral self-devotedness by the willingness of the shepherd to give his life for the sheep (cf. Jn 10:11-15). Now Christ's emphasis at the Last Supper on the new commandment (cf. Jn 15:13) defines more fully the nature of the shepherd's pastoral charity. During his visit to Jerusalem in March 2000, reflecting on the many generations of priests who were fruit of that first ordination in the Upper Room, John Paul II recalled the memory of all those who gave their lives as blood martyrs. But he also remembered the martyrdom of priestly lives given faithfully day by day in heroic service of souls. This is the life-sacrifice that God normally asks of his priests, a sacrifice that is hidden and silent but which is equally effective in its own way.

## UNION WITH CHRIST: THE VINE AND THE BRANCHES

As we read through St John's gospel we find those graphic assertions which Jesus makes about himself and which in some way have to find an echo in the

Dublin, 1986, p 172. See also HTL, 2000, no. 8. **16** Cf. HTL, 2000, no.15.

life and ministry of priests: 'I am the bread of life' (6:35); 'I am the light of the world' (8:12); 'I am the door' (10:9); 'I am the good shepherd' (10:11); 'I am the resurrection and the life' (11:25); 'I am the way, the truth, and the life' (14:6). To these self-definitions Jesus now adds a last one: 'I am the vine' (15:5). To be fruitful, he tells us, we have to be joined to the new, true, vine: Christ. By living his life, the life of grace which nourishes the faith of the believer, we are enabled to yield fruits of eternal life for ourselves and for those entrusted to our care (cf. Jn 6:54-56). The image of the vine, often used as a symbol of the Eucharist, also helps priests to understand how the unity of Christ's mystical Body, the Church, is built up through the Eucharist so that all the members are intimately united to their head and thereby to one another (cf. 1 Cor 12:12-26). He also makes the point: 'Every branch that does bear fruit he prunes that it may bear more fruit' (Jn 15:2): this is a reminder that God is not satisfied with a half-hearted commitment, and therefore he purifies his own by means of contradictions and difficulties which are a form of pruning, to enable them produce more fruit. Here we see an image and an explanation of the purpose of suffering. Christ tells us very clearly that separated from him we can do nothing that is supernaturally effective (cf. Jn 15:5). On the other hand, intimacy with Christ brings a double benefit – great pastoral fruitfulness, and the promise that whatever we ask in prayer will be granted (cf. Jn 15:5, 7).


### THEOLOGY OF EUCHARISTIC MINISTRY

Having reviewed the scriptural basis for the Eucharist, we now examine some aspects of the theology of Eucharistic ministry and its relationship with the Cross. The Vatican II decree on the ministry and life of priests affirms that 'the first task of priests ... is to preach the Gospel of God to all men'.[17] People need to hear the word of God clearly articulated before the grace of faith can take root in their souls. Preaching is, then, the priest's first duty in the logical/cronological order because it is a necessary preparation for the exercise of the priest's most important role – the celebration of the Eucharist. This primary responsibility of the priest is described as follows by Vatican II:

> It is in the Eucharistic cult or in the Eucharistic assembly of the faithful (*synaxis*) that they [bishops and priests] exercise in a supreme degree their sacred functions; there, acting in the person of Christ and proclaiming his mystery, they unite the votive offerings of the faithful to the sacrifice of Christ their head, and in the sacrifice of the Mass

17 *Presbyterorum ordinis*, 4. 18 *Lumen gentium*, 28.

they make present again and apply, until the coming of the Lord (cf. 1 Cor 11:26), the unique sacrifice of the New Testament, that namely of Christ offering himself once for all a spotless victim to the Father (cf. Heb 9:11–28).[18]

Thus all the pastoral activity of the priest is a preparation for the Eucharistic sacrifice and finds its fulfilment in it. Administration of the other sacraments, 'and indeed all ecclesiastical ministries and works of apostolate are bound up with the Eucharist and are directed towards it'.[19] Why is this? Because 'in the Blessed Eucharist is contained the whole spiritual good of the Church'.[20] The priest's principal task is therefore 'to teach the faithful to offer the divine victim to God the Father in the sacrifice of the Mass and with the victim to make an offering of their whole life'.[21] As we are reminded in the letter *Dominicae coenae*:

> Our Eucharistic worship, both in the celebration of Mass and in our devotion to the Blessed Sacrament, is like a life-giving current that links our ministerial priesthood to the common priesthood of the faithful, and presents it with its vertical dimension and its central value. The priest fulfils his principal mission and is manifested in all his fullness when he celebrates the Eucharist, and this manifestation is more complete when he himself allows the depth of that mystery to become visible, so that it alone shines forth in people's hearts and minds, through his ministry. This is the supreme exercise of the 'kingly priesthood', 'the source and summit of all Christian life'.[22]

Since the Eucharist as sacrament and sacrifice is the 'the source and summit of the Christian life',[23] it is only natural that the priest should consistently and progressively catechize his people in the fullness of this great mystery. For this reason,

---

19 *Presbyterorum ordinis*, 5. 20 Ibid. Scheeben describes the import of the Eucharist in the following way: 'The significance of the Eucharist comes to this, that the real union of the Son of God with all men is ratified, completed, and sealed in it, and that men are perfectly incorporated in him in the most intimate, real, and substantial manner, so that, as they are his members, they may also partake of his life. The concept of our real and substantial incorporation in Christ is the fundamental idea of the mystery of the Eucharist. It is from this basic idea that we may trace out the relationship of the Eucharist to the mysteries of the Trinity, the Incarnation, and grace' (Matthias Joseph Scheeben, *The mysteries of Christianity*, St Louis, MO, 1946, p. 482). 21 *Presbyterorum ordinis*, 5. 22 HTL, 1980, no. 2. 23 *Sacrosanctum Concilium*, 2.

formation of the faithful concerning the essence of the Holy sacrifice of the Altar is vitally important as is the need to encourage them to participate fruitfully in the Eucharist. Insistence must be made on the observance of the Sunday obligation and on frequent, if not daily, participation in the celebration of the Mass and Holy Communion. Emphasis must be placed on the grave obligations to fulfil the spiritual and corporeal conditions governing the reception of the Body of Christ – especially individual sacramental confession for those conscious that they are not in a state of grace.[24]

*The priest and the third Christian millennium* goes on to point out that since the strength of Christian life in each parish community depends on the rediscovery of the great gift of faith in the Eucharist and its adoration, the new evangelization entails the recovery and consolidation of pastoral practices which manifest belief in the Real Presence of our Lord in the Tabernacle.[25] The priest has therefore a mission to promote Eucharistic worship outside the time of Masses, thereby making his church 'a Christian "house of prayer"'.[26] The spread of Eucharistic adoration in many churches is a welcome sign of this renewal. In this context it can be said that a very effective form of catechesis on the Eucharist is the material care of everything connected with the church, especially the altar and the tabernacle – cleanliness and decor, worthy vestments and sacred vessels, reverence in celebrating the liturgical ceremonies, etc. We are reminded that attention to these details is not a form of esoteric pietism but derives 'from a well-tested theological tradition of devotion to the Blessed Eucharist'.[27]

The guiding objective of the priest's different commitments is, then, to build up a Eucharistic community which sees the Mass as 'the root and the centre of the Christian life'.[28] It is the *centre* in that the faithful, exercising their baptismal priesthood, learn to place on the paten all the events of their lives so that the priest can gather them up and present them to the Father in his offering of the Eucharistic sacrifice. It is through the Mass that they make an offering of their daily work, their crosses, family needs, and a remembrance of the faithful departed.[29] The Mass is the *root* of the interior life because Christians draw from it all the graces and spiritual energy they need to sanctify their daily lives and to bring Christ to the world. The Mass provides the strength necessary to respond to all the moral demands of the present life: 'By sharing in the sacrifice the Cross, the Christian partakes of Christ's self-giving love and is

24 *The priest and the third Christian millennium*, III, 2. 25 Cf. ibid. 26 John Paul II, Address, 12 May 1993. 27 Ibid. 28 *Presbyterorum ordinis*, 14. 29 Cf. *Lumen gentium*, 34; *Christifideles laici*, 14.

equipped and committed to live this same charity in all his thoughts and deeds'.[30]

This point of the relationship between Mass and evangelization is well developed by John Paul II in his letter *Keeping the Sunday holy*:

> Receiving the Bread of Life, the disciples of Christ ready themselves to undertake with the strength of the Risen Lord and his Spirit *the tasks which await them in their ordinary life*. For the faithful who have understood the meaning of what they have done, the Eucharistic celebration does not stop at the church door. Like the first witnesses of the Resurrection, Christians who gather each Sunday to experience and proclaim the presence of the Risen Lord are called *to evangelize and bear witness* in their daily lives. Given this, the Prayer after Communion and the Concluding Rite – the Final Blessing and the Dismissal – need to be better valued and appreciated, so that all who have shared in the Eucharist may come to a deeper sense of the responsibility which is entrusted to them. Once the assembly disperses, Christ's disciples return to their everyday surroundings with the commitment to make their whole life a gift, a spiritual sacrifice pleasing to God (cf. Rom 12:1).[31]

From the Mass, then, come all the supernatural resources which are necessary to generate a vibrant Christian commitment at the personal, family, and community levels. That is why formation for fruitful participation in the Eucharistic sacrifice is a priority for every pastor.

As John Paul II encourages us, we have to repeat to men and women of the Third Millennium this extraordinary message: the Son of God became man

---

30 John Paul II, Encyclical, *Veritatis splendor*, 107 (6 August 1993). The Mass has always been the principal support of Christian families and communities, especially in difficult times. It was very much so in the past. Augustine Birrell, son of a non-conformist minister, was appointed Chief Secretary of Ireland in 1907. He was a keen observer of the religious situation in the country at the beginning of the twentieth century, and he left us his reflections on the significance of Mass for the Irish: 'Our children ... will have to make up their minds what happened at the Reformation. My suggestion is that they will do so in a majority of cases by concentrating their attention upon what will seem to them most important. And especially will they bend their minds upon the Mass. Nobody nowadays, except for a handful of vulgar fanatics, speaks irreverently of the Mass. It is the Mass that matters. It is the Mass that makes the difference; so hard to define, so subtle it is yet so perceptible between a Catholic country and a Protestant one, between Dublin and Edinburgh. Here I believe is one of the battlefields of the future' (Fr Augustine, OFM Cap., *Ireland's loyalty to the Mass*, London, 1933, pp 206, 208-9). 31 John Paul II, Apostolic Letter, *Dies Domini: on keeping the Sunday holy*, 31 May 1998, no. 45 (italics in original).

for us and offered himself in sacrifice for our salvation. He gives us his Body and Blood as the food of a new life, of a divine life that is no longer subject to death. Through the words 'do this in remembrance of me' the infinite riches of salvation, including the power to rehabilitate human freedom destroyed by sin, are made available to humanity for all time.[32] This same command, associated with the event of Calvary, surpasses the limits of history, allowing the person of Christ to accompany the new People of God on their journey until the end of time.[33]

In a way, the miracle of the loaves and fishes marks the beginning of a long historical process: the uninterrupted multiplication in the Church of the Bread of new life for the people of every race and culture. Priests, faithful to the divine Master's command, never cease to break and distribute the Eucharistic bread from generation to generation. With this bread of life, countless saints and martyrs were nourished and from it drew strength to resist even harsh and prolonged sufferings because they believed in the words spoken by Jesus in Capernaum: 'if any one eats of this bread he will live forever' (Jn 6:51).[34] This same Eucharistic bread will provide the spiritual nourishment to energize the programme of evangelization proposed by the Holy Father for the new millennium.

### EUCHARISTIC IDENTITY

The priest 'can submerge himself every day in this mystery of redemption and grace by celebrating the Holy Mass'[35] an action which defines the Eucharistic identity of the priest:

> The Eucharist is the principal and central *raison d'être* of the sacrament of the priesthood, which effectively came into being at the moment of the institution of the Eucharist, and together with it ... Through our ordination we are united in a singular and exceptional way to the Eucharist. In a certain way we derive from it and exist for it. We are also in a special way responsible for it.[36]

Priesthood, then, cannot be understood without the Eucharist. It is our principal ministry and our greatest power is in relation to it:

> The Eucharist could not exist without us; but without the Eucharist we do not exist, or we are reduced to lifeless shadows. The priest there-

32 Cf. Address, 25 June 2000, no. 4. 33 Cf. *The Eucharist and freedom*, ibid., no. 14. 34 Cf. John Paul II, homily, 22 June 2000, no. 3. 35 HTL, 1999, no. 6. 36 HTL, 1980, no. 2.

fore can never reach complete fulfilment if the Eucharist does not become the centre and root of his life, so that all his activity is nothing but an irradiation of the Eucharist.[37]

The Eucharist will continue to have a great novelty and attraction for the priest if he tries to penetrate this mystery more deeply every day through prayer, study, and devotion. Certainly the rich tradition of the Church has much to tell us about the content of this sacrament, but

> we can say with certainty that, although this teaching is sustained by the acuteness of theologians, by men of deep faith and prayer, and by ascetics and mystics, in complete fidelity to the Eucharistic mystery, it still reaches no more than the threshold, since it is incapable of grasping and translating into words what the Eucharist is in all its fullness, what is expressed by it and what is actuated by it. Indeed, the Eucharist is the ineffable Sacrament![38]

Nevertheless, the centrality of the Eucharist in the life of the priest goes well beyond the sphere of personal devotion:

> It constitutes the directing criterion, the permanent dimension of all his pastoral activity, the indispensable means for the authentic renewal of the Christian people.[39]

### THEOLOGICAL ERRORS

Because of the shortage of priests in some countries since Vatican II, theological opinions began to circulate which reinterpreted the role of the minister of the Eucharist. In summary these erroneous positions held that the power to confect the Eucharist does not absolutely require sacramental ordination conferred through the imposition of the bishop's hands. On the basis of this approach it was claimed that a remedy for the lack of ordained priests, causing people to be deprived of the Eucharist over long periods, could be achieved by

37 Address, 16 February 1984, no. 2. 38 John Paul II, Encyclical, *Redemptor hominis*, 20. 39 Ibid, no. 4. John Paul II continues: 'Therefore, if we want Christian love to be a reality in life; if we want Christians to be a community united in the apostolate and in the common attitude of resistance to the powers of evil; if we want ecclesial communion to become an authentic place of encounter, of hearing the Word of God, of revision of life, of becoming aware of the problems of the Church – every effort must be made to give the Eucharistic celebration its entire power to express the event of the salvation of the community'.

the community designating from among their number a president who, by virtue of such designation, would have all the faculties to lead it, including that of consecrating the Eucharist.[40] In response to this claim, a 1983 letter from the Congregation for the Doctrine of the Faith pointed out how such an attitude is 'absolutely incompatible with the faith as it has been handed down, since not only does it deny the special power conferred on priests, but it undermines the entire apostolic structure of the Church and distorts the sacramental economy of salvation itself'. The letter warns that 'Catholics who attempt to celebrate the Eucharist outside the sacred bond of apostolic succession established by the Sacrament of Orders exclude themselves from participating in the unity of the single body of the Lord: they neither nourish nor build up the community, they tear it apart'.[41] In articulating clearly the traditional doctrine of the Church on this point, the magisterium was defending not only the irreplaceable role of the sacramentally ordained minister in the celebration of the Eucharistic sacrifice, but the very identity of the Catholic priesthood.

To arrive at the identity of the priest from another perspective, it is revealing to study the process by which, at the beginning of the Reformation in England, Thomas Cranmer, archbishop of Canterbury, gradually eliminated the traditional profile of the Catholic priest from the doctrine and liturgy of the Church in England. Since the new religion of the fledgling *Ecclesia Anglicana* was based on justification by faith alone, the Mass and the sacramental system had effectively become redundant. Consequently, in the revised Edwardine ordinal (1552), Cranmer replaced the concept of the priest as mediator by the Lutheran notion of the priest as minister of the word. There was no further reference to the priest as sacrificer; Mass altars were torn down and replaced by communion tables.[42] This evisceration of the liturgical books created a discontinuity in the effectiveness of Anglican orders, eventually leading to them being declared null and void by Leo XIII.[43]

## MINISTRY OF THE EUCHARIST

It is clear that the priest has always sanctified himself through the celebration of the Eucharist, and it is from here, the Holy Sacrifice of the Mass, that the

40 Cf., for example, the March 1980 edition of *Concilium*, with the introduction by E. Schillebeeckx and J-B. Metz. See also E. Schillebeeckx, *Ministry: a case for change*, London 1981; idem, *The Church with a human face: a new and expanded theology of ministry*, London, 1985. 41 Letter from the Congregation for the Doctrine of the Faith on 'Certain questions concerning the minister of the Eucharist' (*Sacerdotium ministeriale*), 6 August 1983. 42 Cf. Eamon Duffy, *The stripping of the altars: traditional religion in England 1400-1580*, New Haven, 1992; Diarmaid McCulloch, *Thomas Cranmer: a life*, London, 1996. 43 Cf. Leo XII, Apostolic letter, *Apostolicae curae*, 13 September 1896.

most specific aspect of his spirituality is born. This of course applies to all Christians in that for them, as Vatican II affirms, the Mass is the centre of the interior life, but it applies to the priest in a special way.[44]

> Priests as ministers of the sacred mysteries, especially in the sacrifice of the Mass, act in a special way in the person of Christ who gave himself as a victim to sanctify men. And this is why they are invited to imitate what they handle, so that as they celebrate the mystery of the Lord's death they may take care to mortify their members from vices and concupiscences.[45]

In the Mass the priest discovers the depths of the mystery of Christ and, as a consequence, he grows in appreciation of the mystery of his own priesthood by which he has been configured sacramentally to Christ the Priest, to the point of being able to act *in persona Christi*. In symmetry with what *Lumen gentium* says to all the faithful, asking them to unite themselves to Christ at Mass[46], *Presbyterorum ordinis* counsels priests that

> when they unite themselves with the act of Christ the Priest they daily offer themselves completely to God, and by being nourished with Christ's Body they share in the charity of him who gives himself as food to the faithful.[47]

It is a matter of making what he does on the altar a reality in his own life. On Calvary Christ was priest and victim. In the sacrifice of the Mass the priest exercises the sacred power of Christ the priest, but he is also required, by the very nature of the priesthood, to become identified with Christ the victim. While it is true that all the faithful, in virtue of their baptismal priesthood, are invited to reproduce in their lives the sentiments of Christ, nevertheless, the spirituality of the priest should be marked in a special way by these sentiments, both for his own sake and for the sake of the people for whom he offers the sacrifice of the altar.[48]

'To form and rule the priestly people' – that is the basic reason of his priesthood, such that through the exercise of his ministry the royal priesthood of the laity reaches its fullness in the Eucharistic sacrifice.[49] When the priest

44 Cf. *Lumen gentium*, 10, 34; *Sacrosanctum Concilium*, 10. 45 *Presbyterorum ordinis*, 13. 46 Cf. *Lumen gentium*, 10, 11. 47 *Presbyterorum ordinis*, 13. 48 Cf. *Lumen gentium*, 10. 49 Looking back on fifty years of priesthood, John Paul II helps us penetrate more deeply into this central element of priestly identity and priestly spirituality: 'The priest, as steward of the "mysteries of God", is at the service of the common priesthood of the faithful. By proclaiming the word and celebrating the sacraments, especially the Eucharist, he makes the

truly appreciates the nourishment he receives from the Body of Christ, he will encourage the faithful to receive regularly as a means to grow in the Christian life. He will also take special care to see that no one is deprived of the great spiritual assistance of the Viaticum as they approach the definitive stage of their journey to eternal life.

Commenting on his experience as a priest for half a century, John Paul II affirms,

> *The priest is a man of the Eucharist.* In the span of nearly fifty years of priesthood, what is still the most important and the most sacred moment for me is the celebration of the Eucharist. My awareness of celebrating *in persona Christi* at the altar prevails. Never in the course of these years have I failed to celebrate the Most Holy Sacrifice. If this has occurred, it has been due entirely to reasons independent of my will. *Holy Mass is the absolute centre of my life and of every day of my life.* It is at the heart of the theology of the priesthood, a theology I learned not so much from text books as from the living example of holy priests.[50]

Consequently, when the priest begins to forget that the celebration of the Mass is the most important part of his ministry and the source of all his effectiveness, he runs the risk of losing sight of the central meaning of his life. This is because,

whole People of God ever more aware of its share in Christ's priesthood, and at the same time encourages it to live that priesthood to the full. When, after the consecration, he says the words *Mysterium fidei*, all are invited to ponder the rich existential meaning of this proclamation, which refers to the mystery of Christ, the Eucharist, and the priesthood. *Is this not the deepest reason behind the priestly vocation?*... Fifty years after my ordination, I can say that in the words *Mysterium fidei* we find ever more each day the meaning of our own priesthood. Here is the measure of the gift which is the priesthood, and here is also the measure of the response which this gift demands'(*Gift and mystery*, p. 79 [italics in original]). 50 Address, 27 October 1995, no, 4 (italics in original). Summing up half a century of priestly life, John Paul II explains why offering the Eucharist sacrifice is totally rewarding even at the human level: 'In our world, is there any greater fulfilment of our humanity than to be able to re-present every day *in persona Christi* the redemptive sacrifice, the same sacrifice which Christ offered on the Cross? In this sacrifice, on the one hand, the very mystery of the Trinity is present in the most profound way, and, on the other hand, the entire created universe is "united" (cf. Eph 1:10) ... This is why in the thanksgiving after Holy Mass the Old Testament canticle of the three young men is recited: *Benedicite omnia opera Domini Domino.* For in the Eucharist all creatures seen and unseen, and man in particular, bless God as Creator and Father; they bless him with the words and the action of Christ, the Son of God' (*Gift and mystery*, ibid., pp 73-4).

priestly identity shines forth in a very special way in the Eucharist. Assimilation to Christ hinges on it; it is the basis of an ordered life of prayer and genuine pastoral charity.[51]

The Pope explains why offering the sacrifice of the Mass in all its cosmic reality is the key to the identity of the priest:

> The priesthood, in its deepest reality, *is the priesthood of Christ*. It is Christ who offers himself, his Body and Blood, in sacrifice to God the Father, and by this sacrifice makes righteous in the Father's eyes all mankind and, indirectly, all creation. The priest, in his daily celebration of the Eucharist, goes to the very heart of this mystery. For this reason, the celebration of the Eucharist must be the most important moment of the priest's day, the centre of his life.[52]

Thus the priest needs to become totally immersed in the supernatural action of the Mass because there is a real danger that his attention to horizontal interaction with the congregation could create a distraction, causing him to lose focus on the profound mystery taking place in his hands.[53] It goes without saying that a deep understanding of the liturgy is essential for the priest's personal identification with Christ in the Mass and an effective ministry of the Eucharist.[54]

## EUCHARISTIC DEVOTION

At the end of his long discourse at the Last Supper (cf. Jn 13-16), we have in chapter seventeen of St John the priestly prayer of Jesus. It is given that name because our Lord addresses the Father in a moving dialogue in which as priest he offers him the immanent sacrifice of his passion and death. It shows us the

51 Idem, Address, 22 October 1993, no. 3. 52 *Gift and mystery*, ibid., p. 75. 53 Scheeben offers a penetrating insight into the mystery of the Mass: 'The mystery of the Eucharist is ontologically joined to the mystery of the Incarnation, just as the mystery of the Incarnation is joined to the Trinity. The Incarnation is the presupposition and explanation of the Eucharist, just as the eternal generation from the bosom of the Father is the presupposition and explanation of the Incarnation, regarded as the stepping forth of God's Son into the world. These mysteries disclose a remarkable analogy and relationship with one another. All three show us the same Son of God: the first in the bosom of his eternal Father, whence he receives his being; the second in the womb of the Virgin, through which he enters the world; the third in the heart of the Church, where he so sojourns by an enduring, universal presence among men and unites himself to them' (Scheeben, ibid., pp 477-8). 54 Cf. Chapter 12 below for a development of this aspect of the theology of priestly ministry.

essential elements of his redemptive mission and provides us with teaching and a model for our own priestly prayer. In the course of his conversation with his Father (Jn 17:11-19) Jesus prays for his disciples, his first priests, and asks the Father for four specific favours for them: unity, perseverance, joy, and holiness. We can be sure that Jesus prayed then, not only for those who were with him in the Upper Room, but for all those priests who would follow in their footsteps across the centuries. We should never doubt that each of us was present to his mind as he prepared to offer himself in sacrifice for mankind.

Contemplation of the Eucharist helps us to penetrate more deeply into the Incarnation and the Redemption, and convinces us of the validity of the Church's sacramental system entrusted to it by Christ, and 'the whole sacramental style of the Christian's life'.[55] 'Eucharistic worship', John Paul II adds, 'is not so much worship of the inaccessible transcendence as worship of the divine condescension, and it is also the merciful and redeeming transformation of the world in the human heart'.[56]

The Pope devotes his 1980 Holy Thursday letter (*Dominicae coenae*) in its entirety to the theme of the Eucharist. It is, theologically, a very rich document which goes to the core of priestly ministry, reminding us that we have primary responsibility for the Eucharist – for its consecration, its distribution, its reservation and adoration. The deepening of Eucharistic worship, the Pope tells us in this letter, is the central point, and proof of the authentic renewal which Vatican II set itself as its aim.[57]

The Curé of Ars was the subject of the Pope's 1986 Holy Thursday letter to commemorate the bicentenary of the birth of this remarkable priest. The extent of his pastoral work was enormous, yet he spent long hours every day in adoration before the Blessed Sacrament. Although he was a man who practised a rigorous personal poverty, he did not hesitate to spend generously to embellish his church. As a consequence, his parishioners quickly developed the habit of praying before the Blessed Sacrament, 'discovering through the attitude of their pastor, the grandeur of the mystery of faith'.[58]

Through the centuries, countless priests have found in the Eucharist the consolation promised by Jesus on the evening of the Last Supper (cf. Jn:16:22). Here is the secret to overcoming solitude, the strength to bear sufferings, the fortitude to make a new beginning after every discouragement, and the inner energy to confirm our resolution to be faithful no matter what the difficulties.[59]

---

55 HTL, 1986, no.7.  56 Ibid.  57 Cf. HTL, 1980, no. 3. He gives the reasons why: 'The Church and the world have a great need of Eucharistic worship. Jesus waits for us in this Sacrament of Love. Let us be generous with our time in going to meet Him in adoration and in contemplation that is full of faith, and ready to make reparation for the great faults and crimes of the world. May our adoration never cease' (ibid).  58 HTL, 1986, no.8  59 Cf. HTL, 2000, no. 14.

The need to pray, and the claim that Christ has on our friendship, can find practical expression in a daily period of meditation before the Tabernacle. If the priest is to live his dedication faithfully, 'he must find time to remain alone with God, listening to what he tells us in silence. It is therefore necessary to be prayerful souls, Eucharistic souls'.[60] We need to make a definite, generous commitment in this regard.

> Never believe that the yearning for intimate conversation with the Eucharistic Jesus, the hours spent on your knees before the tabernacle, will halt or slow down the dynamism of your ministry. What is given to God is never lost for man. The profound demands of spirituality and the priestly ministry remain substantially unchanged throughout the centuries, and tomorrow, just as today, they will have their fulcrum and their reference point in the Eucharistic mystery.[61]

If the deepening of Eucharistic worship is the central aim of the Council renewal, how can this become a reality if priests do not lead the way by the example of their own Eucharistic piety? Pope John Paul II's vision of Eucharistic worship is surely impressive if measured against the target he sets in his 1980 letter: 'it should fill our churches also outside the timetable of Masses'.[62]

The Eucharist has been entrusted to us for the benefit of the faithful who have a right to 'expect from us a particular witness of veneration and love towards this Sacrament',[63] because 'the Eucharist writes the history of human hearts and of human communities'.[64] Hence, this identity will be confirmed for people when they see their priests do a thanksgiving after Mass, pray before the tabernacle, and make visits to the Blessed Sacrament.[65]

J.R.R. Tolkien, reflecting on a period when he had nearly ceased practising the faith, intimates how he was rescued by 'the never-ceasing, silent appeal of the Tabernacle, and the sense of starving hunger'.[66] Writing to his son about marriage, Tolkien, in a revealing account of his own soul, advises him:

> Out of the darkness of my life, so much frustrated, I put before you the one great thing to love on earth: the Blessed Sacrament ...There you will find romance, glory, honour, fidelity, and the true way of all

60 John Paul II, Address, 11 June 1982. 61 Idem, Address, 16 February 1984, no. 2, 3. 62 HTL,1980, no.3 63 Ibid. 64 Address, 29 September 1979, no. 2. 65 The responsibility of the priest to prepare well for Mass is specified in canon 909 of the Code of Canon Law: 'A priest is not to omit dutifully to prepare himself by prayer before the celebration of the Eucharist, nor afterwards to omit to make thanksgiving to God'. 66 J.R.R. Tolkien, *Letters*, ed. H. Carpenter, London 1981, p. 340.

your loves on earth, and more than that: Death: by the divine paradox, that which ends life, and demands the surrender of all, and yet by the taste (or foretaste) of which alone can what you seek in your earthly relationships (love, faithfulness, joy) be maintained, or take on that complexion of reality, of eternal endurance, which every man's heart desires.[67]

Tolkien's deep appreciation of the Real Presence was the foundation of his faith. It also had a profound influence on his literary philosophy.[68]

We can never afford to forget those majestic and demanding words addressed to us by the bishop on ordination day: *Agnosce quod agis, imitare quod tractabis, et vitam tuam mysterio dominicae crucis conforma.*[69] Love for the Eucharist, nourished by our daily prayer before the Tabernacle, will teach us to treat the bread and wine become the Body and Blood of Christ with great liturgical refinement. Our hands have been anointed to make them worthy to cradle Christ's Body, and so we understand well why the Holy Father, with exquisite humility, 'would like to ask forgiveness ... for everything which, for whatever reason, through whatever human weakness, impatience or negligence ... may have caused scandal and disturbance concerning the interpretation of the doctrine and the veneration due to this great Sacrament'.[70]

Despite all the supernatural evidence for the Real Presence, there is still perhaps a reluctance to face the Tabernacle, to live out the full demands of this aspect of our faith. As priests we have a duty not to abandon our Eucharistic Lord, but to try to respond generously to the immense love that his continuous Presence implies.[71] We will make many discoveries about ourselves there, but none more important than the fact that we are co-redeemers. Eucharistic meditation deepens our awareness of the evil of sin as a rejection of Christ's personal love. Until we place ourselves totally in his hands, ready to suffer cheerfully, we will never experience the fullness of the joy of the priesthood.[72]

The Eucharistic liturgy is a pre-eminent school of Christian prayer, especially through adoration of the Blessed Sacrament by which the faithful can enjoy the experience of the 'abiding' love of Christ (cf. Jn 15:5).[73] The Eucharist is a mystery of presence and this is experienced particularly in silent prayer before the tabernacle and in the traditional forms of Eucharistic adora-

---

67 Ibid., pp 53-4. 68 Cf. Joseph Pearce, *Tolkien: man and myth: a literary life*, London, 1999. 69 'Know what you are doing, and imitate the mystery you celebrate; model your life on the mystery of the Lord's cross' *(Pontificale Romanum. De ordinatione diaconi, presbyteri et episcopi*, ed. typica, 1968, p. 93). 70 HTL, 1980, no.12. 71 Cf. John Paul II, Address, 9 June 1993, no. 6. 72 Cf. Sheen, *Those mysterious priests*, p. 182. 73 Cf. HTL, 1999, no. 6.

tion. However, in contemporary culture the perception of mystery has been greatly diminished, since activism is generally regarded as the only real form of fulfilled living. The attitude of meditation, reflection and wonder has been lost to a large extent and thus, even for believers, it is difficult for them to remain in God's presence in a spirit of adoration, thanksgiving, reparation and dedication. Yet because the human person can only recognize his true self in something beyond himself, that is, in the mystery of God, it is only in the truth about the Eucharist and its transcendence that we can fully discover and understand the mystery of our own being.[74] Contemplation before the Blessed Sacrament makes it possible for us to rediscover the mystery of Christ, and our own involvement in it, away from the bustle and superficiality in which at times we are immersed.[75] Prayer before the tabernacle awakens a response of service and love to our Eucharistic Lord and from it will come many graces. It is generally in the good spiritual soil created by this Eucharistic environment that the seed of vocation takes root and grows to recognition and commitment.

### THE CROSS IN THE LIFE OF THE PRIEST

The Eucharist is, of course, inextricably linked to the mystery of the Cross. Through the Incarnation Christ introduced something entirely novel to the priesthood of the Old Testament because, unlike the line of Levi, he united in himself the role of priest and victim (cf. Jn 10:18; Heb 5:9-10). As priest, Christ, who was sinless, offered his life for us. As a victim he was identified with sinners: 'For our sake he made him to be sin who knew no sin, so that in him we might become the righteousness of God' (2 Cor 5:21). On the cross he speaks first as priest: 'Father, forgive them for they know not what they do'(Lk 23:34). As victim he experiences all the loneliness and alienation of sinners:

---

74 In response to post-modernism's agnosticism about meaning, Catherine Pickstock affirms the significance of the Eucharistic mystery for recovering the grounds for meaningful language : 'The Eucharist underlies all language, since in carrying the secrecy, uncertainty, and discontinuity which characterize every sign to an extreme (no body appears in the bread), it also delivers a final disclosure, certainty, and continuity (the bread is the Body) which alone makes it possible now to trust every sign. In consequence we are no longer uncertainly distanced from the "original event" by language, but rather, we are *concelebrants of that event* in every word we speak (the event as transcendental category, whose transcendentality is revealed to be the giving of the Body and Blood of Christ). The words of Consecration "This is my Body" therefore, far from being problematic in their meaning, *are the only words which certainly have meaning, and lend this meaning to all other words'* (*After writing: on the liturgical consummation of philosophy*, Malden, Mass., 1998, pp 262-3, italics in original). 75 Cf. *The Eucharist and freedom*, ibid., nos. 25, 26.

'My God, my God, why have you forsaken me' (Mt 27:45).[76] Hence the inspiration of our priesthood needs to be nurtured by those dramatic words of St Paul to the Philippians:

> Have this mind among yourselves, which was in Christ Jesus, who, though he was in the form of God, did not count equality with God a thing to be grasped, but emptied himself, taking the form of a servant, being born in the likeness of men. And being found in human form he humbled himself and became obedient unto death, even death on a cross (Phil 2:5-8).

To be truly priests after the manner of Christ we should also be ready to offer ourselves as victims for sin as Christ did. Yet, how often we tend to return to the style of the Levitical priesthood in the sense that we see ourselves as priests, but not as victims. Do we at times, as Fulton Sheen asks, offer Mass as if we presented a victim for sin who was totally unrelated to us, like the scapegoat of the Old Testament?[77] Do we offer the Christ-Saviour to the Father as if we were not dying with him? If we are to be truly other Christ's, we cannot escape reproducing in ourselves the mystery enacted on the altar. On the other hand 'if we at Mass eat and drink Divine Life and bring no death of our own to incorporate into the death of Christ through sacrifice, we deserve to be thought of as parasites on the Mystical Body of Christ'.[78] Trenchant criticism that must give us pause.[79]

In the Mass we relive those dark mysterious hours when Christ, dying on the Cross, cried out: 'My God, my God, why have you abandoned me?' (Mk 15:34), and then, 'All is accomplished' (Jn 19:30). These expressions are familiar to every Christian, but especially to the priest. As John Paul II reminds us, they speak of our living and dying, and resonate with those other words of the Liturgy of the Hours which we pray at the end of every day: 'Into your hands, Lord, I commend my Spirit', to prepare ourselves for the great mystery of our passage, of our own personal exodus. Then, nourished by the Eucharist, pledge of eternal life, Christ by virtue of his resurrection will take us to himself to present us to the heavenly Father.[80]

One of the Pope's abiding memories from his seminary days in Krakow is the custom of reciting the 'Litany of our Lord Jesus Christ, priest and victim', especially on the eve of a priestly ordination. All the rich symbolism of its biblical images, taken especially from the Letter to the Hebrews, calls to mind many aspects of Christ's priesthood. He tells us that he has often recited it dur-

---

76 Cf. Fulton Sheen, *Those mysterious priests*, p. 46.  77 Cf. Fulton Sheen, *The priest is not his own*, London 1964, p. 7.  78 Ibid., p. 9.  79 Cf. McGovern, *Priestly celibacy today*, p. 180.  80 Cf. HTL, 1999, no. 2.

ing his fifty years as a priest, leading him to a deeper understanding of the truth about redemption and the Redeemer which 'has been central to me; it has been with me all these years, it has permeated all my pastoral experiences, and it has continued to reveal new riches to me'.[81]

The grace of ordination gives the priest the sense of spiritual fatherhood, yet, as John Paul II points out,

> it is Eucharistic love that daily renews his fatherhood and makes it fruitful, transforming him ever more into Christ and, like Christ, makes him become the bread of souls, their priest, yes, but also their victim, because for them he is gladly consumed in imitation of him who gave his life for the salvation of the world[82]... The priest, among all the faithful, is especially called to identify himself mystically – as well as sacramentally – with Christ in order to be himself in some way *Sacerdos et Hostia*, according to the beautiful expression of St Thomas Aquinas (cf. *Summa Theol.*, III, 83, 1, ad 3).[83]

We never offer our Mass as individuals. It is an action of the whole Mystical Body of Christ, and the more the priest is conscious of this great supernatural reality when he ascends the altar, the deeper will be his awareness of the extraordinary intercessory power of the Mass.[84] It is here that the priest can pre-eminently find the grace to be a co-redeemer with Christ if he sincerely asks for this gift.[85] If we seriously try to appropriate and to reproduce in

81 *Gift and mystery*, ibid., pp 80, 81, 82. 82 Address, 16 February 1984, no. 3. 83 Address, 12 May 1993, no. 2. 84 'In the mystery of the Eucharistic sacrifice, in which priests fulfil their principal function, the work of our redemption is continually carried out. For this reason the daily celebration of it is earnestly recommended. This celebration is an act of Christ and the Church even if it is impossible for the faithful to be present. So when priests unite themselves with the act of Christ the priest they daily offer themselves completely to God, and by being nourished with Christ's Body they share in the charity of him who gives himself as food to the faithful' (*Presbyterorum ordinis*, 13). 85 'When we celebrate the Eucharist, we hold God's grain of wheat in our hands: the bread that is Christ, the Lord, himself; the fruit that has grown a hundredfold from the death of the grain of wheat, and has become the bread of the entire world. Thus the bread of the Eucharist is for us at once the sign of the Cross and the sign of God's great and joyful harvest. It looks back to the Cross, to the grain of wheat that died. But it also looks forward to God's great wedding feast to which many will come from east and west, from north and south (cf. Mt 8:11); indeed, the wedding feast has already begun here in the celebration of the holy Eucharist, where men and women of all races and classes can be God's happy guests at table. It is the priest's finest and most sublime ministry that he can be the servant of this holy meal, that he may transform and distribute this bread of unity. For him, too, this bread will have a double meaning. It will, to start with, remind him too of the Cross. At the end he, too, must somehow be God's grain of wheat: he cannot be content with giving only words and external actions, he must

our lives Christ's role as Victim, then we will have greater confidence that the fruits of the redemption will be applied more efficaciously to our pastoral tasks.

> It is suffering, more than anything else, which clears the way for the grace which transforms human souls. Suffering, more than anything else, makes present in the history of humanity the powers of the Redemption. In that 'cosmic' struggle between the spiritual powers of good and evil, spoken of in the Letter to the Ephesians (cf. Eph 6:12), human sufferings, united to the redemptive suffering of Christ, *constitute a special support for the powers of good*, and open the way to the victory of those salvific powers.[86]

### MORTIFICATION

In order to become other Christs we will perseveringly try to subdue the passions and sinful impulses of our nature (cf. Gal 5:24), because we realize that we have a duty to fill up those sufferings which are wanting in the passion of Christ to apply them to individual souls (cf. Col 1:24), our own in the first place. St Paul speaks about carrying about in his body the death of Jesus, so that the life of the same Jesus may be manifested in our bodies (cf. 2 Cor 4:10). To ensure that his preaching is effective, Paul treats his body severely: 'I pummel my body and subdue it, lest after preaching to others I myself should be disqualified' (1 Cor 9:27).[87]

Mortification is the prayer of the body and without it our priestly prayer is incomplete. Perseverance in priestly tasks despite tiredness, regular small acts of self-denial in areas of comfort, food and entertainment, the effort to maintain a constant programme of parish visitation – these are fruitful sources of daily sacrifice. Through mortification we need to redeem our emotional ambiguities and the often contradictory desires of the heart. This is not a merely negative enterprise in purification, but one which has an essentially positive objective – to create the space and dispositions to share more deeply in the love of the heart of Christ. If we want to become spiritual stones, suitable for building up the spiritual edifice of the Church,

add a piece of his heart's blood – himself. His fate is tied to God' (Cardinal Joseph Ratzinger, *Ministers of joy: meditations on priestly spirituality*, Slough, 1989, pp 20-1). **86** John Paul II, Apostolic Letter, *Salvifici doloris*, 27 (11 February 1984) (italics in original). **87** During the persecutions of the early Christians, St Ignatius of Antioch encouraged his fellow bishop Polycarp in the same way: 'Stand your ground like an anvil under the hammer. The mark of a true champion is to stand up to punishment and still come out victorious. It is our duty, we must accept the fate of being cut and carved. In order to be suitable for the house we must let ourselves be bent into shape for the places where we are needed. Those who want to be stones in and for the whole must let themselves be bound to the whole. They can no longer just do whatever comes to mind and seems worthwhile. They can no longer go just wherever they want. They must accept that their belt will be fastened by another and they will also be led where they do not want to go (cf. Jn 21:18). In John's Gospel we find another image for this – the vine that is to bear fruit must be pruned; it must let itself be cut. Only the pain of being pruned produces a greater harvest (cf. Jn 15:2).[88]

We need to express our gratitude to God for the sublime gift of the priesthood. 'But', as St Paul points out very clearly, 'we have this treasure in earthen vessels, to show that the transcendent power belongs to God and not to us' (2 Cor 4:7) – our pastoral effectiveness comes from God, and not as a result of our talents or personal efforts. True identification with Christ means that we have to be ready to bear with the suffering and tribulation as a normal part of life 'so that the life of Jesus may be manifested in our mortal flesh' (2 Cor 4:11). An early ecclesiastical writer put it this way:

> If it is your ambition to win the esteem of men, if you desire to be well regarded and seek only a life of ease, you have gone astray ... In the city of the saints, entrance is given, and rest and eternal rule with the King, only to those who have made their way along the rough, narrow way of tribulation.[89]

In summary, suffering is necessary for us because it is the normal way to grow in virtue (cf. Jas 1:2-4; 1 Pet 1:5-7), and to win grace for the conversion of souls.[90] That is why it is providential (cf. Phil 1:19; Col 1:24), leading to joy

particularly when the cause is God's, to accept trials of all kinds, if we ourselves are to be accepted by him' *(Letter to Polycarp,* III, 1). 88 Ratzinger, *A new song for the Lord,* p.164. 89 Pseudo-Macarius, *Homilies,* 12,5. 90 The life of the St Jean Marie Vianney is a great example in this regard. John Paul II describes it as follows: 'Many were the crosses which presented themselves to the Curé of Ars in the course of his ministry: calumny on the part of the people, being misunderstood by an assistant priest or other confrères, contradictions, and also a mysterious struggle against the powers of hell, and sometimes even the temptation to despair in the midst of spiritual darkness. Nonetheless he did not content himself with just accepting these trials without complaining; he went beyond them by *mortification,* imposing on himself continual fasts and many other rugged practices in order "to reduce his body to servitude", as St Paul says. But what we must see clearly in this penance, which our age unhappily has little taste for, are his motives: love of God and the conversion of sinners.

and happiness (1 Thess 1:6). St Thomas Aquinas, who spent all his life among books reading the great inheritance of classical and patristic wisdom, or composing his many volumes on philosophy and theology, said that for him the most important book was the Crucifix. By contemplating it he acquired insights which he could never glean from intellectual enquiry alone. This is the wisdom of the Cross which cannot be acquired in any other school. As icons of the Crucified One we cannot shy away from the challenge of the Cross in our lives. The fortitude to respond to its demands is always available through the intercession of her who was pre-eminently a co-redeemer on Calvary. But the Cross is always the prelude to the Resurrection – the light, joy, and serenity found in self-surrender and its visible fruitfulness in the life of the Christian community.

Perseverance in this love, and keeping faith with the Master, is what will bring joy and happiness, a joy that will be complete even in the midst of difficulties (cf. Jn 15:11). It is inevitable that, following Christ, the priest would experience the cross in his life, just as his first priests did. Our faith may be tested by the experience of our own weaknesses and pastoral failures. In such circumstances we will find strength and consolation in Christ's words to the disciples, after alerting them to the difficulties that lay ahead: 'but I will see you again and your hearts will rejoice, and no one will take your joy from you' (Jn 16:22). If a priest lacks joy in his life it will normally be due to one reason – a refusal to take the cross generously on board. The risen Christ is always available to us, especially in the Mass, Holy Communion, and in the tabernacle. After the Resurrection 'the disciples were glad when they saw the Lord' (Jn 20:20), and they never subsequently lost that inner peace because it was grounded on Christ's promise: 'I am with you always, to the close of the age' (Mt 28:20).

> The Eucharist looks backward in time to the Last Supper and the death and Resurrection of the Lord, and, more remotely, to the Passover and Exodus. It also looks forward to the eternal life that was won for us by Christ on the cross: '*et futurae gloriae nobis pignus datur*; the promise of future glory is given to us'. The Eucharist images the eternal banquet that is the fruit of our Redemption.[91]

Thus he asks a discouraged fellow priest: "You have prayed ..., you have wept ..., but have you fasted, have you kept vigil ...?" Here we are close to the warning of Jesus to the Apostles: "But this kind is cast out only by prayer and fasting" (Mt 17:21)' (HTL, 1986, no. 11). **91** Sokolowski, op. cit., p. 3.

# 7

## Some priestly virtues

Christ, who was perfect God, was also perfect man.[1] Hence the priest cannot neglect the practice of the human and the social virtues. People are attracted by his humanity and his capacity for empathy with their difficulties. They should detect the presence of Christ in his optimism, gentleness, and his ready availability in their needs. To facilitate his role as good shepherd, *Presbyterorum ordinis* says that priests should cultivate 'those virtues which are rightly held in high esteem in human relations. Such qualities as goodness of heart, sincerity, strength and constancy of mind, careful attention to justice, courtesy and others which the apostle Paul recommends' (Phil 4:8).[2] As the present Holy Father has pointed out:

> What are needed are heralds of the Gospel who are experts in humanity, who know the depths of the human hearts of today, participate in their joys and hopes, their anxieties and sorrows, and who are themselves true contemplatives, men who are in love with God.[3]

Since every priest should try to reproduce Christ in himself, he will endeavour to build up the supernatural virtues on a solid human foundation. Thus he will always strive to be cheerful, welcoming and kind. He will not allow provocation, indifference, or bad manners in others to undermine his commitment to be refined and courteous, even when he has to confront people with difficult truths about themselves – above all when he is ministering to them in confession. At the same time he has to try his best to ensure that there is nothing in his personality which conflicts with the personality of Christ.[4]

> In order that his ministry may be humanly as credible and acceptable as possible, it is important that the priest should mould his human personality in such a way that it becomes a bridge and not an obstacle for

1 *Symbolum Athanasium*, DS 76. 2 *Presbyterorum ordinis*, 3. 3 Discourse to European bishops, 11 October 1985. 4 Cf. Sheen, *The priest is not his own*, pp 37-9.

others in their meeting with Jesus Christ the Redeemer of man. It is necessary that, following the example of Jesus who 'knew what was in man' (Jn 2:25; cf. 8:3-11), the priest should be able to know the depths of the human heart, to perceive difficulties and problems, to make meeting and dialogue easy, to create trust and co-operation, to express serene and objective judgements.[5]

The priest will more easily build bridges if he is a person of balanced judgement and behaviour, genuinely compassionate and a man of his word. If he is to be a 'man of communion' he needs to be sincere and affable, open to friendship, quick to understand and forgive. We find a full programme for human formation in the recommendations of St Paul to the Philippians: 'whatever is true, whatever is honourable, whatever is just, whatever is pure, whatever is lovely, whatever is gracious, if there is any excellence, if there is anything worthy of praise, think about these things' (Phil 4:8). It is interesting to note that Paul does not hesitate to offer himself as a model for these profoundly human qualities (cf. Phil 4:9).[6]

Through his daily contact with people the priest learns to sharpen his human sensitivity so as to understand more clearly their needs and to respond to their often unvoiced questions. He knows how to share their hopes and expectations, their joys and disappointments. People today are often trapped in situations of loneliness, especially in the larger urban areas. This applies not just to people who are materially poor. Because of the breakdown of community spirit, human isolation and spiritual poverty are becoming increasingly more common among the not-so-poor also. In such situations parish visitation by priests is in general deeply appreciated, and is often very effective in drawing people back to the practice of the faith.[7]

To be an effective pastor of souls, the different talents and abilities required of a priest have been likened to the virtues that bond a family together:

> He must guide people so that they become capable of reconciliation, forgiving and forgetting, endurance and generosity. He must help them to tolerate others in their otherness, to have patience with others, to exhibit trust, prudence, discretion, and openness to the right degree, and to do still a lot more. Above all, he must be capable of standing by people in their pain – in physical suffering as well as in all the disappointments, debasements, and fears that no one can escape.[8]

5 PDV, 43. 6 Cf. ibid. 7 Cf. PDV, 72. 8 Ratzinger, *A new song for the Lord*, pp 164-5. 9 'The ability to accept and weather suffering is a fundamental condition for succeeding as a human being. Where it is never learned, existence is doomed to failure. Being up-in-arms about

Clearly, the priest will not be able to respond to the needs of people unless he has acquired these virtues beforehand.[9]

The acquisition of these priestly virtues begins in the seminary[10], but the effort to mature them has to continue right through our lives. In the metaphor of St Peter (cf.1 Pet 2:5), we have to become living stones capable of building up the spiritual edifice of the Church. The cutting of these stones to the right shape is a work of great skill which can be achieved only with the help of an expert spiritual guide.[11]

*Pastores dabo vobis* offers a challenging perspective on the virtues and attitudes which should characterize the priest who is trying to sanctify himself in his role as good shepherd of souls:

> This ministry demands of the priest an intense spiritual life, filled with those qualities and virtues which are typical of a person who 'presides over' and 'leads' a community, of an 'elder' in the noblest and richest sense of the word: qualities and virtues such as faithfulness, integrity, consistency, wisdom, a welcoming spirit, friendliness, goodness of heart, decisive firmness in essentials, freedom from overly subjective viewpoints, personal disinterestedness, patience, an enthusiasm for daily tasks, confidence in the value of the hidden workings of grace as manifested in the simple and the poor (cf. Tit 1:7-8).[12]

Let us examine more closely some of these desirable priestly virtues and qualities.

## COMPASSION

To be a priest is not just to have a privileged relationship with God and to be able to speak in his name. If he is to be a mediator between man and God, the priest must, as Hebrews emphasizes, be able to sympathize with human weakness (cf. Heb 4:15). Compassion is then an eminently priestly virtue, and par-

---

everyone and everything contaminates the ground of the soul, so to speak, and turns it into barren land. The priest must learn how to cope with pain ... Everyone knows that without training, and the will-power that goes with it, there is no success. Nowadays one trains for all kinds of skills with enthusiasm and persistence, and in this way record performances in many areas are possible that were once deemed inconceivable. But why does it seem so outlandish to train for real life, for the right life – to practise the arts of denial, of self control, and of freeing ourselves from our addictions' (Ratzinger, ibid., p. 145). **10** Cf. *Optatam totius*, 11; PDV, 43, 44. **11** See Chapter 11 below. **12** PDV, 26.

ticularly of priests of the New Testament.[13] However, compassion on its own is not enough – through holiness of life the priest must be at the same time acceptable to God.

As we have already seen, a characteristic element of the shepherd image in the Old Testament is the exercise of the virtue of compassion. We are told that Jesus, who claimed the title of Good Shepherd (cf. Jn 10 :14), had compassion on the multitude because they were 'like sheep without a shepherd'. Moved by concern for their religious ignorance 'he began to teach them many things' (Mk 6:34). All through the Gospels we recognize in Christ a constant solicitude for the needs of people, material as well as spiritual. We see him moved by the hungry crowd who followed him, giving dead children back to their parents, weeping for the death of Lazarus. As John Paul II explains:

> The charity of the Good Shepherd was revealed not only by his gift of salvation to mankind, but also by his desire to share our life: thus, the Word who became 'flesh' (cf. Jn 1:14) desired to know joy and suffering, to experience weariness, to share feelings, to console sadness. Living as a man among and with men, Jesus Christ offers the most complete, genuine and perfect expression of what it means to be human.[14]

The priest not only makes Christ visible – he has also to make him attractive, spreading around him the *bonus odor Christi*, the sweet fragrance of Christ (cf. 2 Cor 2:15). He makes Christ loveable by being accessible, available. People get to know fairly quickly if a priest is welcoming, or if he consciously or unconsciously erects communication barriers. He can do this by his inability to empathize with others, by always seeming to be in a hurry, by his reluctance to do parish visitation, or by his limited availability for confession. The 'sweet fragrance of Christ' is reflected in his cheerfulness, politeness, and care for the sick. The urbanity and refinement of his conversation should give witness to the fact that he speaks frequently with Christ. As somebody who feeds on the Body and Blood of Christ every day, he should mediate the mind and the sentiments of Jesus.[15]

Some people don't want to look at suffering because it creates responsibility. In the parable of the Good Samaritan (cf. Lk 10 :29-37) the priest and the Levite walked on the other side of the road to avoid having to answer for the needs of their neighbour – they simply didn't want to know. Mother Teresa of

---

13 As Vanhoye points out, compassion was not a characteristic of the Temple priesthood – cf. *Old Testament priests and the new priest*, op. cit., pp 115-16. 14 PDV, 72. 15 Fulton Sheen, *Those mysterious priests*, pp 218-20.

Calcutta expressed the joy experienced at being able to show compassion to others in the following way:

> Being happy with Christ means: loving as He loves, helping as He helps, giving as He gives, serving as He serves, rescuing as He rescues, being with Him twenty-four hours, touching Him in His distressing disguise.[16]

Seeing Christ in others helps us to empathize with them and makes us vulnerable to their needs. As Sheen aptly reminds us, 'love exposes the heart to being broken'.[17] The same admonition was given by a good mother to her priest son: 'Josemaría, you are going to suffer a lot in life, because you put your whole heart into whatever you do'.[18]

From whom do we learn compassion? Because Christ's love and self-giving saved us from our sins, we learn from him how to become unprotected from the demands of others. All through our priestly life we have to face the challenge of availability and accessibility on countless occasions – the unannounced calls about so many different things, perhaps objectively trivial yet so important to the caller; the sick calls which do not adapt to any timetable, day or night; requests for Masses for different intentions; calls about school activities; queries about marriage preparation; the professional spongers often exhaling a cloud of alcohol; the long-suffering wife who can no longer cope with an obnoxious husband.

Christ did not distance himself from the lepers who came to be cleansed, nor from the blind and the lame. He responded generously to the sorrow of the widow of Nain (cf. Lk 7:11-17), to those troubled by demonic possession. He inspired such confidence that the intrepid bearers of a paralyzed man didn't hesitate to rip off the roof of a house to ensure their man was deposited in front of Jesus (cf. Mk 2:1-5).

A very relevant expression today of the shepherd's compassion is his concern for those who have ceased to practise the faith. He cannot remain passive or aloof from whose who have distanced themselves from the Church. If Christ described his mission as one to 'the lost sheep of the house of Israel' (Mt 15:24); if there is more joy in heaven over the one sinner who repents than over the ninety-nine who did not need repentance (cf. Lk 15:7); if the good shepherd can call his sheep by name and they follow him because they recognize his voice (cf. Jn 10 :3, 7, 27) – for all these reasons it is clear that the priest has to use his resourcefulness and apostolic zeal to establish pastoral contact with

16 Malcolm Muggeridge, *Something beautiful for God*, New York, 1971, p. 68. 17 Cf. Sheen. op. cit., p. 72. 18 A. Vázquez de Prada, *The founder of Opus Dei*, vol. 1, Princeton NJ, 2001, p. 120.

drop-outs from the Church and try to reintegrate them into the life of the parish. This will require not only persevering pastoral visitation but also a lot of prayer and sacrifice offered both by the priest himself and the local Christian community.


## HUMILITY

Following the example of Christ, priests 'will most gladly spend themselves and be spent (cf. 2 Cor 12:15) in whatever office is entrusted to them, even the humbler and poorer'.[19] The more occupied we are with Christ and his priorities, the less will we be concerned with personal interests. It is then that the words of the Baptist – 'He must increase, but I must decrease'(Jn 3:30 ) – become more meaningful. We need humility to allow ourselves be appropriated by Christ, to become like him (cf. 2 Cor 3:18) so that we in turn can really bring him to others. As the priest empties himself of the desire to be loved and praised, he will no longer be agitated by anxiety – the very limitations he endures will be a source of spiritual joy if he is united to Christ. Only the spiritually fit can carry the spiritual burdens of others.[20] And to be fit we must acquire the simplicity and humility of children, becoming the servant of all (cf. Mk 9:35; Lk 9:46-48).

The fact that in the Roman Canon priests pray for themselves with the words *nobis quoque peccatoribus* (for us sinners also) is not without significance:

> The official self-description of clerics when facing God does not bespeak dignity; it goes to the heart of the matter. We are 'sinful servants'... It is the same awareness that frightens Peter in the face of the miraculous catch of fish and makes him say: 'Go away from me, Lord, for I am a sinful man' (Lk 5:8) ... The preparation that is required to be able to run the risk of professional nearness to the mystery of God can find its valid expression in the command to Moses to take off his shoes ... We must free ourselves from what is dead so that we can be in proximity to the One who is life. The dead – these are, first of all, the excessive amount of possessions with which people surround themselves. They are also those attitudes which oppose the paschal path: only those who lose themselves find themselves. The priesthood requires leaving bourgeois existence behind; it has to incorporate the losing of oneself in a structural way.[21]

19 *Presbyterorum ordinis*, 15. 20 Cf. Sheen, op. cit., p. 62. 21 Ratzinger, *A new song for the Lord.*, pp 172-3. Ratzinger goes on to affirm the justification for priestly celibacy in this context: 'The Church's connecting celibacy and priesthood is the result of such considerations:

In our therapeutic society we are encouraged to have 'a good self-image' and to reject as weakness a willingness to accept our actual limitations or any admission of failure. We are, of course, made to the image of God and, as a consequence of Baptism, are raised to the dignity of his adopted children, the real foundation for a proper self-esteem. But to achieve a sober estimation of ourselves we have to learn from the humility of Christ who offered himself as an example of this virtue (cf. Mt 11:29). On the other hand Scripture is strewn with examples of those who, blinded by pride, failed to recognize their own self-centredness (cf.. Lk 18:10 -14; 14:7-11) or, as in the case of David, his own egregious sinfulness (cf. 2 Sam 11-12).[22] A balance between an authentic self-esteem and Christian humility can best be acquired through regular spiritual guidance.

## CHEERFULNESS, OPTIMISM

In a priest lack of joy is not so much sadness as an expression of something deeper – a certain lack of faith and hope.[23] For a Christian, optimism is perfectly compatible with the cross, pain, and suffering. 'The only sadness in the world', writes Léon Bloy, 'is the sadness of not being a saint'.[24]

We will often have been edified by the cheerfulness of a hospital patient suffering from a terminal illness. A priest should, must, be able to reflect this same optimism to those who come to him looking for light and encouragement. Christian joy is a response to the fact that God loved us and redeemed us before we ever existed or had any knowledge of him ( cf. 1 Jn 4:10 ). It comes from knowing that we have been selected by Christ in a special way: 'You did not choose me, but I choose you and appointed you that you should go and bear fruit and that your fruit should abide; so that whatever you ask the Father in my name, he may give it to you' (Jn 15:16).

An optimistic view of life is directly related to the theological virtue of hope.[25] What the Christian hopes for at the deepest level is the beatific vision,

celibacy is the strongest contradiction to the ordinary fulfilment of life. Whoever accepts the priesthood deep down inside cannot view it as a profession for making a living; rather he must somehow say 'yes' to the renunciation of his life project and let himself be girded and led by another to a place where he really did not want to go ... Along the entire path, there remains the condition of keeping contact with the Lord alive. For if we turn our eyes from him, we will inevitably end up like Peter on his way to Jesus across the water: only the Lord's gaze can overcome gravity – but it really can. We always remain sinners, but if his gaze holds us the waters of the deep lose their power' (ibid., pp 173-4). **22** Cf. Benedict M. Ashley OP, *Living the truth in love: a biblical introduction to moral theology*, New York, 1996, pp 224-31. **23** Cf. Sheen, op. cit., p. 225. **24** Léon Bloy, *Pilgrim of the Absolute*, London 1947, p. 237. **25** Cf. James T. O'Connor, *Land of the living: a theology of the last things*, New York, 1992, when the full promise of our divine filiation will be achieved. Even in the consciousness of our own weaknesses we are buoyed up by the knowledge that Christ has overcome sin and death (cf. Jn 17:33). The virtue of hope responds to the aspiration for happiness which God has placed in the heart of every human being. It sustains us during times of discouragement and opens up the soul to the expectation of eternal happiness. Even more, it shows us how to find joy in the Cross in the present life. If the priest allows his life to be shaped by this vision, he will communicate hope to others, especially when they are discouraged by the burdens of life.[26] The ground of hope is God's goodness and mercy, which for a Christian is a filial hope in the power of a loving Father. In a world racked by loss of faith and uncertainty about the future, and where depression afflicts increasing numbers of people, the priest should be a beacon of hope, offering light and a sense of security based on the promises of Christ.[27]

Blessed Josemaría Escrivá derived a deep peace and security from reflecting on those graphic words of the Old Testament: 'I have redeemed you, and called you by your name; you are mine' (Is 43:1).[28] To know that we are needed and appreciated for what we are – that is the basis of real happiness. But this is something the priest cannot keep for himself – of its nature authentic joy overflows, it communicates itself to others. We always have cause for optimism, for not being depressed (cf. 2 Cor 6:3-10 ), if we learn not to take ourselves too seriously. The person who knows that he needs redemption has the capacity to laugh at himself.[29]

## OBEDIENCE

Christ redeemed by obeying, by making his human will perfectly identified with the divine will (cf. Rom 5:19) – he had come down from heaven to fulfil the mission entrusted to him by the Father (cf. Jn 6:38). This was the dynamic of all his redemptive work (cf. Jn 4:34), 'becoming obedient unto death, even death on a cross' (Phil 2:7). Suffering and death, which came into the world through the disobedience of sin, have now been transformed into an opportunity to obey and to love.

pp 24-7. **26** Cf. CCC, 1817-21. **27** Cf. Ashley, ibid., p. 165. **28** Cf. Blessed Josemaría Escrivá, *The forge*, London, 1988, nos. 7, 12. **29** Reinhold Niebuhr captured some of this element of the joy of the faith as follows: 'Humour is the prelude to faith; and laughter is the beginning of prayer. Laughter must be heard in the outer courts of religion; and the echoes of it should resound in the sanctuary, but there is no laughter in the holy of holies. There laughter is swallowed up in prayer, and humour is fulfilled in faith': *Discerning the signs of the times*, New York, 1946, as quoted in Sheen, op. cit., p. 238.

As we have seen, one of the expressions of sacramental communion in the life of the priest is the bond that unites him with his bishop. From the bishop he receives sacramental power and hierarchical authorisation for exercising his ministry. Following the example of Jesus, the bishop's authority and the obedience of his co-workers should be exercised in a context of true and sincere friendship. Charity and obedience should characterize the priest's relationship with his bishop.[30] As we read in *Presbyterorum ordinis*:

> Among the virtues especially demanded by the ministry of priests must be reckoned that disposition of mind by which they are always prepared to seek not their own will but the will of him who has sent them (cf. Jn 4:34; 5:30 ; and 6:38).[31]

Obedience can sometimes be difficult when there is a clash of opinions, but the priest, imbued with an attitude of faith, has to try to see God's will in the bishop's decisions. It is not a blind obedience but one, which because of the confidence and friendship which exist between priest and bishop, encourages the priest to open his heart to communicate his difficulties, doubts and concerns. Nevertheless, in the long run, he must be always prepared to follow the indications of his bishop. In this context we should never forget that the merit of the redemption derived in the first place from Christ's obedience to his Father's will.[32]

Because ecclesial obedience is not at times an easy virtue to practice, it is helpful to be aware of its deep theological justification:

> This common bond of obedience is also common freedom: it offers protection against arbitrariness, and guarantees the authentically christological character of ecclesial obedience. Ecclesial obedience is not positivistic; it is not simply paid to a merely formal authority, but rather to someone who obeys on his own part, too, and personifies the obedient Christ. And yet such obedience does not, of course, depend on the virtue and holiness of the office-holder, precisely because it refers to the objectivity of faith, a gift from our Lord that transcends all subjectivity. In this sense, obedience to one's bishop always transcends the local Church: it is a catholic obedience. The bishop is obeyed because he represents the *universal* Church in this specific place.[33]

---

30 Cf. *Lumen gentium*, 28; *Presbyterorum ordinis*, 7. 31 *Presbyterorum ordinis*, 15. 32 Cf. St Thomas Aquinas, S Th., III, 47, 2. 33 Cardinal Joseph Ratzinger, 'The ministry and life of priests', in *Homiletic and pastoral review*, August-September 1997, p. 14.

But obedience has a relevance not just for the present – its supernatural reach engages the whole of salvation history:

> And such obedience also points beyond the current moment, since it is directed to the totality of the history of the faith. It is based on all that has grown to maturity in the *communio sanctorum*, and thus opens itself up to the future, in which God will be all in all, and we will all be one. From this point of view, the demand of obedience makes a very serious demand on the one who holds authority. This does not mean, again, that obedience is conditional. It is very concrete. I do not obey a Jesus that I or some others have constructed out of Sacred Scripture; in that case, I would only be obeying my own favourite notions: by adoring the image of Jesus I have invented, I would be adoring myself. No! To obey Christ means to obey his body, to obey him in his body.[34]

*Pastores dabo vobis* highlights some other characteristics of this virtue. For the priest, obedience is *apostolic* in that it is an expression of his love for, and service to, the Church in her hierarchical structure. Such obedience is the best guarantee that he will contribute to safeguarding the truth of the mystery of the Church and better serve the Christian community. Priestly obedience is much more than a personal exercise of this virtue; it has a *community* dimension in that it also expresses and reinforces the unity of the presbyterate. Another aspect of obedience is that which derives from *pastoral charity*. Here it shows itself in a constant availability to the real needs of the people entrusted to our care, and a willingness to adapt personal priorities to the pastoral demands of the community.[35]

---

34 Ibid. Ratzinger develops some of the ascetical reasons for this virtue: 'Ever since the Letter to the Philippians, Jesus' obedience, understood as victory over the disobedience of Adam, has been at the centre of the history of salvation. In the priest's life, this obedience should be incarnated in obedience to the Church's authority, and concretely, that means to the bishop. Only then is there a real rejection of the idolatry of self. Only then will the Adam within us be overcome, and the new humanity formed. Today, when emancipation is considered as the essence of redemption, and freedom is presented as the right for me to do everything I want to do, and nothing I don't want to do, the very concept of obedience has, so to speak, been anathematised. It has been eliminated not only from our vocabulary, but also from our thinking. But this erroneous notion of freedom makes unity and love impossible. It makes man a slave. A rightly understood obedience must be rehabilitated, and assume once more its true value at the centre of Christian and priestly spirituality' (ibid.).
35 Cf. PDV, 28.

## SELF-GIVING AND SERVICE

We have already seen that the concept of mission is at the core of the New Testament definition of priestly ministry. The commission to become somebody sent by Christ touches the very being of the priest in that he now ceases to belong to himself. It implies preaching Christ and not oneself, and being simultaneously at the service of all to whom he is sent.

> It means withdrawing from the limelight to make way for the one who is being represented ... And this involves the realisation that one's own person is not the core of the message.[36]

In a word, it implies being ready to decrease so that He might increase (cf. Jn 3:30 ). Learning to do this involves training and ascetical reshaping which has fundamental implications for the priest's spiritual life. Addressing priests in Chile about vocation, John Paul II told them:

> The only fitting response to this gift is nothing other than total surrender: an act of complete love. The voluntary acceptance of the divine call to the priesthood was, without doubt, an act of love which makes each of us a lover. Perseverance and fidelity to the vocation we have received consists, not only in ensuring that this love never weakens or dies, but rather intensifying it so that it will grow greater each day.[37]

Only by regular reflection on the self-giving of Christ as witnessed in the Gospel will the priest acquire the dynamic to nurture in his own life an unfolding vision of personal dedication.

The nature of the priest's vocation is essentially one of service. Following the teaching and example of Christ, it couldn't be otherwise. When the mother of James and John came to ask Jesus to give her sons the first places in the kingdom, the Master used the opportunity to explain the real nature of service to his disciples: in the new dispensation to be great meant to be a servant, to be first one had a be a slave. The Son of Man, he told them, had come 'not to be served but to serve, and to give his life as a ransom for many' (Mt 20: 28). On another occasion, to get across this same point, he posed a rhetorical question for his disciples, 'Which is the greater, one who sits at table, or one who serves?'. His own answer – 'I am among you as one who serves' (Lk 22: 27) – would have opened up a whole new horizon for his disciples on the nature of the service expected of them in their ministry.

36 Cf. Ratzinger, *Priestly ministry: a search for its meaning*, p. 11. 37 Address, 13 April 1987.

Christ did not just preach about having a spirit of service: it was a permanent and striking feature of his life. His washing of the feet of the disciples at the Last Supper was no mere parting gesture, but the logical culmination of a life of dedication to the spiritual and material needs of his closest followers. Yet this last act of service has a special significance. It was done with a specific purpose as St John relates:

> When he had washed their feet, and taken his garments, and resumed his place, he said to them, 'Do you know what I have done to you? You call me Teacher and Lord; and you are right, for so I am. If I then, your Lord and Teacher, have washed your feet, you also ought to wash one another's feet. For I have given you an example, that you also should do as I have done to you' (Jn 13:12-15).

Christ wanted to make sure that, by performing what for the Jews was regarded as a most menial task, all future generations of priests would have before them a graphic example of the spirit of service he expected from them. At the same time, he made the additional significant point, 'If you know these things, blessed are you if you do them' (v.17): true happiness comes from a generous self-giving to others.

In a homily to priests during his 1987 visit to Poland, to illustrate the spousal aspect of their service, John Paul II recalled some words of the revered primate of that country:

> Commissioned as we are by God for the service of the People of God, we have become their property. All the energies of our soul and body ought to serve the people who have the right to our life, to our eyes, and to our priestly lips, to our hands which offer the sacrifice, and to our apostolic feet. So we must dedicate them entirely to unceasing work, while it is still daylight.[38]

The theology of priestly service has been eloquently stated by Cardinal Ratzinger. Taking an image from St Augustine, he develops the idea of the priest as *servus Dei* (servant of God) or *servus Christi* (servant of Christ):

> This expression, 'the servant of Christ,' which is taken from the ecclesiastical language of his time, has a background in the christological hymn of the Letter to the Philippians (2:5-11): Christ, the Son who is equal to God, took on the condition of a servant, and became a slave

38 Cardinal Wyszynski, *Letter to my priests*, Paris, 1969, quoted by John Paul II in his homily in Tarnow, Poland, 10 June 1987.

for us ... What is pertinent to our theme is that 'servant' is a relational concept. One is a servant only in relation to another. If the priest is defined as a servant of Jesus Christ, this means that his existence is essentially determined as relational. The essence of his ministry consists in his *having been ordained* for the service of the Lord, and this reaches into his very own being. He is a servant of Christ in order to be from Him, through Him, and with Him, a servant of men. His being in relation to Christ is not opposed to his being ordained for the service of the community (of the Church); rather, it is the foundation that alone gives depth to that service. Being related to Christ means to be taken up into His existence as servant, and staying with Him, at the service of the 'body', that is, the Church. Precisely because the priest belongs to Christ, he belongs, in a thoroughly radical sense, to men. Otherwise, he would be unable to dedicate himself profoundly and absolutely to them. This means, in turn, that the ontological concept of the priesthood, which affects the priest's being, is not opposed to his important function as a minister to the community. In fact, the ontological aspect creates a service too radical to be conceived in any merely profane terms.[39]

This disposition of service is then a primary expression of that pastoral charity which is the dynamic of priestly ministry. 'The gift of self', John Paul II reminds us, 'has no limits, marked as it is by the same apostolic and missionary zeal of Christ, the Good Shepherd'.[40]

The faithful see and observe the priest not only when he is preaching the Word of God, celebrating at the altar, and administering the sacraments, but also in many other ordinary encounters. They should be encouraged by his warm humanity, his courtesy, his simplicity in dealing with people of every rank in society.

> The grace and charity of the Altar are diffused at the ambo, in the confessional, in the parish office, in the schools and oratories, in the homes of the faithful, in the streets and at the hospitals, on public transport and in the media. The priest has an opportunity to fulfil his role as Pastor everywhere. In every instant it is his Mass which is diffused. His spiritual union with Christ, Priest and Host, causes him to be the grain of God that is to become the true bread of Christ – as St Ignatius of Antioch says (*Epist. ad Romanos*, IV, I) – for the good of the brethren.[41]

39 Ratzinger, 'The ministry and life of priests', pp 11-12. **40** PDV, 23. **41** John Paul II, Address, 7 July 1993. 'The priest is, therefore, *a man of charity*, and is called to educate oth-

Hence the theological virtues of faith, hope, and charity are exercised in a special way in the celebration of the Eucharist. The Mass is the *Mysterium fidei* (mystery of faith) which allows us to look beyond the appearances of bread and wine and to adore the Body and Blood of Christ. Nourished by the flesh of Christ we are given a pledge of eternal life even in this world. And we leave the altar ready to live each day by the love of the heart of Christ we bear within us.[42]

ers according to Christ's example and the new commandment of brotherly love (cf. Jn 15:12)' (PDV, 49) [italics in original]. 42 'The virtues of faith, hope, and charity are to be exercised in all spheres of life, but they are exercised in a concentrated way in the celebration of the Eucharist. The Eucharist does more that merely symbolise and remind us of the saving action of God. It makes that action present again through the quoted words and gestures of Christ, the words and gestures he used when he anticipated and accepted the death by which we were saved. It is in faith, hope, and charity that we take part in the Eucharistic celebration, as we see beyond the looks of bread and wine and acknowledge the presence of the God who created us and who could be, in undiminished goodness and greatness, even without the world; we recognize his presence not just as the eternal God, but as the God who acts in the sacraments to bring about our Redemption' (Sokolowski, op. cit., p. 233).

# 8

## The priest as evangelizer

In the conciliar decree on the life and ministry of priests, we see a harmonious integration of the priest as evangelizer, proclaiming Christ's mission to all men, and the cultic aspect of priestly ministry with its emphasis on the worship and adoration of God.[1] To the Upper Room, where he had so recently consecrated the Eucharist, Christ returned on Easter evening to invest the apostles with their mission. The simple greeting, 'Peace be with you' (Jn 20:21) has overtones of forgiveness and reconciliation, and sets the scene for imparting to the apostles, in solemn words, their new assignment: 'As the Father has sent me, I also send you' (Jn 20:21). This is a fundamental, constitutive element of the definitive priesthood of the New Covenant. They, and all priests through the apostolic succession, are given a mission that is universal in scope because it shares in Christ's priesthood, which extends to all men and to all times (cf. Mt 28:19-20). They were to preach repentance and forgiveness of sins to all nations (cf. Lk 24:47).

In undertaking their new mission, the first generation of priests would have the preaching of Jesus as a basic point of reference for their proclamation of the Gospel. They had an intense apprenticeship of three years, listening to the Master speak on the different aspects of the message of salvation to a variety of audiences. But it wasn't just a listening exercise. Christ also sent them out to preach in the towns and villages, with specific instructions about how they were to approach their task (cf. Mt 10:5-23; Mk 6:7-12; Lk 9:1-6; 10:1-12). From the record of the New Testament we see how well they learned the lesson from the Master's example, and how they became effective communicators of the word of God.

The Vatican II constitution on divine Revelation affirms that all preaching should be nourished and guided by sacred Scripture.[2] Priests are therefore

---

1 Cf. *Presbyterorum ordinis*, 4-5.  2 Cf. *Dei Verbum*, 21. This is recommended not only because the life and teaching of Jesus should form the basic content of preaching, but also because the New Testament offers many pointers about method as well. 'There is no true evangelization if the name, the teaching, the life, the promises, the kingdom and the mystery of Jesus of Nazareth, the Son of God are not proclaimed' (*Evangelii nuntiandi*, 22).

encouraged to immerse themselves in the inspired texts by constant reading and diligent study.[3] As John Paul II invites them:

> I urge you, then, to take special care that your preaching be inspired by the word of God, just as it is proposed by the Magisterium of the Church. It is a word revealed by God, inspired by the Holy Spirit, preached by the Church, celebrated in the liturgy, lived by the saints, and converted by you into a subject of contemplation, to illuminate the events of daily history. For that reason try to take up the word of God devoutly in prayer and contemplation, so that it be the object of study and life-experience shared with one's brothers. Speak courageously, preach with a deep faith and with a hopeful tone, as witnesses of the risen Lord who has transformed and continues to transform creation and history.[4]

The missionary presence of the priest in the world is more necessary than ever today for building up the Church. In a society saturated by materialism, where people are often isolated and alienated from God, they need to be approached as Jesus approached the disciples on the road to Emmaus. The salvific truth of the Scriptures has to be opened up to them so that, with rejuvenated faith, they will eventually be able to recognize the Master 'in the breaking of bread', in Eucharistic communion with the glorified Christ (cf. Lk 24:13-35). It is the grace of the Holy Spirit which confers on the priest the prophetic task of preaching and explaining the word of God with authority. It also gives him the fortitude to proclaim the full demands of the Christian faith without trying to dilute them to make them more palatable.

Priests could ask themselves if they aspire to the same dispositions when preaching as those which motivated St Paul: 'My speech and my message', he tells the Christian community in Corinth, 'were not in plausible words of wisdom, but in the demonstration of the Spirit and power' (1 Cor 2:4). Certainly the priest should try to cultivate a positive style, seasoned with lively examples. But he can never forget that the power of his preaching depends primarily on the action of the Holy Spirit, evincing a response in individual souls. The Curé of Ars moved the hardest of hearts to repentance and tears, not by his eloquence but by his holiness of life – the fact that he allowed himself to be totally appropriated by the Holy Spirit. By means of his christocentric lifestyle and through his pastoral zeal, the priest gives witness to the transcendence of the Gospel message, and is a constant reminder to the faithful of the spiritual meaning of their lives.[5]

---

3 Cf. ibid., no. 25. 4 Address, 1 July 1986. 5 Cf. del Portillo, op. cit., p. 33.

To fulfil his mission of preaching in a responsible way, the priest should bear in mind the guidelines offered by the Pope:

> The preaching of priests is not a mere exercise of the word that answers to a personal need to express oneself and to communicate one's own thought, nor can it consist solely in sharing one's personal experience. This psychological element, which can have a didactic-pastoral role, is neither the reason for, nor the principal element in preaching ... The mission of preaching is entrusted by the Church to priests as a sharing in Christ's mediation, to be exercised by virtue of and according to the demands of his mandate.[6]

What we preach is the divine word, which is not ours, and which therefore 'cannot be manipulated, changed or adapted at will, but must be proclaimed in its entirety'.[7] John Paul II adds, in summary, that the role of priests as evangelizers is 'not to preach their own wisdom but the word of God and to issue an urgent invitation to all people to conversion and holiness'.[8]

> Indeed, he reminds us, if it is true that the word and the sacraments work through the power of the Spirit they impart, it is also true that, when they transform the life of the minister, he himself becomes a kind of living Gospel. The best evangelizer is always a holy one.[9]

In his Second Letter to the Corinthians Paul defends himself vigorously against accusations made about his preaching and his apostolic authority. He contrasts the sincerity of his preaching with the way false apostles adulterate the word of God. What alone makes his message important is that he is an ambassador of God: 'So we are ambassadors for Christ, since God is making his appeal through us; we entreat you on behalf of Christ, be reconciled to God" (2 Cor 5:50). It has been pointed out that

> these words of Paul remain the valid definition of the basic form and fundamental mission of priestly existence in the Church of the New Covenant. I have to deliver the message of another, and this means first of all that I must know what it is, I have to have understood it, and I have to make it my own ... This proclamation, however, requires more than merely the posture of a telegram messenger who passes on for-

---

6 Address, 21 April 1993, no. 3.  7 Ibid.  8 Ibid., no. 4.  9 Address, 22 October 1993, no. 7. Paul VI explained this idea as follows: 'Modern man listens more willingly to witnesses than to teachers, and if he does listen to teachers, it is because they are witnesses' (Address, 2 October 1974).

eign words faithfully without being affected by them in any way. Instead, I must pass on the words of another in the first person and in a very personal way, and must commit myself to them in such a way that they become my words entirely. For these words require not a telex operator but a witness.[10]

At a practical level this means that in the study of theology the intellectual and spiritual dimensions are inseparable from each other.

Following the example of Christ, the priest should know how to illustrate the truths of the faith with lively illustrations, metaphors, comparisons, and events from everyday life. We are reminded by the evangelists that Christ invariably spoke in parables to the people – the Gospels record over a hundred such stories told by Christ. In chapter thirteen of Matthew we notice how many different similes he used to elucidate the concept of the kingdom of God – the story of the sower and the different types of ground on which the seed fell to illustrate the mystery of grace and human freedom; the parable of the wheat and the cockle to explain how saints and sinners belong to the same Church and the eschatological nature of God's kingdom; the metaphor of the mustard seed and the leaven to explain the interior growth of the Church and its effect on the whole of society. We can also see the power of such parables as the treasure hidden in the field and the pearl of great price to illustrate the nature of the Christian vocation. Even though congregations now may in some ways be more sophisticated than the crowds Christ preached to, the level of religious ignorance encountered at present is often on a par with what Christ experienced. Hence the need in today's preaching for incisive, relevant parables to respond to the contemporary catechetical illiteracy.

Because we live in a society which is highly influenced by the communications media, the priest has, in a very real sense, to compete for attention with many different messages in the air-waves. Consequently he needs to cultivate the formal aspects of his preaching in order to present the message of the Gospel in as persuasive a manner as possible. At the same time, the priest's own conviction about the attraction of the Christian message, and its capacity to put a sense of purpose and security into people's lives, is his most cogent resource for effective preaching.[11]

10 Cf. Ratzinger, *A new song for the Lord*, pp 168-9.  11 'Elegant accurate language, comprehensible to contemporary men and women of all social backgrounds, is always useful for preaching. Banal commonplace language should be eschewed. While preachers must speak from an authentic vision of faith, a vocabulary must be employed which is comprehensible in all quarters and must avoid specialised jargon or concessions to the spirit of materialism. The human "key" to effective preaching of the Word is to be found in the professionalism of the preacher who knows what he wants to say and who is always backed up by serious remote and proximate preparation. This is far removed from the improvisation of the dilet-

## PREACHING ABOUT HOLINESS

In his Letter for the New Millennium John Paul II says that, having reflected on many aspects of the Christian life during the Jubilee year, we need to start out on a new enterprise of evangelization. It is not a question of inventing a new programme because such a programme already exists:

> it is the plan found in the Gospel and in the living Tradition, it is the same as ever. Ultimately, it has its centre in Christ himself, who is to be known, loved and imitated, so that in him we may live the life of the Trinity, and with him transform history until its fulfilment in the heavenly Jerusalem. This is a programme which does not change with shifts of times and cultures, even though it takes account of time and culture for the sake of true dialogue and effective communication. This programme for all times is our programme for the Third Millennium.[12]

What is striking about John Paul II's proposal for pastoral revitalisation in the Church is his insistence that the programme be based on a rediscovery of 'the full practical significance of ... the universal call to holiness'.[13] However, this, he affirms, cannot be just 'a spiritual veneer', but a commitment to make the call to holiness 'an intrinsic and essential part' of Church teaching.[14] He repeats the teaching of Vatican II, that 'all the Christian faithful, of whatever state or rank, are called to the fullness of the Christian life and to the perfection of charity'.[15] In the light of the full theological and ascetical consequences of our baptismal vocation, it would, he tells us, 'be a contradiction to settle for a life of mediocrity, marked by a minimalist ethic and a shallow religiosity'.[16]

Therefore 'the time has come to re-propose wholeheartedly to everyone this high standard of ordinary Christian living: the whole life of the Christian community and of Christian families must lead in this direction'.[17] In his Holy Thursday Letter to priests for 2001, he again underlined this idea saying that

tante. Attempts to obscure the entire force of truth are insidious forms of irenicism. Care should therefore be taken with the meaning of words, style and diction. Important themes should be highlighted without ostentation, after careful reflection. A pleasant speaking voice should be cultivated. Preachers should know their objectives and have a good understanding of the existential and cultural reality of their congregations. Theories and abstract generalisations must always be avoided. Hence every preacher should know his own flock well and use an attractive style which, rather than wounding people, strikes the conscience and is not afraid to call things for what they really are' (*The priest and the third Christian millennium*, II, 2). 12 John Paul II, *Novo millennio ineunte*, 29 (6 January 2001). 13 Ibid., no. 30. 14 Cf. ibid. 15 Ibid., quoting *Lumen gentium*, 40. 16 Ibid., no. 31. 17 Ibid.

Evangelization in the third millennium must come to grips with the urgent need for a presentation of the Gospel message which is dynamic, complete and demanding. The Christian life to be aimed at cannot be reduced to a mediocre commitment to 'goodness' as society defines it; it must be a true quest for holiness.[18]

This is not a new approach in the teaching of John Paul II. Many years ago he had already pointed out that it was not enough to evangelize – it is also necessary to sanctify.[19]

The Holy Father's renewed call to holiness is a challenge to priests to evangelize and form the faithful in the fullness of their baptismal vocation. This 'training in holiness' requires that in the first place pastors teach people how to pray.[20] Indeed, the Holy Father maintains, education in prayer should become 'a key-point of all pastoral planning' with a view to encouraging both popular piety and liturgical prayer.[21] Growth in a spirit of prayer is what in turn will lead on to more fruitful participation in the Sunday Eucharist and in the Sacrament of Reconciliation, the great sources of Christian holiness.[22]

DIVINE FILIATION

As an integral part of 'training in holiness', a regular theme of preaching should be the Fatherhood of God. If the most important truth about our existence is that, as a consequence of Baptism, we are truly sons and daughters of God,[23] then this is a topic to which priests should find themselves returning

---

18 HTL, 2001, no. 15. 19 Cf. Address, 19 October 1985. 20 Cf. *Novo millennio ineunte*, 32-34. An important part of the priest's mission is to be a 'teacher of prayer' (cf. PDV, 47). 21 Cf. ibid., no. 34. On a previous occasion, John Paul II had outlined to a meeting of bishops the reasons why the development of a spirit of prayer among the people is essential to guarantee the effectiveness of the priest's pastoral activity: 'We must convince the people that prayer is indispensable, quite simply because it is a case of doing the *work of God*, and not our own work. We must carry it out in accordance with *his inspiration*, and hence with his Holy Spirit, not in accordance with our own feelings. We must draw on sources which are other than those from which the world seeks to draw power. We must find our strength in *the grace of God. Our methods* are inspired by evangelical love. Yes, it is grace alone that permits us to carry out well the work of salvation, which implies the *conversion* of persons: only the Spirit of God can make people aware of sin, and give the desire to abandon sin; he alone leads to faith or to reconciliation with God. We give our testimony, which is an appeal that respects freedom, and God alone can awake an interior attraction ... It is obvious that only grace leads to holiness': Address, 22 January 1987. 22 Cf. *Novo millennio ineunte*, 35-9. 23 Cf. CCC, 683, 1997. See also Blessed Josemaría Escrivá, *Friends of God*, Dublin 1981, no. 26.

again and again to discover its rich ascetical implications. We can draw on many incidents in the Gospel to illustrate this aspect of the Christian life – our Lord's teaching on the fatherly providence of God even in our most material needs (cf. Mt 6:25-33; 10:29), prayer to God as Father (cf. Mt 6:6-13); living as children of God (cf. Mk 10:13-16); becoming children of God through faith in Christ (Jn 1:12-13). But, above all, we will find in the story of the prodigal son, told by the Master himself, a powerful illustration of God as a merciful Father (cf. Lk 15: 11-32). A growing conviction that we have a Father who loves us, ready to give us all the graces we need, will not only make the call to holiness meaningful, but will speed us along that path. St Paul has much to say about this doctrine, especially in Romans and Galatians, which deserves our attention.[24]

The life of a Christian is a sharing in the life of Christ, God's only Son. By becoming, through adoption, true children of God we have, as it were, a right to share also in Christ's inheritance – eternal life in heaven. This divine life in us, begun in Baptism through rebirth in the Holy Spirit, will grow under the guidance of this Spirit who makes us ever more like Christ. So, our adoption as children is already a fact but only at the end of time, when our bodies rise in glory, will it reach fulfilment. Meanwhile we are in a waiting situation, not free from suffering and trials.[25]

### HARD SAYINGS

To preach Christ crucified is a challenge for the priest. But through the folly of such preaching Christ saves those who believe (cf. 1 Cor 1:18-25). Hence the priest cannot allow his agenda to be set by what the media consider to be the important issues of the day, since media concerns are often ephemeral and superficial. The driving ethos is generally secularist, frequently portraying and affirming moral values which undermine the Christian view of life. Media attitudes are invariably hostile to Catholic institutions and values. There is normally little sympathy with the Christian concept of marriage and the family; indeed sexual permissiveness is the norm. This is the background which the priest has to take account of in setting out the teaching of the Master. Convinced that the full truth revealed by Christ is the only message which will satisfy the deepest longings of the human heart, he has to know how to present the challenge and adventure of the Christian way of life. At the same time, he has a duty to alert the faithful to those influences which undermine faith,

---

24 Some of his classic texts include Rom 8:14-25; Gal 4:4-7. 25 Cf. *The Navarre Bible: Romans and Galatians*, Dublin, 1990, pp 115-18.

and equip them to defend the values which are central to their dignity as children of God.

Christ said he was the truth (cf. Jn 14:6). It is the knowledge of this truth that does not pass away which gives the priest the self-confidence to preach those 'hard sayings' which do not sound very harmonious to modern ears. Consequently, as John Paul II does for the whole Church, the priest in his parish will need to constantly affirm the idea that freedom without an anchorage in objective truth and permanent moral values is a spurious freedom, which in the end will lead only to personal unhappiness and social disorder.[26] To fulfil our role as effective evangelizers we need to take to heart the Holy Father's advice:

> As we proclaim the truth in love, it is not possible for us to avoid all criticism; nor is it possible to please everyone. And so we are humbly convinced that God is with us in our ministry of truth and that he 'did not give us a spirit of timidity but a spirit of power and love and self control' (2 Tim 1:7).[27]

Christ knew that his teaching would cause divisions, separating father from son and mother from daughter, because his message was opposed to the wisdom of the world. That is why he said he had come to bring a sword, not peace (cf. Mt 10:34-35). Thus the priest cannot be surprised if his preaching at times fails to satisfy everybody. But to be loyal to the Gospel he has to have the courage to 'preach the word ... in season, and out of season', to 'convince, rebuke, and exhort ... unfailing in patience and in teaching' (2 Tim 4:2). To heal people of their sins it is sometimes necessary to cause a certain amount of pain. To do otherwise would rightfully draw down on us the admonition of Jeremiah: 'Dressing my people's wound, but skin deep only, with them saying, "All is well." All well? Nothing is well' (Jer 8:11). The purpose of an anaesthetic is to make surgery less painful. Not all pain, however, can be spared – there is usually some element of suffering in the healing process. Nevertheless, the result is generally the recovery of health and vitality. On the other hand, superficial preaching, which does not go to the root of evil, is akin to administering an anaesthetic without performing the surgery which is essential to the promotion of spiritual good health.

Perhaps the greatest disservice to the faithful today is the loss of nerve on the part of priests to preach the full truth about God's plan in two specific areas – about chastity, marriage and the family, and about the Last Things. Taking a lead from the Pope, I think it can said that, at the present time, Church teaching on the family and on sexual morality needs to be affirmed in

26 Cf. Encyclical Letter, *Veritatis splendor* (6 August 1993), 31-34.   27 Address, 5 October 1979.

all its positive dimensions. To undo the immense damage caused to individuals and families by a philosophy of hedonism and sexual permissiveness, it is vital to recover all the attractive and enduring values of the Christian virtue of chastity.[28]

Since we live at a time which has lost the sense of sin,[29] with consequent disinterest about the future life, a new emphasis is required in evangelizing people about the Last Things. These topics were very much at the core of Christ's own preaching.[30] Nevertheless, the cult of pleasure and hedonism sweeps out of sight the consideration of death. The concept of penance, discipline, and self-denial is alien territory, something to be kept out of sight and out of mind.[31] Although the priest is a witness to the presence of God in history and to the eschatological dimension of human existence, many priests seem to be reluctant to preach about the realities of death, judgement, heaven and hell. Yet we all need to be reminded regularly that the only important objective in this life is to attain salvation through the grace of Christ, and to live our lives accordingly – everything else is superfluous (cf. Lk 10:42). In this sense the priest must be a sign of contradiction, not being afraid to repeat those sobering words of Christ, 'whoever would save his life will lose it, and whoever loses his life for my sake will find it' (Mt 16:25).

In *Crossing the threshold of hope* John Paul II answered a number of searching questions about different aspects of Church teaching in relation to the present day. In putting the question 'Does Eternal Life exist?', Vittorio Messori drew attention to the vast amount of documents produced over the past twenty years at every level of the Church. And yet, he commented, 'this very loquacious Church seems to be silent about what seems most essential: eternal life'. Why, he asked, 'do many Churchmen comment interminably about topical issues, but hardly ever speak to us about eternity, about that ultimate union with God that is ... man's vocation, man's destiny, and ultimate end?'[32] In reply the Pope agreed that, to some extent, in pastoral practice the connection between the life of the Church on earth and personal eschatology had been lost sight of. He recalled that not so long ago, in sermons during retreats and missions, the Last Things were always a standard part of the preaching programme and that many people were drawn to conversion and confession by these reflections. On the other hand, he pointed out, the emphasis in *Lumen gentium* is on the eschatological character of the pilgrim Church rather than on individual eschatology. He admits that to a certain degree

28 This topic is discussed in detail in Chapter 9 below.   29 Cf. Apostolic exhortation, *Reconciliatio et paenitentia*, 18 (2 December 1984).   30 Cf. CCC, 1020–1060; see also John Paul II, Addresses, 21 July 1999 (on Heaven); 28 July 1999 (on Hell); 4 August 1999 (on Purgatory).   31 Cf. Sheen, ibid., p.162.   32 John Paul II, *Crossing the threshold of hope*, London, 1994, p. 178.

preachers, catechists and teachers got lost in this cosmic view of eschatology 'and, as a result, they no longer have the courage to preach about the threat of hell'.[33] This amnesia about the Last Things is, he suggests, the consequence of a consumerist mentality focusing on the enjoyment of earthly goods. Nevertheless, he affirms that while to some degree eschatology has become irrelevant to contemporary man, faith in God as Supreme Justice remains, faith that Someone, in the end, will be able to speak the truth about the good and evil man has done, Someone who is able to reward the good and punish the bad.

John Paul II suggests an approach for priests to speak about the Last Things. His point is that eschatology is not something that will take place in the future after earthly life has finished. Rather, eschatology began with the coming of Christ and especially with his redemptive death and Resurrection.[34] Christ himself reminds us that whoever lives from the Eucharist *has* eternal life (cf. Jn 6:54) – it is a present reality rather than a possibility for the future.[35]

Our understanding and preaching about the Last Things has to take as its point of departure St Paul's teaching that God desires 'all men to be saved and to come to the knowledge of the truth' (1 Tim 2:4). Yet the Gospel witness to the existence of eternal punishment is unequivocal (cf. Mt 5:22; 8:12; 25:41, etc.).[36] The difficult question is, how can God, who loved man so much, permit those who reject him to be condemned to eternal torment? Yet, on the other hand, can he tolerate that terrible crimes go unpunished? This is truly a great mystery which involves man's freedom and the holiness of God. Nevertheless, the Holy Father says, there is something in man's moral conscience which rebels against any loss of the conviction that the God who is love is also the God of ultimate justice, and that final punishment is in some way necessary to re-establish moral equilibrium in human history.

One of the principal themes underlined by the 1999 synod of bishops for Europe was the need, in the new evangelization, to speak about eternal life as Jesus Christ did. People must be told, the bishops said, that after this life there is another life, and that this eternal life should define our way of living on earth. Some pointed out that eternal life was one of the topics which had been 'lost' in preaching. Other bishops adverted to the fact that if the transcendent dimension of the faith is forgotten about, people end up seeing Christianity as merely good advice about how to organize society. [37]

---

33 Ibid., p. 183. 34 Ibid., pp 184-6. 35 Cf. James T. O'Connor, *Land of the living*, pp 126, 154. 36 Cf. *Lumen gentium*, 48. 37 Cf. reports of contributions to Second Special Assembly for Europe of the Synod of Bishops in the English weekly edition of *Osservatore Romano*, for October and November 1999. As John Paul II points out in his encyclical, *Redemptoris missio*, 'The temptation today is to reduce Christianity to merely human wisdom, a pseudo-science of well-being. In our heavily secularized world a "gradual secularization of salvation" has taken place, so that people strive for the good of man, but man who is truncated,

## OBSTACLES TO EVANGELIZATION

Christ did not shy away from confronting his hearers with uncomfortable truths – his very first sermon was about repentance (cf. Mk 1:15). He called things by their names: 'For from within, out of the heart of man, come evil thoughts, fornication, theft, murder, adultery, coveting, wickedness, deceit, licentiousness, envy, pride, slander foolishness. All these evil things come from within, and they defile a man' (Mk 7:20-23). And according to St Paul these same sins exclude from the kingdom of heaven (cf. Gal 5:19-21; 1 Cor 6:9-10). John Paul II has put this aspect of the priest's role into perspective:

> As minister of the essential saving acts, he places at the service of all men not perishable goods, nor socio-political projects, but supernatural and eternal life, teaching how to read and interpret the events of history in a Gospel perspective. This is the primary task of the priest.[38]

In this context it has to be noted that widespread moral and doctrinal dissent constitute perhaps the most serious obstacle to effective evangelization. Speaking to representatives of European episcopal conferences the Pope put the issue in context:

> In the delicate and difficult task of creating a renewed synthesis between Gospel and life, between the gospel message and modern culture, our pastoral duty imposes on us, in this regard, a particularly delicate, demanding and vigilant exercise of discernment. From this point of view, we must point out that the phenomenon of dissent represents a great obstacle to evangelization. Doctrinal and moral dissent appear to be symptoms rather characteristic of the 'rich' West, and thus of Europe as well. In certain respects it seems to have found its origins in a transposition of models of civil life and political contestation into the religious and ecclesial realm; in other respects it can well denote a human spirit which is proud and intolerant before the demands of the Gospel and before the necessity of God's 'grace' to accept them and live them. A necessary condition for evangelization will be that of reaching and utilizing – beyond and in spite of dissent – the authentic sense of the faithful, who accept the Gospel in that fullness which distinguishes it from the spirit of the world, according

reduced to his merely horizontal dimension. We know, however, that Jesus came to bring integral salvation, one which embraces the whole person and all mankind, and opens up the wondrous prospect of divine filiation' (no. 11) (7 December 1990). **38** Address, 22 October 1993, no. 2.

to the exhortation of St Paul: *nolite conformari huic saeculo* ('Do not be conformed to this world') (Rom 12:2).[39]

Resistance or even hostility to the teachings of the Gospel should not inhibit its full and courageous proclamation.[40] In most cases such opposition or dissent is given disproportionate coverage by the media and thus a climate of opinion is created which does not at all represent the general attitude of the faithful. In his many pastoral visits during the past twenty years John Paul II, by preaching directly to countless millions of people in every part of the world, bypassed the media spin so often put on many aspects of Church teaching, and thus allowed people to hear the fullness of the faith with remarkable pastoral results, especially among young people.

MINISTRY OF THE WORD

In the ministry of the word, identification with Christ the Teacher becomes a real source of sanctification for priests because they are 'guided by his Spirit in the very act of teaching the Word'.[41] This implies not only preaching in the presence of Christ, but also being identified with his very sentiments since we make him present by our preaching. In his encyclical *Redemptor hominis*, John Paul II refers to some of the ascetical implications of the ministry of the word, such as the practical demands of preaching the truth, and of love for the truth in our own lives.[42] There is also the awareness that the truth we preach is not our own, but God's, which is to be found in its fullness in the Church.[43]

---

39 Address, 11 October 1985. 40 Paul VI says that evangelization is not only a question of preaching the Gospel to ever greater numbers of people, 'but also of affecting and as it were upsetting ... humanity's criteria of judgement, determining values, points of interest, lines of thought, sources of inspiration and models of life which are in contrast with the word of God and the plan of salvation' (*Evangelii nuntiandi*, 19). 41 *Presbyterorum ordinis*, 13. 42 Cf. Encyclical, *Redemptor hominis*, 12. 43 Cf. ibid., no.19, which, among other things, affirms: 'Faith as a specific supernatural virtue infused into the human spirit makes us sharers in knowledge of God as a response to his revealed word. Therefore it is required, when the Church professes and teaches the faith, that she should adhere strictly to divine truth (cf. *Dei Verbum*, 5, 10, 21), and should translate it into living attitudes of "obedience in harmony with reason" (Vatican I, *Dei Filius*, ch. 3). Christ himself, concerned for this fidelity to divine truth, promised the Church the special assistance of the Spirit of truth, gave the gift of infallibility ... Being responsible for that truth also means loving it and seeking the most exact understanding of it, in order to bring it closer to ourselves and others in all its saving power, its splendour and its profundity joined with simplicity'. See also the Declaration of the Congregation for the Doctrine of the Faith, *Dominus Jesus*, on the *Unicity and salvific universality of Jesus Christ and the Church*, 6 August 2000.

This responsibility for the truth, which the priest has as preacher, requires meditation and study. It demands an effort to acquire a deeper understanding of the truths of salvation which will at the same time make this doctrine more influential in his own life. *Presbyterorum ordinis* describes it this way:

> For, by seeking more effective ways of conveying to others what they have meditated on (cf. St Thomas, *Summa Theol.*, II-II, q 188, a 7) they will savour more profoundly the 'unsearchable riches of Christ' (Eph 3:8) and the many-sided wisdom of God.[44]

This personal appropriation of the Gospel inevitably leads to a deeper identification with the teaching and sentiments of the Master (cf. Phil 2:5) and, consequently, to greater personal holiness.

In the context of the ministry of the word, linguistic and exegetical knowledge of Scripture, while necessary, is not sufficient. Prayerful meditation is what gives a real, personal familiarity with the word of God, so that the priest's speech and attitudes become a reflection and a witness to the Gospel:

> Only if he 'abides' in the word will the priest become a perfect disciple of the Lord. Only then will he know the truth and be set truly free, overcoming every conditioning which is contrary or foreign to the Gospel (cf. Jn 8:31-32). The priest ought to be the first 'believer' in the word, while being fully aware that the words of his ministry are not 'his', but those of the One who sent him. He is not the master of the word, but its servant ... Precisely because he can and does evangelize, the priest, like every other member of the Church, ought to grow in awareness that he himself is continually in need of being evangelized.[45]

As a guarantee that he possesses and transmits the Gospel in its entirety, the priest is asked to develop a special sensitivity and docility to the living Tradition of the Church and to her Magisterium. This is essential for the proper interpretation of the word of God and to preserve its authentic meaning.[46]

---

44 *Presbyterorum ordinis*, 13. 45 PDV, 26. See also PDV, 47. 'The priest must be a man who lives off the Word, who is impregnated by the Word, totally at home in the Word. He must concretely find in the Word the centre around which he builds his existence. Somewhat drastically expressed: the priest has to be a living contemplation of the Word and not simply a cultic technician or manager' (Ratzinger, *Priestly ministry: a search for its meaning*, p. 19). 46 Cf. *Dei Verbum*, 8 and 10.

## WINNING VOCATIONS

Looking at Jesus' pastoral ministry we see that he gave a particular priority to seeking out those who would be his immediate disciples and co-workers. His call to Peter and the others was direct and peremptory: 'Follow me, and I will make you fishers of men' (Mt 4:19). Their response was rapid and unconditional – 'Immediately they left their nets and followed him' (Mt 4:20). At other times the invitation was more open-ended: 'come and see' was his response to John and Andrew who had asked him where he stayed. After spending the day with Jesus the seed of vocation had taken deep root in their souls (cf. Jn 1:38-39). We see that call repeated frequently and in different circumstances throughout the Gospels. Sometimes Christ met with a negative response as in the case of the young man who went away sad because he did not have the generosity to respond to the Master's call – his heart was too enmeshed in material wealth (cf. Mt 19:22). Indeed, reflecting on Christ's public life we can say that the whole of his ministry was characterized by his constant challenge to people to engage with the new life of grace he was offering them. His entire ministry was, in a very real sense, a vocations ministry. Hence we can say that only if the priest's pastoral activity as a whole has this vocational dimension will there be vocations to the priesthood.[47]

If the priest is to be truly an icon of Christ then his concern for the vitality and future of the Church will be reflected in pastoral initiatives to personally call young men to the priesthood. An attitude of 'passive expectation' falls short of the example of Christ and the standards set by John Paul II.[48] Zeal to promote candidates for the seminary is a significant indicator of the priest's appreciation of his own vocation and his practical love for the Church.

*Pastores dabo vobis* affirms that priests should be active in the promotion of vocations. Indeed concern for vocations is a connatural and essential dimension of the priest's pastoral work.[49] As a guide to efforts in this regard we are offered the example of Andrew, who not only told his brother Simon about the Messiah whom he had just met, but 'brought him to Jesus' (Jn 1:42). Christ used Andrew as a human instrument to facilitate that first encounter of Simon Peter with the Lord. This bringing of possible candidates face to face with

---

47 'All our initiatives aimed at an adequate ministry for vocations to the priesthood and its irreplaceable, specific meaning for the Church will be rewarded only if we do not see it as an isolated aspect, but rather regard the whole of pastoral activity as a vocations apostolate. Being human always means being called by God, which takes place in the most diverse ways. Only then can Christianity be experienced as the inter-relationship between God's call and a personal response. A vocation and a community-orientated response always go together in the priesthood' (John Paul II, Address, 14 December 1992). 48 Cf. *Letter for Vocations Day*, 1986. 49 Cf. PDV, 34.

Christ is the very heart of the Church's work to promote vocations. Since the present crisis in vocations is rooted in an even more radical crisis of faith, promoting vocations means, at the same time, working towards restoring a Christian mentality grounded on faith and sustained by it.[50]

In Western society at present the fall-off in vocations to the priesthood is one of the deepest concerns of Church authority. How can this trend be reversed? In the first place it is useful to identify the real obstacles to an effective vocations ministry. These derive mainly from the cultural environment. *Pastores dabo vobis* highlights three such negative influences – the lure of a consumerist society which traps people in a materialist interpretation of life; a utilitarian and hedonistic approach to sexuality which stunts the growth of human personality; and, finally, a distorted sense of freedom disconnected form objective truth.[51]

> In this context it is difficult not only to respond fully to a vocation to the priesthood but even to understand its very meaning as a special witness to the primacy of 'being' over 'having', and as a recognition that the significance of life consists in a free and responsible giving of oneself to others, a willingness to place oneself entirely at the service of the Gospel and the Kingdom of God as a priest.[52]

What role do priests have in fostering vocations? The priest who is convinced that he is another Christ, and who cherishes the dignity of his calling, will be committed to winning vocations for the seminary even in the present difficult circumstances. This means, among other things, knowing promising boys at local schools, having a keen eye to developing the spiritual life of altar boys, being aware of those families which have an environment conducive to nurturing vocations. As John Paul II, speaking to the bishops of Western France, reminds us:

> The first milieu that must be aided to awaken vocations is obviously the family. It is very much easier to set out for a life consecrated to the Church when the family bears witness to a living faith and has been generous enough to transmit life to several children ... In concrete terms, there is no doubt that we as bishops and priests must express even more directly to young people the call to the priesthood.[53]

The young need to hear the call of God if they are going to consider the priesthood seriously. Many potential vocations, however, never respond because they

---

50 Cf. ibid., no. 37. 51 Cf. ibid., no. 8. 52 Ibid. 53 Address, 13 February 1987, nos. 7, 8.

cannot distinguish the gentle intimations of the Holy Spirit above the noise created by all the other voices in the airwaves which claim their attention. The option of a life of service to God tends to be crowded out because it receives little echo in the social environment, or because it is so caricatured that it offers scant attraction for generous souls.

While the Christian family continues to be essential to fostering vocations, in today's world, where role models exercise such a strong influence on the young, a boy's esteem for, and attraction to, the priesthood probably depends largely on the impression priests themselves create. The full reality of the priestly vocation, if properly conveyed, is immensely attractive to idealistic souls at both the human and supernatural levels. The very life of priests, their unconditional dedication to God's flock, their witness of loving service to the Lord and to his Church, their fraternal unity and zeal for the evangelization of the world – these are the first and most convincing factors in the growth of vocations.[54] The Holy Father puts this aspect of things into perspective in his Message for the World Day of Vocations for the year 2000:

> I am aware that the pastoral care of vocations constitutes a less than easy ministry, but how can one not remember that there is nothing more uplifting than an enthusiastic witnessing to one's own vocation? He who lives this gift joyfully and nourishes it daily in his encounter with the Eucharist will know how to sow in the hearts of many young people the good seed of faithful adherence to the divine call.[55]

Consequently, if there are few applicants for the seminary, we priests have perhaps ourselves to blame in the first place because we have failed to spark that interest which is the initial stage in the development of a vocation. Could it be that potential vocations do not find in our own personal lifestyle the clearly etched image of Christ which always attracts and inspires?[56]

A fruitful source of vocations has traditionally been from among the boys who serve at our Masses. Nevertheless, their response will depend largely on the image of priesthood we project. Will they find in us that initial perception of the greatness of the priestly calling, of that ideal of service which so appeals to the generosity of a youthful heart? Will they grasp something of the awesome nature of the Holy Mass in our preparation for it, in our liturgical refinement, in the fact that we always do a few moments thanksgiving afterwards? In a word do they see that the Mass is the dynamic and the great love of our lives?

As he sent them out two by two, Christ reminded his disciples that the harvest was plentiful but the labourers few. The immediate conclusion he drew

---

54 Cf. PDV, 41.  55 *Osservatore Romano*, 1 December 1999.  56 Cf. Sheen, *The priest is not his own*, p. 57.

for them was: 'pray therefore the Lord of the harvest to send out labourers into his harvest' (Lk 10:2). The Lord will grant what we pray for earnestly, so the search for vocations has to begin on our knees. How often do I pray for this intention in my Mass, in my Rosary? How frequently do I remind others to pray for vocations – the parish congregation, mothers of families, generous souls?[57] As John Paul II puts it:

> there is no use in complaining about the lack of priestly and religious vocations. Vocations cannot be humanly 'made'. *Vocations are obtained from God through prayer.*[58]

Prayerful expectation of vocations has to become a more central aspect of the life of parish communities.[59]

The Pope spoke to a group of bishops from central France about the question of priestly vocations which is a critical issue in that country at the present time. His tone, as always, is optimistic and, while he is also fully aware of the shortage of vocations, he cautions against any solutions which would be contrary to the living Tradition of the Church:

> Your priests are fewer in number and their average age is rising. Young priests are coming and they are zealous, but there are not enough of them to ensure replacement! This is your daily concern. I share your anxiety in getting through this bleak period. But I am convinced that the decline is not irreversible and that this situation does not call into question the fundamental structure of the People of God as it has been established, in accord with the will of Christ, since the apostolic foundation and throughout Tradition. The history of France, as of many other countries, has not been without periods of scarcity; history also shows us that the vitality of the priestly corps has not been snuffed out. The Lord will not leave his flock without shepherds: 'I am with you always, until the end of the age' (Mt 28:20). This is a conviction which all the members of God's People must bring to their prayer and

57 'In his pastoral work, each priest will take particular care concerning vocations, doing his best in the work of catechetics, and taking care of the formation of the ministers. He will promote appropriate initiatives through a personal rapport with those under his care, allowing him to discover their talents and to single out the will of God for them, permitting a courageous choice in following Christ. Above all, a clear knowledge of one's specific identity, a unity of life, a transparent cheerfulness, and a missionary zeal are the indispensable elements of the vocational work that must be an integral and organic part of ordinary pastoral action ... It would be desirable that every priest be concerned with inspiring at least one priestly vocation which could thus continue the ministry' (DMLP, 32). 58 Homily, 20 June 1998 (italics in original). 59 Cf. PDV, 38.

which must inspire them to new action so that the call to young people may be made insistently and credibly.[60]

We have seen the primary role of prayer in nurturing vocations. However, prayer in itself is not enough: 'We need a direct preaching on the value of the ministerial priesthood, on God's people's urgent need of it ... The time has come to speak courageously about priestly life as a priceless gift and a splendid and privileged form of Christian living'.[61] Priests, John Paul II encourages us, 'should not be afraid to set forth explicitly and forcefully the priestly vocation as a real possibility for those young people who demonstrate the necessary gifts and talents'.[62] We need to take more to heart those unambiguous words of Christ: 'Put out into the deep and let down your nets for a catch' (Lk 5:4). We too have to return to the work of vocations ministry with the faith of Peter (cf. Lk 5:5). By trusting Christ's words we can go forward in hope (cf. Lk 5:6).[63]

> Today, every possible effort must again be made to encourage vocations, to form new generations of priests. This must be done in a genuinely evangelical spirit ... The full reconstitution of the life of seminaries throughout the Church will be the best proof of the achievement of the renewal to which the Council directed the Church.[64]

A priestly vocation is a gift from God but since it is also a gift to the Church as a whole, 'all the members of the Church, without exception, have the grace and responsibility to look after vocations'.[65] Priestly vocations are the guarantee of the future of the Church, so this ministry has to be treated as the jewel in the crown of pastoral care. Addressing priests directly, John Paul II tells them:

> Through you the Good Shepherd continues to teach, to sanctify, to guide and to love all peoples of every culture, every continent and every age. For this reason you alone enjoy the title of pastor and, since there is no salvation except in Christ and since he must be proclaimed to the ends of the earth, it is impossible to cross the threshold of the third millennium without making the pastoral care of vocations a priority. If the world cannot do without Christ, it also cannot do without priests.[66]

---

60 Address, 13 January 1992, no. 2. 61 *Pastores dabo vobis*, 39. 62 Ibid. 63 Cf. *Novo millennio ineunte*, 1, 58. 64 HTL, 1979. 65 *Pastores dabo vobis*, 41. 66 Message to priests, 19 June 2000, no. 4. 67 These figures, which have been rounded off for ease of comparison, are taken from the *Osservatore Romano*, 31 July 1996. A more recent summary, published in *Seminarium*, XXXIX (1999), no. 4, provides seminarian statistics up to 1997 with the arti-

## CHANGING SEMINARIAN PROFILE

While it is true that there has been a serious decline in priestly vocations in the developed countries of the West, this is not the case in other parts of the world. In Africa the number of seminarians (diocesan and religious) increased five-fold between 1970 and 1997. There was a three fold increase in Central and South America in the same period, while candidates for the priesthood in South East Asia more than doubled. The story for the Western world is very different. Seminarians in North America are about a third of what they were twenty years ago. Although in Europe the rate of decline was less marked, numbers decreased from 34,000 in 1974 to a low of 23,000 in 1977. Nevertheless, since 1978, the year John Paul II was elected Pope, the situation has recovered with a gradual increase to 28,000 by 1997.[67]

A review of the vocations situation in some of the developed Western countries over the twenty years 1978 to 1997 provides interesting reading. During this period the number of seminarians in Germany dropped by 40%, in the Low Countries by 28%, and in Britain by 26%. On the other hand in Italy the number increased by 15%, in Portugal by 18%, and in Poland by 30%. In 1978 France had 1280 seminarians, a figure which rose to 1603 by 1997, an increase of 25%. Ireland had roughly the same number of seminarians as France in 1978 - a total of 1120. However, over the next twenty years this figure would decrease to 386, a drop of 65%, the sharpest rate of decline in the whole of Europe.[68]

Yet, there are good reasons for hope in the West as we can see from the healthy developments in some dioceses in the US and elsewhere. Peoria in Illinois, Arlington near Washington DC, Denver (Colorado), and Lincoln (Nebraska) have been singularly successful in attracting young men to the priesthood. Atlanta, which in 1985 had nine seminarians, now boasts sixty-one. Arlington, with a Catholic population of 275,000, has nearly fifty seminarians and ordained fifty-five men to the priesthood in the period 1991-98. Bishop John Myers of Peoria (230,000 Catholics), who also has fifty young men preparing for the priesthood, has advised his people to prepare for the 're-priesting' of the diocese, having ordained seventy eight priests in the period 1991-98.[69]

Another diocese with a healthy seminary situation is Omaha, Nebraska (fifty-six men ordained in 1991-98 for a diocese of 215,000 Catholics).

cle *Dimensione quantitativa della Chiesa Cattolica alle soglie dell'Anno giubilare*, pp 591-740. The same trends continue between 1994 and 1997. 68 Cf. *Seminarium*, ibid., table no. 14 for Europe, p. 720. 69 Cf. Michael F. Flach, 'What priest shortage?', *Catholic World Report*, June 1996, pp 36-41; John F. Quinn, 'Priest shortage panic', *Crisis*, October 1996, pp 40-4; Michael Rose, 'A self-imposed shortage', in *Catholic World Report*, February 2001, p. 60.

Archbishop Curtiss, the ordinary of Omaha, told the Serra international convention that, in his experience, young people 'do not want to commit themselves to dioceses or communities which permit or simply ignore dissent from Church doctrine. They do not want to be associated with people who are angry with the Church's leadership or reject magisterial teaching'. He urged his audience to

> take heart by what is happening in certain dioceses and religious communities throughout the world which are experiencing increasing numbers of candidates. There is a remarkable similarity in the reasons which are given for these successes: unswerving allegiance to the Pope and the magisterial teaching of the Church; adoration of the Blessed Sacrament in parishes, with an emphasis on praying for vocations; a strong effort by a significant number of priests and religious who extend themselves to help young men and women remain open to the Lord's will in their lives; and a growing number of laity who support vocation ministry.[70]

These are obviously useful desiderata to be taken into account in any strategy for vocations promotion.

Seminary authorities in the West have commented in recent years on the change in the profile of seminarians entering the priesthood at present by comparison with those of twenty-five years ago. Generally they are older, usually with a university degree and some years work experience. They come to the priesthood by many different routes, but always as a result of a deeper personal conversion to Christ. Often they have been powerfully attracted by the discovery of the integral faith of the Church as reflected in the life and teaching of John Paul II. As one American seminary rector commented:

> Most of them have experienced some significant conversion in their lives, and this is the hermeneutical key to understanding their attachment to a solid and unambiguous faith. They have lived through the passage from confusion to certainty, from a state of indifference and conformity with the world's moral compromises to embracing Christ and his way of living. The distinctive moral and doctrinal notes of Catholic Christianity are for them, not impediments to the happiness they anticipate in the mainstream culture, but are the salutary means for deliverance from the damage the culture and its promises have

---

70 *Origins*, 8 October 1995, p. 167.  71 Bishop Allen H. Vigernon, rector of Sacred Heart Seminary, Detroit, 'A new breed of seminarians', in *Crisis*, May 1999, p. 38.

done to them and their buddies, by means of all the excesses of the age.[71]

Another seminary rector, referring to the confusion and uncertainty of twenty-five years ago, says that the current crop of seminarians

> have a pretty clear sense of direction and are very guided by the teachings of John Paul II. What I see now more than ever is a very strong apostolic spirit. They're eager to get out and preach the Gospel and they're eager to find ways of communicating the faith to people.[72]

John Paul II himself has been a great promoter of priestly vocations because of his compelling witness to a priesthood which reflects the person of Christ so clearly. He generates a deep conviction about priestly identity – this is why he attracts many young men to the priesthood. It was in this context that one ecclesiastic commented, 'A man will give his life for a mystery but not for a question mark'.[73] As we have seen, it is not without significance that in Europe as a whole vocations have increased significantly since John Paul II's accession to the papacy in 1978.

## NEW EVANGELIZATION

Over the years the Holy Father has frequently called for a re-evangelization, especially in countries of long-standing Christian tradition which have succumbed to the inroads of secularism and materialism. In his encyclical *Redemptoris missio* he speaks about a new spring of evangelization and outlines the modern equivalents of the Areopagus (cf. Acts 17:23-31) which need to be evangelized – the world of communications, culture, scientific research and international relations.[74] What is at stake here, he tells us, is the struggle for the world's soul because of a powerful 'anti-evangelization' at work in the world, which is well organized and with the resources 'to vigorously oppose the Gospel'.[75] This evangelization is essentially a task for the lay faithful who through the sanctification of their work are baptismally called to christianize secular realities. But to do so effectively they need to be serviced by a ministerial priesthood which will supply them with the formation and means of grace to equip them for this apostolic enterprise.

72 Monsignor Kenneth Roeltgen, former rector of Mount St Mary's Seminary, Emmetsburg, Maryland, in an interview with David Wagner, *Crisis*, October 1997, p. 35. 73 Cf. Weigel, ibid., p. 658. 74 *Redemptoris missio*, 37 (7 December 1990). 75 John Paul II, *Crossing the threshold of hope*, p. 112.

At the beginning of this new millennium John Paul II repeats his invitation 'to put out into the deep' (Lk 5:5), asking us to rekindle the zeal of the early Christians and 'to allow ourselves to be filled with the ardour of the apostolic preaching which followed Pentecost'.[76] If priests are imbued with this vision it will stir up a new sense of mission in the Church. To do this

> Christ must be presented to all people with confidence. We should address adults, families, young people, children, without ever hiding the most radical demands of the Gospel message.[77]

The Pope asks that our efforts would be inspired, sustained, and guided by the example of those men and women from very different backgrounds who were remembered during the Jubilee year, newly recognised saints and martyrs, who in different ways were able to live the Gospel heroically in ordinary life or who were ready to give witness to the faith in an environment of hostility and persecution.[78]

While the Church should use all the available technical resources to communicate effectively the Christian message of salvation, it can never be forgotten that technology is no substitute for the witness of a holy life. John Paul II, referring specifically to the re-christianization of Europe, affirms that 'the saints were the great evangelizers of Europe. We must pray the Lord to increase the spirit of holiness in the Church and to send us new saints to evangelize the contemporary world'.[79] Philosophical and theological formation are a necessary foundation for priests to present the faith constructively, by means of personal dialogue. But the proclamation of the Gospel cannot be reduced to dialogue alone. What is also required is the courage to communicate the full demands of Christ's message, and not shy away from confronting people with unsettling truths about their lives. The objective of evangelization is always the same – on the one hand, to instruct and to encourage the intelligence towards conversion (cf. Mt 9:36; 4:17), and, on the other, to move hearts to sorrow and repentance, opening the way to sacramental forgiveness.[80]

The spirit of the new evangelization which should animate priests is perhaps best summed up by John Paul II in the pastoral challenge issued in his document on the Church in the third millennium:

> At the beginning of the new millennium ... our hearts ring out with the words of Jesus when one day, after speaking to the crowds from Simon's boat, he invited the Apostle to 'put out into the deep' for a catch: '*Duc in altum*' (Lk 5:4). Peter and his first companions trusted

76 *Novo millennio ineunte*, 40.  77 Ibid.  78 Cf. ibid, no. 41.  79 John Paul II, Address to European bishops, 11 October 1985.  80 Cf. *The priest and the third Christian millennium*, I.

Christ's words, and cast the nets. When they had done this, they caught a great number of fish' (Lk 5:6) ... *Duc in altum!* These words ring out for us today, and they invite us to remember the past with gratitude, to live the present with enthusiasm and to look forward to the future with confidence: 'Jesus Christ is the same yesterday and today and for ever' (Heb 13:8).[81]

---

81 *Novo millennio ineunte,* 1.

# 9

# Preaching about chastity, marriage and
## *Humanae vitae*

We live at a time when traditional Church teaching on sexual morality is widely rejected or obscured. There is also much evidence to indicate that many Catholics ignore this teaching both inside and outside of marriage. Consequently preaching about chastity today is in many ways an exercise in rowing against the current. At the present time particular areas of the social environment are quite hostile to the living of this virtue, with the emphasis on an exaggerated sense of personal freedom rooted in a climate of permissiveness. It is not that this is a new challenge for preachers. Down through history the Church has always had to contend with the problem of sexual immorality. St Paul, and the Fathers of the Church after him, did not hesitate to use vigorous language to inculcate the virtue of chastity and to keep the early Christians away from immoral forms of entertainment common in their day.[1]

Man is endowed with a strong sexual instinct which with difficulty is amenable to control. It has also become abundantly clear that experiments in social engineering do not provide answers in this area. People are in fact rediscovering that only by the cultivation of a moral sense, in keeping with man's dignity as a being made to the image and likeness of God, can the sexual dynamic be channelled towards its proper objective. Thus the priest has a particular responsibility to remind people that sexuality is a gift from God, and that what we do with it forms a very definite part of God's plan for us in this life. It is his privilege to bring out in his preaching the fully positive and liberating implications of the Master's affirmation 'Blessed are the pure in heart for they shall see God' (Mt 5:8). The regulation of the sexual instinct by the virtue of chastity is not a form of repression. On the contrary, it is a rational discipline which respects human dignity and which with the help of grace facilitates a human love that is faithful, fruitful and fulfilling.

To preach convincingly about the virtue of chastity, the priest needs to be

---

1 Cf., for example, the homilies of St John Chrysostom on the book of Genesis and on St John's Gospel, *passim* (*Commentary on St John the Apostle and the Evangelist*, vol. 1 (nos. 1-47), vol. 2 (nos. 48-88), Catholic University of America Press, Washington 1960; *Homilies on Genesis*, vol. 1 (nos. 1 -17), vol. 2 (nos. 18-45), vol. 3 (nos. 46-67), Washington, 1986).

able to present coherent arguments from Christian anthropology and Sacred Scripture. John Paul II in his extensive catechesis on the 'nuptial meaning of the body' has developed these arguments with a depth and coherence which has rarely been attempted before. Any priest who takes the trouble to familiarize himself with this catechesis will have his Christian vision of man reaffirmed, and will be encouraged to present Christ's teaching on chastity in a positive and confident way.[2]

We are reminded by Vatican II that all preaching 'should be nourished and ruled by Sacred Scripture'.[3] So, familiarity with the biblical understanding of human sexuality is essential to give an integral presentation of God's revelation in this area of Christian morality. Just about every expression of sexual activity is mentioned in the Old Testament, but the only form which is recognized as legitimate is that of marital intercourse within a lifelong covenant of love, a covenant which accepts both the sensuousness of the Song of Songs and the self-obligation of 1 Corinthians 13 as constitutive of married love.[4]

### NEW TESTAMENT TEACHING

The incomplete teaching of the Old Testament on chastity is brought to fulfilment by Christ and explained with remarkable clarity in the preaching of St Paul. The New Testament brings everything human, including man's sexuality, within the context of the Incarnation and Christ's saving grace. Jesus shows compassion for the woman taken in adultery, but leaves her in no doubt about the seriousness of the sin (cf. Jn 8:3-11). His condemnation of adultery of the heart (cf. Mt 5:28) expresses a datum which is at the core of Christ's moral teaching – sin is not just a matter of external behaviour but stems primarily from the internal dispositions of the heart and the will. These inclinations are the cause of that catalogue of vices, including the sins of adultery, fornication and sensuality enumerated by Christ, which defile the human person and exclude from the kingdom of Heaven.[5]

St Paul repeats the same teaching in similar words as he voices his deep concern for the Christian converts in swinging Corinth.[6] The Pauline teaching

2 This series of weekly addresses by John Paul II, which ran intermittently from 1979 to 1984, have been published in four volumes by St Paul Editions, Boston, as follows: *Original unity of man and woman: catechesis on the book of Genesis* (1981); *Blessed are the pure of heart: catechesis on the sermon on the mount and the writings of St Paul* (1983); *Reflections on Humanae vitae: conjugal morality and spirituality* (1984); *The theology of marriage and celibacy: catechesis on marriage and celibacy in the light of the resurrection of the body* (1986). These addresses are also available in one volume: *The theology of the body: human love in the divine plan*, Boston, 1997. 3 *Dei Verbum*, 21. 4 Cf. John F. Kippley, 'A covenant theology of sex', in *Homiletic and Pastoral Review*, Aug.-Sept. 1983, p. 25. 5 Cf. Mt 15:19; Mk 7:21-22; Gal 5:19-21. 6 Cf. 1 Cor 6:9-10. See also Heb 13:4.

on human sexuality takes as its starting point the effects of baptism by which the person is united to Christ in a very intimate way and, as a consequence, becomes a temple of the Holy Spirit (cf. 1 Cor 6:13-20). It was in this context that Pope John Paul II, in an address to an audience of young people, described chastity as 'a primary expression of caring for one's baptismal identity'.[7]

St Paul's development of the covenant theme of married love is one of the gems of sacred Scripture and is rich in ideas for preaching on this topic (cf. Eph 5: 21-33). In the same letter he sets high standards with regard to purity in conversations and actions (cf. Eph 5:3-14), but he also reminds us that the fruits of a life lived in the Holy Spirit include modesty, continence and chastity (cf. Gal 5:22-23). This Pauline doctrine on human sexuality is developed with balance and clarity in the pastoral letter of the Irish bishops, *Love is for life*.[8]

PREACHING PROGRAMME

Since no particular virtue can be acquired in isolation, effective communication of the importance of, and the need for, chastity in the spiritual life requires that it be seen in the broader context of the Christian vocation in general. Indeed, the document of the Pontifical Council for the Family on sex education says that formation in chastity should always be given in the light of the universal call to holiness, either as vocation to marriage or as vocation to celibacy or virginity.[9]

Obviously the presentation of such a programme will be determined to some extent by the needs of particular congregations, their social and age structure, etc. Nevertheless, whatever the audience, a proper understanding and appreciation of chastity always requires effective evangelization in the programme of Christian living outlined by Jesus Christ in the Sermon on the Mount, an appreciation of the importance of prayer and sacramental life for growth in holiness, the need for self-denial and its relationship to the Cross in our daily lives, and an elucidation of the Decalogue in the light of the words of the Master: 'If you love me, you will keep my commandments' (Jn 14:15).

The needs of the present time require that in preaching about chastity we do so with clarity. A great bishop has said:

> Today a vigorous recall is needed to the basic virtue of chastity. There must be new respect for the gift of human sexuality and for the laws of

7 Homily, 27 September 1986. 8 Cf. paras. 43-46 and 128-136, published Lent, 1985. 9 Cf. *The truth and meaning of human sexuality*, 26 (8 December 1995).

God which govern its use ... It is necessary to call things once again by their true names – fornication, adultery, lustful desires, immoral displays in cinemas, videos, etc. All these are a serious offence against human dignity.[10]

Pastoral charity does not mean being silent in face of sin or error. Tolerance is an admirable virtue but it is never an excuse for turning a blind eye to particular practices or behaviour which undermine the teaching of Christ. A priest must be ready to unmask the euphemisms of our day which disguise immorality or indeed real crimes. A person may be in a 'stable relationship', or have a 'partner' in addition to a lawfully wedded spouse, or may 'terminate a pregnancy'. But it is only when things are called by their real names – fornication, adultery, etc. – as Christ described such acts, that people learn to face up fully to the moral demands of their lives as Christians. Priests need to be clear but also refined in their presentation; they have to teach positively but also with courage: 'Proclaim the message, welcome or unwelcome, insist on it ... But do all with patience and the intention of teaching' (2 Tim 4:12).

In addition, it is necessary to approach this task with humility in the knowledge that we are all made of the same clay. Our efforts to live this virtue faithfully will give us the insight and understanding appropriate to persons and circumstances. Apart from the suggestions outlined above, Christian wisdom down through the centuries has indicated specific means by which the virtue of holy purity can be more easily acquired: practice of the virtue of temperance, guard of the heart and the senses, avoiding idleness and occasions of sin, living those other virtues which cluster around and protect chastity such as modesty, refinement in thought and conversations, rejection of temptations to vanity and pride, etc.

### JOHN PAUL II'S EXAMPLE

An eloquent example of this kind of preaching is that given by the Holy Father in his encounter with the youth of Holland during his visit to that country in May 1985. In reply to a number of questions which he was asked by these young people, the Pope said: 'You still have many prejudices and suspicions in encountering the Church. You have let me know that you often consider the Church an institution which does nothing but promulgate regulations and laws. You think that she puts up barriers in many fields: sexuality, the structure of the Church, the place of women in the Church..' Then he goes on to put their objections into context:

10 Archbishop K. McNamara, 'The role of the laity in the Church' in *Osservatore Romano*, 12 May 1986.

Dear friends, allow me to be very frank with you. I know that you speak in perfectly good faith. But are you really sure that the idea you have of Christ fully corresponds to the reality of his person? The Gospel, in truth, presents us with a very demanding Christ who invites us to a radical conversion of heart (cf. Mk 19:3-9) ... In particular, concerning the sexual sphere, the firm position taken by him in defence of the indissolubility of marriage (cf. Mt 19:3-9), and the condemnation pronounced even regarding simple adultery of the heart (cf. Mt 5:27) are well known. And how can one fail to be struck by the precept 'to gouge out one's eye' or 'cut off one's hand' if these members are an occasion of 'scandal' (cf. Mt 5:29)?[11]

With these specific Gospel references as background, the Pope then asks his listeners,

is it realistic to imagine a 'permissive' Christ in the realm of married life, in the question of abortion, or pre-marital, extra-marital, or homosexual relations? The early Christian community, taught by those who had personally known Christ were certainly not permissive. Suffice it here to allude to the numerous passages of the Pauline letters which touch upon these matters (cf. Rom 1:26 ff; 1 Cor 6:9; Gal 5:19; etc). The words of the Apostle are certainly not lacking in clarity and vigour. And they are words inspired from on high. They remain normative for the Church of every age ... Permissiveness does not make man happy ... A human being fulfils himself only to the extent that he knows how to accept the demands that have their origin in his dignity as a creature made 'in the image and likeness of God' (Gen 1: 27).[12]

If preaching about chastity were suffused by this gospel clarity, priests would be making a real contribution to forming people in the truth about an integral part of their lives, a truth that would make them free to love in an authentic way (cf. Jn 8:32).

GENERAL CONTEXT

In preaching about the virtue of chastity there are certain fundamental concepts which should under-pin and permeate any discourse on this topic. Briefly these are:

11 Address to youth of Holland, 14 May 1985.  12 Ibid.

- the gift of personal freedom and what this implies for human actions and our responsibility for them;

- the call to Christian holiness stemming from our baptismal vocation;

- the inherent frailty of the human condition as a consequence of original sin;

- the redemptive and transforming power of divine grace.

Bearing these elements in mind will help us avoid approaches which suffer from either a naive optimism on the one hand, or a kind of manichean pessimism on the other; it will help us steer the middle course of Christian realism.

Education in a true sense of freedom is an essential part of a programme for formation in chastity.[13] For some, freedom simply means doing what one feels like doing, leading on to the idea that real happiness is to be found only by a release from all obligations, duties or limits. Yet authentic freedom is in fact achieved when one can freely choose to live according to God's plan.[14] The point has been well made: 'there is no sexual freedom without chastity, without the proper ordering of our sexual faculty which does not easily accept control'.[15]

The doctrine of the transforming action of grace in the human soul is ultimately the basis of the priest's confidence that his preaching about chastity will be effective.[16] It is encourging to remind oneself, and to remind others as well, that when St Paul complained about his own struggle against the flesh, he was told by Christ 'my grace is sufficient for you, for my power is made perfect in weakness' (2 Cor 12:9).

### OVERALL PASTORAL PROGRAMME

The question of preaching about chastity has to be seen in the context of an overall pastoral programme. Effective formation in chastity would seem to be constituted by three main elements:

a) regular preaching, on appropriate occasions, on different aspects of chastity inside and outside of marriage, as an integral part of the homily programme for the liturgical cycle;[17]

13 Cf. *Familiaris consortio*, 37.  14 Cf. CCC, 1731-42.  15 Anthony J. Mastroeni, 'The freedom of the sons of God', in *Homiletic and Pastoral Review*, February 1983, p. 33.  16 Cf. CCC, 1996-2005.  17 This, and the catechesis in home and school, can be based on the relevant sections of the *Catechism of the Catholic Church*: cf. Sacrament of Matrimony, nos. 1601-66; The Sixth Commandment, nos. 2331-400; The Ninth Commandment, nos. 2514-

b) a progressive catechesis in this virtue in the school and in the home, which will also include a programme of Christian sex education as outlined in the Pontifical Council for the Family document *The truth and meaning of human sexuality*;

c) the catechetical and preaching programme needs pastoral back-up through spiritual counselling and sacramental participation, especially by means of the sacrament of Reconciliation.[18]

These three elements are complementary and mutually supportive, and are essential if adolescents in particular are to acquire this virtue in the context of normal emotional development. They will thus come to terms with their God-given sexuality in a personality that reflects a balance of both the human and supernatural virtues. However, to achieve this objective is not an easy task at the present time. The findings of surveys of young people's attitudes to sexual morality seem to indicate a failure to assimilate, or a tendency to reject some of the basic Christian moral values in this area.[19] The reality of this change in attitude is in fact substantiated by the rapid growth in the levels of abortion and out-of-wedlock births over the past thirty years.[20]

## CHASTITY WITHIN MARRIAGE

While preaching about chastity in general has its own importance, from the perspective of marriage and family responsibilities it takes on a renewed significance at the present time. The theology of married love has been developed from rich scriptural sources and this has been reinforced by Catholic tradition. Nevertheless, the memory of this tradition has been lost to many contemporary Christians. There are, for example, very few people today who seem to be aware that until the 1930 Lambeth Conference no Christian church had ever accepted contraception as morally permissible.

A subjective approach to marriage is a common feature of contemporary society, in the sense that the quality of the affective life of the partners often becomes the dominant measure for assessing everything related to marriage. Viewed, however, from a Christian perspective there are, of course, other, and

---

33. **18** Cf. Chapter 11 below. **19** Cf. *Religious beliefs, practice and moral attitudes:* a comparison of two Irish surveys 1974-1984, by Council for Research and Development, Maynooth College, with particular reference to the 18-30 age group, under headings of attitudes to: Use of contraceptives, Pre-marital sex, Abortion, and Divorce; Christopher W. Whelan (ed.), *Values and social change in Ireland*, Dublin, 1994. **20** Out-of-wedlock births in the Republic rose from 1709 in 1970 to 16,451 in 1999, representing an increase from 2.6% to 30.9% of live births. Abortions increased from 261 in 1970 to 6214 in 1999, representing 11.6% of live births. Sources: annual reports of CSO, Dublin and OPCS, Britain.

deeper, factors which must also be given adequate consideration – the role of marriage in extending the kingdom of Christ, the responsibility of parents for transmitting the faith from one generation to the next, the contribution of children to the human and spiritual maturity of the parents.

In a permissive society there is a tendency to assume that sexual gratification constitutes the greatest human fulfilment. To counteract this erroneous and selfish perspective there is a need to reaffirm the liberating and healthy joy that comes from service to others, from noble human ambitions and work well done, from family and friendships. It is also essential to emphasise that earthly happiness is not the only happiness open to man.

Independently of subjective attitudes to marriage, it needs to be understood that marriage is of divine institution and serves particular purposes in God's plan. The more people are aware of this, the better they will understand the nature of marriage and the expectations they can have of it. The Church teaches that 'happiness in marriage is normally and in the long run more likely to depend on having and rearing children than on the mutual love between husband and wife, and its expressions'. This is because nature has designed married love to become family love, and thus 'growth in love will normally be in function of growth in fruitfulness'.[21]

To preach adequately about marriage it is not enough for the priest to be familiar with the theology and the pastoral aspects of the sacrament. He also needs to be able to articulate what Christian anthropology teaches us about marriage. John Paul II in his weekly catechesis on the theology of the body has developed a rich Christian anthropology based on Scripture and the reality of the Incarnation.[22] As he graphically points out, consequent to the fact that the Word of God became flesh, 'the body entered theology through the main door'.[23] In this sense the Incarnation is the source of the sacramentality of marriage.[24]

The importance of the theology of the body is measured by the fact that, for most Christians, marriage is a vocation and a way to holiness.[25] Consequently the teaching of revelation on the body has to be the basis of the theology of vocation to marriage. This awareness of the transcendent meaning of the body is even more necessary today in a culture which is increasingly influenced by a utilitarian and materialistic way of seeing things. Modern science can supply a great deal of precise information about human sexuality. However, man has to have recourse to other sources to get to know the dignity

21 Cf. Cormac Burke, *Covenanted happiness*, Dublin, 1990, pp 17-22. **22** Cf. footnote no. 2. 23 Address, 2 April 1980, no.4. **24** While still auxiliary bishop of Krakow, John Paul II had developed his anthropology of marriage in *Love and responsibility*, London, 1981 (originally published in Polish in 1960). **25** Cf. *Gaudium et spes*, 48, 50; *Apostolicam actuositatem*, 11; *Familiaris consortio*, 34.

of the human body and sexuality, primarily what the Word of God Himself has revealed about it.[26]

John Paul II, for the duration of his pontificate, and for may years before, has dedicated his best energies to persuading us of the truth and the richness of the Church's teaching on marriage and the family. His constant attention to this theme is a consequence of his conviction that stable marriages and happy family life are essential to human well-being and that, if this objective is achieved, many other evils in society would be eradicated. After he completed his long series of talks on the theology of the body (1979-1984), he has continued to give special attention to moral and pastoral questions related to marriage and the family. In his many journeys abroad the affirmation of the Christian concept of the family has always been high on his agenda. Indeed in 1984 he identified the defence of marriage and the family as his first pastoral priority,[27] because for him 'the story of mankind and the history of salvation passes by way of the family'.[28] A fundamental part of his programme of evangelization is geared to making Christians rediscover once again the full implications of his exhortation: 'Family, become what you are'.[29]

During his pontificate we have seen the publication of several important documents on the family, including *The Christian family in the modern world* [*Familiaris consortio*] (1981); the *Charter of the rights of the family* (1983); and the *Letter to families* (1994). Awareness of these writings of John Paul II will enable the priest draw on many rich insights to illustrate his preaching on this topic.

PURPOSES OF MARRIAGE

Up to the time of Vatican II the Magisterium of the Church spoke about a hierarchy in the ends or purposes of marriage. Thus it maintained that the procreation and education of children was the *primary* purpose of marriage – this was the objective, ontological basis and explanation of marriage as an institution. The *secondary* end was the mutual love and personal development of the spouses. However, the Vatican II constitution *Gaudium et spes* avoids this terminology and affirms of marriage that 'its nature as an indissoluble compact between two people and the good of the children demand that the mutual love of the partners be properly shown, that it should grow and mature'.[30]

In the 1983 Code of Canon Law, marriage is described as a covenant by

---

26 Cf. John Paul II Address, 2 April 1980, no.5. 27 Cf. Address, 22 March 1984. 28 John Paul II, *Letter to families*, 23; see also *Familiaris consortio*, 86. 29 *Familiaris consortio*, 17. 30 *Gaudium et spes*, 50.

which a man and woman establish a life-long partnership 'which of its very nature is ordered to the well-being of the spouses and to the procreation and upbringing of children'.[31] The same definition is repeated in the new *Catechism of the Catholic Church*.[32] This is a development of the doctrine taught in the 1917 Code of Canon Law, and subsequently by Pius XI and by Pius XII.[33] Rather than a hierarchy of ends, the Church now defines marriage with two equal but interrelated primary ends: the good of the spouses and the transmission of life. As one noted canon lawyer has put it, 'it is their mutual interdependence and inseparability which are now emphasized'.[34]

This integrated statement of the ends of marriage reflects the Christian anthropology and personalism which are characteristic of the teaching of John Paul II, as well as of Vatican II. The rich theological and ascetical implications of this renewed vision of marriage have been well put by Blessed Josemaría Escrivá, both from the institutional and vocational points of view:

> It is important for married people to acquire a clear sense of the dignity of their vocation. They must know that they have been called by God not only to human love but also to a divine love through their human love. It is important for them to realize that they have been chosen from eternity to cooperate with the creative power of God by having and then bringing up children. Our Lord asks them to make their home and their entire family life a testimony to all the Christian virtues.[35]

The personalist values inherent in this restatement of the purposes of marriage focus, as we have already seen, on the innate dignity of the individual made to the image and likeness of God. A consequence of this attitude is the mutual self-giving of the spouses through the marriage covenant which nurtures the growth of maturity, generosity, and the capacity to trust each other. In summary, each spouse becomes a means and a source of holiness for the other, facilitating the growth of those marital values reflected in the Song of Songs, the book of Tobit, and chapter five of the Ephesians.

Marriage as a 'communion of persons' is central to the doctrine of John Paul II on this area.[36] This, he says, can only be achieved by total self-giving, that sustained effort to suppress the selfish tendencies of the human soul which are constantly inclined to reassert themselves. In this context he has fre-

---

31 Code of Canon Law, 1055§1.  32 Cf. no. 1601.  33 Cf., for example, the encyclical *Casti connubii* of Pius XI (1931), Address of Pius XII, 29 October 1951.  34 Cf. Cormac Burke, 'Love and the family in today's world' in *Homiletic and Pastoral Review*, March 1995, p. 28.  35 *Conversations with Monsignor Escrivá*, Manila, 1977, no. 93.  36 Cf. *Familiaris consortio*, 15.

quently repeated a phrase of Vatican II: 'man can fully discover his true self only in a sincere giving of himself'.[37]

## CHILDREN AND MARRIAGE

Clearly there is a direct connection between total self-giving in marriage and generosity in accepting the children God sends to spouses. The Church sees children as 'the supreme gift of marriage'[38], and affirms that it is in them marriage 'finds its crowning glory'.[39]

Yet nowadays there is a tendency to see children as a mixed blessing. Often they are considered more as a burden and a strain on material and psychological resources rather than a gift from God. The loss of the Christian sense of the unique value of children in themselves, as well as a declining awareness of the contribution of children to healthy family relationships, has caused spouses to deprive themselves of the very means which God intended to enable them grow in love for each other. In the context of the current anti-child propaganda the priest has a serious duty to reaffirm the importance of the role of children from a human and Christian point of view.[40] There is a need to recover an awareness of the great blessing children are for parents, not only in terms of the joy they bring them but, more fundamentally, of the role children play in leading them to holiness. Every child is another reason for the couple to mature their love for each other, to grow in generosity, and to co-operate in the redemptive work of God.

## PREACHING ABOUT *HUMANAE VITAE*

In preaching about chastity and marriage, one of the great challenges is the presentation of the moral teaching of *Humanae vitae*. Perhaps no other encyclical in the history of the Church has been the subject of such comment and controversy. After it was published in 1968 there were a number of forces already pushing for its rejection. Vatican II presented people with changes which were profound and often confusing. A change in the teaching on artificial contraception was, according to some theologians, just another change. With the availability of the contraceptive pill in the sixties the 'sexual revolution' was in full swing, and media hype was producing a neurotic fear about 'overpopulation'. For five years people had been led to believe by Vatican watchers and dissident theologians that the teaching would change. And so in

37 *Gaudium et spes*, 24.  38 Ibid, no. 50.  39 Ibid, no. 48.  40 Cf. John Paul II, Homily in Washington D.C., 7 October 1979.

1968 when the Pope's answer did finally come, and there was no change, many reacted with dissent and disbelief.[41]

Any suggestion that the encyclical was a provisional statement on the morality of contraception was conclusively dispelled by Pope John Paul II in an authoritative commentary on *Humanae vitae*.[42] The difficulties involved in teaching and accepting the doctrine of the encyclical are not underestimated by the Holy Father, but this does not in any way take away from its certainty:

> In their effort to live their conjugal love correctly, married couples can be seriously impeded by a certain hedonistic mentality widespread today, by the mass media, by ideologies and practices contrary to the Gospel. This can also come about, with truly grave and destructive consequences, when the doctrine taught by the encyclical is called into question, as has sometimes happened, even on the part of some theologians and pastors of souls. This attitude, in fact, can instil doubt with regard to a teaching which for the Church is certain; in this way it clouds the perception of a truth which cannot be questioned. This is not a sign of 'pastoral understanding' but of *misunderstanding the true good of persons.* Truth cannot be measured by majority opinion.[43]

In a world which has scant esteem for generosity in this area, and where trust in God's providence finds little practical echo, preaching the doctrine of Paul VI's great encyclical requires faith and courage.

### JOHN PAUL II AND *HUMANAE VITAE*: ANTHROPOLOGICAL CONSIDERATIONS

To preach effectively about *Humanae vitae* it is essential to put it in context. One of the most important insights of Vatican II was the articulation of the fact that marriage is a divine vocation.[44] Pope John Paul II developed this theme during his visit to Ireland in 1979. 'Married people', he urged, 'must

41 Cf. Bishop John J Myers, 'The rejection and rediscovery by Christians of the truths of *Humanae vitae'* in Russell Smith (ed.), *Trust the truth: a symposium on the twentieth anniversary of the encyclical,* Braintree, Mass. 1988, pp 65-78. 42 Cf. John Paul II, *Reflections on Humanae vitae,* Boston 1984; a series of fourteen addresses delivered between 11 July and 28 November 1984. There are also very helpful commentaries on *Humanae vitae* in chapters 9 and 10 of *Christian marriage* (Pastoral letter of Irish hierarchy for Lent 1969), and in *Human life is sacred* (Pastoral letter, 1 May 1975), particularly paragraphs nos. 93-127. 43 John Paul II, Address, 14 March 1988 (italics in original). 44 Cf. *Gaudium et spes,* 48 and 50; see also Decree on the lay apostolate (*Apostolicam actuositatem*), no. 11; *Familiaris consortio,* 34.

believe in the power of the sacrament to make them holy; they must believe in their vocation to witness through their marriage to the power of Christ's love'.[45] It is in this context that chastity in marriage has to be preached if it is to be truly meaningful to Christians of today. It demands on the part of the priest a deepening perception of the vocation of the laity who, the Holy Father reminds us in the same homily, 'are called to the heights of holiness'.[46] Otherwise there is the danger that priests will sell the laity short in relation to God's expectation of them and the vocational dynamic that should inspire their lives.[47]

The priest should know how to present the Church's attitude to human life as protective and affirmative of married love. Perhaps the most important point he has to get across at the present time is that the Church has an eminently positive approach to human love, sexuality and marriage, and that it is essentially pro-love and pro-life.[48] The Church reaffirms that no real contradiction can exist between fulfilling the divine laws pertaining to the transmission of life and those which foster authentic conjugal love.[49] The teaching of Christ in the Sermon on the Mount and the Pauline doctrine taught in 1 Corinthians demonstrate a real awareness of the practical difficulties involved in being faithful to the Christian moral norms related to marital chastity. However, they are also a confirmation of man's capacity to live this holiness of life by means of grace.[50]

Diligent priests will glean many new and penetrating insights from the writings of John Paul II for a more persuasive presentation of the teaching of *Humanae vitae* based on Scripture, Christian anthropology, and natural law. On 11 July 1984 he began a series of reflections on the encyclical in continuity with the addresses which he initiated in 1979 on the theology of the body.[51] In these fourteen addresses he applies the anthropological principles he had already developed to facilitate a deeper understanding of Paul VI's document on the transmission of human life. He focuses particularly on the central affirmation of this encyclical, that is, on the inseparable connection established by God between the unitive and procreative significance of the marriage act.[52]

45 *The Pope in Ireland: addresses and homilies,* Dublin, 1979, p. 80 (Homily in Limerick, on 1 October 1979). 46 Ibid., p. 76. 47 Cf. *Lumen gentium,* 31, 40, 41. These ideas are powerfully developed by John Paul II in his post-synodal exhortation, *The vocation and mission of the laity in the Church and the world (Christifideles laici),* nos. 16 and 17, 30 December 1988. 48 Cf. Charles M. Mangan, 'The homily that never was', in *Homiletic and Pastoral Review,* November 1991, pp 67-70. 49 Cf. *Humanae vitae,* 20. 50 Cf. Address, 25 July 1984, no. 6. 51 Cf. *Reflections on Humanae vitae,* Boston, 1984. 52 'The Church teaches as absolutely required that in any use whatever of marriage there must be no impairment of its natural capacity to procreate human life ... This particular doctrine, often expounded by the Magisterium of the Church, is based on the inseparable connection, established by God, which man on his own initiative may not break, between the unitive significance and the

In a world which is invaded by a hedonistic philosophy, it is not sufficient, John Paul II tells us, that the teaching of *Humanae vitae* be faithfully and fully proposed. Deeply conscious of the intellectual and moral confusion of our times, he affirms that it is also necessary to demonstrate its deepest reasons.[53] Where these deepest reasons were to be found he had already adumbrated in *Familiaris consortio* when he called on theologians to 'commit themselves to the task of illustrating ever more clearly the biblical foundations, the ethical grounds and the personalist reasons behind this doctrine'.[54] No-one has done more than the present Pope to explain the reasons for the moral teaching of the Church on human sexuality and procreation. Starting with the datum that man is made to the image and likeness of God he demonstrates how the use of contraceptives is opposed to the 'full truth about man'. It is this truth about our human nature, our bodies, and especially our identity as persons, all reflecting God's truth, which is the ultimate basis for the moral norms on marriage and procreation articulated in *Humanae vitae*.[55]

## SCRIPTURAL BASIS

While there is no direct prohibition of contraception in Scripture, there are several converging themes in the moral teaching of the Bible which the priest can use to support his preaching on the encyclical:[56]

- the exceptional value given to procreation – Christ himself pointed to the great joy which spontaneously follows childbirth;

- the portrayal of sterility as a big cross, a deprivation;

- the condemnation of all sexual acts, including onanism, that are not designed to protect the good of procreation;

- the likening of Christ's relationship with his Church to that of a bridegroom with his bride – a union that is meant to be a fruitful relationship, one that will bring forth many sons and daughters for God.

Once God had created man, male and female, to his own image and likeness, his first directive to them was: 'Increase and multiply, and fill the earth and subdue it' (Gen 1:27). Fertility and fruitfulness are seen as part of the

procreative significance which are both inherent to the marriage act' (*Humanae vitae*, 11 and 12). 53 Cf. Address, 17 September 1983. 54 *Familiaris consortio*, 31. 55 Cf. John Crosby, 'The personalism of John Paul II as the basis of his approach to the teaching of *Humanae vitae*' in Janet Smith (ed.), *Why Humanae vitae was right: a reader*, San Francisco, 1993, pp 195-226. 56 Cf. Janet Smith, *Humanae vitae: a generation later*, Washington, 1991, p. 130.

covenant that man has with God. When God renews his covenant with Noah and Abraham, he repeats the same mandate: 'Be fruitful and multiply and fill the earth' (Gen 9:1). Throughout the Old Testament fertility and family are portrayed as great goods, as evidence of faithfulness to God (cf. Gen 13:16; 17:6). Children were not viewed as a burden but as a sign of favour and wealth (cf. Ps 127). Sterility and barrenness were considered a severe hardship and a curse, as confirmed by the stories of Sarah, Hannah, Rachel and Elizabeth.

Scripture also repeatedly praises the good of marriage. In the Old Testament it is often compared to the relationship between God and the Chosen People. In so far as married couples are to image the relationship between Christ and his Church (cf. Eph 5:21-32), contraception would seem to be a violation of that unique image. 'The value that Scripture puts on human life because of both its nature and its destiny, the view of God as author of life, the view of God as author of nature, and the understanding of God as an "unconditional" lover - all illuminate and enrich natural law arguments'[57] against contraception.

Even though this law is not found literally in Scripture, it is, John Paul tells us, fully in accord not only with the sum total of the moral doctrine contained in the Bible, its essential premises, and the general character of its content. It also integrates with that fuller context of the biblical anthropology which the Holy Father developed when speaking about the theology of the body.[58]

In the light of the foregoing we can see that preaching about *Humanae vitae* has to be set in the broader context of the Christian life as a whole if its teaching is to be understood properly and appropriated at a personal level. Presenting this wider ascetical canvas in a preaching programme would require covering the following topics among others:

- marriage as a divine vocation and a call to holiness expressing the spousal love of Christ for his Church;

- how the sacramental grace of marriage enables couples overcome all the difficulties and challenges of married life together;

- fulfilment in marriage comes through generosity and self-giving in the little events of each day;

- the procreation of children provides new members of the People of God who will be able to glorify the Trinity in eternity;

- the blessings each new child brings, especially as a God-given means to provide a deeper bonding between the couple;

- a Christian perspective on life means having trust in the paternal providence of God to care for the needs of the future;

57 Ibid., p. 134.  58 Cf. Address 18 July 1984.

- the weakness of our nature which requires to be healed by regular reception of the sacraments of Penance and the Eucharist;

- generous acceptance of the Cross as a normal part of Christian living which brings its own rewards;

- the need for daily prayer to see and accept God's will.

If the scriptural, moral, and personalist arguments supporting *Humanae vitae* are outlined against this background, there is no doubt that consciences will be enlightened and opened to accept its teaching.

In his recent Apostolic Letter outlining a pastoral programme for the Church for the new millennium, John Paul II says that such a programme has to be based on a rediscovery of 'the full practical significance' of the universal call to holiness proposed by Vatican II.[59] In the context of the demands of our Baptismal vocation, it would, he says

> be a contradiction to settle for a life of mediocrity, marked by a minimalist ethic and a shallow religiosity ... The time has come to re-propose wholeheartedly to everyone this high standard of ordinary Christian living: the whole life of the Christian community and of Christian families must lead in this direction.[60]

This, he continues, calls for a genuine 'training in holiness' adapted to people's needs.[61] Priests, clearly, have a major role to play in this demanding enterprise. An essential element in leading families to holiness is the recovery of that spirit of generosity which allows Christian couples to be ready to welcome the gift of new life in the home.[62]

### CONTRACEPTION AND CONSCIENCE

Good intentions, however, are not enough to guide spouses in this matter of responsible parenthood – the objective moral criteria must also be used to bring their consciences into conformity with the law of God as taught by the Magisterium of the Church.[63] Those are considered 'to exercise responsible

---

59 Apostolic Letter, *Novo millennio ineunte*, 30 (6 January 2001). 60 Ibid., no. 31. 61 Cf. ibid. 62 *Letter to families*, 12. 63 As Vatican II points out: 'Married people should realize that in their behaviour they may not simply follow their own fancy but must be ruled by conscience – and conscience ought to be conformed to the law of God in the light of the teaching of the divine law. For the divine law throws light on the meaning of married love, protects it and leads it to a truly human fulfilment. Whenever Christian spouses in a spirit of sacrifice and trust in divine providence carry out their duties of procreation with generous

parenthood who prudently and generously decide to have a large family, or who, for serious reasons and with due respect to the moral law, choose to have no more children for the time being or even for an indeterminate period'.[64] Thus the couple cannot act arbitrarily; on the contrary they 'must act in conformity with God's creative intention'[65], on the basis of the 'inseparable connection of the two significances of the conjugal act'.[66]

One of the chief responses to *Humanae vitae* after it first appeared was that Catholics were entitled to use contraception if their conscience allowed them.[67] Responsibility for preaching the demands of marital chastity has often been abdicated by priests by telling people to *follow* their conscience, without at the same time alerting them to the serious duty they have to *form* their conscience in accordance with the Church's teaching to ascertain the moral implications of what one is doing. As a consequence, a new interpretation of the meaning of conscience has grown up among Catholics since the publication of *Humanae vitae*. For many, conscience has become separated from the teaching of the Church, so that individual opinion is the ultimate arbiter of right or wrong, the ultimate standard of morality. People feel justified in using contraceptives because they see the 'good' of their marriage relationship as taking precedence over the demands of Church teaching. This is a principle which is constantly advocated in the media about many aspects of morality. Consequently, it is essential that, in the light of John Paul II's ground-breaking encyclical on the fundamentals of Christian morality (*Veritatis splendor*), people would be formed in a correct understanding of the authentic relationship between conscience and truth, and the consequences this has for the morality of human actions.[68] This is not a mere academic question – it has profound consequences for the stability and happiness of married life.

## THE VOCATION OF MOTHER

One of the more recent pressures which makes the teaching of *Humanae vitae* difficult to accept for some families is the increasing tendency for mothers to

human and Christian responsibility, they glorify the Creator and perfect themselves in Christ' (*Gaudium et spes*, 50). **64** Cf. *Humanae vitae*, 10. **65** Cf. ibid. **66** Cf. ibid., no.12. **67** While this was the reaction of a number of theologians, it was an argument which also found support in the initial responses of various episcopal conferences e.g. those of France, Canada and Austria. However, subsequently both Canada and Austria repudiated their 1968 statements, suggesting that effectively it would be almost impossible for a Catholic to reject *Humanae vitae* in good conscience (cf. Smith, ibid., pp 148-60). **68** Cf. *Veritatis splendor*, published 6 August 1993, nos.54-64. John Paul II sums up the essence of this teaching as follows: 'Christians have a great help for the formation of conscience *in the Church and in her Magisterium*. As the Council [Vatican II] affirms: "in forming their consciences the

work outside the home. In many cases this is a consequence of financial constraints. In recent decades, however, the tendency to downgrade the value and status of work in the home, a product largely of feminist ideology, has also accelerated the exodus of mothers into the workplace in search of what they are assured will be a more fulfilling job than that of being a full-time mother and homemaker.

An integral part of the defence of the family and family values is the need for society to recover an awareness of the exceptional importance and dignity of a mother's work in the home. While recognising the equal right of women with men to work in external professional activity, it is imperative to identify at the present time the reasons why domestic work has a higher priority in terms of fundamental values. No-one has done this better than John Paul II. Woman, he reminds us, is 'the heart of the family community. It is she who gives life, it is she who is the first educator'. In the same way that the heart is essential to the human organism, 'she who is the heart of the family cannot be missing from it'.[69] What the Church asks first of all is that 'all the activity of a woman in the home, as mother and educator, be fully esteemed as work. This important work', the Holy Father warns, 'cannot be socially scorned, but must constantly be reaffirmed in its value, if society does not wish to act against its own interests'[70] because, among other things, the vocation of mother is integrally united to the vocation of transmitting 'the truths of the faith and ethical values' in the home.

'Doubt is frequently cast', he continues, 'on this natural mission of the woman-mother by positions which emphasise the social rights of women. At times their professional work is seen as social advancement, while total dedica-

---

Christian faithful must give careful attention to the sacred and certain teaching of the Church. For the Catholic Church is by the will of Christ the teacher of truth. Her charge is to announce and teach authentically that truth which is Christ, and at the same time with her authority to declare and confirm the principles of the moral order which derive from human nature itself"(Declaration on religious freedom *Dignitatis humanae*, 14). It follows that the authority of the Church, when she pronounces on moral questions, in no way undermines the freedom of the conscience of Christians. This is so not only because freedom of conscience is never freedom "from" the truth but always and only freedom "in" the truth, but also because the Magisterium does not bring to the Christian conscience truths which are extraneous to it; rather it brings to light the truths which it ought already to possess, developing them from the starting point of the primordial act of faith. The Church puts herself always and only at the *service of conscience*, helping to avoid it being tossed to and fro by every wind of doctrine proposed by human deceit (cf Eph 4:14), and helping it not to swerve from the truth about the good of man, but rather, especially in more difficult questions, to attain the truth with certainty and to abide in it' (*Veritatis splendor*, 64). See also CCC, 1777-85. **69** Address, 13 June 1987, no. 4. **70** Ibid., no. 5. See also John Paul II, Encyclical, *Laborem exercens*, 19 (14 September 1981).

tion to family matters and the education of children is held to be a renunciation of the development of their own personalities'. While proclaiming that the
equal dignity of women with men justifies their access to all public responsibilities, he nevertheless strongly reaffirms that

> the true advancement of women demands of society a particular
> recognition of maternal and family responsibilities because they con-
> stitute *a value superior* to all other public tasks and professions ...
> Children have a particular need of the dedication of a mother in order
> to develop as persons who are responsible, religiously and morally
> mature and psychologically well-balanced. The good of the family is
> so great that it urgently requires of today's society *a reaffirmation of the
> value of maternal duties,* in the sphere of the advancement of women
> and among those who hold that they must do remunerative work out-
> side of the home.[71]

Roundly proclaiming the mother's work in the home as superior to all
other external professions is a strongly counter-cultural statement, but a necessary one if the importance of the family is to be truly recognized. In 1981
John Paul II had already called for a renewed theology of work to shed a deeper light on the 'original and irreplaceable meaning of work in the home and in
rearing children'.[72] Thus he says the Church

> can and should help modern society by tirelessly insisting that the work
> of women in the home be recognized and respected by all in its irre-
> placeable value. Furthermore, the mentality which honours women more
> for their work outside the home than for their work within the family
> must be overcome. This requires that men should truly esteem and love
> women with total respect for their dignity, and that society should create
> and develop conditions favouring work in the home.[73]

Here we have many clearly defined principles and practical pointers to
guide the pastoral work of the priest in relation to the family. This is not a topic
that should come up just for occasional comment in preaching and catechetical
activity. Because of the vulnerable situation of many families today, and a
media philosophy which is increasingly subversive of family values, these
ideas, in the words of John Paul II, need to be insisted on tirelessly if people
are to retain a Christian concept of marriage, and nurture families which will
be stable and psychologically mature. The impressive commitment of the Holy

71 Address, 13 June 1987, no. 7 (italics in the original). **72** *Familiaris consortio,* 23. **73** Ibid.

Father to the defence of the family all during his pontificate is an example and a cogent reminder to priests of the pastoral effort required of them in this area.

Another aspect of rechristianising married life is to educate couples to see that marriage is not just a human reality, but also a sacred one. Marriage, with its specific ends and characteristics, has been made by God and its sacramental nature gives it a supernatural purpose. Thus understood it will be more easily appreciated as a mission to cooperate with God in the task of transmitting, by procreation, the divine image from person to person.[74] The loss of the supernatural perspective on marriage results in its success being measured primarily in terms of personal gratification. In this context children tend to be regarded very much as of secondary importance. Only when marriage is understood as a sacred reality will parents be in a position to respond generously to the challenges which rearing a large family involves. With this outlook they will enter marriage as Tobias and Sarah did, motivated by love for posterity so that in them the Lord would be blessed eternally (cf. Tob 8:7 ff).

## CHRISTIAN SEX EDUCATION

If the priest is to fulfil his responsibility of giving an effective formation in chastity, his preaching needs to be complemented by what is being taught in the home and at school by way of catechesis and sex education. That there is a real need for such education was affirmed by Vatican II.[75] John Paul II emphasises that parents have the primary responsibility to give sex education to their children, and he states clearly that, for a Christian, sex education is fundamentally formation in the virtue of chastity. Consequently the Church is firmly opposed to sex education as information dissociated from moral principles.[76]

The document of the Pontifical Council for the Family, *The truth and meaning of human sexuality*, provides a systematic development of the principles laid down by the Holy Father in *Familiaris consortio*[77]. *Human sexuality* puts the present difficulties with sex education into perspective. In the past the general culture was permeated by respect for the values of sexuality and human intimacy and, consequently, tended to protect and maintain them. However, with the decline in these traditional values in recent decades, human sexuality has been 'demythologized' and depersonalized by reducing it to the commonplace. It is precisely because of the dangers of these influences that parents have a greater responsibility to form their children in positive convictions about chastity and sexuality, and thus enable them to protect themselves from the corrosive effects of the social environment.

74 Cf. *Familiaris consortio*, 28. 75 Cf. *Gravissimum educationis*, 1. 76 Cf. *Familiaris consortio*, 37. 77 Ibid., no. 37. *The truth and meaning of human sexuality* is subsequently abbreviated to *Human sexuality*.

In summary, this document of the Pontifical Council for the Family can be regarded as the *magna carta* for Christian sex education. It is eminently positive in tone and sets the parameters for the current debate on this topic. Discussion of sex education is lifted out of the positivistic and naturalistic context in which it is normally debated and raised to a new level. The document outlines very clearly how, for a Christian, sex education only makes sense in the much broader context of formation in the virtue of chastity and the vocation to holiness to which all are called. Every priest should be familiar with the content and the methodology of *Human sexuality*. They will thus be in a position to give effective pastoral guidance to parents to enable them fulfil their role as educators of their children in this very important area.

CONCLUSION

John Paul II says that his document *Familiaris consortio* 'can be considered the *magna carta* of the apostolate to families'.[78] From it priests will learn how to develop new pastoral methods to meet the needs of the family in contemporary society. Indeed this is an apostolate which should have a particular priority because, as the Pope reminds us, 'the pastoral care of the family – and I know this from personal experience – is in a way the quintessence of priestly activity at every level'.[79] Thus the promotion of family prayer is one of the first tasks if priests are to bring forward the apostolate with families, family prayer which should be encouraged on the basis of drawing out the implications of Christ's promise, 'For where two or three are gathered in my name, there am I in the midst of them' (Mt 18:20). This apostolic enterprise should be undertaken with a deep awareness of the power of children's prayer (cf. Mt 18:2-5), apart from the fact that teaching children to pray inevitably leads mothers and fathers to pray, which for the latter is often the prelude to a return to the sacraments. Priests should remember too how much they benefit from the prayer of families, and the extent to which new priestly vocations are the product of such family prayer.[80]

In the life of the priest there is a strong connection between conviction about celibacy and preaching effectively about chastity. The priest who appreciates the charism of celibacy will put before his people the full demands of God's law on sexual morality, because he knows that only by living a chaste life, both inside and outside marriage, will there be truly Christian and authentically happy lives. He is convinced that pre-marital chastity is what will best prepare young people for marriage as a life-long commitment. He is also per-

78 HTL, 1994, no. 2.  79 Ibid.  80 Cf. ibid., no. 4.

suaded that only when conjugal life within marriage is lived according to God's laws will there be strong Christian families generously open to new life, which in turn will be graced with the vocations the Holy Spirit will grant and which the Church needs so urgently.

The Christian message is a radical one, above all in relation to sexual morality. It is necessary to convince people that to live by it they have to be prepared to go against the current of conventional wisdom and accepted mores. This is not something new; Christ went against the current of his time, the apostles and the early Christians did, and so will all who want to be loyal to Jesus Christ. But chastity brings its own rewards – stable marriages; joy in family life; vocations; and a cluster of grandchildren to light up old age.

Central to the truth of *Humanae vitae* is that each and every marital act should be open to the procreation of new life. However, a convincing presentation of the teaching of this encyclical requires that it be placed in a broader context. It is essential to preach *Humanae vitae* in the light of marriage as a Christian vocation and a call to holiness if people are to be able to perceive the theological depth and the rich Christian anthropology which it implies. John Paul II asks us frequently in his writings on marriage to promote and defend the interests of the family as a pastoral priority. A synthesis of much that he has been saying about the family, and his vision for its future, is perhaps best provided in the encyclical *Centesimus annus:*

> The first and fundamental structure for 'human ecology' is the family, in which man receives his first formative ideas about truth and goodness, and learns what it means to love and to be loved, and thus what it actually means to be a person. Here we mean the family founded on marriage, in which the mutual gift of self by husband and wife creates an environment in which children can be born and develop their potentialities, become aware of their dignity and prepare to face their unique and individual destiny ... It is necessary to go back to seeing the family as the sanctuary of life. The family is indeed sacred: it is the place in which life – the gift of God – can be properly welcomed and protected against the many attacks to which it is exposed and can develop in accordance with what constitutes authentic human growth. In the face of the so-called culture of death, the family is the heart of the culture of life.[81]

The preacher is always aware that no particular Christian virtue can be developed in isolation. There cannot be chastity without, for example, the virtues of faith, prudence and fortitude. In addition, the priest will be con-

81 Encyclical Letter, *Centesimus annus,* 39 (1 May 1991).

scious that all the moral virtues, including chastity, are at root different speci-
fications of the virtue of charity, different applications of love for God to particular human acts. To be chaste is to impose order on the sexual tendency for
love of God, not in the sense of suppressing it, or treating it as something negative, but of doing something positive, of exercising virtuous control for the
sake of love of other. In this deeper sense chastity is a virtue that relates not
only to external acts but to the internal dispositions also, in consonance with
the words of the Master, 'Blessed are the pure in heart for they shall see God'
(Mt 5:8).

To appreciate chastity in a positive manner, it is important to emphasise
that this virtue is necessary to develop friendship with God, and to live a truly
Christian and apostolic life.[82] Chastity leads to optimism, joy and fortitude in
the service of God. While it is true that original sin introduced disorder into
our faculties, chastity is the virtue which in a special way facilitates the recovery of that unity of moral purpose for the Christian.[83]

Revelation teaches us that chastity is possible, even in adverse circumstances. So we need to communicate this conviction to people who live in an
environment which depreciates and is often hostile to chastity, in order to
encourage them and give them confidence. This, as we have seen, implies
ongoing formation to help people understand the importance of the means
which Christian tradition and experience have always recommended to acquire
and mature in holy purity – prayer, guard of the heart and the senses, a spirit
of self-denial, and the courage to avoid occasions of sin. Because it is a supernatural virtue, we need the grace of the sacraments, especially Penance and the
Eucharist, to enable us persevere in the effort to live chaste lives. In particular,
the Church has always counselled devotion to Mary as a powerful means to live
that cleanliness of heart which, Christ tells us, enables us to see with clear
vision the action of God in our lives.[84]

---

82 'The virtue of chastity blossoms in *friendship*. It shows the disciple how to follow and imitate him who has chosen us as his friends (cf. Jn 15:15), who has given himself totally to us
and allows us to participate in his divine estate. Chastity is a promise of immortality.
Chastity is expressed notably in *friendship with one's neighbour*. Whether it develops between
persons of the same or opposite sex, friendship represents a great good for all. It leads to
spiritual communion' (CCC, 2347). 83 'Indeed it is through chastity that we are gathered
together and led back to the unity from which we were fragmented into multiplicity' (St
Augustine, *Confessions* 10, 29). 84 As Blessed Josemaría Escrivá puts it: 'Without God's help
it is impossible to live a clean life. God wants us to be humble, and to ask him for his help
through our Mother who is his Mother. You should say to our Lady, right now, speaking
without the sound of words, from the accompanied solitude of your heart: "O, my Mother,
sometimes this poor heart of mine rebels, but if you help me..." She will indeed help you to
keep it clean and to follow the way God has called you to pursue. The Virgin Mary will
always make it easier for you to fulfil the Will of God' (*The forge*, London, 1988, no. 315).

# 10

# The Holy Spirit, sin, reconciliation

Christ was anointed by the Spirit at his baptism in the Jordan (Lk 4:18-19; Mk 1:10) as prefigured by Isaiah (Is 11:1-3; 61:1ff). He affirmed the relevance of that text to himself: 'Today this scripture has been fulfilled in your hearing' (Lk 4:21). Thus the Gospel reveals the Holy Spirit as the intimate source of the life and messianic activity of Jesus Christ. And so the priest, if he is to be truly an icon of Christ, must be enlivened by the power of the same Spirit. As a consequence of sacramental ordination the seal of the Holy Spirit is imprinted on his soul, giving him a character which marks him out for all time as a priest of Jesus Christ. Infidelity to his vocation, even laicization, can never remove this priestly configuration which will accompany him into eternity.

In the celebration of the liturgy the priest acts through the Holy Spirit on behalf of the Church. Catholic tradition has always seen the Paraclete at work in a unique way in the Holy Mass where the priest renews Christ's sacrifice of Calvary. 'By the power of the Holy Spirit', writes St John Damascene, 'the transformation of the bread into the Body of Christ takes place'.[1] And Scheeben develops this point by telling us that 'under the veil of the sacramental species the Holy Spirit re-enacts the miracle that he once wrought in the womb of Mary, and again in the darkness of the sepulchre'.[2] According to the ancient liturgies the Eucharistic act of sacrifice is effected by the fire of the Holy Spirit when the priest invokes the divine blessing on the offerings in the epiclesis. Being the instrument of such a profound and mysterious action, the priest is invited to grow in intimacy with the Paraclete in order to penetrate more deeply the great mystery of his vocation and identity.

In his Apostolic Letter, outlining how the Church should prepare for the Jubilee Year 2000, Pope John Paul II appealed for 'a renewed appreciation of the presence and activity of the Spirit'. In particular he would like us to grow in our awareness of the role of the Holy Spirit as the 'principal agent of the new evangelization',[3] and of the need to call on his grace when faced with the obstacles of agnosticism, prejudice, and religious indifference.[4] At the Last

1 *De fide orthodoxa*, 13: PG 94, 1139. 2 Matthias J. Scheeben, *The mysteries of Christianity*, p. 509. 3 Cf. *Tertio millennio adveniente*, 45 (10 November 1994). 4 Cf. Address, 21 April

Supper Christ referred to the role and the action of the Holy Spirit in the life of the apostles and of his future priests. The Paraclete will make the teaching of the Master clear to them, recalling what he had preached over the previous three years and gradually leading them into the fullness of truth (cf. Jn 14:26; 16:13). They will be persecuted for their loyalty to Christ but they will not lack the friendship and solace of the Comforter (cf. Jn 15:20-26). The Holy Spirit will, from day to day, open up to the priest new dimensions of the meaning of Christ's life as he attends to the multiple demands of his pastoral work. In this way he will learn how to find Christ in the most material, the most insignificant duties of each day, and how to give to all of them a redemptive value.[5]

The same Holy Spirit, who is the Sanctifier, communicates the merits of the Redemption in a special way through the Catholic priesthood. This was uniquely evident on the first Easter evening. To the great joy of the disciples, Christ appeared to them in the Upper Room and greeted them with the words 'Peace be with you'. 'Receive the Holy Spirit', he said, and then, breathing on them, invested the apostles with an incredible power: 'If you forgive the sins of any, they are forgiven; if you retain the sins of any, they are retained' (Jn 20:21-23). The forgiveness of sins is an immediate consequence of the gift of the Spirit by Christ to his priests. 'This', John Paul II points out, 'is one of the most awe-inspiring innovations of the Gospel'.[6]

### THE HOLY SPIRIT AND SANCTITY

We are reminded by the same Pope that 'the Holy Spirit is the principal agent in our spiritual life'.[7] The conviction that the grace of the Holy Spirit will never be lacking is the foundation of the priest's confidence that he will persevere in his vocation and that his work will be effective. Hence we are encouraged to return often to that prayer which we heard in the rite of priestly ordination: 'Almighty Father, give these your sons, the dignity of the priesthood. Renew in them the outpouring of your Spirit of holiness'.[8]

> Herein lies supernatural wisdom, above all as a gift of the Holy Spirit, who makes it possible to exercise good judgement in the light of the 'ultimate reasons', the 'eternal things'. Wisdom thus becomes the principal factor in identifying with Christ in thought, judgement, the evaluation of any matter however large or small, so that the priest (like

1993, no. 8.  5 Cf. Blessed Josemaría Escrivá, *Conversations*, Manila, 1977, no. 114.  6 *Reconciliatio et paenitentia*, 29.  7 PDV, 33.  8 Cf. ibid.

every Christian only more so) reflects the light, obedience to the Father, practical zeal, rhythm of prayer and action and, one could almost say, the spiritual breath of Christ.[9]

The priest needs to listen to the voice of the Holy Spirit in his meditation if he is to follow the thrust of grace and appropriate the inspirations that will lead him to a more intimate friendship with Christ. Because of increased bureaucracy, activism is a real danger for the priest today. Nevertheless, if his plan of work is nurtured in prayer, he will learn to identify the intimations of the Paraclete active in his soul, helping him establish the pastoral priorities of each day: 'It is the Spirit who makes us more priestly day by day, because he takes the things of Christ and reveals them to us, bringing to remembrance all the words of Christ (cf. Jn 16:14; 14:26)'.[10]

The Holy Spirit feels at home in the souls of those who allow themselves to be guided by his inspirations. This is why, the Curé of Ars tells us, so many unlettered and simple people are wiser than the learned. The Paraclete is light and strength and, guided by him, one cannot go astray. The Curé's life was surely a striking confirmation of this profound truth. 'With the Holy Spirit', he tells us, 'we see everything in its true proportions; we see the greatness of the least actions done for God, and the greatness of the least faults'. So, 'if we are not led by the Holy Spirit, we labour in vain, and there is no substance, no savour in anything we do'. On the other hand he maintains that if the saints were asked why they were in heaven they would reply, 'For having listened to the Holy Spirit'.[11] The Consoler, who comes to us as the fruit of the Cross,[12] manifests himself above all as the gift that 'helps us in our weakness'. St Paul develops this profound thought in his letter to the Romans: 'For we do not know how to pray as we ought, but the Spirit intercedes for us with sighs too deep for words' (Rom 8:26). Hence the Paraclete not only enables us to pray but also guides our prayer from within.

Although the Sanctifier urges us to journey further each day along the path of love of Christ, we will always encounter the obstacles created by our over-attachment to the things of this world. We are still fragile, earthenware vessels, and the sublime gift of the priesthood which has been deposited in us does not eliminate the threefold concupiscence identified by St John – the lust of the eyes, the lust of the flesh, and the pride of life (cf. 1 Jn 2:16). What the action of the Holy Spirit does is to make the priest more conscious of sin, of the conflict between good and evil within himself so graphically described by

9 John Paul II, Address, 2 June 1993, no. 4. 10 Sheen, *The priest is not his own*, p. 80. See also *Summa theologiae*, III, 23, 2, ad 3. 11 From 'Catechism on the Holy Spirit', as published in *Thoughts of the Curé d'Ars*, Rockford, Ill., 1984. 12 Cf. Blessed Josemaría Escrivá, *Christ is passing by*, Dublin 1982, no. 137.

St Paul (cf. Rom 7:14-16).[13] Awareness of this interior spiritual conflict is not a neurosis, but a characteristic of the life of every priest sincerely striving for holiness.

### THE HOLY SPIRIT AND SIN

Over centuries the Christian mind has acquired a deep awareness of the sense of sin which is rooted in man's moral conscience. However, in his document on penance and reconciliation, John Paul II says there are many signs today which show such a deformation of conscience that one can speak about a loss of the sense of sin. In his analysis of contemporary culture he suggests four reasons for this progressive weakening of the sense of God in consciences:

• A pervasive secularism in many countries which advocates a humanism totally disconnected from God. Its practical expression is rampant consumerism and pleasure seeking, unconcerned with the danger of 'losing one's soul'.

• Currents of psychology which avoid creating guilt feelings or placing limits on freedom, often associated with a sociology which puts the blame for personal failings on society, or which too easily asserts that environmental and historical conditioning take away personal responsibility.

• The rejection of the idea of intrinsically evil acts independent of the circumstances in which they were performed.

• The sense of sin disappears when it is wrongly identified with a morbid feeling of guilt, or with the mere transgression of legal norms and precepts.

Loss of the sense of sin can also arise when one exaggeration is replaced by another, as for example, by changing from emphasis on the fear of eternal punishment to preaching a love of God that excludes any punishment deserved by sin. The confusion caused in consciences by differences of opinions in theology, preaching, catechesis and spiritual guidance, on serious and delicate questions of Christian morals, ends up by diminishing a true sense of sin almost to

---

13 'We know that the law is spiritual, but I am carnal, sold under sin. I do not understand my own actions. For I do not do what I want, but I do the very thing I hate ... For I delight in the law of God, in my inmost self, but I see in my members another law at war with the law of my mind and making me captive to the law of sin which dwells in my members. Wretched man that I am! Who will deliver me from this body of death?' (Rom 7:14-24).

the point of eliminating it altogether. John Paul II affirms that the restoration of a proper sense of sin, through a clear reminder of the unchangeable principles of the Church's moral teaching, is the first stage of facing up to the grave spiritual crisis which looms over humanity today.[14]

Christ explained at the Last Supper how it will be for the Paraclete 'to convince the world of sin' (Jn 16:8) so that it recognizes its need for redemption. Through the Fall, man refused to answer God's call to communion with him, and proposed to decide for himself what constituted good and evil.[15] The work of the Holy Spirit in the world is to open consciences so that man rediscovers his original vocation and follows the path of conversion, forgiveness and reconciliation, thereby restoring communion among men and with their Father God.[16]

> One never understands the enormity of sin except through the Spirit, a truth which Our Lord explained to his priests the night of the Last Supper. Sin is best treated and overcome, not solely in relation to the breaking of a commandment, but in terms of the breaking of our bonds with the Father, Son, and Holy Spirit. Sin disrupts our ties with the Heavenly Father because it alienates us as sons. Such is the message of the parable of the prodigal son (Lk 15:11-32). Sin also re-enacts Calvary: 'Would they crucify the Son of God a second time, hold him up to mockery a second time, for their own ends?' (Heb 6:6) ... Sin must be seen as resisting the Spirit of Love (Acts 7:51); as stifling the Spirit of Love (1 Thes 5:19); and as distressing the Spirit of Love (Eph 4:30).[17]

Man can reject the action of the Holy Spirit through the loss of the sense of sin and remain impenitent. This resistance in the internal forum of conscience also takes on an external dimension in society as philosophies of materialism or death. The world's refusal to recognize its need for redemption has resulted in a litany of crimes which constitute the 'culture of death', epitomized today by the crime of abortion. These are different forms of enslavement, and it is the work if the Holy Spirit to lead man back from this degradation of his original purpose to experience once more 'the freedom of the children of God'. Thus the priest, through the work of the confessional, has the power to restore to man the greatest freedom of all – liberation from sin.[18] The vocation of the Church, through the power of the Spirit, is to restore hope to man and the divine meaning of human life.[19]

14 Cf. *Reconciliatio et paenitentia*, 18. See also PDV, 47.  15 Cf. John Paul II, Encyclical, *Dominum et vivificantem*, 35, 36, 38 (18 May 1986).  16 Cf. ibid., nos. 42, 43, 44.  17 Sheen, *The priest is not his own*, p. 133.  18 Cf. *Dominum et vivificantem*, 57.  19 Cf. ibid., nos. 62, 67.

Because one of the fruits of the Holy Spirit is to lead us to a deeper understanding of the Cross, it follows that priests should have a keen sense of reparation – reparation for their own sins and those of the people entrusted to their
care. This is also a logical consequence of our role as mediators. How often do
we imitate Christ in his petition, 'Father forgive them, for they know not what
they do' (Lk 23:34)? By prayer such as this we will merit the effective action of
the Holy Spirit in people to inspire them to contrition and a return to the
sacrament of Reconciliation.


### THE GOOD SHEPHERD AND FORGIVENESS

Reading the gospel narrative we observe how Christ lives out the role of the
Good Shepherd. From the very beginning of his public life his ministry was
carried out among sinners. We see how he makes use of the opportunity of a
rest at the well of Sichar to win over the Samaritan woman and how, through
her, he converts a whole village. We observe his compassion in dealing with the
woman taken in adultery (cf. Jn 8:3-11), with the woman repenting of her sins
(cf. Lk 15:11-32), and with the Good Thief on Calvary (cf. Lk 23:43). Christ
invites all to conversion, encouraging sinners, but he never forces anyone's
freedom. Turning back to God has to be a free response to grace accompanied
by a humble recognition of sinfulness. The response of the publican – 'God,
be merciful to me a sinner'(cf. Lk 18:13) – is a paradigm of the attitudes needed to win God's mercy. For Christ, children, the sick, and sinners are three
types which summarize those who are indigent before God and who draw
down the mercy of Christ in a special way. The priest should be guided by the
same principle in his pastoral work.

Because the priest shares in a special way in the likeness of Christ the
Good Shepherd, he should feel compassion for people because they are
harassed by the difficulties of life. His pastoral charity will impel him to go in
search of dropouts from the faith, and to try to recover for Christ those who
have ceased to live according to his teachings.

> The solicitude of every good shepherd is that all people 'may have life
> and have it to the full' (Jn 10:10), so that none of them may be lost (cf.
> Jn 17:12), but should have eternal life. Let us endeavour to make this
> solicitude penetrate deeply into our souls; let us strive to live it. May
> it characterize our personality, and be at the foundation of our priest-
> ly identity.[20]

See also Weigel, ibid., p. 517. **20** HTL, 1979, no. 7.

## SACRAMENT OF RECONCILIATION

In the Old Testament the sinner was considered a debtor before God and was justified by some external action. Christ, however, introduces a whole new approach to sin when, in the Sermon on the Mount, he speaks about the idea of pardon and forgiveness and interior conversion (cf. Mt 5-7).

On Easter evening, as the disciples waited in the Upper Room, depressed by their infidelity and sceptical about the news of the Resurrection, Christ appeared greeting them with the words, 'Peace be with you' (Jn 20:19). With his presence and his affectionate greeting he recovered their souls and their renewed commitment to the great adventure of spreading the Gospel. At the same time, showing his unfailing confidence in them, he invested the apostles with his own mission from the Father including the unique power of forgiving sins through the Holy Spirit (cf. Jn 20:21-23). The forgiveness of sins is at the very core of the priest's mission. As John Paul II has pointed out:

> Christ desired to place the great treasure of redemption, the forgiveness of sins, in our priestly hands. I urge you not to neglect this saving reality. Always show a particular appreciation for the sacrament of Reconciliation through which Christians receive the forgiveness of their sins. You must encourage pastoral activity which will bring the faithful towards personal conversion; with generosity and the patience of authentic 'fishers of men' you must dedicate all the time necessary to this ministry of forgiveness.[21]... The experience of centuries confirms the importance of this ministry. If priests have a profound understanding of that close collaboration which, by means of the sacrament of Penance, they offer to the Saviour in the work of conversion, they will give themselves with a greater zeal each day to this ministry. Other works can be postponed, or even abandoned, for lack of time, but never the work of confession.[22]

In the sacrament of Reconciliation the priest is the instrument for fulfilling the Isaian prophecy, 'If your sins be as scarlet, they shall be made as white as snow; and if they be red as crimson, they shall be white as wool' (Is 1:18), because they are washed clean in the blood of the Lamb.[23] Sacramental confession not only forgives sins, but also restores the foundation for peace and serenity in people's lives. Despite external appearances, sin can and does weigh people

---

21 Address, 1 April 1987. See also CCC 1464. 22 Address, 21 April 1979. See also, Address, 31 March 2001, no. 5. 23 Cf. Edwin Gordon, 'The Good Shepherd: the ideal of the priest', *Homiletic and Pastoral Review*, December 1991, p. 29.

down. That is why catechesis on the sacrament of Reconciliation should convey Christ's own sentiments that whose who come to him burdened with guilt will recover peace and serenity (cf. Mt 11:28-30).[24]

In Sheehan's novel, *My new curate*, the parish priest reflects on the greatness of the sacrament of Penance as he observes the scene in his church, where the young priest is hearing First Friday confessions in the dark of a winter's evening:

> [The church] was lit by the one red lamp that shone like a star in the sanctuary, and by the two dim waxlights in tin sconces, that cast a pallid light on the painted pillars, and a brown shadow farther up, against which were silhouetted the figures of the men, who sat in even rows around Fr Letheby's confessional. Now and again a solitary penitent darkened the light of the candles, as he moved up to the altar rails to read his penance or thanksgiving; or the quick figure of a child darted rapidly past me into the thicker darkness without. Hardly a sound broke the stillness, only now and then there was a moan of sorrow, or some expression of emphasis from the penitents; and the drawing of the slides from time to time made a soft sibilance, as of shuttles, beneath which were woven tapestries of human souls that were fit to hang in the halls of heaven. Silently the mighty work went forward; and I thought, as there and then the stupendous sacrifice of Calvary was brought down into our midst, and the hands of that young priest gathered up the Blood of Christ from grass, and stone, and wood – from reeking nails and soldier's lance, and the wet weeping hair of Magdalen, and poured it softly on the souls of these young villagers – I thought what madness possesses the world not to see that this sublime assumption of God's greatest privilege of mercy is in itself the highest dogmatic proof of the divine origin of the Church; for no purely human institution could dare usurp such an exalted position, nor assume the possession of such tremendous power.[25]

The scene is obviously from an earlier era than ours, but it nonetheless captures the enduring essence of the great drama of the confessional.

---

24 'To acknowledge one's misery in the sight of God is not to abase oneself, but to live the truth of one's own condition and thus to obtain the true greatness of justice and grace after falling into sin, the effect of malice and weakness; it is to rise to the loftiest peace of spirit, by entering into a living relationship with God who is merciful and faithful. The truth thus lived is the only thing in the human condition that truly makes us free: this is attested by the word of God (Jn 8: 31-34)' ( John Paul II, Message to Cardinal Penitentiary, 22 March 1996, no. 2). 25 P. A. Canon Sheehan, *My new curate*, Cork (1989 reprint), pp 128-9.

## FORGIVENESS OF SIN

Over the years there has been a significant fall-off in the numbers going to confession. At the same time it is clear that, by Christian ethical standards, immoral life-styles are now regarded as normal, particularly in the area of sexual morality. Recovery of the practice of regular confession is therefore essential for a vibrant Christian life both at the community and personal levels. Consequently it is not surprising that in his recent Apostolic Letter to commemorate the beginning of the new millennium, John Paul II appeals for 'renewed pastoral courage in ensuring that the day to day teaching of Christian communities persuasively and effectively presents the practice of the Sacrament of Reconciliation'.[26] While the symptoms of the crisis which he drew attention to in 1984 have not disappeared[27], he encourages priests to trust in God's power to change the human heart and to bring about a recovery of this sacramental practice through a rediscovery of the 'compassionate face of Christ'.[28]

As the Pope points out in his encyclical, *Dives in misericordia*, the sacrament of penance 'opens the way for everyone, especially those borne down by grave sin, individually to experience mercy, that love which is stronger than sin'.[29] Recovery of the sense of sin and, as a consequence, a deeper awareness of the need for confession and forgiveness, requires adequate preaching on the different elements of the Christian moral life. From his pastoral experience, the priest will also be aware that the faithful need to be reminded regularly of particular aspects of the Church's moral doctrine.

One of the central teachings of Vatican II, as seen above, is that all are called to holiness.[30] If the priest is conscious that this is the Church's vision of Christian commitment for the faithful, he realizes that he will have to inspire them to something more than spiritual and moral minimalism, and that one way he can facilitate this is by his generous availability for confession. Experience teaches that people will come to this sacrament if the priest is regularly available.

In October 1983, in St Peter's Square, Pope John Paul II canonized a Capuchin priest, St Leopold Mandic. This small, diminutive priest had spent the entire span of his priestly life in the ministry of the confessional, day after day for fifty-two years. In this demanding work he was noted for his patience, gentleness, his ability to listen and to form consciences. His greatness, the Holy Father said, lay 'in his fading into the background to give place to the true Shepherd of souls'.[31]

There is also the danger that when the practice of confession diminishes,

26 *Novo millennio ineunte*, 37. 27 Cf. *Reconciliatio et paenitentia*, 18. 28 Cf. *Novo millennio ineunte*, 37. 29 John Paul II, Encyclical *Dives in misericordia*, 13 (30 November 1980). 30 Cf. *Lumen gentium*, 39-42. 31 Homily, 16 October 1983.

it will be followed by a decline in the theological and pastoral quality of the exercise of this ministry.[32] Such an attitude is reflected in reconciliation services where the need for integrity in confession is played down with a view to making the sacrament more accessible for people. This approach betokens a false pastoral zeal because it undermines the conditions for the validity of the sacrament. Confession is, then, no longer a real, personal encounter with Christ because it does not express that complete conversion of heart which is an essential condition for forgiveness.[33] On the other hand, the priest will make confession easier for the penitent by emphasising the unlimited mercy of God, by his kindness, understanding and encouragement, and by giving the penitent all the time he needs, as well as the anonymity which most people still prefer by confessing through the grille.

## ROLE OF THE PRIEST IN CONFESSION

In confession the priest fulfils several roles including that of father, physician, teacher, and judge:[34]

*As father*, he should receive the penitent with gentleness and affection, showing even more understanding to those who have greater need of God's mercy, encouraging them to begin again on the path of a Christian life. People should experience in their encounter with the priest those qualities of a loving father which St Luke brings out so well in his record of the parable of the prodigal son (cf. Lk 15:11-32).[35] He will try to make it easy for the penitent to admit his sins by tempering the demand for formal integrity with not making confession burdensome.

The priest is a *physician* of souls and, like Jesus Christ, he has to heal those who are spiritually sick, and bind up wounds as the Good Samaritan of the parable did on the road to Jericho (cf. Lk 10:25-37).[36] Experience indicates that there are increasing numbers of morally wounded who need this kind of attention. As physician he should prudently diagnose the roots of deviation and failure, and apply the appropriate medicine to heal the scars left by sin, so that the penitent can live a life more in conformity with his or her dignity and responsibility as a son or daughter of God. To be effective in this ministry St John Chrysostom advises priests:

---

32 *The priest and the Third Christian millennium*, III, 3. 33 Cf. CCC, 1456; *Reconciliatio et paenitentia*, 31, II; Address, 31 March 2001, no. 3. 34 Cf. CCC 1464/5. 35 Cf. also John Paul II, *Dives in misericordia*, 5 and 6; *Reconciliatio et paenitentia*, 5 and 6; CCC 1439. 36 The idea of Christ as Divine Physician is a favourite metaphor of St Augustine: cf. Rudolf Arbesmann OSA, 'The concept of "Christus Medicus" in St Augustine', *Traditio*, 10 (1954), 1-28.

> In this you should act like good physicians. When they see that the sickness does not respond to the first treatment, they try another and then yet another. Sometimes they cut and sometimes they use bandages. You too must be physicians of souls and use every remedy in accordance with Christ's laws. Then you will be rewarded by your own health and that of others.[37]

As *teacher* he will, where necessary, educate the conscience of the penitent so that he or she will be aware of the moral principles to be applied in a particular situation. In recent years, surveys show that there has been a high degree of failure, particularly on the part of young people, to assimilate basic moral principles,[38] so the priest should be prepared to carry out a work of formation of conscience in the confessional.[39]

Due to the influence of different strands of contemporary culture, the confessor will frequently have to guide the penitent out of a subjective moral morass into a deeper awareness of objective moral criteria, and help him or her see how these principles determine the morality of actions. As teacher, he will often have to instruct the penitent to obtain material integrity in confession. The dangers of leaving a person in ignorance about important aspects of the moral life are obvious. To do so would seriously jeopardize his or her capacity to respond to God's call to holiness. Obligations with regard to Sunday Mass, duties of justice at work and in the home, the demands of sexual morality for the single person as well as for those who are married, the implications of mortal sin – these are recurring topics which priests do well to be prepared to give practical advice on.

They will also be conscious of the dominant influences in society which are an obstacle to a meaningful Christian life – consumerism, materialism, worldly success, self-indulgence, sensuality –influences which have often been

---

37 St John Chrysostom, *In Matthaeum homiliae*, 29, 3. 38 Cf. *Religious belief, practice and moral attitudes: a comparison of two surveys 1974-1984*, Council for Research and Development, Maynooth College, Report no.21; Thomas F. Inglis, 'Dimensions of Irish Students' Religiosity', *Economic and Social Review*, 11, no. 4, July 1980, pp. 237-56; Christopher W. Whelan, ed., *Values and social change in Ireland*, Dublin, 1994; Julian MacAirt, 'Religion among Irish university students', in *Doctrine and Life*, 40, April 1990, pp. 172-83. 39 John Paul II adverts to this difficulty in his Holy Thursday Letter to priests for 2001: 'There is also the fundamental problem of catechetical teaching about moral conscience and about sin, so that people can have a clearer idea of the radical demands of the Gospel. Unfortunately, there exists a minimalist tendency which prevents the Sacrament from producing all the benefits that we might hope for. Many of the faithful have an idea of sin that is not based on the Gospel but on common convention, on what is socially "acceptable". This makes them feel not particularly responsible for things that "everybody does", and all the more so if these things are permitted by civil law' (no. 15).

referred to by John Paul II. The priest has, of course, a prior responsibility to be well grounded in the moral teaching of the Church and recent developments in moral theology, especially the principles outlined in papal documents such as *Reconciliatio et paenitentia, Veritatis splendor*,[40] *Evangelium vitae*,[41] and the vademecum for confessors on aspects of conjugal morality.[42]

As *judge* he has to weigh things according to the truth and not according to appearances. Hence he has to know the sins committed and, consequently, he will encourage integrity of confession. At the same time he will be concerned, no matter what else is at issue, to help the penitent understand that there is always a place in God's paternal heart for him or her.[43] The priest, then, as confessor, should never show surprise at the sins the penitent confesses however serious or inconceivable, so to speak, they may be.[44]

To recover regular practice of this sacrament, with great benefit not only for individual souls but also for the whole parish community, the priest should preach regularly on the parables of God's mercy – the lost sheep, the lost coin, and the prodigal son (cf. Lk 15). The story of the prodigal son (cf. Lk 15:11–32) is not only one of the most beautiful episodes in the whole of the New Testament, but also contains rich material for catechesis about forgiveness and reconciliation with God. People need to hear, and to be reassured by Christ's promise that 'there will be more joy in heaven over one sinner who repents than over ninety-nine righteous persons who need no repentance' (Lk 15:7).[45] Christian life is not so much a matter of chalking up brownie points for good behaviour as a constant series of conversions, of returning once and again through contrition to our Father God.[46] Hence priests should not only be generously available to hear confessions,

---

40 John Paul II, encyclical, *Veritatis splendor*, 6 August 1993. 41 John Paul II, encyclical, *Evangelium vitae*, 25 March 1995. 42 Pontifical Council for the Family, *Vademecum for confessors concerning some aspects of the morality of conjugal life*, 12 February 1997. 43 Address, 12 November 1990. 44 John Paul II gives the priest the following practical advice for confession: 'He should never use words that seem to condemn the sinner rather than the sin. He should never instil terror but rather reverential awe. He should never enquire into aspects of the penitent's life when this knowledge is not needed to evaluate his actions. He should never use words that offend, even delicate feelings, even if, properly speaking, they do not violate justice and charity. He should never seem impatient or begrudging of his time, humiliating the penitent by asking him to hurry (except, of course, when the confession is being made with useless wordiness). Regarding his external attitude, the confessor should appear calm and avoid expressions that could indicate astonishment, censure or ridicule' (Address to Roman confessors, 27 March 1993, no. 5). 45 In his encyclical *Dives in misericordia* and the post-synodal document *Reconciliatio et paenitentia*, John Paul II draws out the full implications of the teaching in parable of the prodigal son, which will provide the priest with many insights for preaching on this topic. 46 Cf. Blessed Josemaría Escrivá, *Christ is passing by*, Dublin 1982, no. 64.

but also, continually, in liturgical homilies, catechesis, spiritual direction and every possible form our ministry to the truth may take, train [the faithful] to benefit with better dispositions from this great gift of God's mercy, which is the sacrament of Penance.[47]

At the present time catechesis about different aspects of confession is a pastoral priority.

The penance the priest imposes should be appropriate but never burdensome.[48] Often, conscious of the fragility of the penitent, he will take responsibility for most of the penance himself to 'complete what is lacking in Christ's afflictions for the sake of his body, that is, the Church' (Col 1:24). Like Christ, the priest should be able to close his conversation with the penitent with a sentiment reflecting the Lord's infinite mercy (cf. Jn 8:11), giving him grounds for confidence that he will receive the absolution fruitfully and be encouraged in his resolution to embark on a more committed Christian life.

47 John Paul II, Message to Cardinal Penitentiary, 22 March 1996, no. 7. 48 'Sacramental satisfaction must first of all be prayer: it praises God and detests sins as an offence against him, confesses the sinner's malice and weakness, and humbly and confidently asks for help, recognising man's incapacity for any salutary deed, unless he is so disposed by the Lord's supernatural aid, which is implored precisely in prayer – but if imploring, it means the theological hope of obtaining it, and thereby experiencing God's goodness as it were and being led to conversation with him. The confessor will take care to help the penitent understand all this, when the latter's spiritual resources are modest. Obviously, then, along with a certain quantitative proportion between the sin committed and the satisfaction to be made, the penitent's level of piety, his spiritual formation, his very capacity for understanding and attention and, possibly, his scrupulous tendency, must be taken into account. Therefore, while sacramental penance must be used as an opportunity to encourage penitents to pray, ordinarily one must also hold to the principle that a moderate penance done with fervour is better than a huge, unfinished one, or one done with annoyance. When the penance is to consist not only of prayers but also of deeds, they should be chosen in such a way as to enable the penitent to succeed in the practice of virtue and, in this respect, to acquire a connatural inclination along with the supernatural habit infused by grace, and thus be assisted in doing good and avoiding evil. In this regard, a certain "retribution" should ordinarily be applied, a reverse therapy as it were, the more that the sin has harmed basic goods: for example, an appropriate penitential response to the crime of abortion, so tragically widespread today, might be involvement in efforts to aid and defend life, in all the ways charity can devise in relation to the needs of individuals and society. A fitting response to the sins against justice that today so taint personal relations and defile society could be, presupposing the duty of restitution to the victim, a generous charity that more than compensates for the loss inflicted on one's neighbour, following the example of Zacchaeus, who told Jesus: "Behold, Lord, the half of my goods I give to the poor; and if I have defrauded any one of anything, I restore it fourfold" (Lk 19:8). It will not be difficult, when considered with the criteria of the faith, to find similar answers for other sins' (John Paul II, Address to Roman confessors, 18 March 1995, nos. 4-5).

G. K. Chesterton used to say that one of the main reasons why he became a Catholic was to get rid of his sins, and that the Church of Rome was the only religious system that professed to do so. He went on to explain:

> It is confirmed by the logic, which to many seems startling, by which the Church deduces that sin confessed and adequately repented is actually abolished; and that the sinner does really begin again as if he had never sinned. When a Catholic comes from Confession, he does truly, by definition, step out again into the dawn of his own beginning, and look with new eyes across the world ... He believes that in that dim corner, and in that brief ritual, God has already remade him in His own image. He is now a new experiment of the Creator. Thus the Sacrament of Penance gives a new life, and reconciles a man to all the living, but it does not do it as the optimists and the hedonists and the heathen preachers of happiness do. The gift is given at a price, and is conditioned by a confession. In other words, the name of the price is Truth, which also may be called Reality; but it is facing the reality of oneself.[49]

He admits that psychoanalysts and other groups have rediscovered the advantages of a secular form of confession, but, he points out, not without irony, 'none of them professes to provide the minor advantage of Absolution'.[50] This is why approaching the sacrament as a substitute for psychotherapy would be to deprive it of its essential supernatural purpose and meaning.[51] At the same time we should never underestimate the humanising effect which confession well received has on the penitent.[52]

John Paul II's personal witness to the importance of this aspect of the priest's pastoral work is worth recalling. Reflecting on the fruitfulness of the life of the Curé of Ars, he commented:

> It was his heroic service in the confessional which particularly struck me. That humble priest, who would hear confessions more than ten hours a day, eating little and sleeping only a few hours, was able, at a

49 G.K. Chesterton, *Autobiography*, London, 1937, pp 329-30. 50 Ibid., p. 330. 51 'The truth, which comes from the Word and must lead us to him, explains why sacramental confession must not stem from and be accompanied by a mere psychological impulse, as though the sacrament were a substitute for psychotherapy, but *from sorrow based on supernatural motives*, because sin, which violates charity towards God, the Supreme Good, was the reason for the Redeemer's sufferings and causes us to lose the goods of eternity' (John Paul II, Message to Cardinal Penitentiary, 22 March 1996, no. 3 [italics in original]). See also Address, 31 March 2001, no. 4. 52 Cf. HTL, 2001, 13.

difficult moment in history, to inspire a kind of spiritual revolution in France, and not only there. Thousands of people passed through Ars and knelt at his confessional. Against the background of attacks on the Church and the clergy in the nineteenth century, his witness was truly revolutionary. My encounter with this saintly figure confirmed me in *the conviction that a priest fulfills an essential part of his mission through the confessional* – by voluntarily 'making himself a prisoner of the confessional'. Many times, as I heard confessions in my first parish at Niegowic and then in Krakow, my thought would turn to this unforgettable experience. I have always tried to maintain this link to the confessional, both during my years of teaching at Krakow ..., and now in Rome, even if only symbolically, when every year on Good Friday I sit in the confessional in Saint Peter's Basilica.[53]

This service is one of the highest expressions of the dignity of the priest, one in which he finds his deepest sense of fulfilment.

John Henry Newman gave a series of public lectures in Birmingham in 1851 which were later published under the title, *The present position of Catholics in England*. He had recently converted to Rome and these lectures were an effort to respond to the prejudices and hostility of the British public towards the Catholic Church, prejudices which he painfully experienced at a personal level. One of the deepest misconceptions of those outside the Church concerned the practice of sacramental confession. In his lecture, 'Ignorance concerning Catholics', he explains the essentials of this sacrament and conveys, with deep supernatural and psychological insight, something of the great human and spiritual consolation of this personal encounter with Christ. He speaks about the need souls have to pour out their feelings unheard by the world to someone who is strong enough to bear their burdens, yet who is not so strong as to despise them, but someone to whom they can go to gain solace and to receive assurance.[54] Thus when people receive the sacrament of Penance with a contrite heart, this reconciliation with God and the Church brings peace and serenity of conscience, a restoration of lost dignity and a strong sense of spiritual consolation.[55]

53 John Paul II, *Gift and mystery: on the fiftieth anniversary of my priestly ordination* , London, 1996, p. 58 (italics in original). 54 J. H. Newman, *The present position of Catholics in England*, London, 1913, pp 351-2. 55 Cf. CCC, 1468.

PERSONAL RECEPTION OF THE SACRAMENT OF RECONCILIATION

In *Pastores dabo vobis* it is interesting to note the priority of emphasis which the Holy Father gives to personal reception by the priest of the sacrament of Reconciliation.[56] In doing so he repeats what he had already said in his exhortation *Reconciliatio et paenitentia* : that the quality and fervour of the priest's pastoral and spiritual life depends greatly on frequent and conscientious reception of the sacrament of Penance. If through negligence or some other reason he fails to receive this sacrament regularly, his whole priestly existence, John Paul II affirms, will suffer an inevitable decay.[57] On the other hand, priests who are good penitents make the best confessors and are zealous about promoting this ministry.

We should see the grace of the priesthood as a superabundance of mercy, not least because, like Peter and Paul, we too are sinners who have been called by Christ (cf. Jn 15:16), and like them we should abandon ourselves to the Father's mercy in the sacrament of Reconciliation with sincere repentance for our frailties. In a very real sense, Jesus's words to Peter, 'If I do not wash you, you have no part in me' (Jn 13:8), apply also to us. Only by regularly encountering God's mercy in confession will we be able to pass on to others the warmth of the Father's embrace when we administer this sacrament to others.[58] Regular confession helps us to have a realistic image of our selves, that we too are sinners in need of forgiveness.[59]

Priests have a primordial duty of helping souls be converted, of showing them how to offer a receptive mind and heart to the grace of God, so that they encounter him personally in the sacraments, especially in the sacrament of Reconciliation. To do this effectively priests also need to be converted, to experience in their lives that daily return 'to the very grace of our vocation'.[60] What in practical terms does this 'being converted' mean? The Holy Father spells it out as follows:

56 Cf. PDV, 26. 57 'All priestly existence undergoes an inexorable decline if the priest, through negligence or whatever other reason, neglects frequent recourse, inspired by genuine faith and devotion, to the Sacrament of Penance. If a priest no longer goes to confession or makes a bad confession, very quickly this will affect his priestly ministry and be noticed by the community of which he is pastor' (*Reconciliatio et paenitentia*, 31). In *Gift and mystery*, John Paul II emphasises that being a privileged witness of the working of divine mercy in the confessional imposes a special responsibility on the priest: 'It is necessary ... that every priest at the service of his brothers and sisters in the confessional should experience this same divine mercy by going regularly to confession himself and by receiving spiritual direction' (p. 86). See also, Address, 31 March 2001, no. 5. 58 Cf. HTL, 2001, nos. 6 and 10. 59 Cf. John Paul II, Address, 26 May 1993, no. 4. 60 HTL, 1979, no. 10.

It means meditating on the infinite goodness and love of Christ, who has addressed each of us and, calling us by name, has said: 'Follow me'. Being converted means continually 'giving an account' before the Lord of our hearts about our service, our zeal and fidelity, ... of our negligences and sins, of our timidity, of our lack of faith and hope, of our thinking only 'in a human way' and not in a 'divine way' ... Being converted means, for us, seeking again the pardon and strength of God in the sacrament of Reconciliation, and thus always beginning anew, and every day progressing, overcoming ourselves, making spiritual conquests, giving cheerfully 'for God loves a cheerful giver' (2 Cor 9:7).[61]

As we reflect on the import of these words we begin to understand more deeply the practical implications of conversion in our lives. It requires a sincere recognition of areas of neglect, and a commitment to strive for personal holiness grounded on the grace and light of the Holy Spirit.

61 Ibid.

# Spiritual guidance for priest and laity

The responsibilities of the priest to the community entrusted to his care are summarized in the Vatican II decree on the ministry and life of priests as follows:

> In the name of the bishop they gather the family of God as a brother-hood endowed with the spirit of unity and lead it in Christ through the Spirit to God the Father.[1]

Parish ministry involves a multiplicity of activities at group level, but as John Paul II points out, 'the community dimension of pastoral care cannot overlook *the needs of the individual faithful'*.[2]

Not very much attention has been given to this aspect of the priest's pastoral role, but the social crises of our time, with their consequences for the individual and the family, make personal spiritual guidance a keenly felt need.[3] From another perspective, the affirmation by the Council of the universal call to holiness for all Christians poses the question of the role of personal spiritual attention in this demanding enterprise.

At a time when consultants and counsellors abound for nearly every aspect of human activity, it is surely unexceptional that, in the context of priestly responsibility for the personal sanctification of the laity, specific consideration be given to the question of spiritual counselling. Priests are primarily concerned with the health of the human soul. If a good relationship between physician and patient is considered an important aspect of medical treatment, how much more should not this be the case in the task of the priest whose responsibility it is to lead souls to spiritual health and holiness.

## HISTORICAL BACKGROUND

One could say that spiritual guidance, from a Christian point of view, began with the work of personal formation Jesus gave to his disciples as he taught,

1 Cf. *Presbyterorum ordinis*, 6. 2 Address, 19 May 1993, no. 4 (italics in original).

corrected, and encouraged them, not only as a group but individually as well (cf. Mt 16:23; Lk 22:31; Jn 21:16; etc). They spent three years in close company with the Master, a period during which they learned as much from his example as from his teaching. At times he rebuked them sharply as when he said to Peter, 'get behind me Satan' (Mt 16:23), but in general his attitude was one of immense patience, deep affection and limitless understanding. Before he left them he promised to send the Holy Spirit who would recall to their minds all that he had taught them, and lead them into the fullness of truth (cf. Jn 14:26; 16:13). It is clear from this teaching that the sanctification of souls is in a special way the work of the Paraclete, and thus the role of the spiritual counsellor could be summarized by saying that his task consists essentially in helping people identify, and back up, the action of the Holy Spirit at a personal level.

St Paul gives us many insights into the role of spiritual guidance which could be summarized as follows: Christian life consists in discerning the will of God according to faith in Jesus Christ. But how are we to know if our faith and commitment are authentic? We do so through the action of the Holy Spirit (cf. Rom 8:14.26; Gal 4:6) as experienced in the Church (cf. 1 Cor 12; Eph 4:11-12), of which the believer forms a part. This action of the Holy Spirit is a complex of gifts and graces the greatest of which is charity (cf. 1 Cor 13; Rom 5:5); this is the touchstone which unites interior experience with life. The role of the director of souls is to facilitate the growth of this charity so that it finds increasing practical expression according to the great Pauline hymn articulated in 1 Corinthians 13. Paul's own docility in accepting the guidance of Ananias as to how to serve Jesus Christ is a prime example of the virtues needed to accept spiritual guidance, and, indeed, of its effectiveness (cf. Acts 9:6). In general, all those who have wanted to be faithful to divine inspirations have tried to have a spiritual guide who would help them to know the will of God, to avoid the deceits of the devil, and to persevere in the ascetic struggle.

The practice of spiritual guidance was widespread among the first monastic communities as it developed under the influence of the writings of St Basil, St Gregory the Greek and, later, St Bernard. From the middle ages we have the unusual example of St Catherine of Siena giving spiritual guidance by letter to popes and cardinals, confronting them courageously and very effectively with their ecclesiastical and spiritual responsibilities. Another woman saint, who was also proclaimed a Doctor of the Church, St Teresa of Avila, was a great director of souls and recorded for posterity her spiritual experiences in the *Way of perfection* and the *Interior castle.*

3 Cf. John Paul II, Address, 22 September, 1993.

In the nineteenth century, the magisterium of the Church reaffirmed its position on the importance of spiritual guidance when it reprobated the doctrine of *Americanism*, which, among other things, devalued spiritual direction, appealing to a simulated respect for the freedom of interior action of the Holy Spirit in souls. In rejecting this opinion Leo XIII wrote:

> God has disposed matters so that, normally, men are saved by the help of other men; and thus, for those whom he calls to a higher level of holiness, he also provides men who will guide them towards this goal.[4]

### NEED FOR SPIRITUAL GUIDANCE

Modern authors take up this traditional teaching, outlining the need for spiritual guidance for those starting out on the spiritual life, as well as for those who are well advanced in it. Blessed Josemaría Escrivá, speaking particularly to lay people, writes in *The way* that to become holy we need to listen to and follow the promptings of the Holy Spirit.[5] He then goes on to explain the advantages of having a director:

> Here is a safe doctrine that I want you to know: one's own mind is a bad adviser, a poor pilot to steer the soul through the storms and tempests and among the reefs of the interior life. That is why it is the will of God that the command of the ship be entrusted to a Master who, with his light and his knowledge, can guide you to a safe harbour.[6]

In one of his Holy Thursday Letters to priests, John Paul II, taking cognisance of the many different ways in which we fulfil our priestly vocation, reminds us, nevertheless, that the care of souls is the one responsibility we can never renounce. Here he recalls the penetrating words of St Gregory the Great: 'The supreme art is the direction of souls'.[7] This, he affirms, was the distinguishing characteristic of men such as St Vincent de Paul, St John of Avila, the Curé of Ars, St John Bosco, St Maximilian Kolbe and many other outstanding priests.

While this task is certainly an art, it is grounded on a solid scientific basis in that its effective exercise requires a sound knowledge of the principles of dogmatic, moral, and ascetical theology. It also demands familiarity with the basics of Christian anthropology. While it is true that people can reach sancti-

4 *Testem benevolentiae*, 22 January 1899; ASS 31 (1898–99) 481.  5 *The way*, Dublin, 1977, nos. 57 and 58.  6 Ibid, no. 59.  7 HTL, 1980, no. 6.

ty without the benefit of personal spiritual guidance, nevertheless, when we look at the history of Christian asceticism, we see that invariably the saints were men and women who entrusted the guidance of their souls to a spiritual director. Although the practice of spiritual guidance was never laid down by Church authority as a general requirement for Christians, it has frequently been recommended, not least by John Paul II, as we have already seen.

## SCOPE OF SPIRITUAL GUIDANCE

St Paul tells us that God wishes all men to be saved and to come to the knowledge of the truth (cf. 1 Tim 2:4). But man needs to be guided if he is to discover this message of salvation for himself and appropriate it. To do so he must encounter Christ, the fullness of revelation. In this way he enters on the life of grace, becoming a sharer in the divine life of Christ. Man as pilgrim will encounter many difficulties in his efforts to respond to his Christian vocation, difficulties which have their origin as much in his own soul as in the external circumstances of his life. At times he will meet with darkness and misunderstanding, and experience the brittleness of his own fragile flesh. It is precisely because of these limitations that he needs the light of Christ which comes to him through prayer, the sacraments and the teaching of the Church, as well as through personal spiritual counselling.

The aim of spiritual guidance is to help individual souls live the Gospel fully, and to encourage them in the practice a committed Christian life according to their specific vocation and context. For most it will be to sanctify themselves through the responsibilities of married life.

Spiritual guidance implies a progressive growth in the knowledge of the truths of the faith and in personal piety, as well as a deeper sacramental and apostolic commitment. However, since maturity in the spiritual life consists largely in having a well formed conscience, effective spiritual guidance helps one acquire the moral criteria appropriate to the particular vocation God has given to each. In this sense the spiritual guide is one who indicates the direction, one who leads, or, like John the Baptist, one who points out Jesus to his disciples as the Way they ought to follow (cf. Jn 1:29-42). The authority of a spiritual director is, then, the authority of a teacher and guide, not that of a superior to whom one owes obedience. The spiritual director, formally speaking, helps the person not only to acquire a Christian conscience in the strict sense, but also to apply Christian principles to every aspect of his life – family, work, social commitments, etc.

Spiritual direction also means pointing out the hidden obstacles to be overcome. It is to encourage people in difficult times, teaching them how to use the means God has given us to become holy. Clearly the person directed needs to have the virtues of docility and sincerity in order to be perfectly open with his or her director – to hide any part of the soul from a spiritual guide is a recipe for stagnation in the spiritual life, if not for regression and failure. Little by little directees have to learn to make themselves known to the priest. It is also important that they reflect with him on aspects of their past life that might have a bearing on present or future plans.

The spiritual director is teacher and friend. At a first stage he tries to guide the soul along the ways of prayer, that is, teaching them to have a sincere dialogue with God through examination of conscience, petition for grace, and a spirit of penance and thanksgiving. Hence the initial elements of spiritual guidance will normally include instruction on how to pray, how to do an examination of conscience, and how to get maximum benefit from the sacrament of Reconciliation.

A second stage generally involves training the will to respond generously and with good hope to doing God's will. This means, among other things, developing a spirit of confidence in God as Father, and a love for the Mass and the Eucharist. These are the sources of the spiritual energy needed to cultivate the theological virtues in everyday life. To develop the intelligence in the service of God, the spiritual director should recommend suitable reading material, especially books related to the New Testament. This facilitates and encourages a deep knowledge and love for the Sacred Humanity of Christ.

It is important to build up in souls confidence in the capacity of God's grace to help them overcome any defect or obstacle. That is why inculcating the conviction that they are children of God is one of the most important tasks of the director. To help directees acquire this outlook, the priest should encourage them to meditate on the parable of the prodigal son[8], and on those texts which Christ used to teach his listeners how to live imbued with a deep sense of God's fatherly providence.[9] As one experienced spiritual writer has put it, the Christian who is unaware that he is a child of God is ignorant of the deepest truth about his life.[10]

### UNITY OF LIFE

In the context of spiritual guidance, one of the best services a priest can offer lay people is to help them acquire unity of life. As John Paul II points out:

---

8 Cf. Lk 15: 11-32.  9 Cf., for example, Mt 6:25-33; 10:29-33; Mk 10:13-16; Jn 1:12-13. See also Rom 8:14-30; Gal 4:6-7; 2 Cor 6:17-18; Eph 1;5; 1 Jn 3:1-2; 1 Pet 1:17, etc.  10 Cf. Blessed Josemaría Escrivá, *Friends of God*, London, 1981, no. 26.

> There cannot be two parallel lives in their existence: on the one hand, the so-called 'spiritual' life, with its values and demands; and on the other, the so-called 'secular' life, that is, life in a family, at work, in social relationships, in the responsibilities of public life and in culture.[11]

The Pope makes his own what the 1987 synod of bishops said about this fundamental reality in the spiritual life:

> The unity of life of the lay faithful is of the greatest importance: indeed they must be sanctified in everyday professional and social life. Therefore to respond to their vocation, the lay faithful must see their daily activities as an occasion to join themselves to God, fulfil his will, serve other people and lead them to communion with God in Christ.[12]

If the human soul is engrafted into Christ through grace, there is no aspect of their lives that cannot be an occasion for an encounter with God. Consequently,

> every activity, every situation, every precise responsibility – as, for example, skill and solidarity in work, love and dedication in the family and the education of children, service to society and public life and the promotion of truth in the area of culture – are the occasions ordained by Providence for a 'continuous exercise of faith, hope and charity'.[13]

The separation between faith and the ordinary circumstances of life, a kind of spiritual schizophrenia, was considered by the Fathers of Vatican II as among the more serious errors of our age.[14] It is precisely by overcoming this dichotomy between Gospel and life that the laity will be able to have an integrated approach to their Christian responsibilities in the family, at work, and in society.[15] This very important teaching was cogently developed by one of the great modern pioneers of lay spirituality:

> Everyday life is the true setting for your lives as Christians. Your ordinary contact with God takes place where your fellow men, your yearnings, your work and your affections are. There you have your daily encounter with Christ. It is in the midst of the most material things of the earth that we must sanctify ourselves, serving God and all mankind ... You must understand now more clearly that God is calling you to

---

11 *Christifideles laici*, 59. 12 Ibid., no. 17. 13 Ibid., no. 59. 14 Cf. *Gaudium et spes*, 43. 15 Cf. *Christifideles laici*, 34.

serve him *in and from* the ordinary, material and secular activities of human life.[16]

Manifestly this doctrine has immense implications for the spiritual life of lay people, and that is why Blessed Josemaría Escrivá goes so far as to say, 'either we learn to find our Lord in ordinary, everyday life, or else we shall never find him'.[17]

John Paul II points out how achieving unity of life requires formation at three levels.[18] In the first place he emphasises spiritual formation. Obviously, the personal guidance offered by the priest will contribute greatly in this regard. Secondly, he says there is an increasing urgency in relation to the doctrinal formation of the lay faithful, which requires a systematic approach to catechesis and education in the Church's social teaching. Experience, in fact, confirms how progress in the spiritual life is very closely linked to an increasing catechetical and theological literacy. Thirdly, the Holy Father insists on the need for a deeper human formation in the context of unity of life, quoting the Vatican II decree on the lay apostolate:

> the lay faithful should also hold in high esteem professional skill, family and civic spirit, and the virtues related to social behaviour, namely, honesty, a spirit of justice, sincerity, courtesy, moral courage; without them there is no true Christian life.[19]

If grace builds on nature, then a good spiritual director will help souls develop these human virtues as a solid foundation for progress in the spiritual life.

The need for spiritual guidance which provides this unity of life for the laity is implicit in what John Paul II says when developing the teaching of *Presbyterorum ordinis* on this topic:[20]

> Thanks be to God, we know that there are many faithful – in the Church today and often outside her visible organisation – who are devoted or who want to devote themselves to prayer, meditation, penance (at least that of tiring, everyday work, done with diligence and patience, and that of difficult living situations), with or without the

16 Blessed Josemaría Escrivá, *Conversations*, Manila, 1977, nos. 113, 114 (italics in original). 17 Ibid., no. 114. 18 Cf. *Christifideles laici*, 60. 19 *Apostolicam actuositatem*, 4, quoted in *Christifideles laici*, 60. 20 The following is the passage from *Presbyterorum ordinis*, 9, which John Paul II refers to in this context of encouraging personal spiritual direction of the laity: 'Among other gifts of God which are found abundantly among the laity, special attention ought to be devoted to those graces by which a considerable number of people are attracted to greater heights of the spiritual life.'

direct involvement in an active apostolate. They often feel the need for a priest counsellor or even a spiritual director, who welcomes them, listens to them, and treats them with Christian friendship, in humility and charity. One could say that the moral and social crisis of our time, with the problems it brings to both individuals and families, makes this need for priestly help in the spiritual life more keenly felt. A new recognition of, and a new dedication to the ministry of the confessional and of spiritual direction are to be strongly recommended to priests, also because of the new requests of lay people who more greatly desire to follow the way of Christian perfection set forth by the Gospel.[21]

## CONFESSION AND SPIRITUAL GUIDANCE

It might well be objected that the demands of other work leave very little time for the priest to make himself available for the ministry of the confessional and personal spiritual guidance so strongly recommended by the Pope. However, if people are to acquire that mature knowledge of the faith, and the personal commitment to it which the Church expects of the laity at the present time, there is no alternative but to make time for it by a readjustment of priorities. This effort is demanded especially by the current rather tenuous and fragile bonding of many Catholics with the Church, especially among the younger generation.

How can the priest respond to this situation? How can he make progress in providing a more personalized pastoral service to the people entrusted to his care? While there are, doubtless, many valid approaches to this question, the pastoral service of spiritual guidance through confession offers considerable scope. Obviously there is an element of spiritual counselling inherent in every confession. Nevertheless, effective spiritual guidance requires a certain continuity, and encouraging people to have regular confession is one way of facilitating this. The sacramental context is a privileged opportunity for the priest to exercise his role as spiritual director.[22] At such times there is, on the part of the penitent, a ready disposition to communicate his difficulties, and a willingness to accept advice about the direction his life should take in the future. At the same time, spiritual guidance is not necessarily tied to confession – these two functions of the priest can be exercised separately. The focus of the different roles is clear: in spiritual guidance the priest is a teacher, counsellor, guide. In confession he is all these things also, but he is primarily a judge

21 Address, 22 September 1993. 22 Infrequent confession, or the socializing of it through overemphasis on the sacrament as a communal penitential rite, could obscure or undermine the perception of it as an opportunity for spiritual guidance.

endowed with powers related to the internal forum, and as such can impose spiritual or ascetical obligations on the penitent. His essential task in the sacrament of Reconciliation is to forgive sins in the name of the Trinity. In spiritual guidance, on the other hand, the priest can advise and encourage, but he cannot obligate the person. This follows logically from the requirement to respect the freedom of those who come for spiritual counselling, leading them gently to a closer identification with Jesus Christ.[23]

Pope John Paul II says spiritual guidance can readily be linked with confession by means of which souls can check on their spiritual progress, discern their vocation more accurately, and get rid of spiritual apathy.[24] On other occasions he has described confession well prepared for, and well administered, as 'a very high form of spiritual guidance',[25] as 'an instrument of development and growth, a school of sanctity, a training ground for new vocations'.[26] When we consider the Pope's own apostolate of the confessional, we are not surprised that those who had him as a confessor during his early years as a priest would describe him as a great confessor. As one of his biographer's recalls, for Fr Karol Wojtyla

> the sacrament of Penance was a deeply personal encounter in which confessor and penitent explored the unique drama of a Christian's life-situation through the prism of the Gospel. Wojtyla always stressed the responsibility of choice: 'You must decide' was the hallmark of his counsel. But at the same time he stressed the responsibility of choosing wisely. The goal was to live vocationally and to sanctify all of life through one's choices. Thus the pastoral strategy of 'accompaniment' continued in the confessional: the confessor was less a judge going through a checklist of prohibitions than a companion assisting the penitent to a deeper discernment of his or her spiritual life.[27]

All during his priestly life John Paul II gave particular priority to this ministry of confession and 'accompaniment'.

## THE MIND OF THE CHURCH

It is instructive to note in the Vatican II document on the training of priests what the mind of the Church is on this topic of spiritual guidance. It affirms that seminarians

23 Cf. Jordan Aumann, *Spiritual theology*, London 1985, p. 381. Aumann's section on 'Spiritual direction' (pp 380–89) is a helpful summary of the basic principles of this task. 24 Cf. *Reconciliatio et paenitentia*, 32. 25 Address, 30 January 1981. 26 Address, 5 October 1983. 27 George Weigel, 'Prepared to lead', in *Crisis*, October 1998, p. 15.

should receive precise instruction in the art of directing souls. They will thus be able, first of all, to form all the members of the Church in a Christian life which is fully conscious and apostolic, and so facilitate them in fulfilling the duties of their state.[28]

While the priest has to cater for the requirements of all ages, he has also to consider in a special way the specific needs of adolescents, married couples, the sick. All are in different situations; all have different duties. The very multiplicity of circumstances would seem to make what is asked of the priest a daunting task. However, John Paul II is not unaware of this when he says in *Pastores dabo vobis*:

Children, adolescents and young men are invited to discover and appreciate the gift of spiritual direction, to look for it and experience it, and to ask for it with trusting insistence from those who are their educators in the faith. Priests for their part should be the first to devote time and energies to this work of education and personal spiritual guidance: they will never regret having neglected or put in second place so many other things which are themselves good and useful, if this proved necessary for them to be faithful to their ministry as cooperators of the Spirit in enlightening and guiding those who have been called.[29]

For the priest to exercise his role as a 'teacher of prayer'[30] and to provide the 'training in holiness'[31] requested by John Paul II in his pastoral programme for the New Millennium, personal spiritual guidance will inevitably be a required part of that programme.

### SECULAR SPIRITUALITY

We have already outlined in a general way the scope and content of spiritual counselling. Nevertheless, an obvious question arises at this stage – Are there some clearly defined paths along which lay people should be guided? Are there specific objectives which we should seek to attain? Priests have been considerably helped by the documents of Vatican II in defining for them the goals they should have in mind for developing the spiritual lives of lay people, and the tar-

28 *Optatam totius*, 19. In preparing seminarians for directing souls, the reception of regular spiritual guidance right from the beginning of seminary training is an equally important part of this formation (cf. PDV, 45-8). 29 PDV, 40. 30 Cf. PDV, 47. 31 Cf. *Novo millennio ineunte*, 31.

gets they can propose to them as achievable in their relations with God. The basic parameters of lay spirituality are outlined very clearly in two chapters of *Lumen gentium*, the dogmatic constitution on the Church, especially in chapter IV on the laity,[32] and in chapter V on the universal call to holiness.[33] These principles are further developed in the conciliar document on the lay apostolate, *Apostolicam actuositatem*,[34] and in subsequent papal documents such as *Evangelii nuntiandi*,[35] *Laborem exercens*,[36] *Familiaris consortio*,[37] *Christifideles laici*,[38] and *Centesimus annus*.[39]

In general what is striking about the spirituality proposed in these documents is the high level of Christian commitment demanded, based on a vibrant sacramental life and a mature knowledge of the faith. As Pope John Paul II has recently pointed out, since Baptism is a true entry into the holiness of God,

> it would be a contradiction to settle for a life of mediocrity, marked by a minimalist ethic and a shadow religiosity.[40]

The following, then, would seem to be the more important parameters outlined in the documents referred to above about the vocation and spirituality of the laity:

a) Their specific vocation is to bring the values of the Gospel into all temporal activities – into the world of work, family, and social life, and to direct them according to God's plan of creation and redemption.[41] The laity have a particular vocation to make the Church present and fruitful in those places and sectors of life where it is only through them that she can be the salt of the earth.[42]

b) They have to be a leaven to sanctify the world from within through the conscientious fulfilment of their secular duties.[43] This point was developed in a very practical way by the Holy Father in his homily in Limerick.[44]

---

32 Cf. nos. 30-8.  33 Ibid., nos. 39-42.  34 Cf. *Decree on the apostolate of lay people* (*Apostolicam actuositatem*).  35 Cf. Paul VI, Apostolic Exhortation, *Evangelization in the modern world*, 8 December 1975.  36 John Paul II, Encyclical, *Human work*, 14 September 1981. 37 John Paul II, Apostolic Exhortation, *Christian family in the modern world*, 22 November 1981.  38 John Paul II, Apostolic Exhortation, *The vocation and mission of the lay faithful in the Church and the world*, 30 December 1988.  39 John Paul II, Encyclical on the Hundredth Anniversary of *Rerum novarum*, 1 May 1991.  40 *Novo millennio ineunte*, 31.  41 Cf. *Lumen gentium*, 31.  42 Cf. ibid., 33.  43 Cf. ibid., 31.  44 'It is their specific vocation and mission to express the Gospel in their lives and thereby to insert the Gospel as a leaven into the reality of the world in which they live and work. The great forces which shape the world - politics, the mass media, science, technology, culture, education, industry and work - are precisely the areas where lay people are especially competent to exercise their mission. If these forces are guided by people who are true disciples of Christ, and who are, at the same time,

c) All Christians in any state or walk of life are called to holiness and have an equal privilege of faith.[45]

d) All have a common dignity in building up the Church.[46]

e) Through Baptism and Confirmation all the laity are called to the apostolate by Christ himself.[47]

f) Christian marriage is a divine vocation; the family is a school of sanctity and a centre of apostolate.[48]

g) The laity have a right to receive in abundance the sacraments and the word of God; and they should disclose to pastors their needs and desires with that liberty and confidence which befits those who are children of God and brothers and sisters of Christ.[49]

h) Priests should encourage the laity to undertake apostolic works on their own initiative, not just through parochial structures, recognising their freedom in this area.[50]

i) All are obliged to do an individual, personal apostolate which is the foundation of every apostolate.[51]

j) To achieve this, each of the faithful should receive the sacraments frequently; take part in prayer and self-denial, and the practice of the virtues.[52]

fully competent in the relevant secular knowledge and skill, then indeed will the world be transformed from within by Christ's redeeming power' (See *The Pope in Ireland: addresses and homilies*, Dublin, 1979, p. 77). **45** Cf. *Lumen gentium*, 32; *Christifideles laici*, 16; *Novo millennio ineunte*, 30–31. **46** Cf. *Lumen gentium*, 32; *Christifideles laici*, 17. **47** Cf. *Lumen gentium*, 33. 'In fact, the Christian vocation is, of its very nature, a vocation to the apostolate as well' (*Apostolicam actuositatem*, 2); 'Inserted as they are in the Mystical Body by baptism and strengthened by the power of the Holy Spirit in confirmation, it is by the Lord himself that they are assigned to the apostolate ... On all Christians, accordingly, rests the noble obligation of working to bring all men throughout the whole world to hear and accept the divine message of salvation' (ibid., no. 3). **48** 'In virtue of the sacrament of Matrimony by which they signify and share (cf. Eph 5:32) the mystery of the unity and faithful love between Christ and the Church, Christian married couples help one another to attain holiness in their married life and in the rearing of their *children' (Lumen gentium*, 11). Cf. also ibid., 35 and 41; *Gaudium et spes*, 48 and 52; *Apostolicam actuositatem*, 11. In *Familiaris consortio* the Holy Father comes back to the same idea: 'In God's plan all husbands and wives are called in marriage to holiness, and this lofty vocation is fulfilled to the extent that the human person is able to respond to God's command with serene confidence in God's grace and in his or her own will' (no. 34). See also *Christifideles laici*, 51, 52. **49** Cf. *Lumen gentium*, 37. See also *Novo millennio ineunte*, 32–39. **50** Cf. *Lumen gentium*, 37; *Apostolicam actuositatem*, 3, 7, 13; *Christifideles laici*, 43, 44. **51** 'The apostolate to be exercised by the individual – which flows abundantly from a truly Christian life (cf. Jn 4:11) – is the starting point and condition of all types of lay apostolate, including the organized apostolate; nothing can replace it. *The individual apostolate is everywhere and always in place; in certain circumstances it is the only one appropriate, the only one possible. Every lay person, whatever his condition, is called to it, is obliged to it, even if he has not the opportunity or possibility of collaborating in associations'* (*Apostolicam actuositatem*, 16) (emphasis added). **52** Cf. *Lumen gentium*, 42; *Apostolicam*

These general principles deriving from the documents of Vatican II have, as already noted, been developed in detail in subsequent documents of the Holy Father, particularly *Familiaris consortio* on the vocation of marriage (1981), and *Christifideles laici* on the vocation and mission of the laity in the Church and the world (1988). More recently we find a reaffirmation of these criteria in the apostolic letter *Novo millennio ineunte* (2001).

### SPIRITUAL GUIDANCE FOR MARRIED COUPLES

The increasing incidence of marriage breakdown suggests that guidance for married couples is an area which requires urgent pastoral attention. This escalating marital fragility is not unconnected with the fact that, in recent years, the institution of marriage and the family has been undermined in many different ways. Divorce legislation seriously erodes the concept of permanent, life-long commitment. Premarital and extramarital sex are portrayed in the media as normal behaviour and are acquiring a greater social acceptability. As already noted, the contraceptive mentality is becoming more widespread to judge by the very significant fall in family size over the past twenty years. All of these elements ask for recognition in preaching and in spiritual guidance.

Marriage counsellors can offer specific expertise and have a useful role to play in this context. However, since a high proportion of marital difficulties have their roots in what are essentially moral and spiritual problems, they can often be more effectively addressed by the priest in spiritual guidance or in confession. Usually marital problems can be reduced to fundamental issues such as lack of generosity and self-giving, contraceptive practices, lack of effort in communication, poor prayer life, a materialistic outlook, infidelity. The priest has to have the conviction that correspondence with sacramental grace will overcome most of these difficulties.

This point was eloquently made by the Holy Father in his homily in Limerick in 1979:

> Above all, hold high the esteem for the wonderful dignity and grace of the sacrament of marriage. Prepare earnestly for it. Believe in the spiritual power which this sacrament of Jesus Christ gives to strengthen the marriage union, and to overcome all the crises and problems of life together. Married people must believe in the power of the sacrament to make them holy; they must believe in their vocation to witness through their marriage to the power of Christ's love ... Dear fathers

*actuositatem*, 4; *Novo millennio ineunte*, 32-40. **53** *The Pope in Ireland*, p. 80.

and mothers of Ireland, believe in your vocation, that beautiful vocation of marriage and parenthood which God has given to you.[53]

As a means to holiness in married life, John Paul II has developed the doctrine of *Humanae vitae* and demonstrated the deep human and supernatural wisdom contained in that much controverted encyclical, a document which has, over the past thirty years, been seen to be a prophetic defence of the truth and dignity of conjugal love.[54] Priests need to be fully persuaded of the validity of this teaching at the scriptural, ethical, and personalist levels if they are to be able to explain it to couples and show them how the Church is essentially pro-love and pro-life.[55]

Effective guidance in this area will require the priest to educate people in the importance of prayer, the idea that marriage is a vocation to holiness, and how real self-fulfilment in marriage can only be achieved through self-giving. He will need to affirm the blessings which each new child brings, especially as a means to a deeper bonding of the couple's love. Practical trust in the providence of God, and generous acceptance of the cross as a normal part of the Christian life, constitute a fundamental aspect of spiritual guidance for married couples.

Many people come to marriage expecting too much from it, more than it can realistically deliver. Often their preparation and approach to the sacrament leaves much to be desired. Consequently priests have to teach couples to work at their marriage, and encourage them to mature in their relationship so as to make it a truly Christian and fulfilling partnership.[56] Indeed they should be gradually formed to see that marriage is a divine vocation and a specific way to holiness.[57]

## QUALITIES OF SPIRITUAL DIRECTOR

A priest by reason of his training in theology, his experience in the work of the confessional and general pastoral involvement, is normally a suitable candidate

54 Cf. John Paul II, Address, 14 March 1988. 55 For a more detailed treatment of this topic, see Chapter 9 above. 56 While in general women may be more receptive to spiritual guidance than men, Christian wisdom and common sense have always indicated practical norms of prudence which should guide priests in giving spiritual guidance and hearing the confessions of women. The priest in his dealings with women penitents should be vigilant to avoid anything which would encourage undue familiarity or attachments. The recent Vatican guidelines for confessors in relation to conjugal matters is helpful for priests (Pontifical Council for the Family, *Vademecum for confessors*, 12 February 1997). 57 Cf. *Constitution on the Church in the modern world*, 48, 50; *Decree on the lay apostolate*, 11; *Familiaris consortio*, 34.

to be a spiritual director.[58] Because of his mission and responsibility to sanctify souls, every priest should be alert to opportunities to give personal spiritual guidance, especially in the context of the sacrament of Reconciliation.

To offer effective spiritual counselling certain aptitudes are required on the part of the priest. We find a clear statement of these basic competencies in the writings of St Teresa of Avila:

> It is of great importance that the director should be a prudent man –
> of sound understanding, I mean – and also an experienced one: if he
> is a learned man as well, that is a very great advantage.[59]

St Francis de Sales, drawing on his own extensive experience, says that a good director of souls should excel in three particular qualities or virtues - charity, knowledge, and prudence.[60]

Apart from a solid grounding in moral, dogmatic and ascetical theology, a spiritual director should be very familiar with Scripture, especially the New Testament. If Christ is for all 'the way , the truth, and the life' (Jn 14:6), and holiness is essentially friendship with Christ, a spiritual director should know how to 'open the Scriptures' for his directees in such a way that they, like the two disciples on the road to Emmaus, will find that little by little their vision of the spiritual life is deepened by contemplating the life and teaching of the Master (cf. Lk 24:13-35).

The influential spiritual director will learn much from the lives of the saints about Christian holiness and the very different paths along which the Holy Spirit leads souls. This has two important consequences. In the first place, because sanctification is primarily a work of the Spirit, the priest will be more effective when he realizes that his role is essentially that of an instrument, to be a channel for the action of the Paraclete. Hence he has a special need of those gifts of the Spirit such as wisdom, understanding and counsel in order to guide people along the most suitable ascetical path in keeping with their personal circumstances.

Secondly, because each soul is unique, the priest cannot try to impose a preconceived ascetical programme or structure. While there are common, fundamental elements in every spiritual life, a person's particular circumstances – family, work, social situation – will to a large extent determine where he or she starts and the contours of the spiritual road to be followed. This approach is also demanded by respect for the freedom of the individual.

58 In saying this, I am not unaware of the fact that many people other than priests can give effective spiritual guidance. 59 *The complete works of St Teresa of Jesus* (trans. E. Allison Peers), vol. 1, London, 1975, p. 80; see also, ibid., pp 79-83; vol. 2, pp 19-26. 60 *Introduction to the devout life*, Part I, ch. 4.

## OTHER REQUIREMENTS FOR EFFECTIVE SPIRITUAL GUIDANCE

To respond adequately to the needs of souls, the priest must be able to identify the basic psychological structure of each person he deals with. Thus he should be familiar with the requirements of different temperaments, and be aware of the manner in which emotions influence the spiritual life. It is also important that he would be able to recognize common nervous or emotional disorders so that he would know when to recommend medical advice. A director should treat souls with great refinement, and always encourage no matter how poor the response to previous advice may seem to have been. His humility will be reflected in his approachability and understanding.

*Prudence* Because of the variety of human situations, a measure of prudence is a basic requirement to make sound judgements about what is the best advice to give a person. Such wisdom comes in different ways. In the first place the priest learns a lot from the experience of dealing with souls at a personal level in his normal pastoral work. If he hears confessions regularly and tries to get to know each penitent well, he will acquire the necessary confidence for giving practical spiritual guidance.

A good director knows how to listen; he will also ask questions to get to the root of difficulties. The frequency of these conversations will depend on the needs of people and their circumstances. A prudent director won't necessarily offer immediate solutions to problems; often it will be advisable to wait to get to know the person better and, if necessary, to ask another priest for advice.

An important element in developing the requisite prudence is that the priest himself would receive spiritual guidance regularly. The experience of striving for holiness in a committed way, with its successes and failures, and the effort to respond faithfully to the specific points of guidance he receives from his own spiritual director, will enable the priest to more easily empathize with the interior struggle of those he himself guides.[61]

*Prayer-life of priest* The priest's ability to lead people along the road to holiness depends very much on his own prayer-life. He should ask the Holy Spirit for light before any session of spiritual guidance and pray about the difficulties of those who entrust their spiritual needs to him. A consequence of this approach is that in helping others he will give more importance to supernatural arguments than to merely human considerations. Since prayer, conversation with God, is the foundation of the spiritual life, unless the priest is seriously trying to develop his own prayer-life, he would lack the indispensable

61 This aspect will be developed in more depth later in this chapter.

experience and conviction to be a competent guide for souls. He should be familiar with the different approaches to prayer so as to be able to adapt his advice to the needs and the varying circumstances of individuals.

*Respect for freedom*  The priest should not approach his task with a predetermined spiritual programme which he tries to superimpose on souls, or present an ascetical straight-jacket into which he tries to slot people. Because every soul is unique, the director should have great respect for the insights of people into their own lives. He should be open-minded about the different practices of piety, and not try to impose a personal preference or prejudice with regard to a particular devotion. He has to allow the Holy Spirit full freedom and space to act – this means never forcing situations. Only rarely should he exact obedience to his specific indications.

*Patience*  Patience is essential for progress in the spiritual life – the director should be ready to lift souls and encourage them to start again as often as necessary. With time he will get to know people – their strengths and weaknesses, particular circumstances of life, temperament, and interests. He will learn the difficulties they encounter in their spiritual life, temptations, etc. He will also be able to assess any lacunae that might exist in their moral or doctrinal education. Little by little, as a result of a deeper formation, the directee will learn how to take more decisions on his or her own initiative. While the priest needs to empathize with people to fully understand their situation, at the same time he has to maintain a certain reserve to avoid the danger of creating a dependency or attachment. He should keep an appropriate emotional distance so as to lead souls to God and thus avoid seeking human consolation in his relationship with them. It is not the role of the spiritual director to solve family, professional, or financial problems. Consequently, he should never allow a person to transfer on to him such responsibilities, just as Christ refused to get involved in sorting out a family dispute about the division of a family property (cf. Lk 12:14).

*Holiness of the director*  In summary, the best service a priest can offer others is the quality of his own holiness, or, at least, a serious commitment to the quest for it. Zeal for souls will give the priest the impetus to help many towards holiness. His example will inspire others to be ambitious for a deeper friendship with God. If he reflects the sentiments of the Good Shepherd in his own person, he will attract many to spiritual guidance by the example of his own life.

## SPIRITUAL GUIDANCE FOR PRIESTS

One of the dangers in pastoral action is that, contrary to what the Vatican II documents expect, priests would underestimate the capacity of people to respond to a vocation to holiness. However, the present Holy Father has put the matter in very clear perspective:

> The conviction we need to share and to spread is that the call to holiness is addressed to all Christians. It is not the privilege of a spiritual elite. It is not the preoccupation of just a few who feel a sense of heroic courage. Still less is it a kind of peaceful refuge, adapted to a certain kind of piety or to certain original temperaments. It is a grace proposed to all the baptized, according to different modalities and degrees.[62]

Failure to encourage people to strive for holiness could well mean that the priest lacks real challenge in his own spiritual life. On the other hand,

> familiarity with one's own soul, with its difficulties in making progress towards sanctity, its struggles and temptations, inclinations and opportunities, its anxiety and inner peace, is one of the greatest helps towards a deep understanding and knowledge of others. Experience shows that it is very difficult to direct others if one has not had direction oneself, for few things are as beneficial in dealing with others as the memory of how one was treated oneself.[63]

Among the helps recommended by Vatican II to achieve priestly holiness is that of receiving spiritual guidance, for which, we are reminded, we 'should have a high regard'.[64] This point is reiterated by John Paul II in *Pastores dabo vobis*: 'It is necessary to rediscover the great tradition of personal spiritual guidance which has always brought great and precious fruits to the Church's life' [65] and 'which contributes in| no small way to the ongoing formation of priests ... It ensures spiritual formation. It fosters and maintains faithfulness and generosity in the carrying out of the priestly ministry.'[66]

62 Address to Council of Laity, 7 June 1986. 63 Federico Suarez, *About being a priest*, Dublin, 1979, p. 122. 64 *Presbyterorum ordinis*, 18. 65 PDV, 40. 66 PDV, 80. Pius XII exhorted priests not to trust just their own lights for the development of their spiritual lives. Rather, he tells them, 'humbly and with docile mind accept advice and seek help from those who can direct you with wise counsel, warn you in advance against the dangers that threaten and, at the same time, prescribe suitable remedies, and in all difficulties, interior or exterior, guide you correctly and direct you to the daily increasing perfection to which the exam-

Scripture tell us 'a brother helped by a brother is as strong as a walled city' (Prov 18:19). This principle applies not only at the general level of priestly fraternity, but even more so when availing of the support that a priest colleague can offer through regular spiritual guidance. Every priest needs what is so accurately conveyed by the Irish word *anam-chara*, a soul-friend in whom he can confide, with whom he can share the successes and failures of his spiritual struggle, to whom he can go for encouragement and objective advice.[67]

One might ask why are we priests reluctant at times to do something which has been so strongly recommended for our good? Is it because we feel uncomfortable about doing so, or because we think our freedom would be limited as a result? We have no reason to be embarrassed because the Holy Spirit works effectively through that brother priest who has feet of clay like ourselves. He is a man who, by and large, experiences the same temptations and, as a consequence, will never think he has reason to feel more secure. We would also have a false idea of personal freedom if we felt that spiritual guidance would restrict it in any way. On the contrary, guidance is one of the helps available to us to use our freedom properly. Through it we create more space for the Holy Spirit to act in us and, as St Paul states categorically, 'where the Spirit of the Lord is, there is freedom' (2 Cor 3:17).

Underlying our reluctance to let ourselves be known by a brother priest there may be an element of fear – fear that he may get to know us as we really are, fear that we my lose our 'prestige' in the eyes of another; fear perhaps of going too deeply into ourselves. There may even be a certain fear of holiness itself because we are a little uneasy about the demands it might make on us – the danger, as we have already suggested, of losing our so-called 'independence'. However, as priests we have given our lives to Christ and he in turn has called us to intimacy with him (cf. Jn 15:12). It is this intimacy which opens up to us the full potential of our vocation and, one might add, the fullness of the joy of being a priest of Jesus Christ. All the accumulated wisdom of the Church points to spiritual guidance as one of the most effective ways of attaining this deeper friendship with the Master.

---

ple of the saints in heaven and the approved masters of Christian asceticism attract and call you. For without these prudent directors of conscience, it is generally very difficult to respond as one should to the supernatural promptings of the Holy Spirit and divine grace' (Apostolic exhortation, *Menti nostrae*, 23 September 1950). **67** What are we to say, how are we to approach a spiritual director? Again St Francis de Sales points the way: 'Treat him with an open heart, in all sincerity and fidelity, manifesting clearly to him your good and your evil without feint or dissimulation: and by this means your good will be examined and rendered better, and your evil will be corrected and remedied' (*Introduction to the devout life*, I, 4). There, in a nut shell, we have the content and objective of spiritual guidance.

## OBJECTIVE SELF-KNOWLEDGE

One of the basic reasons for spiritual guidance is that the way we should follow in our interior life is not always clear and obvious. We are too close to ourselves to be objective in something so personal as the pursuit of holiness. The priest knows from the experience of trying to guide others the dangers of subjective self-will. This results in us being blind to the real needs of our own spiritual life. Indeed one of the peculiar weaknesses of the human condition in matters spiritual is the tendency to allow ourselves to be over-influenced by self-regarding motives rather than by reasons which are grounded on faith or supernatural considerations. Working on the basis of human impulse alone, even heroically so, is ultimately a recipe for burn-out and disillusionment

To avoid shying away from the demands of holiness, the priest needs somebody to point the way objectively, a kind and understanding mentor who will call his spiritual bluff when necessary, and help him be sincere with himself. Since we all tend to avoid being over-stretched and to work comfortably within our limits, a good spiritual guide will help us get the best out of ourselves and thus keep a proper balance between work and prayer, relaxation and pastoral zeal. He will encourage us to make the Holy Mass the real centre of our day, and show us how to draw out of it all the spiritual resources we need to sanctify the multiplicity of seemingly insignificant things that claim our attention, and which appear to have very little to do with effective pastoral action. He will gently prompt us that we need to spend time in prayer every day. Spiritual guidance is seen by *Pastores dabo vobis* as an integral part of the priest's ongoing formation.[68]

A spiritual director will perhaps tell the priest little that he doesn't know already at a theoretical level. Hence his most effective contribution will often be to help the priest face up to himself, and to motivate him to do something practical about those ideas which he collects from one retreat to the next, and which, because of a certain apathy or surfeit of activism, he never actually gets round to doing anything about. Spiritual counselling will encourage him to

[68] The essential content of this formation, which was detailed in *Optatam totius*, 8, was reiterated again by John Paul II in *Pastores dabo vobis* : 'Those who are to take on the likeness of Christ the priest by sacred ordination should form the habit of drawing close to him as friends in every detail of their lives. They should live his Paschal Mystery in such a way that they will know how to initiate into it the people committed to their charge. They should be taught to seek Christ in faithful meditation on the word of God and in active participation in the sacred mysteries of the Church, especially in the Eucharist and the Divine Office, to seek him in the Bishop by whom they are sent and in the people to whom they are sent, especially the poor, little children, the weak, sinners and unbelievers. With the confidence of sons they should love and reverence the most Blessed Virgin Mary, who was given as a mother to the disciple by Jesus Christ as he was dying on the Cross' (PDV, 45).

acquire that subjective moral authenticity which comes from a growing identification with Christ the Good Shepherd.

A logical consequence of spiritual guidance is that a priest learns to make
good use of his time, plan his work better, and fulfil responsibilities promptly.
A committed and orderly work schedule, inspired by unity of life, provides a
context for human and spiritual fulfilment and in this way contributes effectively to fidelity in the area of celibacy. Overall we can see that personal spiritual guidance is an opportunity for communicating at the deepest and most
intimate level of our being. It provides an awareness of being understood, supported and appreciated. This kind of intimacy is a powerful defence against
the dangers of pessimism and frustration which can undermine the commitment of the priest.

While psychology can provide some insights about the religious dimension
of people's behaviour, discernment of spirits and the pedagogical wisdom of
the saints offer a much more profound source of knowledge for the guidance
of priests and seminarians. It is the attractive profile of the saint, reflecting
natural and supernatural virtues forged by grace, that should be offered as the
model rather than the narrow reductive framework of psychoanalysis which
emerges from the now largely discredited Freudian interpretation of human
behaviour.[69]

CONCLUSION

In summary, the pastoral challenge of today is, as Vatican II points out, to transmit to the laity a greater awareness of their Christian vocation, and a deeper personal commitment to it through the development of an authentic lay spirituality. As priests we need to know the parameters of that spirituality so that we give
the proper focus to our work of evangelization, putting before people all the
demands of their vocation, and at the same time providing them with the necessary sacramental and pastoral resources to rise to these demands.[70] The work of
spiritual guidance offers immense potential in any pastoral strategy, and can be
truly effective when integrated with regular confession.

69 Cf. John Farrell, *Freud's paranoid quest*, New York, NY, 1996. Dietrich von Hildebrand
warns us that 'Freud's thesis, on which the so-called psychoanalytic method is based,
embodies a completely erroneous view of the structure of human personality, which betrays
the influence of an exploded sensationalism'. One of its radical errors, he tells us, 'is that it
regards the body and physiological life as the "form" of the soul, not the spiritual soul as the
"form" of life and the body' (*In defence of purity*, London, 1937, p. 17). 70 To help focus on
the needs of different age groups, the priest will find the *General directory for catechesis*, nos.
171-88, a useful resourse (Congregation for the Clergy, 11 August 1997).

On the other hand, there is a direct connection between the holiness of the priest and his pastoral effectiveness.[71] Consequently he needs to take seriously the invitation of Christ to follow him closely. Regular reception of spiritual guidance is one of the most effective means available to us to become priests to the measure of the heart of Christ. This, the Holy Father has often reminded us, is what is so much needed in the Church today.

71 'The very holiness of priests is of the greatest benefit for the fruitful fulfilment of their ministry. While it is possible for God's grace to carry out the work of salvation through unworthy ministers, yet God ordinarily prefers to show his wonders through those men who are more submissive to the impulse and guidance of the Holy Spirit and who, because of their intimate union with Christ and their holiness of life, are able to say with St Paul: "It is no longer I who live, but Christ who lives in me"(Gal 2:20)' (*Presbyterorum ordinis*, 12).

# The priest and the liturgy

The identification of the priest with Christ finds its supreme expression in the celebration of the Eucharistic sacrifice.[1] When he takes the host in his hands and says 'This is my Body,' the priest challenges himself to the deepest possible involvement in the redemptive sacrifice of Christ, while at the same time ensuring the historical continuity of the Incarnate Word among men. As we have seen, these two aspects of the priestly life are mutually interactive.

As a result of his consecration the priest's most important task is the celebration of Eucharistic sacrifice. Since it is primarily through the sacramental ministry that the work of redemption is carried out, the priest needs to have a profound knowledge of all those elements which constitute the liturgical action in order to facilitate its salvific effectiveness. Devout celebration of the liturgy has always has a profound influence on the piety of the faithful, but this is particularly necessary at the present time when authoritative voices have articulated considerable concern about irregularities and a loss of the sense of reverence in liturgical celebrations.

### CRISIS IN THE LITURGY

The fact that there has been a certain crisis in the liturgy since the 1970s is well documented. In 1980 a Vatican statement spoke about frequent abuses being reported from different parts of the world. These deficiencies referred to a confusion of roles of priest and laity, an increasing loss of the sense of the sacred (characterized by a lack of respect for the Blessed Sacrament and the abandonment of liturgical vestments), and the improvisation of liturgical

1 Cf. *S. Th.* III, 82, 1. **2** The abuses reported included : 'confusion of roles, especially regarding the priestly ministry and the role of the laity (indiscriminate shared recitation of the Eucharistic prayer, homilies given by lay people, lay people distributing communion while the priests refrain from doing so); an increasing loss of the sense of the sacred (abandonment of liturgical vestments, the Eucharist celebrated outside church without real need, lack of reverence and respect for the Blessed Sacrament, etc.); misunderstanding of the

texts.[2] Eight years later, in his review of the Vatican II mandated liturgical reform, John Paul II does not hide the fact that many of the same abuses continued to exist, abuses which, he says, disfigure the liturgy and deprive the people of the true treasures of Christian worship.[3]

As recently as 1998, in an address to American bishops, the Pope went so far as to assert that some of the liturgical changes introduced since Vatican II 'show a misunderstanding of the very nature of the liturgy, leading to abuses, polarization and sometimes even grave scandal'.[4] Monsignor M Francis Mannion, a keen observer of the American liturgical scene, explains that the severe problems in the Church's liturgical life in the US arise because of the effort to adapt the liturgy to American popular culture, an approach which includes 'the trivialisation of rites and symbols, the ascendancy of an entertainment and therapeutic ethos in liturgical celebrations, an exaggerated, neo-

ecclesial character of the liturgy (the use of private texts, the proliferation of unapproved Eucharistic Prayers, the manipulation of liturgical texts for social and political ends). In these cases we are face to face with a real falsification of the Catholic liturgy ... None of these things can bring good results. The consequences are – and cannot fail to be – the impairing of the unity of faith and worship in the Church, doctrinal uncertainty, scandal and bewilderment among the People of God, and the near inevitability of violent reactions' (Instruction, *Inaestimabile donum*, Congregation for the Sacraments and Divine Worship, 17 April 1980). 3 'On occasion there have been noted illicit omissions or additions, rites invented outside the framework of established norms; postures or songs which are not conducive to faith or to a sense of the sacred; abuses in the practice of general absolution; confusion between the ministerial priesthood, linked with Ordination, and the common priesthood of the faithful, which has its foundation in Baptism. It cannot be tolerated that certain priests should take upon themselves the right to compose Eucharistic prayers or to substitute profane readings for texts from Sacred Scripture. Initiatives of this sort, far from being linked with the liturgical reform as such, or with the books which have issued from it, are in direct contradiction to it, disfigure it and deprive the Christian people of the genuine treasures of the Liturgy of the Church' (John Paul II, Apostolic letter, *Vicesimus quintus annus*, on the 25th anniversary of the promulgation of the Vatican II conciliar constitution, *Sacrosanctum Concilium*, on the Sacred Liturgy, 4 December 1988, no. 13). 4 Address, 9 October 1998, no. 1. Aidan Nichols traces current difficulties to the assimilation of Enlightenment ideas in the liturgical domain, resulting in a demand for simplification of the liturgy with the emphasis on its socially useful or community-building character, and the insistence on as complete an intelligibility as possible so as to edify morally those who worshipped by means of it (cf. *Looking at the liturgy*, San Francisco, 1996, p. 22). In Cardinal Ratzinger's estimation the source of many of the difficulties is an overemphasis on antiquity as the liturgical norm while regarding subsequent developments as decadent accretions. From time to time one hears a call for a return to the 'simplicity' of the domestic liturgy which is supposed to have characterised the early Christian communities, a proposal that at times is justified by forced interpretations of Scripture. Behind such calls lies not only a skewed perception of Church history, but also a deficient understanding of the majesty and transcendence of God. (Cf. *The spirit of the liturgy*, San Francisco, 2000, p. 82).

clerical style of priestly presidency and an individualistic and consumerist spirituality'.[5]

John Paul II has also warned against the tendency of dumbing down the liturgy in the interests of intelligibility. 'Conscious participation' he tells us, calls for proper instruction in the mysteries of the liturgy, but, he asserts,

> *It does not mean a constant attempt within the liturgy itself to make the implicit explicit*, since this often leads to a verbosity and informality which are alien to the Roman rite and end by trivializing the act of worship. Nor does it mean the suppression of all subconscious experience, which is vital in a liturgy that thrives on symbols that speak to the subconscious just as they speak to the conscious.[6]

The challenge now, he affirms, is to move beyond the misunderstandings and to return to a deeper appropriation of the universal, the vertical and the eternal aspects of the liturgy, that is, to a greater appreciation of the cosmic and eschatological dimensions of Catholic worship.[7] The purpose of this chapter is to help priests do what John Paul II recommended in his 1998 address, that is, 'to enter more deeply into the contemplative dimension of worship' so as to recover 'the sense of awe, reverence and adoration which are fundamental attributes in our relationship with God'.[8] This is not a question of nostalgia for the past, but of faithfully implementing the richness of Vatican II's vision of the liturgy as outlined in the constitution *Sacrosanctum Concilium*. It has been well said in this regard that

> when celebrated with attentiveness to ritual and text, with spiritual profundity, nobility and solemnity, with well-formed ministerial leadership, and with rich musical, artistic and architectural elaboration, the present liturgy is pastorally most edifying and deeply expressive of Catholic fullness.[9]

To try to penetrate more deeply this contemplative dimension of worship, I will first of all consider the nature of the liturgy as revealed by God himself in

5 M. Francis Mannion, 'The catholicity of the liturgy: shaping a new agenda' in Stratford Caldecott (ed.), *Beyond the prosaic: renewing the liturgical movement*, Edinburgh, 1998, p. 35. 6 John Paul II, Address, 9 October 1998, no. 3 (italics in original). 7 Cf. Address, 9 October 1998, no. 2. Mgr Mannion also affirms that the most comprehensive dimensions of Catholic liturgy – eschatological, cosmic, and doxological – 'are, in fact, today in something of a critical condition'. While 'these three elements were highly important in the modern liturgical movement ... [they] underwent considerable neglect in the aftermath of the Second Vatican Council' ('Liturgy for the third millennium', in *Priest and people*, December 1999, p. 458). 8 Cf. Address, 9 October 1998, no. 2. 9 Mannion, 'The catholicity of the liturgy', p. 36.

the Old Testament, a liturgy which undergirds so much of the worship of the New. It was in fact during the celebration of the Passover, the most solemn of the feasts of the Old Covenant, that the new Christian liturgy was born. This will help us to understand why the liturgy is an ecclesial responsibility and, thus, why it cannot be fabricated or modified by the creativity of priests or planning groups. We will then examine what precisely Vatican II says about the liturgy and see how this theology of the liturgy is developed in the *Catechism of the Catholic Church*, particularly the nature of signs and symbols used in worship and its sacramental character. Subsequently we will reflect on the eschatological and cosmic dimensions of Catholic liturgy, the laity's participation in it, and the relevance of silence and song to worship. Because a church is the house of God, the sacred place in which the Eucharistic sacrifice is celebrated and where the Real Presence is enshrined, we will try to identify some of those general characteristics of church furnishing and design which facilitate a sense of reverence and transcendence, and see why a spirit of splendour and largesse is appropriate to the celebration of the Paschal mystery. If the identity of the priest is expressed primarily through his celebration of the Eucharistic sacrifice, we see how all these elements of the liturgy have a clear relevance for defining that very identity.

In this context it is appropriate to point out that the recent publication of the revised *General instruction on the Roman missal* provides guidelines for stabilizing the liturgy with a clear intention of highlighting the sacred dimension of Catholic worship.[10] This purpose is underscored by the sacral vocabulary used in the revised Instruction. Thus we have repeated use of 'sacred liturgy', 'sacred rites', 'sacred ministers', 'sacred place'. etc. The Instruction also points out that 'greater attention needs to be paid to what is laid down by liturgical law and by the traditional practice of the Roman rite, for the sake of the common spiritual good of the people of God rather than to personal inclination and or arbitrary choice'.[11]

## OLD TESTAMENT LITURGY

The Church reads the books of the Old Testament in the light of the Paschal event to discover the testimony they bear to the history of salvation. This has implications not only for the theology, but also for the liturgy of the New Covenant. The institution of the Passover feast, the making of the Sinai

10 Approved by John Paul II on Holy Thursday, 2000, and issued by the Congregation for Divine Worship and the Sacraments, 28 July 2000 (subsequently abbreviated to GIRM). 11 GIRM, 42. See Jerry J. Pokorsky, 'Saving the Roman rite?', in *Catholic World Report*, October 2000, pp 50-5.

covenant, and the establishment of religious worship for the people of Israel find their fulfilment in the liturgy instituted by Christ.

Liturgical legislation was an essential element of the Sinaic covenant. Since the Chosen People were to be 'a priestly kingdom and a holy nation' (Ex 19:6), the whole of life was to come under the influence of religion and be sanctified. The Mosaic religion in fact inculcated a profound reverence for God: his majesty was symbolized by the extraordinary care exercised in the preparation of the Hebrew cult with reference to the sanctuary, the Ark, and the Holy of Holies. The need for absolute ritual purity impressed on the Hebrews this sense of God's sanctity. There was a clear perception among the Israelites of the need for redemption and of the offering of sacrifice for this purpose. By means of the different sacrifices – holocaust, peace and sin offerings, etc. – the Hebrew people would now be able to glorify the God who delivered them from Egypt.

In the Old Testament we find detailed instructions given by Yahweh to Moses relating to every aspect of the liturgy of the covenant – the feasts, the sanctuary, prescriptions about the different types of sacrifice.[12] Here too we encounter comprehensive legislation about the ordination of priests, the different liturgical rites – nothing is left to chance, nor is there any scope for personal innovation.[13] The book of Leviticus prefigures what becomes a reality in the Redemption. Many passages in the New Testament, particularly in the letter to the Hebrews, use Leviticus as a reference point. The minute details as regards design and dimensions, and the specific indications about the quality of materials, fabrics and furniture to be used in the construction of the tabernacle, emphasise on the one hand the transcendence of God and on the other his closeness to his people. At the same time we see that the liturgy of the Old Covenant is fulfilled in the New with several points of continuity – listening to the word of God, offering sacrifice, praying the psalms in the Divine Office, the tabernacle as the locus par excellence of God's presence among men.

It is salutary to reflect on the fact that all these indications were given directly by God himself for a liturgy which was infinitely inferior to that of the Christian era. Under the old dispensation Temple worship was focussed on the sacrifice of mere animals. However, in the cult of the New Covenant, where the principal act of worship is the renewal of the sacrifice of the Son of God, we intuit how much more worthy the liturgical arrangements for the celebration of the Eucharistic sacrifice should be. It is a revealing lesson for us on the importance of everything the Church lays down about the liturgy, especially the celebration of the Eucharist. As we are reminded in *Dominicae coenae*:

12 Cf. Ex 25-31.  13 Cf. Lev.

The Eucharist is a common possession of the whole Church as the sacrament of her unity. And thus the Church has the strict duty to specify everything that concerns participation in it and its celebration.[14]

What is obvious too is that the liturgy of the Old Testament is not a humanly crafted worship; it is made present through God's revelation to Moses. Consequently authentic liturgy implies that it is God himself who reveals how best we can worship him. In the same way that Scripture is a work inspired by the Holy Spirit and an expression of God's self-revelation, so also the liturgy is a work of God and an integral part of the living Tradition of the Church which has to be transmitted and interpreted with the same fidelity and attention as the word of God.[15]

Many of the current criticisms of the liturgy relate to the need for a deeper sense of reverence and transcendence, and the elimination of informality, improvisation, and over-emphasis on horizontal engagement. There is also an increasing awareness that this will not come about without the recovery of a more profound sense of the eschatological dimension of the liturgy expressed in church music, art and design. Reflection on the ideas of redemption, transcendence, holiness, and splendour which characterized the Old Covenant worship will also help to reclaim whatever may have been lost to the liturgy through too humanistic an interpretation of how divine worship should be offered to God.

## THE *CATECHISM OF THE CATHOLIC CHURCH* AND THE RENEWAL OF THE LITURGY

The teaching of the *Catechism of the Catholic Church* fosters a clear perception of the transcendent nature of the liturgy. Here we find the best insights of the Liturgical Movement and the permanently valid elements of this tradition.[16] The *Catechism* makes its own the definition and description of the liturgy contained in *Sacrosanctum Concilium*:

The liturgy then is rightly seen as an exercise of the priestly office of Jesus Christ. It involves the presentation of man's sanctification under the guise of signs perceptible by the senses and its accomplishment in ways appropriate to each of these signs. In it full public worship is per-

14 John Paul II, Letter, *Dominicae Coenae*, 4 February 1980, no. 12. 15 Cf. Ratzinger, *The spirit of the liturgy*, pp 21, 22. 16 Cf. Ratzinger, *A new song for the Lord*, New York, 1997, p. 133.

formed by the Mystical Body of Jesus Christ, that is, by the Head and his members. From this it follows that every liturgical celebration, because it is an action of Christ the priest and of his Body which is the Church, is a sacred action surpassing all others. No other action of the Church can equal its efficacy by the same title and to the same degree.[17]

While the liturgy has an essentially Trinitarian dimension, the priest will be particularly conscious of the christological aspect.[18] Christ, now seated at the right hand of the Father, acts through the sacraments he instituted to communicate his grace, making present his own Paschal Mystery. He always associates the Church with himself in offering worship to the Father.[19]

The ordained priesthood, which is at the service of the priesthood of all the baptized, guarantees that it really is Christ who acts in the sacraments. By means of the apostolic power transmitted from one generation of bishops to the next, the priest is the sacramental bond which ties the liturgical action to the words and actions of Christ, the source and foundation of the sacraments.[20] In this way the priest sees himself inserted by divine gift and grace into the source of that spiritual energy which is the Paschal Mystery, entrusted with the responsibility to channel these graces to souls in the most efficacious manner possible.

17 CCC, 1070, quoting *Sacrosanctum Concilium* 7. §2-3.   18 'In the liturgy of the New Covenant every liturgical action, especially the celebration of the Eucharist and the sacraments, is an encounter between Christ and the Church. The liturgical assembly derives its unity from the "communion of the Holy Spirit" who gathers the children of God into the one Body of Christ. This assembly transcends racial, cultural, social – indeed all human affinities. The assembly should *prepare* itself to encounter its Lord and to become "a people well disposed"' (CCC, 1097, 1098).   19 Cf. CCC, 1084 –89. 'The liturgy is not celebrated by the individual, but by the body of the faithful. This is not composed merely of the persons who may be present in the church; it is not the assembled congregation. On the contrary, it reaches out beyond the bounds of space to embrace all the faithful on earth. Simultaneously it reaches beyond the bounds of time, to this extent, that the body which is praying upon earth knows itself to be at one with those for whom time no longer exists, who, being perfected, exist in Eternity. Yet this definition does not exhaust the conception of the universality and the all-embracingness which characterise the fellowship of the liturgy. The entity which performs the liturgical actions is not merely the sum total of all individual Catholics. It *does* consist of all those united in one body, but only in so far as this unity is of itself something, apart from the millions which compose it. And that something is the Church' (Romano Guardini, *The spirit of the liturgy*, London, 1937, pp 37-8). 20 Cf. CCC, 1120.

### SIGNS AND SYMBOLS: THE SACRAMENTAL
### CHARACTER OF THE LITURGY

In everyday life signs and symbols serve an important function. Because we are social beings we need them to communicate with each other through language, gestures and actions. The same holds true for our relationship with God. He speaks to us through his visible creation, and these realities in turn can be a means for man to offer worship to God. The liturgy of the Church presupposes and sanctifies elements from creation and human culture, conferring on them the dignity of signs of grace. This is the basis of the sacramental principle – as a creature of body and soul man perceives spiritual realities through signs and symbols. In the Old Testament the Chosen People received from God distinctive signs that marked their liturgical life. These included purifications, anointings, sacrifices of crops and animals, but especially the Passover meal. In the sacraments of the New Covenant, Christ gives natural elements such as water, oil, bread and wine a new supernatural dimension so that they transmit specific graces when they are taken up into the liturgical action and specified by the consecrating words.[21] Thus all the signs and actions of the liturgy should lead to the mystery beyond the visible. Since Pentecost, it is through the sacramental signs of the Church that the Holy Spirit carries on the work of sanctification.

St Thomas tells us that the liturgy expresses in concrete images what it is difficult for the mind to grasp.[22] To maintain and encourage the perception of the liturgy as sacramental, it is celebrated with ceremonial language, is punctuated by symbolic actions, and is focused on the transcendence of the redemptive action of Christ.

> It speaks measuredly and melodiously; it employs formal, rhythmic gestures; it is clothed in colours and garments foreign to everyday life; it is carried out in places and at hours which have been co-ordinated and systematized according to sublimer laws than ours. It is the highest sense of the life of a child, in which everything is picture, melody and song.[23]

21 Cf. ibid., 1145-52. As Guardini points out: 'In the liturgy the faithful are confronted by a new world, rich in types and symbols, which are expressed in terms of ritual, actions, vestments, implements, places, and hours, all of which are highly significant ... The people who really live by the liturgy will come to learn that the bodily movements, the actions, and material objects which it employs are all of the highest significance. It offers great opportunities of expression, of knowledge, and of spiritual experience; it is emancipating in its action, and capable of presenting a truth far more strongly and convincingly than can the mere word of mouth' (*The spirit of the liturgy*, pp 70, 84). 22 Cf. *S. Th.* II-I, 101, 2, obj 2 ad 2. 23 Guardini, ibid., pp 101-2.

In the liturgy 'man, with the aid of grace, is given the opportunity ... of really becoming that which according to divine destiny he should be and longs to be, a child of God'.[24] Developing this analogy, Ratzinger says that the liturgy should be a reminder that 'we are all children, or should be children, in relation to that true life towards which we yearn to go'. In this sense the liturgy should be a prelude to eternal life, 'a rediscovery within us of true childhood, of openness to greatness still to come, which is still unfilled in adult life ... Thus it would imprint on the seemingly real life of daily existence the mark of future freedom, break open the walls that confine us, and let the light of heaven shine down upon earth'.[25]

If there is faith in the sacramental reality, a conviction grows that something happens which is altogether exceptional – Christ has become really present among us. Because man wants to transcend himself, the solemnity of the liturgy appeals to something deep in his soul, raising up his mind and heart to the contemplation of the divine and the infinite.[26] The early Christians had a deep conviction that when celebrating the *Dominicum* they were participating in something of such an exalted nature that the catechumens were required to depart the assembly before the liturgy of the Eucharist proper began. Only those who had the fullness of the faith could remain and adore.[27]

When there is a failure to grasp the sacramental character of the sacred actions, this is the main reason why for some, especially the young, the Mass is boring or meaningless. It is only through faith that the meaning signified by the words is perceived as objective reality. This is to recognize that Christ's true Body is present at Mass, and that the nourishment of soul which comes from communicating with it derives not from a sense of community, but exclusively

24 Ibid., p. 102. 'Such is the wonderful fact which the liturgy demonstrates: it unites art and reality in a supernatural childhood before God. That which formerly existed in the world of unreality only, and was rendered in art as the expression of mature human life, has here become reality. These forms are the vital expression of real and frankly supernatural life. But this has one thing in common with the play of the child and the life of art – it has no purpose, but it is full of profound meaning. It is not work, but play. To be at play, or to fashion a work of art in God's sight – not to create but to exist – such is the essence of the liturgy. From this is derived its sublime mingling of profound earnestness and divine joyfulness. The fact that the liturgy gives a thousand strict and careful directions on the quality of the language, gestures, colours, garments and instruments which it employs, can only be understood by those who are able to take art and play seriously' (Guardini, ibid., pp 102-3). 25 Ratzinger, *The spirit of the liturgy*, p. 14. 26 This is why a priest is not doing his congregation any favour when, in the interests of a supposed community bonding, he greets them with a cheery 'good-morning'. From the very beginning of the liturgy he thus sends a signal to the congregation that they are participating in something almost trite and banal. It undermines the conviction that they have come to participate in a divine action, confusing the distinction between the sacred and the profane. 27 Cf. Georges Chevrot, *Our Mass*, London, 1948, p. 189.

from the power of God in the Eucharist.[28] A true and deep sense of the sacramental is one of the best defences against the desacralisation of the liturgy.

## THE ESCHATOLOGICAL DIMENSION OF THE LITURGY

A fundamental element of the Christian theology of worship is the perception that Christ is the Lamb of God who takes away the sin of the world. When John the Baptist used this description to identify Jesus for the two disciples (cf. Jn 1:29-31) he was well aware of the Old Testament references which prefigured the true Lamb (cf. Ex 12:6-7; Is 53:7), Christ, the victim in the sacrifice of Calvary. This is why St Paul will say, 'Christ, our paschal lamb, has been sacrificed' (1 Cor 5:7). The book of Revelation presents Jesus victorious and glorious in heaven as the sacrificed lamb (cf. Rev 5:6-14), surrounded by saints, martyrs and virgins (cf. Rev 7:9, 14; 14:1-5) who offer him the praise and glory due to him as God (Rev 7:10). Through Christ's sacrifice the heavenly liturgy is made present in the world.

This essentially eschatological nature of the liturgy, which is a basic point of reference for the Church's worship, is richly developed in the documents of Vatican II:

> In the earthly liturgy we take part in a foretaste of that heavenly liturgy which is celebrated in the Holy City of Jerusalem toward which we journey as pilgrims, where Christ is sitting at the right hand of God, Minister of the holies and of the true tabernacle. With all the warriors of the heavenly army we sing a hymn of glory to the Lord; venerating the memory of the saints, we hope for some part and fellowship with them; we eagerly await the Saviour, Our Lord Jesus Christ, until he our life shall appear and we too will appear with him in glory.[29]

A wider dogmatic base is given to this understanding of the liturgy in *Lumen gentium*:

> It is especially in the sacred liturgy that our union with the heavenly church is best realized; in the liturgy, through the sacramental signs, the power of the Holy Spirit acts on us, and with community rejoicing we celebrate together the praise of the divine majesty, when all those of every tribe and tongue and people and nation (cf. Apoc. 5:9) who have been redeemed by the blood of Christ and gathered together into

28 Cf. Pieper, ibid., p. 28. 29 *Sacrosanctum Concilium*, 8.

one Church glorify, in one common song of praise, the one and triune God. When, then, we celebrate the Eucharistic sacrifice we are most closely united to the worship of the heavenly Church; when in the fellowship of communion we honour and remember the glorious Mary ever virgin, St Joseph, the holy apostles and martyrs and all the saints.[30]

Do we priests normally celebrate Mass with this vision of the liturgy? It this the kind of worship that the faithful usually experience on Sundays? In all honesty we would have to say that such eschatological transcendence is rarely transmitted with the clarity and significance given it by Vatican II.

There are historical reasons for this.[31] The cultural and social dynamic of the post-Vatican II years led to a secularisation of eschatological themes. Excessive importance was given to liturgy as a service to culture and society, often resulting in its reductive instrumentalizaton for narrowly socially-conscious ends.[32] However, the task of the Church is not to adapt the teaching of Christ to the *Zeitgeist*, the seemingly progressive insights of the age, but rather to announce to the world why and how it should open out to the values of the Gospel in the light of the New Jerusalem.

A greater awareness of the eschatological dimension of the liturgy will allow the priest to celebrate Mass with a deeper spirit of its transcendence, and thus avoid the danger of parish worship being reduced to the human dimensions of the local community. If people understand that every Mass is a participation in the eternal liturgy which is celebrated in heaven, it will evince a deeper sense of reverence and promote the conviction that the Eucharist is truly a pledge of future glory. Since the true glory of the liturgy is to be 'a window onto the eternal Trinitarian love',[33] everything that goes on in the sanctuary area should be in function of this noble objective.


### CHURCHES AND THE MASS

In churches of East and West we find the great masterpieces of art – in painting, sculpture, and stained glass – reflecting a profound eschatological vision of the liturgy. With the secularisation caused by post-Enlightenment thinking, the culture lost its anchorage in the eternal truths and this loss of reference is clearly reflected not only in secular art, but in many of the churches which are being built today. Minimalist spaces, banal exteriors, and disfigured religious art reflect a jarring discontinuity with the accumulated artistic wisdom of the

30 *Lumen gentium*, 50. 31 Cf. Mannion, 'Liturgy for the third millennium', pp 458-9. 32 Cf. ibid., p. 459. 33 Nichols, *The service of glory*, p. 7.

past. Because Christianity is a historical religion, as such it must identify itself with the past to bring Christ into the present: 'Jesus Christ is the same yesterday, today, and forever' (Heb 13:8). New and original work should be inspired by this tradition so as to connect artistic and architectural contributions of previous with future generations.[34]

A church should reflect the fact that it provides an environment for the most sacred and sublime action which takes place on this earth. People behave with respect and reverence when they are conscious of being in a sacred place. In contemporary culture, which has been infected with 'the virus of desacralization',[35] the concept of the sacred is becoming less clear and needs to be affirmed in more specific language. Hence the requirement at present to emphasise rather than dilute the tradition of Christian art and architecture so that churches immediately communicate the sense of transcendence.

The fact that a church is build to surround an altar on which is re-enacted the sacrifice of Calvary is what distinguishes it from every other type of building where people foregather. The history of the liturgy shows how the insight and ingenuity of the Christian people down through the centuries has developed many different styles of church architecture. From a conviction of faith as to what happens there, certain boundary lines are laid down as regards physical orientation, furniture and behaviour. While such markers will have a clear significance in relation to the local culture, at the same time, because the celebration of the liturgy has a common universal dimension, it is not surprising that some elements of church architecture are reflected in every nation. Nor is it surprising that for a people, who live by faith and see the Mass as the centre of existence, the challenge of church architecture would inspire buildings of permanent artistic merit. Vatican II has reaffirmed this aspiration:

> Holy Mother Church has always been the patron of the fine arts and has ever sought their noble ministry, to the end especially that all things set apart for use in divine worship should be worthy, becoming, and beautiful, signs and symbols of things supernatural[36] ... Thus in the course of the centuries she has brought into existence a treasury of art which must be preserved with every care.[37]

The worship of God unites people and gives their being together its true liturgical meaning. Down through history this transcendental bonding has taken place in the sacred space set aside for worship, whether in the Temple or

34 Cf. Duncan Stroik, 'Displaced tabernacles', in *Crisis*, June 2000, p. 27.  35 Cf. Pieper, op. cit., p. 26.  36 *Sacrosanctum Concilium*, 122.  37 Ibid., no. 123.

synagogue of the Old Testament or, under the New Covenant, in an oratory, church or cathedral. There is a strong parallel between the liturgical arrangements of the sacred places of the two covenants since, in both, people came together to hear the word of Scripture and to seal the covenant by means of sacrifice.[38] Christianity has also learned from the Temple liturgy how to surround the holy place of the sanctuary with signs of reverence which befit the mysterious presence of God. When the Jewish synagogue had to be reshaped for Christian worship, we see both a continuity and an newness in the relationship of the Old Covenant to the New.[39]

One of the challenges of liturgical reform is the recovery of the sense of reverence in churches. Why do many people no longer genuflect passing in front of the tabernacle? Witness, too, the chatter before Mass which is common in churches. This loss of the sense of the transcendent is due to several factors, not least a dilution of faith in the Real Presence of Christ in the Blessed Sacrament. Church design which gives priority to functionalism over beauty does little to encourage people to remain to pray. Certainly *Lumen gentium* envisages a higher architectural concept when it uses metaphors such as 'the dwelling place of God among men', 'the holy temple', 'the image of the Holy City', 'the New Jerusalem' to describe a church building.[40] Sacred architecture should make the world of the spirit perceptible through material construction. Thus John Paul II affirms that the church should be

> a worthy place for prayer and sacred functions both for its good order, cleanliness, the neatness with which it is maintained, and for the artistic beauty of its environment, which has a great importance for the way it forms and inspires prayer. For this reason the Council recommends that the priest 'properly cultivate liturgical knowledge and art' (*Presbyterorum ordinis*, 5). I have called attention to these aspects because they too belong to the complex picture of a good 'care of souls' on the part of priests.[41]

### MUNIFICENCE AND SPLENDOUR IN THE LITURGY

Liturgy down through the ages has not just been a vehicle for reverence, worship and prayer. It has also manifested another aspect, that of 'abundance and enthusiasm, of generosity and almost extravagance'.[42] The liturgy has in fact inspired many of the highest expressions of Western culture in architecture, metalwork, painting and sculpture. It was motivated by the conviction that the

38 Cf. Ratzinger, *The spirit of the liturgy*, p. 63. **39** Cf. ibid., p. 75. **40** Cf. *Lumen gentium*, 6.
41 John Paul II, Address, 12 May 1993, no. 6. **42** Cf. Pieper, op. cit., p. 43.

sacred action of the liturgy transcended all other human activity, and was therefore deserving of the richest expressions of man's artistic imagination and skill. Hence we see why Christ would praise the generosity of the woman who used a flask of expensive ointment to prepare his body for burial. He described what she did as 'a beautiful thing', and he promised that her story would be told wherever the Gospel was preached (cf. Mk 14:3-9; Mt 26:6-13).

What is also striking about the Mosaic liturgy is the largesse and splendour which characterized everything related to the worship of Yahweh. We see this particularly in the instructions Moses received from God for the construction of the Ark and the Tabernacle which were to be the physical expression of Yahweh's presence among the Chosen People (cf. Ex 25-31). The plates and dishes, flagons and bowls used in the sacrifices were to be of pure gold (cf. Ex 25:23-30). The seven-branch candle-stick was clearly a work of exceptional craftsmanship (cf. Ex 25:31-40). Not only were the candle snuffers to be fashioned in gold, but also the very trays on which they rested. The tabernacle was to be made of silver.

The tabernacle in which the Blessed Sacrament is reserved takes the place previously occupied by the Ark of the Covenant and is the complete fulfilment of what it represented: it is the new Holy of Holies. The centrality of the Ark to the sanctuary, its beauty of design, and the reverence with which it was held by the Chosen People are all pointers to the very special consideration which should be given to the artistic, architectural and liturgical presentation of the tabernacle in the churches of the New Covenant. If the Ark housed merely the symbolic presence of Yahweh, how much more significant is the new Holy of Holies which contains the Real Presence of the Incarnate Son of God. In the revised *General instruction on the Roman missal*, there is a renewed emphasis on the need for the tabernacle to have a prominent location in churches.[43]

When we come to the question of the priest's vestments in the Old Testament we find a description of garments designed for beauty and glory (cf. Ex 28). They are to be made of the richest material and only by the most accomplished craftsmen. The quality of vestments worn by the Temple priests is a pointer to the significance of vestments for the celebration of the liturgy of the New Covenant. The visible appearance of the priest on the altar, the way he is vested, the reverence of his approach to the liturgy – all this can have a profound effect on the people present at Mass. This is because liturgical vestments took their specific form, not because of any practical need stemming from their specific use, but as a consequence of historical association and the cultural environment. And yet, they proclaim loud and clear that, for a certain span of time, their wearer is speaking and acting *not* as the individual named

---

43 Cf. GIRM, 315.

and described on his driver's license but *in persona Christi*.[44] Vestments are a reminder of that Pauline image of 'putting on Christ' (Gal 3:7). They

> are a challenge to the priest to surrender himself to the dynamism of breaking out of the capsule of self and being fashioned anew by Christ and for Christ. They remind those who participate in the Mass of the new way that began with Baptism and continues with the Eucharist, the way that leads to the future world already delineated in our daily lives by the sacraments[45] ... The liturgical vestment has a meaning that goes beyond that of external garments. It is an anticipation of the new clothing, the risen Body of Jesus Christ, that new reality which awaits us when the 'earthly' tent is taken down and which gives us a 'place to stay' (cf. Jn 14:2).[46]

In this context we can understand more clearly why neglecting to wear appropriate liturgical vestments is one of the abuses censured by Church authority.


### PARTICIPATION OF THE LAITY IN THE LITURGY

The participation of the laity in the liturgy is one of the most visible consequences of the liturgical renewal since Vatican II. Being a priestly people, called to offer spiritual sacrifices, they are empowered to participate actively in the liturgy. The Mass for them, as for priests, is the 'root and centre'[47] of the spiritual life. Thus their very vocation demands a profound participation in the Eucharistic sacrifice. However, a deep understanding of what the Mass is about is the basis of any meaningful involvement in it. But this is not something which can be improvised. As John Paul II advises:

> *Conscious participation* calls for the entire community to be properly instructed in the mysteries of the liturgy lest the experience of worship degenerate into a form of ritualism.[48]

The *Catechism of the Catholic Church* provides a wealth of teaching about this central element of the faith which the priest does well to communicate to his people if they are to appreciate what full and conscious participation in the liturgy means.[49] Without this knowledge, absent this transcendental approach

---

44 Cf. Pieper, op. cit., p. 73. 45 Ratzinger, op. cit., p. 217. 46 Ibid., p. 219. 47 *Presbyterorum ordinis*, 14. 48 Address to US bishops on 9 October 1998, no. 3, in *Osservatore Romano*, 14 October 1998 (italics in original). 49 Cf. CCC 1077-1186; 1322-1405.

to the liturgy, there is a danger that the Mass will be seen in a reductive manner by the participating congregation, often no more than a way of celebrating its own cultural and religious identity rather than the objective historical realisation of the Redemption accomplished by Christ on the Cross.[50]

In this context the Pope clarified a point which has been a bone of contention – the precise implications of the Council's call for a 'full, conscious and active participation in the liturgy'.[51] Full participation, he tells us, means that every member of the community has a part to play in the liturgy. However, if the different roles of priest and people are not respected, this could 'lead to a *clericalizing* of the laity and a *laicizing* of the priesthood'.[52]

For the laity, active participation in the liturgy is expressed primarily by uniting with the sacrifice of the Mass their efforts to sanctify daily work, family life, and social commitments.[53] Their participation in the liturgy is more complete when they draw from it the spiritual energy they need to evangelize the culture, bringing Christ and the values of the Gospel into every aspect of human activity.[54] The essential role of the liturgy for the laity is, then, to make them a priestly people in the middle of the world, to activate their capacity to be witnesses to Christ in the home and work environment and, in this way, to sanctify temporal realities.[55]

John Paul II underscores the relationship between authentic liturgical renewal and effective evangelization:

50 Cf. Nichols, *Looking at the liturgy*, p. 55. 51 *Sacrosanctum Concilium*, 14. 52 Address, 9 October 1998, no. 3 (italics in original). What does the 'active participation' in the liturgy, affirmed by Vatican II, mean that we have to do? Ratzinger explains that unfortunately this *participatio actuosa* was quickly misunderstood to mean something external, entailing a need for general activity, as if as many people as possible should be visibly engaged in action. Since 'participation' refers to a principal action in which everyone has a part, we must first of all determine what that central action (*actio*) is in which people are supposed to take part. Basically this is the Eucharistic Prayer that forms the core of the liturgical celebration. But the Eucharistic Canon is much more than speech – it is *actio* in the highest sense, the *actio divina* (divine action) of God. Because of his ontological bonding with Christ, the being of the priest is mysteriously appropriated by the Word Incarnate and the event of Calvary is represented on the altar in an unbloody manner by means of the words, 'This is my Body', 'This is my Blood' spoken through the mouth of the priest. This is the distinctive character of the Christian liturgy by comparison with that of the Old Testament. God himself acts and does what is essential (cf. Ratzinger, op. cit., pp 171-3). 53 Cf. *Lumen gentium*, 34. 54 Cf. *Dies Domini*, 45. 55 'The true liturgical action is the deed of God, and for that very reason the liturgy of faith always reaches beyond the cultic act into everyday life, which must itself become "liturgical", a service for the transformation of the world. Much more is required of the body than carrying objects around and other such activities. A demand is made on the body in all its involvements in the circumstances of everyday life' (Ratzinger, op. cit., pp 175-6).

In so far as developments in liturgical renewal are superficial or unbalanced, our energies for a new evangelization will be compromised; and in so far as our vision falls short of the new evangelization our liturgical renewal will be reduced to external and possibly unsound adaptation. The Roman rite has always been a form of worship that looks to mission.[56]

Even with the dismissal, the community is sent out to evangelize the world in obedience to Christ's command (cf. Mt 28:19-20).[57]

### SILENCE IN THE LITURGY

Active participation in the liturgy does not, however, preclude 'the active passivity of *silence, stillness and listening*: indeed it demands it'.[58] The Holy Father explains the nature of this active silence as follows:

> Worshippers are not passive, for instance, when listening to the readings or the homily, or following the prayers of the celebrant, and the chants and music of the liturgy. These are experiences of silence and stillness, but they are in their own way profoundly active. In a culture which neither favours nor fosters meditative quiet, the art of interior listening is learned only with difficulty.[59]

It is in this sense that the Pope says the liturgy has to be counter-cultural in an environment where activism is regarded as the essence of being and living.[60] A commentator on this address which John Paul II gave to a group of American bishops has aptly said:

> If we are to foster the awe, reverence, and adoration through which we may know the Word of Christ, then we must love, and not fear silence

56 Address, 9 October 1998, no. 4.  57 Cf. ibid.  58 Ibid., no. 3 (italics in original).  59 Ibid. Guardini's comments in this context are interesting: 'It is in this very aspect of the liturgy that its didactic aim is to be found, that of teaching the soul not to see purposes everywhere, not to be too conscious of the end it wishes to attain, not to be desirous of being over clever and grown-up, but to understand simplicity in life. The soul must learn to abandon, at least in prayer, the restlessness of purposeful activity; it must learn to waste time for the sake of God and to be prepared for the sacred game with sayings and thought and gestures, without always immediately asking "why?" and "wherefore?". It must learn not to be continually yearning to *do* something, to attack something, to accomplish something useful, but to play the divinely ordained game of the liturgy in liberty and beauty and holy joy before God' (ibid., p. 106).  60 Address, 9 October 1998. no. 3.

and stillness in the Mass and in our life. From silence comes the Word. From silence God spoke and created the world. From silence he spoke to Mary and came to dwell in her womb. From silence he sent his Holy Spirit at Pentecost to lead the Church. Meditative quiet, as the pope laments, is neither favoured nor fostered in our culture. Yet there is no getting around the simple fact that only in stillness do we learn to listen with the interior ear. Only in stillness can we build the habit of listening, a habit that, when impeded by the jangle of noise, can never develop. Only in stillness do we calm down enough to sense the Lord's presence. Only in stillness do we find out that the Lord loves us and that we are made to love him. Silence, then, is not a den of terror; it is rather the place where we fall in love.[61]

It is surely no accident that increasing numbers of people are trying out different techniques of meditation in search of a spirituality to empty the mind of the static that clogs it up. This may well be due to the fact that the way the liturgy is celebrated today frequently fails to provide that silence which is so manifestly necessary in the spiritual life. John Paul II reminds us that only a liturgy which produces a 'silence filled with the presence of him who is adored' can respond to the demands and the goals of the Christian life.[62]

It is instructive to note how the revised rite promotes the value of silence in preparation for Mass: 'Even before the celebration itself, it is praiseworthy for silence to be observed in church, in the sacristy, and adjacent areas, so that all may dispose themselves for the sacred rites which are to be enacted in a devout and fitting manner'.[63]

## MUSIC AND THE LITURGY

While prayerful silence is an integral part of the liturgy, song is also required to give human expression to joy, sorrow, consent and complaint, in order to fulfil the vocation to worship and glorify God.[64] The Hebrew people found it necessary to sing the psalms to give fuller voice to their prayer and glorification of Yahweh. These chants, with a new christological interpretation, found continuity in the early Church as a means to praise God for the gift of the Paschal Mystery. This, in a very real sense, is the beginning of the tradition of Christian liturgical music.[65]

61 Anne Husted Burleigh, 'Common wisdom', in *Crisis*, January 1999, p. 58. 62 Cf. John Paul II, Address, 3 May 1996, no. 5. 63 GIRM, 45. 64 Cf. Ratzinger, *A new song for the Lord*, ibid., p. 100. 65 Ratzinger draws out the implications of this basic reference: 'Artistic creation as the Old Testament sees it is something completely different from what the modern

The Vatican II constitution on the Sacred Liturgy strongly recommends that the treasury of sacred music should be preserved and cultivated with great care, and that Gregorian chant should be given pride of place in liturgical services.[66] We are reminded by the *Catechism* that song and music serve their liturgical function when they fulfil certain criteria: that they constitute beauty expressive of prayer; that the music involves participation by the congregation at the designated times; and that it reflects the solemn character of the celebration. In this way liturgical music and song give glory to God and sanctify the faithful.[67] While exceptionally some churches have managed to maintain this tradition, it is hardly an exaggeration to say that there is considerable dissatisfaction with the state of contemporary Church music. The sense of beauty and art has often given way to banality and mediocrity in an effort to try to be more 'meaningful'.

*Sacrosanctum Concilium*, as already noted, encourages the use of Gregorian chant. But is this form of music still relevant to contemporary culture? In this context, the Pope warns against the abandonment of Latin in the liturgy, and especially Gregorian chant, in the interests of intelligibility. Why? Because 'if subconscious experience is ignored in worship, an affective and devotional vacuum is created, and the liturgy can become not only too verbal but also too cerebral'. The genius of the Roman rite, he concludes, is that 'it feeds the heart and the mind, the body and the soul'.[68] Chant thus penetrates the heart where it goes to the core of our being, engaging with the image of the Creator and Redeemer in us. Chant dilates the sacred text and allows it to disclose its specifically theological value.[69]

It has been pointed out that when a certain spirit of worldliness entered into the liturgy, one of the first things that came under attack was the tradition of sacred music and liturgical chant.[70] It is necessary to rediscover this tradition, not out of a sense of nostalgia for the past but rather because the modern experiment in liturgical music has hardly been successful in teaching people to pray. Rapidly emptying churches, especially the exodus from Sunday worship of the younger generation which this music was supposed to attract and hold,

age understands by creativity. Today creativity is understood to be the making of something that is completely one's own and completely new. In comparison with this, artistic creativeness in the book of Exodus is seeing something together with God, participating in his creativity; it is exposing the beauty that is already waiting and concealed in creation. This does not diminish the worth of the artist, but is in fact its justification ... For church music this means that everything the Old Testament has to say about art – its necessity, its essence, and its dignity – is concealed in the *bene cantare* of the psalms ' (*A new song for the Lord*, p. 103). **66** Cf. *Sacrosanctum Concilium*, 114, 116. **67** Cf. CCC, 1157. **68** Address, 9 October 1998, no. 3. **69** Cf. Mark-Daniel Kirby, 'Sung theology: the liturgical chant of the Church' in Caldecott (ed.), ibid., p. 130. **70** Cf. Stratford Caldecott, 'The spirit of the liturgical movement' in *Beyond the prosaic*, p. 157.

suggests that the opposite is the case.[71] It is surely not without significance that in recent years Gregorian chant has been rediscovered as popular music on a massive scale outside of the Church. Consequently, it is perhaps not surprising to note that in the recently revised rite, even in the context of Mass in the vernacular, we are told that 'because the faithful from different countries come together ever more frequently, it is desirable that they know how to sing at least some parts of the Ordinary of the Mass in Latin, especially the profession of faith and the Lord's Prayer'.[72]

### LITURGICAL IMPROVIZATION

The supernatural unity which is generated as a consequence of the celebration of the Eucharistic sacrifice is what gives rise to the sense of Christian community. One of the dangers, however, with liturgical praxis today is the tendency to engender a sense of community as an end in itself through local adaptation of worship. This is a self-defeating exercise since,

> It is by acceptance through faith of our composition into a supernatural unity through a pre-existing rite that community is engendered, not by devising of new or adapted rites that have the creation of community as their immediate end. Like happiness, community is not produced by aiming at it directly; rather, it is a vital, indirect consequences of immersion in other things.[73]

This is because fidelity to the system of signs, symbols and actions is the means of being integrated into the liturgical tradition. Liturgical improvisation on the part of the priest is, therefore, an action of the individual only, disconnected from the official prayer and worship of the Church.[74] In his review of twenty five years of liturgical innovation, John Paul II lays down a clear marker:

71 The point has been made that 'Deprived of the sacred, sometimes without even knowing what it is they instinctively miss, many abandon religious practice. A whole generation of young people is growing up believing that the essential purpose of the liturgy is didactic; they get bored quickly and stay away' (Mark Drew, 'The spirit or the letter? Vatican II and liturgical reform', in Caldecott (ed.), p. 51). 72 GIRM, 41. 73 Nichols, *Looking at the liturgy*, p. 43. 74 Cf. Pieper, op. cit., p. 41. 75 John Paul II, Apostolic Letter, *Vicesimus quintus annus*, 10 (4 December 1988). The trend to downgrade ritual caused by the assimilation of particular philosophical influences has been compounded to some extent by what is happening in society in general. Here we see a slackening of family ties, an excessive emphasis on freedom as individualism disconnected from objective truth, and the levelling, if not

The Liturgy belongs to the whole body of the Church. It is for this reason that it is not permitted to anyone, even the priest, or any group, to add, subtract or change anything whatsoever on their own initiative. Fidelity to the rites and to the authentic texts of the Liturgy is a requirement of the *Lex orandi,* which must always be in conformity with the *Lex credendi.* A lack of fidelity on this point may even affect the validity of the sacraments.[75]

Because the core of the mystery of Christian worship is the sacrifice of Christ offered to the Father, it is essential, John Paul II reminds us, 'that in seeking to enter more deeply into the contemplative depths of worship the inexhaustible mystery of the priesthood of Jesus Christ be fully acknowledged and respected'.[76] The priest, clearly, has a special responsibility to guarantee this authentic dimension of the liturgy. He has to be seen not just as one who presides, or as the inventor or producer of the liturgy, but above all as one who acts in the person of Christ.[77] The revised rite reminds the priest that to be truly a servant of the liturgy he should be very faithful to all the details of the ceremonies as laid down.[78]

## COSMIC DIMENSION OF THE LITURGY

Historically the cosmic dimension of the liturgy is more explicit in the Eastern Christian tradition. However, the intention to recover this perspective for the West is clearly indicated in the *Catechism of the Catholic Church.* In its section on the liturgy we read about those who take part in the service of praise of God and the fulfilment of his plan:

> the heavenly powers, all creation (the four living beings), the servants of the Old and New Covenants (the twenty four elders), the new People of God (the one hundred and forty-four thousand), especially the martyrs 'slain for the word of God', and the all-holy Mother of God (the Woman), the Bride of the Lamb, and finally 'a great multitude which no one could number, from every nation, from all tribes, and peoples and tongues'.[79]

rejection, of hierarchical structure. Coupled with this is a growing amnesia about tradition-al values due to a lack of any real bonding with the past, with consequent ignorance about the need to hand on something of value to future generations. All this leads to lack of appre-ciation if not contempt for rite and ritual: cf. Nichols, ibid., p. 74. **76** Address, 9 October 1998, no. 2. **77** Cf. ibid. **78** Cf. GIRM, 24. **79** CCC, 1138.

Redemption involves the whole of creation where all things have to be made new, as St Paul dramatically describes it in his Letter to the Romans (8:19-24).

Re-establishment of the order willed by God, bringing the whole world to fulfil its true purpose to give glory to God, is part of the mission of the Holy Spirit. But God wants man to co-operate with him in the renewal of creation. As we have already seen, it is particularly the vocation of lay people, called to sanctify the world, to impregnate all temporal realities with the spirit of Christ and in this way allow creation give true glory to the Father.[80]

Because of the different influences – philosophical, cultural, social – which have had the effect of diluting the eschatological and doxological aspects of liturgy, it is not surprising that in recent decades there have been complaints about the loss of the sense of mystery, dignity, and solemnity in Catholic worship. In an increasingly secularized culture, we need to recover a deeper awareness of the eschatological dimension of worship if it is to engage and unfold to the full the expectations for liturgical renewal of Vatican II. Since the visual is an extremely important part of the message and the sentiments which the liturgy is meant to convey, detailed attention to ceremony which reflects the ethos of participation in a profoundly mysterious action is also an integral part of the renewal desired by *Sacrosanctum Concilium*.[81] Clearly the priest has a central role to play in making this vision a reality in the life of the community he serves. But it has to start with a personal assimilation of this vision and the effort to appropriate it in his own spiritual life.

80 Cf. *The Navarre Bible: Romans and Galatians*, Dublin, 1990, p. 117. 81 A very practical help for celebrating the liturgy with reverence and dignity is *Ceremonies of the modern Roman rite*, by Peter J. Elliott, San Francisco, 1994.

# Epilogue

We began our study of the priesthood by adverting to the fact that during the post-conciliar period a crisis of identity affected many priests, a situation which was reflected above all in thousands of defections from the ministry and a significant drop in vocations. We analysed some of the reasons why this occurred and saw that it was primarily due to a deficient theological perception of the nature of the Catholic priesthood. While one can still come across a reductive doctrinal approach to the priestly ministry, it is clear that over the past two decades there has been a significant shift in the articulation of the theology of priesthood. In the years immediately after Vatican II there was a certain tentativeness, not to say ambiguity, in many efforts to restate the identity of the priest. This was a theology which had to a large extent become untethered from the accumulated wisdom of the Church about priesthood, and which was in turn deeply influenced by Protestant scriptural exegesis deriving from the Reformation. However, over the past two decades the theological identity of the priest has been boldly and clearly restated, not only because it draws deeply on the living Tradition of the Church, but also because of genuine doctrinal developments since the Council.

What, we might ask, were the reasons which caused this recovery of the theological richness of the priestly vocation? There were, no doubt, several factors at work, but in my opinion we have to look to the pontificate of John Paul II to discover the driving influences for this renewal of the theology of priesthood. In his annual Holy Thursday Letters to priests, but especially in *Pastores dabo vobis*, he laid the doctrinal foundations for a restatement of the theology of priestly ministry. This teaching is firmly anchored in the documents of Vatican II, especially *Lumen gentium* and *Presbyterorum ordinis*. Yet, as in all other areas of theology he has touched on, sacred Scripture is his primary source for understanding the priesthood instituted by Christ and the foundation he uses for explaining it to the Church. His exceptional capacity to 'open up the Scriptures' is evident in all the major documents of his pontificate.

But John Paul II hasn't just given us a new and enriched doctrine of priesthood. His whole pontificate is in fact an enduring example of who and what a priest of Jesus Christ should be. It is a statement of priestly identity which goes far beyond theological definition. His demanding pastoral journeys, his ability to use every aspect of his ministry to carry out a penetrating work of evangelization, his resourcefulness as regards pastoral initiatives with every segment and age group in society, his sharp focus on family and youth apostolate – all of these activities have defined more clearly than any theology what the image and the identity of the priest should be. While these two elements from the pontificate of John Paul II – the theological and pastoral – have provided a deeply enriched vision of the priesthood, there is, I feel, one other aspect of the present Holy Father's work which has, perhaps more than ever before, highlighted a core element of the nature of priestly ministry. All during his priestly life, whether in Krakow or Rome, John Paul II has insisted that the primary apostolic role of the laity, as a consequence of their baptismal vocation to holiness, is to evangelize the family and the culture – the world of work, media, science, education, politics, art, etc. While this theme is a constant point of reference in all his preaching, he has articulated this vision more specifically in three particular documents – in his encyclical on *Human work,*[1] and his documents on *The vocation and mission of the lay faithful in the Church and the world,*[2] and the *Christian family in the modern world.*[3] These, in a very real sense, constitute John Paul II's magna carta on the vocation of the laity to sanctify all temporal realities.[4] But, as he points out in his pastoral programme for the new millennium,[5] this enterprise of evangelizing secular activities will only become a reality if the laity take their personal vocation to holiness seriously. By outlining more clearly what the ascetical and apostolic objectives of the laity should be, John Paul II is at the same time defining some of the core personal and pastoral demands of the priesthood. Since the role of the priest is to provide the resources of formation and grace to enable the lay faithful live up to the requirements of their baptismal vocation, the challenge for a pastor of souls is very clear. If he is to provide a genuine 'training in holiness',[6] if education in prayer is to become a key point in his pastoral ministry,[7] this imposes very specific demands on the formation and the spiritual life of the priest, a programme which, in fact, has already been explicitly defined in *Pastores dabo vobis.*

1 Encyclical, *Laborem exercens,* 14 September 1981. 2 Apostolic exhortation, *Christifideles laici,* 30 December 1988. 3 Apostolic exhortation, *Familiaris consortio,* 22 November 1981. 4 This assumes that lay people have the basic catechetical formation outlined in the *General directory for catechesis* (published by the Congregation for the Clergy, 11 August 1997). However, there is increasing evidence to suggest that there are serious deficiencies in the catechetical formation of young people, even in those up to about the age of thirty-five. This would perhaps indicate that priests need to be more active in promoting catechesis along the lines suggested in the *General directory,* nos. 224-5. 5 *Novo millennio ineunte,* 6 January 2001, 31. 6 Cf. ibid. 7 Cf. ibid., 34.

The foundations of this formation are, of course, laid in the seminary, but if the priest is to measure up to the pastoral requirements of the New Millennium as outlined by John Paul II, he will need specific on-going pastoral and spiritual formation. This cannot be improvised: it requires careful consideration as regards content and time investment. It is my hope that some of the topics touched on in this book will be of use in devising such a programme. This formation should also provide a vision for redressing any negative pastoral trends that have surfaced since Vatican II, especially in the area of vocations ministry.

These are challenging times but, as John Paul II declared in Maynooth, 'This is wonderful time to be a priest.'[8] Why is the Vicar of Christ so optimistic when in many parts of the world, especially in the economically developed West, the 'culture of death' is pervasive and the human spirit is often drugged by a hedonistic philosophy of life? In the first place, what is abundantly clear about John Paul II is that, since he is a man of deep faith, he is convinced there is no obstacle in the spiritual life, or in evangelization, which cannot be overcome by prayer, apostolic zeal and loyalty to the teaching of Christ. Secondly, his experience of life has also persuaded him of another fundamental truth: man's deep sense of alienation eventually turns him to God when he discovers that his lifestyle fails to provide him with the truth about the meaning and purpose of his existence, when he realizes that the conventional wisdom is subversive of his true happiness. All during his pontificate John Paul II has consistently reaffirmed the direct connection between knowledge of the truth and a sense of authentic Christian freedom.[9] Because Christ is the source of all truth (cf. Jn 14:6), and because man has a deep connatural desire for this truth, it is the Holy Father's deep conviction that preaching the full truth about the Word made flesh will attract men to Jesus and help them rediscover the joy of his liberating love. John Paul II has proclaimed this message from the first days of his priesthood. Not only by his preaching, but also by the witness of his own life, he has made the attraction of the person of Christ shine out in our times in a way that has rarely been achieved before. Looking forward to a new millennium, he invites all his brother priests to be inspired and convinced by these same truths:

> Let us go forward in hope! A new millennium is opening before the Church like a vast ocean upon which we shall venture, relying on the help of Christ. The Son of God, who became incarnate two thousand years ago out of love for humanity, is at work even today: we need discerning eyes to see this and, above all, a generous heart to become the

---

8 Address, Maynooth, 1 October 1979. 9 Cf. for example, *Veritatis splendor*, 84, 85.

instrument of his work ... The missionary mandate accompanies us into the Third Millennium and urges us to share the enthusiasm of the very first Christians: we can count on the power of the same Spirit who was poured out at Pentecost and who impels us still today to start out anew, sustained by the hope 'which does not disappoint' (Rom 5:5).[10]

By making our own John Paul II's vision for the future of the Church, we see how the priestly vocation is not only a great human challenge, but also a divine adventure capable of filling the deepest aspirations of the spirit.

10 *Novo millennio ineunte*, 58.

# Bibliography

DOCUMENTS OF THE MAGISTERIUM

**Council of Trent**
Decree on the sacraments in general (7th session) 3 March 1547.
Decree concerning the sacrifice of the Mass (22nd session), 17 September 1562.
Decree concerning the sacrament of Order (23rd session), 15 July 1563.

**Vatican II**
Decree on the training of priests, *Optatam totius*, 28 October 1965.
Constitution on divine revelation, *Dei Verbum*, 18 November 1965.
Constitution on the Church, *Lumen gentium*, 21 November 1964.
Constitution on the Church in the modern world, *Gaudium et spes*, 7 December 1965.
Decree on the ministry and life of priests, *Presbyterorum ordinis*, 18 November 1965.
Constitution on the liturgy, *Sacrosanctum Concilium*, 4 December 1963.
Decree on the Church's missionary activity, *Ad gentes*, 7 December 1965.
Decree on the pastoral office of bishops in the Church, *Christus Dominus*, 28 October 1965.
Decree on the apostolate of lay people, *Apostolicam actuositatem*, 18 November 1965.
Decree on Christian education, *Gravissimum educationis*, 28 October 1965.

**Papal documents**
Leo XIII, Apostolic letter, *Apostolicae curae*, 13 September 1896.
——Apostolic letter, *Testem benevolentiae*, 22 January 1899.
St Pius X, Apostolic exhortation, *Haerent animo*, 4 August 1908.
Benedict XV, Encyclical letter, *Humani generis redemptionem*, 15 June 1917.
Pius XI, Encyclical letter, *Ad catholici sacerdotii*, 20 December 1935.
——Encyclical letter, *Casti conubii*, 31 December 1930.
Pius XII, Encyclical letter, *Mystici corporis*, 29 June 1943.
——Encyclical letter, *Mediator Dei*, 20 November 1947.
——Apostolic exhortation, *Menti nostrae*, 23 September 1950.
John XXIII, Encyclical letter, *Sacerdotii nostri primordia*, 1 August 1959.
Paul VI, Encyclical letter, *Mysterium fidei*, 3 September 1965.
——Encyclical letter, *Sacerdotalis caelibatus*, 24 June 1967.
John Paul II: Encyclical letter, *Redemptor hominis*, 4 March 1979.
——Encyclical letter, *Dives in misericordia*, 30 November 1980.
——Encyclical letter, *Laborem exercens*, 14 September 1981.

——Apostolic exhortation, *Familiaris consortio*, 22 November 1981.
——Apostolic letter, *Salvifici doloris*, 11 February 1984.
——Apostolic exhortation, *Reconciliatio et paenitentia*, 2 December 1984.
——Encyclical letter, *Dominum et vivificantem*, 18 May 1986.
——Apostolic letter, *Mulieris dignitatem*, 15 August 1988.
——Apostolic letter, *Vicesimus quintus annus*, 4 December 1988.
——Apostolic exhortation, *Christifideles laici*, 30 December 1988.
——Encyclical letter, *Redemptoris missio*, 7 December 1990.
——Encyclical letter, *Centesimus annus*, 1 May 1991.
——Apostolic exhortation, *Pastores dabo vobis*, 25 March 1992.
——Encyclical letter, *Veritatis splendor*, 6 August 1993.
——Apostolic letter, *Ordinatio sacerdotalis*, 22 May 1994.
——Apostolic letter, *Tertio millennio adveniente*, 10 November 1994.
——Encyclical letter, *Evangelium vitae*, 25 March 1995.
——Apostolic letter, *Dies Domini*, 31 May 1998.
——Apostolic letter, *Novo millennio ineunte*, 6 January 2001.
——*Catechism of the Catholic Church*, Dublin, 1994.
——*Letter for vocations day*, 1986.
——*A Priest Forever*, Athlone, 1984.
——Catechesis on the theology of the body (1979–84):
——*Original unity of man and woman: catechesis on the book of Genesis*, Boston, 1981.
——*Blessed are the pure of heart: catechesis on the sermon on the mount and the writings of St Paul*, Boston, 1983.
——*Reflections on Humanae vitae: conjugal morality and spirituality*, Boston, 1984.
——*The theology of marriage and celibacy: catechesis on marriage and celibacy in the light of the resurrection of the body*, Boston, 1986.
——*The theology of the body: human love in the divine plan*, Boston, 1997 (summary volume).
——*Crossing the threshold of hope*, London, 1994.
——*Gift and mystery: on the fiftieth anniversary of my priestly ordination*, London, 1996.
——*Priests for the third millennium*, Chicago, 1995 (series of addresses on priesthood during 1993).
——*Letters to my brother priests 1979–1999*, Chicago, 2000.
——*The Pope in Ireland: addresses and homilies*, Dublin, 1979.

**Other documents of the Magisterium**
1971 synodal document, *The ministerial priesthood*.
Congregation for the Doctrine of the Faith, Instruction, *Inter insigniores*, 15 October 1974.
——*Letter to the bishops of the Catholic Church on certain questions concerning the minister of the Eucharist (Sacerdotium ministeriale)*, 6 August 1983.
——*Instruction on the ecclesial vocation of the theologian*, 24 May 1990.
——*The primacy of the successor of Peter in the mystery of the Church*, 18 November 1998.
——Declaration, *Dominus Jesus*, on the *Unicity and salvific universality of Jesus Christ and the Church*, 6 August 2000.
Congregation for Divine Worship and the Discipline of the Sacraments, *General instruction on the Liturgy of the Hours*, 11 April 1971.
——Instruction, *Inaestimabile donum*, 17 April 1980.
——*General instruction on the Roman Missal* (Revised), 28 July 2000.

——*Responses on the obligation attaching to the recitation of the Liturgy of the Hours*, 15 November 2000.
Congregation for the Clergy, *Directory on the ministry and life of priests*, 31 January 1994.
——*General directory for catechesis*, 11 August 1997.
——*The priest and the third Christian millennium*, 19 March 1999.
Various congregations, *Instruction on certain questions regarding the collaboration of the non-ordained faithful in the sacred ministry of priests*, 15 August 1997.
Pontifical Council for the Family, *The truth and meaning of human sexuality*, 8 December 1995.
——*Vademecum for confessors concerning some aspects of the morality of conjugal life*, 12 February 1997.
Pastoral letters of Irish hierarchy, *Christian marriage*, Lent 1969.
——*Human life is sacred*, 1 May 1975.


OTHER BIBLIOGRAPHY


Antonio Aranda, 'The Christian, *alter Christus, ipse Christus*, in the thought of Blessed Josemaría Escrivá', in M. Belda et al. (eds.), *Holiness and the world*, Dublin, 1997.
Rudolf Arbesmann OSA, 'The concept of "Christus Medicus" in St Augustine', *Traditio*, 10 (1954).
Benedict M. Ashley OP, *Living the truth in love: a biblical introduction to moral theology*, New York, 1996.
Fr Augustine, OFM Cap., *Ireland's loyalty to the Mass*, London, 1933.
Jordan Aumann, *Spiritual theology*, London, 1985.
Benedict Baur, *Frequent confession*, Princeton NJ, 2000.
J. B. Baur (ed.), *Encyclopedia of biblical theology*, vol. 2, London, 1970.
Charles Belmonte, *Understanding the Mass*, Manila, 1989.
Léon Bloy, *Pilgrim of the Absolute*, London, 1947.
Enrique Borda, 'La fraternidad sacerdotal de los presbíteros: fundamentos y formación de los candidatos', in various authors, *La formación de los sacerdotes en las circunstancias actuales*, Pamplona, 1990.
E. Boylan, *The spiritual life of the priest*, Westminster MD, 1959.
Cormac Burke, 'Love and the family in today's world', *Homiletic and Pastoral Review*, March 1995.
——*Covenanted happiness*, Dublin, 1990.
Anne Husted Burleigh, 'Common wisdom', *Crisis* magazine, January 1999.
Stratford Caldecott (ed.), *Beyond the prosaic: renewing the liturgical movement*, Edinburgh, 1998.
Charles J. Chaput, *Pastoral letter*, Denver, 8 September 1999.
G. K. Chesterton, *Autobiography*, London, 1937.
Georges Chevrot, *Our Mass*, London, 1948.
Roman Cholij, *Clerical celibacy in East and West*, Leominister, 1989.
Christian Cochini, *Apostolic origins of priestly celibacy*, San Francisco, 1990.
G. Colombo, 'Fare la verità del ministerio nella carità pastorale', in various authors, *La vita spirituale del presbitero diocesano oggi: Problemi e prospettive*, Bergamo, 1989.

John Crosby, 'The personalism of John Paul II as the basis of his approach to the teaching of *Humanae vitae'*, in Janet Smith (ed.), *Why* Humanae vitae *was right: a reader*, San Francisco, 1993.

Conor T. Cunningham, 'A vision of priesthood for the third millennium: a review of the theologies of priesthood of Yves Congar, Edward Schilebeeckx, and Joseph Ratzinger in the context of the Apostolic exhortation *Pastores dabo vobis* of John Paul II' (unpublished thesis), St Patrick's College, Maynooth, 2000.

*Thoughts of the Curé d'Ars*, Rockford, Ill., 1984.

Elden Curtiss, *Pastoral letter*, Omaha, 1995 (*Osservatore Romano*, 5 August 1998).

Godfried Danneels, 'Una eclesiología de comunión' in various authors, *Iglesia universal, Iglesias particulares*, Pamplona, 1990.

C. Dillenschneider, *Teología y espiritualidad del sacerdote*, Salamanca, 1964.

Mark Drew, 'The spirit or the letter? Vatican II and liturgical reform', in Stratford Caldecott (ed.), *Beyond the prosaic: renewing the liturgical movement*, Edinburgh, 1998.

Eamon Duffy, *The stripping of the altars: traditional religion in England 1400-1580*, New Haven, 1992.

Avery Dulles, *The priestly office: a theological reflection*, New York, 1997.

Patrick J. Dunn, *Priesthood: a re-examination of the Roman Catholic theology of the presbyterate*, New York, 1990.

T.S. Eliot, *Four quartets (Burnt Norton)*, London, 1978.

Peter J. Elliott, *Ceremonies of the modern Roman rite*, San Francisco, 1995.

Blessed Josemaría Escrivá, *A priest forever*, London 1975.

——*The Way*, Dublin, 1977.

——*Conversations*, Manila, 1977.

——*Christ is passing by*, Dublin 1982.

——*Friends of God*, Dublin 1981.

——*The Forge*, London, 1988.

J. Esquerda Bifet, *Historia de la espiritualidad sacerdotal*, Burgos, 1985.

*The Eucharist and freedom*, Pontifical Committee for International Eucharistic Congresses, Rome, *Osservatore Romano*, 13 November 1996.

*The Eucharist: gift of divine life*, Jubilee 2000 Commission, New York, 1999.

M. Evans, '*In Persona Christi*: the key to priestly identity', *Clergy Review*, 71 (1986).

John Farrell, *Freud's paranoid quest*, New York University Press, 1996.

St John Fisher, *The defence of the priesthood*, London, 1935.

Michael F. Flach, 'What priest shortage?', *Catholic World Report*, June 1996.

A. Flannery, (ed.), *Vatican Council II: the conciliar and post conciliar documents*, Dublin, 1981.

Various authors, *La formación de los sacerdotes en las circunstancias actuales*, Pamplona, 1990, pp 1015.

St Francis de Sales, *Introduction to the devout life*.

André Frossard, *Be not afraid!*, London, 1984.

Jean Galot, *Theology of priesthood*, San Francisco, 1985.

Ramón García de Haro, *Marriage and the family in the documents of the magisterium*, San Francisco, 1993.

R. Garrigou-Lagrange, *The three ages of the interior life*, St Louis, MO, 1947.

——*The priest in union with Christ*, Cork, 1961.

Francis George, 'Pastoral charity rooted in priestly fraternity', various authors, *Priests for a new millennium*, USCC, Washington DC, 2000.

Edwin Gordon, 'The Good Shepherd: the ideal of the priest', *Homiletic and Pastoral Review*, December 1991.

Patrick Gorevan, 'Romano Guardini and the liturgy', *New Blackfriars*, vol. 79, no. 926, April 1998;

——'Translation and liturgical tradition', *New Blackfriars*, vol. 79, no. 934, December 1998.

Gisbert Greshake, *The meaning of Christian priesthood*, Dublin, 1988.

Romano Guardini, *The spirit of the liturgy*, London, 1937;

——'Liturgical worship and modern man', *Doctrine and Life*, September 1964.

Alec Guinness, *Blessings in disguise*, London, 1985.

John M. Haas, 'The sacral character of the priest as the foundation for his moral life and teaching' in John M. Haas (ed.), *The Catholic priest as moral teacher and guide*, San Francisco, 1990.

Manfred Hauke, *Women in the priesthood? A systematic analysis in the light of the order of creation and redemption*, San Francisco, 1988.

Stefan Heid, *Celibacy in the early Church*, San Francisco, 2001.

Dietrich von Hildebrand, *Celibacy and the crisis of faith*, Chicago, 1971.

——*In defence of purity*, London, 1937.

J. L. Illanes, 'Naturaleza y figura del ministerio sacerdotal' in J. L. Illanes and M. Belda Plans, *Teología espiritual y sacerdocio*, Mexico City, 1995.

——'Rasgos distintivos de la espiritualidad sacerdotal' in J. L. Illanes and M. Belda Plans, *Teología espiritual y sacerdocio*, Mexico City, 1995.

——'Vocación sacerdotal y seguimiento de Cristo', in various authors, *La formación de los sacerdotes en las circunstancias actuales*, Pamplona, 1990.

Stanley L. Jaki, 'Man of one wife or celibacy', *Homiletic and Pastoral Review*, January 1986.

——*Theology of celibacy*, Front Royal, VA, 1997.

St John Chrysostom, *On the priesthood: a treatise*, Westminister MD, 1943.

——*Homilies on Genesis*, vols I, II, III, Washington, 1986.

——*Commentary on St John the apostle and the evangelist*, vols 1, 2, Washington, 1960.

Roch A. Kereszty, *Jesus Christ: fundamentals of christology*, New York, 1995.

John F. Kippley, 'A covenant theology of sex', *Homiletic and Pastoral Review*, August-September 1983.

Enrique de la Lama, *La vocación sacerdotal: cien años de clarificación*, Madrid, 1994.

E. de la Lama and L.F. Mateo-Seco, 'Sobre la espiritualidad del sacerdote secular', *Scripta Theologica*, 31 (1999), p. 162.

Thomas Lane, *A priesthood in tune: theological reflections on ministry*, Dublin 1993.

Ronald Lawler, Joseph Boyle, William E. May, *Catholic sexual ethics*, Huntington, IN, 1996.

St Alphonsus Liguori, *Dignity and duties of the priest*, New York, 1927.

Henri de Lubac, *The sources of revelation*, New York, 1968.

Diarmaid McCulloch, *Thomas Cranmer: a life*, London, 1996.

Bede McGregor and Thomas Norris, (eds.), *The formation journey of the priest: exploring Pastores dabo vobis*, Dublin, 1994.

Thomas J. McGovern, 'The Christian anthropology of John Paul II: an overview', *Josephinum Journal of Theology*, vol. 8, no. 1, Winter/Spring, 2001.

——*Priestly celibacy today*, Dublin and Chicago, 1998.

John P. McIntyre, '*In persona Christi Capitis*: a commentary on canon 1008', *Studia canonica*, 30 (1996).

Kevin McNamara, 'The role of the laity in the Church', *Osservatore Romano*, 12 May 1986.

Charles M. Mangan, 'The homily that never was', *Homiletic and Pastoral Review*, November 1991.

M. Francis Mannion, 'Liturgy for the third millennium', *Priest and People*, December 1999.

——'The catholicity of the liturgy: shaping a new agenda' in Stratford Caldecott (ed.), *Beyond the prosaic: renewing the liturgical movement*, Edinburgh, 1998.

Anthony J. Mastroeni, 'The freedom of the sons of God', in *Homiletic and Pastoral Review*, February 1983

Lucas F. Mateo-Seco, 'El ministerio, fuente de la espiritualidad del sacerdote', various authors, *La formación de los sacerdotes en las circumstancias actuales*, Pamplona, 1990.

William E. May, *Marriage: the rock on which the family is built*, San Francisco, 1995.

Malcolm Muggeridge, *Something beautiful for God*, New York, 1971.

Maureen Mullarkey, 'Worship gone awry', *Crisis* magazine, July/August 2000.

John J Myers, 'The rejection and rediscovery by Christians of the truths of *Humanae vitae*', in Russell Smith (ed.), *Trust the truth: a symposium on the twentieth anniversary of the encyclical*, Braintree, Mass., 1988.

*The Navarre Bible: St Mark's Gospel*, Dublin, 1986.

——*St John's Gospel*, Dublin, 1987.

——*St Luke's Gospel*, Dublin, 1987.

——*St Matthew's Gospel*, Dublin, 1988.

——*Romans and Galatians*, Dublin, 1990.

——*Corinthians*, Dublin, 1991.

——*Catholic Epistles*, Dublin, 1992.

Reinhold Niebuhr, *Discerning the signs of the times*, New York, 1946.

John H. Newman, *Discourses to mixed congregations*, London, 1886.

——*The present position of Catholics in England*, London, 1913.

Aidan Nichols, *Holy order: apostolic priesthood from the New Testament to the second Vatican Council*, Dublin, 1990.

——*The Holy Eucharist*, Dublin, 1991.

——*Looking at the liturgy*, San Francisco, 1996

——*The service of glory*, Edinburgh, 1997.

J. Nuechterlein, 'Pastoral concerns', *First Things*, 77, November 1997.

F. Ocariz, L. Mateo Seco, J. A. Riestra, *The mystery of Christ*, Dublin, 1994.

Leonid Ouspensky, *Theology of the icon*, Crestwood, NY, 1978.

James T. O'Connor, *The hidden manna: a theology of the Eucharist*, San Francisco, 1988.

——*The Father's Son*, Boston, 1984.

——*Land of the living: a theology of the last things*, New York, 1992.

Colman O'Neill, *Meeting Christ in the sacraments*, Cork, 1964.

Marc Ouellet, 'Priestly ministry at the service of ecclesial communion', *Communio* 23 (Winter 1996).

Joseph Pearce, *Tolkien: man and myth: a literary life*, London, 1999.

J.M. Pero-Sanz, '¿Existe una secularidad sacerdotal?' various authors, *La formación de los sacerdotes en las circunstancias actuales*, Pamplona, 1990.

Catherine Pickstock, *After writing: on the liturgical consummation of philosophy*, Malden, Mass., 1998.

Josef Pieper, *In search of the sacred*, San Francisco, 1996.

Servais Pinckaers, *The sources of Christian ethics*, Edinburgh, 1995.

Jerry. J. Pokorsky, 'Saving the Roman rite?', *Catholic World Report*, October 2000.

Wanda Poltawaska, 'Priestly celibacy in the light of medicine and psychology', various authors, *For love alone: reflections on priestly celibacy*, Maynooth, 1993.

Lawrence B. Porter, 'Sheep and shepherd: an ancient image of the Church and a contemporary challenge', *Gregorianum* 82, 1 (2001).

Alvaro del Portillo, *On priesthood*, Chicago, 1974.

Ignace de la Potterie, 'The biblical foundation of priestly celibacy', various authors, *For love alone: reflections on priestly celibacy*, Maynooth, 1993.

David Power, *A spiritual theology of the priesthood : the mystery of Christ and the mission of the priest*, Edinburgh, 1998.

Various authors, *Priests for a new millennium*, USCC, Washington, DC, 2000.

Michel Quenot, *The icon: window on the kingdom*, London, 1991.

John F. Quinn, 'Priest shortage panic', *Crisis* magazine, October 1996.

Kevin M. Quirk, 'With apologies to Shakespeare: what's in the name "priest"'?, *Josephinum Journal of Theology*, 8, no. 1, Winter/Spring 2001.

Joseph Ratzinger, *Priestly ministry: a search for its meaning*, New York, 1971.

——*Ministers of joy: meditations on priestly spirituality*, Slough, 1989.

——'Some perspectives on priestly formation today', in John M. Haas, (ed.), *The Catholic priest as moral teacher and guide*, San Francisco, 1990.

——'The nature of priesthood', in *Osservatore Romano*, 29 October 1990.

——'The ministry and life of priests', *Homiletic and Pastoral Review*, August-September 1997.

——'Reflections on the instruction regarding the collaboration of the lay faithful in the ministry of priests - 6', *Osservatore Romano*, 29 April 1998.

——*Sing a new song to the Lord*, New York, 1998.

——*Milestones: memoirs 1927-1977*, San Francisco, 1998.

——*The spirit of the liturgy*, San Francisco, 2000.

*Religious belief, practice and moral attitudes:* a comparison of two Irish surveys 1974-1984, by Council for Research and Development, Maynooth (Report no. 21).

'Report of interdicasterial meeting with representatives of the Australian bishops', *Osservatore Romano*, 14 December 1998.

Kenneth Roeltgen, *Crisis* magazine, October 1997.

Michael Rose, 'A self-imposed shortage', *Catholic World Report*, February 2001.

George W. Rutler, *The Curé d'Ars today*, San Francisco, 1988.

——*A crisis of saints*, San Francisco, 1995.

Augusto Saramiento, 'Elementos configuradores de la espiritualidad del sacerdote secular', various authors, *La formación de los sacerdotes en las circunstancias actuales*, Pamplona, 1990.

John Saward, *Christ is the answer: the Christ-centred teaching of Pope John Paul II*, Edinburgh, 1995.

José Antonio Sayes, *Señor y Cristo*, Pamplona, 1995.

Matthias Joseph Scheeben, *The mysteries of Christianity*, St Louis, MO, 1946.

Leo Scheffczyk, 'Laypersons, deacons and priests: A difference of ministries', *Communio*, 23 (Winter 1996).

H. J. Schroeder (trans.), *The canons and decrees of the Council of Trent*, Rockfort, Il., 1978.

Christoph Schönborn, *God's human face*, San Francisco, 1994.

Angelo Scola, 'The formation of priests in the pastoral care of the family', *Communio* 24 (Spring 1997).

Josef Selmair, *The priest in the world*, London, 1954.

Crescenzio Sepe, 'The relevance of priestly celibacy today', various authors, *For love alone: reflections on priestly celibacy*, Maynooth, 1993.

Michael Sharkey (ed.), *International Theological Commission: texts and documents 1969-1985*, San Francisco, 1989.

P. A. Sheehan, *My new curate*, Cork, 1989 (reprint).

Fulton Sheen, *The priest is not his own*, London, 1964.

——*Those mysterious priests: reflections on the meaning of priesthood*, New York, 1974.

Janet Smith, *Humanae vitae: a generation later*, Washington, 1991.

Janet Smith (ed.), *Why* Humanae vitae *was right: a reader*, San Francisco, 1993.

Robert Sokolowski, *Eucharistic presence: a study in the theology of disclosure*, Washington DC, 1993.

J. Francis Stafford, *In the Person of Christ, the head of the body: the mystery of the priestly vocation* (Pastoral letter), Denver, 27 September 1988.

Alfons M. Stickler, *The case for clerical celibacy: its historical development and theological foundations*, San Francisco, 1995.

Duncan Stroik, 'Displaced tabernacles', *Crisis* magazine, June 2000.

Federico Suarez, *About being a priest*, Dublin, 1979.

——*The sacrifice of the altar*, London, 1990.

*The complete works of St Teresa of Jesus* (trans. E. Allison Peers), London, 1975.

Mother Teresa of Calcutta, 'Priestly celibacy: sign of the charity of Christ', various authors, *For love alone*, Maynooth, 1993.

J.R.R. Tolkien, *Letters*, ed. H. Carpenter, London, 1981.

Leo Trese, *A man approved*, London, 1953.

——*Tenders of the flock*, London, 1956.

——*Sanctified in the truth*, London, 1961.

Albert Vanhoye, *Old Testament priests and the new priest*, Petersham, Mass., 1986.

'Sacramentalidad del ministerio y su repercusión en la persona ordenada', various authors, *Espiritualidad del presbítero diocesano secular*, Madrid, 1987.

Albert Vanhoye and Henri Crouzel, 'The ministry in the Church: reflections on a recent publication', *Clergy Review*, 68 (May 1983).

A. Vázquez de Prada, *The founder of Opus Dei*, vol. 1, Princeton NJ, 2001.

Pierre Veuillot, ed., *The Catholic priesthood: papal documents from Pius X to Pius XII* (1903-1954), Dublin, 1962.

Allen H. Vigernon, 'A new breed of seminarians', *Crisis* magazine, May 1999.

George Weigel, 'Prepared to lead', *Crisis* magazine, October 1998.

*Witness to hope: the biography of John Paul II*, New York, 1999.

Christopher W. Whelan, ed., *Values and social change in Ireland*, Dublin, 1994.

Karol Wojtyla, 'Reflections on fatherhood', in *The collected plays and writings on theater*, Berkeley, 1987.

——*Love and responsibility*, London, 1981.

Stefan Wyszynski, *Letter to my priests*, Paris, 1969.

Anton Ziegenaus, 'Identidad del sacerdocio ministerial', various authors, *La formación de los sacerdotes en las circunstancias actuales*, Pamplona, 1990.

# Index

313